A fine exploration of the meaningfulness of arguments from human experience to the reality of God.

Ralph Hood, Jr.
The Psychology of Religion
Handbook of Religious Experience

I0130478

Joseph Hinman has injected some much-needed scientific rigour into the subject of mysticism and religious experience. From a seemingly subjective body of evidence, he has shown how to build a solid argument that theism is philosophically warranted. I recommend this book to anyone interested in the debate over the existence of God.

James Hannam
God's Philosophers: How the Medieval World Laid the Foundations of Modern Science *(shortlisted for the Royal Society Prize for Science Books 2010)*

A great contribution to discussions of the rationality of belief in God

William S. Babcock
Professor Emeritus of Church History
Southern Methodist University

Hinman's book will give you something to think about.

Nick Peters

Christian Answers to This Generation's Questions *(with J. P. Holding)*

I'm glad to see a book report this often-overlooked data with careful analysis.

Jason Pratt

Cry of Justice *(CSPA 2008 Novel of the Year)*

THE TRACE OF GOD

A Rational Warrant for Belief

Joseph Hinman

GRAND VIADUCT

Dallas Colorado Springs   GrandViaduct.com

Cover Image
by Lucas Taylor (CERN)
*The image is a simulated data model of a Higgs boson decaying into two jets of hadrons
and two electrons. The lines represent the possible paths of particles produced by a
proton-proton collision while the energy deposited by the particles is shown in blue.*
Used under the Creative Commons CC-BY-SA 4.0 license (http://creativecommons.org/
licenses/by-sa/4.0/)
Image available at http://cds.cern.ch/record/39444?ln=en (used without modification)

Designed by T Michael Wood

Hinman, Joseph
  The Trace of God: A Rational Warrant for Belief
     p.   cm.
  Includes bibliographical references and index
  ISBN 978-0-9824087-1-1
1. Theology.   2. Religious Experience.   3. Mystical Experience.   4. Trace of God.   I.
Title.

First Edition

GrandViaduct
Dallas | Colorado Springs
Exploring the nature of Civilization and Society
@GrandViaduct
GrandViaduct.com
4419 Centennial Blvd #361, Colorado Springs CO 80907

Dedicated to the memory of my beloved parents A.D. and Virginia Hinman, the best parents anyone ever had, and to the memory of my brother Ray without whom I would not have pursued the life of the mind.

Acknowledgements

I would like to thank Dr. Ralph Hood Jr. I was not his student and he didn't know me from Adam but he gamely endured a thousand stupid questions and discussed and advised on every phase of the work.

Michael Neilsen, who I also met on the net through email, and who has been answering my stupid questions for years, his advice was indispensable.

William G. Barnard, SMU, for valuable advice and consultation on his approach to James and to Proudfoot.

William "Billy" Abraham, my former professor at Perkins, and coffee buddy, who did some of the early research for me and obtained for me some of the major studies I was unable to get hold of.

William Babcock, Perkins School of Theology, former professor and good friend, for his willingness to take time out for some crucial discussions about the chapters on Proudfoot and on Schleiermacher and mystical experience.

Fran Carris, Leslie A. Fox, Kristen Rosser, Dave Stump, Ryan Tufts and Ingrid Wood for their invaluable assistance and advice over the course of this book.

I would like to thank my good friend Jim Bratone for being a constant and valuable sounding board on all matters related to this book.

And I would like to extend my greatest appreciation to the Managing Editor of GrandViaduct Press, Tim Wood. This project has been a long ongoing effort, extending over two years in editorial preparation, involving the coordination of many groups , including readers, editors, and proofreaders. Tim has proven to be a miracle of patience, determination, and perseverance through it all, believing in it more strongly than even I at times, encouraging me through late-night or early-morning phone calls to keep pushing through until the book was in its final form. Without his professionalism and friendship, this book would have never happened.

Contents

Introduction

Arguments for God based upon personal religious experience have always been considered weak by both apologists and skeptics. This has been the case due to prejudices and misconceptions about the nature of religious experiences. These prejudices include: (1) the notion that experiences cannot be studied scientifically because they are subjective, (2) that religious experience is related to emotional instability or mental illness, or, (3) the fear that feelings cannot be trusted. Religious experiences are often wrongly understood to be about voices and visions and God telling people to put their children in ovens.

Over the past thirty years a large body of scientific work demonstrates that religious experience is not just a pathology or trick of the mind. This body of empirical scientific studies demonstrates the validity of religious experience as an actual experience of something, and the effects of having such experiences are indicative of something actually experienced. A vast body of data demonstrates that religious experiences, what some call "mystical" and others refer to as "peak," have positive, long-term effects so dramatic they can only be described as "transformative." In this book I will explore this body of work and apply it to arguments in an attempt to demonstrate how such experience rationally warrants religious belief. One of the most important advances in this scientific work is the development of the M scale, which allows for a control on the actual determination of mystical experience. Being able to control for actual mystical experience is crucial since not all things that involve God are "mystical" and not all religious experiences are "peak" experiences. Researchers who claim to manipulate the brain to produce mystical experience, for example, are not cognizant of the advances in this field and thus don't use experimental controls that can differentiate between what is mystical experience and what is not. We will determine what this scientific work has to say about the work of philosophers who seek to rule out the validity of religious experience. We will examine alternative theories about the source for experiences of the divine.

Over the past three decades we have seen a constantly shifting battle between Christian apologists and promoters of secular atheistic viewpoints. In the 1980's the tide turned heavily in favor of theistic thinkers with all the amazing data about the Big Bang. This renaissance was short lived, however, as secular-minded physicists began moving away from the standard model and concocted new concepts, first inflationary theory and then string theory.[1] In addition to the Big Bang cosmology, the fine-turning argument came into its own and gained many adherents. A major physicist, Paul Davies, known for his atheistic popularizing, converted to theistic viewpoints based upon this argument.[2] In the 1990's, studies such as the one done by Byrd on prayer, were being put forward as confirmations of the positive effects of belief. These studies fall into two categories: double blind studies on the outcome of prayer, and general data of a demographic nature on religious participation and overall health. In the first decade of the new century these findings have been called into question. The double blind studies did not support the early conclusions and atheistic thinkers are now producing works challenging the general participation and health studies.[3] In philosophy, during the ferment of the 60's and 70s, the work of Norman Malcolm, Charles Hartshorne and Alvin Plantinga came to fruition and by the 80's bore real fruit, with a zenith in the late 90's. God arguments became popular again in certain circles, academics began journals devoted to God arguments and the ontological argument made a surprising return in the form of Hartshorne's modal argument (carried on by Plantinga after Hartshorne's death).

All of this foment culminated in the conversion of Antony Flew (perhaps the most important atheist philosopher of the twentieth century after Russell) to the theistic view. However, we have now seen the counter-punch in the form of an aggressive, sometimes vindictive "New Atheism." Most of its major arguments concern scientific notions of origin and health. These arguments have been picked over by both sides, yet both sides have missed a wide range of scientific data that clearly and decisively establishes a rational basis for religious belief.

Although both apologists and their atheist counterparts back away from experience arguments, William P. Alston and Richard Swinburne have notably produced good sound experience arguments that demonstrate the rationality of belief.[4] Yet even these books do not go into depth on this vast corpus of scientific data supporting the validity of religious experience. This vast body of scientific research produced by the social sciences over the course of the past four decades consists of literally hundreds of studies on the nature and outcome of religious experiences. Caroline Franks-Davis wrote a notable book on arguments for the existence of God from religious experience and she did go into detail on this body of work, but she did not cover the social science methodology of the studies in enough depth, and more research has been done since her 1989 venture.[5] I suspect that Christians tend to back away from experience arguments because skeptics tend to balk at them, and the experiences generally tend to be non-Christian religious experiences as often as they are Christian ones. It's hard to make a credible argument for "my subjective experiences and not these others that don't back my tradition, but seem very much the same." Atheist apologists tend to shun experience arguments because they seem to be afraid of subjective phenomenon such as experiences, and on a surface level religious experiences appear (*appear* being the operative word here) to be completely explainable in naturalistic terms. The approach most atheists tend to use in refuting these arguments is to use irrelevant data on brain chemistry and to argue that such experiences can be induced. Since they do not refer to the body of data from the social sciences, their work misses the fact that the major researchers in this field are not impressed by such methodology. The body of scientific

3

research of which I speak tends to concern itself with a certain type of religious experience known as "mystical" or "peak" experience. This experience is characterized not by voices and visions, but by two basic types of sensation: (1) the sense of the numinous: the understanding that there is something transcendent and "sacred" afoot in the universe. This is usually communicated through a sense of totality of love, embodied in a sense of all pervasive presence. (2) Undifferentiated unity: the sense that all differentiation of being is illusory and all things are actually one. While these experiences are beyond words, and mystics find it hard to recount them, they also have a deep and abiding sense of having learned clearly communicable lessons from their experiences. These lessons are called "noetic" and they amount to ideas like "God is love."

Both types of sensation are often experienced by the same person. The former is more clearly associated with Christianity and other theistic-style religious traditions, while the latter is more indicative of eastern religious traditions.[6] The skeptic habitually assumes that these studies are flawed or unscientific, but they have been cross-culturally validated many times. The early classic writings in the field are William James' *The Varieties of Religious Experience*[7], and the first attempt to put that work into the context of mid-twentieth century social science research, Abraham Maslow's *Religion and Peak Experience.*[8] These works, along with W.T. Stace's *Concepts of Mysticism,* were the basis of research by Ralph Hood, Jr., from the 1970's to the early twenty-first century. Hood developed the "M Scale" (Mystical scale) based upon the assumptions of Stace. The M Scale, not a study itself but an instrument (a scale that is actually graded like a student test) used in studies to validate mystical experience, has now been accepted by the entire field of psychology of religion. The M Scale has become the standard method for determining the validity of a mystical experience. By validity I mean the extent to which a person's experiences conform to the typology compiled by Stace from the world's great mystics, or if the experiences are just quasi religious but having not mystical consciousness. In the act of making this sort of validation, the study itself demonstrates that mystical experience is a valid psychological concept and can be studied scientifically; it also demonstrates the effect upon the life of the one having the experience. The M Scale has better demonstrated cross-cultural validation than most studies in the field.[9]

Using this body of work as a base, I will present several arguments which I hope will be helpful to apologists and social scientists as well as to philosophers of religion. My aim is to demonstrate the ultimate rationality of religious belief and to further illuminate, for both scholars and the laity, the value of such experiences and the validity of their study. In Chapter Three, I will develop arguments. For now I will merely say that, based upon the body of work of which I speak, religious belief is rationally warranted. Ultimately, my aim is to demonstrate that the realizations offered by such experiences are indicative of what has been called the religious *"a priori"* and free the believer from the tyranny of the need to prove.[10]

1. Andre Linde, *Scientific American*, Sept. 1999. Linde in this interview doesn't put the problem in the context of a battle between Christian apologetics and secularism, but he clearly acknowledges the problem of explaining origins naturalistically from the standpoint of the Big Bang. Christopher Southgate alludes to an "unease beyond the Christian community." *God, Humanity and the Cosmos,* T&T Clark.1999. Physicist Barry Parker stated "if we accept the Big Bang theory, and most physicists do now, then a creation of some sort is forced upon us." See Barry Parker, *Creation: the Story of the Origin and Evolution of the Universe*, New York, London: Plenum Press, 1988, 202. Steven Hawking stated that a number of attempts to move away from the Big Bang were attempts to avoid implications of divine intervention in origins of the universe. See Hawking, Steven. *A Brief History of Time*, New York: Bantam Books, 1988. 46.

2.	Paul Davies, *The Mind of God*, New York: Simon and Schuster, 1992.

3.	Sloan, Richard P. Blind Faith: the Unholy Alliance of Religion and Medicine, New York: MacMillan Publishing, 2006.See also Randolph Byrd, "Positive Therapeutic effects of Intercessory Prayer in the Coronary Care Unit." Southern Medical Journal (July 1988) vol 81 no 7.

4.	Alston, William P. *Perceiving God: The Epistemology of Religious Experience*. Ithaca and London: Cornell University Press, 1991. see also Swinburne, Richard. *The Existence of God,* N.Y., Oxford University Press, 2004.

5.	Caroline Franks-Davis. *The Evidential Force of Religious Experience*, New York, London: Oxford, Clarendon Press 1989.

6.	Spilka, Bernard, Ralph Hood Jr., Bruce Hunsberger, Richard Gorsuch. *The Psychology of Religion: An Empirical Approach.* New York, London: The Guilford Press, 2003, 332-337. There's a range from "religious feeling" to "perennial philosophy" and various thinkers have proposed various ways of categorizing it.

7.	William James, *The Varieties of Religious Experience, Gifford Lectures, 1901-1902*, New York: Modern Library.

8.	Abraham Maslow, *Religions, Values and Peak-Experiences*, "preface" to the 1970 edition.

9.	Spilka, op. cit.

10.	David Pailin "The Religious a priori" *Westminster Dictionary of Christian Theology,* Louisville Kentucky: Westminster, John Knox Press; Alan Richardson and John Bowden ed., 1983 498.

Preliminary Concepts and Definitions

It is important to define exactly what we are talking about when we speak of "religious experience" and to address other definitional issues.

The religious *a priori*

...Used by philosophers of religion to express the view that the sense of the Divine is due to a special form of awareness which exists alongside the cognitive, moral, and aesthetic forms of awareness and is not explicable by reference to them. The concept of religion as concerned with the awareness of and response to the divine is accordingly a simple notion which cannot be defined by reference other than itself.

> —*David Pailin "Religious a priori"* Westminster Dictionary of Christian Theology *(498)*[1]

The religious *a priori* is not just the experience *per se*. It is more broadly the special form of awareness which results in the religious experience. Thus I will use the term to refer not only to my overall argument but to the conclusion that this rational warrant *frees us from the need to prove*. I use that phrase, even though I am attempting to prove something, because it contains power in its open-ended nature. To be sure, I am arguing for freedom from the need to prove the existence of God, but the studies I draw upon offer more: freedom from

Joseph Hinman

the need to prove the validity of philosophical thought; freedom from
the need to prove that philosophy need not be embarrassed about not
being science; freedom from the need to prove that not all subjectivity
is a sign of mental instability; freedom from the need to fear the
subjective.

The religious *a priori* might be criticized as a misnomer since it is
really derived from the empirical sense rather than by deductive
reasoning. This is at least true in terms of our experience of it. One
might argue that sense experience constitutes an *a priori* truth, but *a
priori* truths are not often derived from a phenomenological basis. For
this reason I suggest an alternate term, the *believer's default*. That is to
say that, similar to the atheist's "default" where the assumption is made
that without devastating proof for God one must make the assumption
there is no God, in this case where devastating evidence demonstrates
that "something is afoot in the universe" (and without devastating
evidence that nothing is afoot), we should assume there is "something"
and that that "something" is probably in some sense what we might call
"God."

Religious Experience

That which is described as mystical experience I refer to as either RE
(religious experience) or ME (mystical experience). I also call it
"mystical consciousness," although that phrase has broader overtones;
it speaks to the consciousness involved in the experience as well as the
experience itself. I call those who have mystical experiences either
"peakers" (ala Abraham Maslow) or "experiencers" or "mystics." I try
to avoid the latter term due to confusion with the saints and great
figures of the Christian Church.

8

Definition of Religious Experience (and examples)

The definition of Religious Experience (RE) is a major issue. While many critics of the research have argued that there is no clear-cut definition, there are many different definitions that have been derived from the data. These definitions all involve basic ideas such as ineffability (beyond words), sensing a universal presence, a sense of unity of all things, noetic qualities (we can learn things from the experiences). The critics are correct in pointing out that there are gray areas; it is not all clear-cut. Just as in the early part of the twentieth century, science disparaged religious experience and the popular movement of intellectuals that focused on mystical experience, so too in the latter twentieth century the situation has been reversed. While study after study demonstrated the validity of RE, philosophers and skeptics mounted a growing opposition to mysticism, an opposition dedicated to tearing apart the concept. That opposition began with Katz[2] and culminates in Wayne Proudfoot. Despite this opposition, the empirical research and the view that emerges from it is a fairly clear guide. Those who argue that it's not clear expect a blow-by-blow account with 100% accuracy and no ambiguities, which we do not have. On the other hand, what we do have tells us that there is some sort of experience with a general range of characteristics, that it can be distinguished from other sorts of experiences, and that the effects of it can be understood empirically. This is all we need to make an argument. The critics are trying to treat these experiences as an illness, while the effects are anything but the symptoms of disease. This issue will be discussed in greater detail in dealing with Wayne Proudfoot's attacks on Schleiermacher. Schleiermacher opens up a vista involving other forms of the *a priori;* peak experience is not the only form. I look at both Proudfoot and Schleiermacher in greater detail in the chapter on the *a priori.*

I define "rational warrant" and terms connected with decision-making paradigms in the second chapter. In the present chapter I deal with "Religious Experience" and what is meant by that term. By RE, I do not mean voices or visions or miracles. These things might or might not accompany RE . By "RE" I indicate the basic core experiences that foster belief and that make up the substance of "mystical" experience. I am proceeding on the assumption that there is a continuum of RE. At one end, we have "ordinary" experiences, which I call "ordinary believer experiences": the basic emotive sense that accompanies belief. At the other end of the spectrum we have full blown mysticism as one finds with saints of the Church such as Teresa of Avila or San Juan de la Cruz. The hallmark of such experiences is a sense of presence; that God is present in the world, right here and now in the moment. This is not the result of voices or visions. In its most basic form it is similar to the feeling one has sitting alone with one's eyes closed, and yet feeling the presence of someone else in the room, but it can also be much more powerful.

Most religious experiences are not only much stronger; they also include a pervasive sense of total peace. Sometimes they include a sense that one understands all things and that the world makes sense; that there is higher meaning to life. In its strongest sense this notion results in a feeling of the undifferentiated unity of all things; God, humanity, the universe, and the self are all one thing. While it may not be wise to base doctrines upon such experiences, (and I do not advocate doing so), the nature of these experiences, especially their effects upon the one experiencing them, is a profound proof of the rational and logically valid nature of belief.

An example of this sort of experience is found in a study by Robinson.[3] Finally, Robinson (1977) found that 15% of his adult respondents spoke of childhood mystical experiences. An example is the following from a 40 year old female:

When I was eleven years old I spent part of a summer holiday in the Wye Valley. Waking up very early one bright morning, before any of the household was about, I left my bed and went to kneel on the window seat, to look out over the curve, which the river took just below the house. The trees between the house and river ... The scene was very beautiful, and quite suddenly I felt myself on the verge of a great revelation. It was as if I had stumbled unwittingly on a place where I was not expected, and was about to be initiated into some wonderful mystery, something of indescribable significance. Then, just as suddenly, the feeling faded. But for the brief seconds while it lasted I had known that in some strange way I, the essential "me", was a part of the trees, of the sunshine, and the river, that we all belonged to some great unity. I was left filled with exhilaration and exultation of spirit. This is one of the most memorable experiences of my life, of a quite different quality and greater intensity than the sudden lift of the spirit one may often feel when confronted with beauty in Nature (p. 37). (quoted by Gackenback)[4]

Here is another example (this one from William James used by William Alston):

...all at once I felt the presence of God —I tell of the thing just as I was conscious of it— as if his goodness and his power were penetrating me altogether... I thanked God that in the course of my life he had taught me to know him, that he sustained my life and took pity both on the insignificant creature and on the sinner that I was. I begged him ardently that my life might be consecrated to the doing of his will. I felt his reply, which was that I should do his will from day to day, in humility and poverty, leaving him the Almighty God, to judge of whether I should some time be called to bear witness more conspicuously. Then, slowly, the ecstasy left my heart; that is, I felt that God had withdrawn the communion, which he had granted.[5]

Still another example, used by Alston:

> There was no sensible vision, but the room was filled by a Presence, which in a strange way was both about me and within me. I was overwhelmingly possessed by Someone who was not myself, and yet I felt I was more myself than I had ever been before.[6]

In the early part of the twentieth century science took a dim view of religion. Freud's assumptions that religion represented pathological states had influenced scientific thinking.[7] At the same time there was a major movement that drew popular attention to mysticism and mystical consciousness. Dean Inge, Evelyn Underhill and Baron Friedrich von Hügel were major leaders of that movement.[8] In the late twentieth century the situation was reversed. A vast body of scientific data was gathered which showed that religious experience is healthy and positive. Even though this conclusion is largely unknown to the general public (to say nothing of the research that backs it up), this insight is widely known to psychologists and in the social sciences. A steady flow of empirical research since the 1970's has yielded some very solid results. Several characteristics have been identified as definitive for these experiences:

This is from the Voyle study and quotes Hood:

> The contemporary interest in the empirical research of mysticism can be traced to Stace, "Demarcation of the Phenomenological Characteristics of Mystical Experiences" (1960, in Hood, 1975). In Stace's conceptualization, mystical experiences had five characteristics (Hood, 1985, p.176):
>
> 1. The mystical experience is noetic. The person having the experience perceives it as a valid source of knowledge and not just a subjective experience.
> 2. The mystical experience is ineffable; it cannot simply be described in words.

3. The mystical experience is holy. While this is the religious aspect of the experience it is not necessarily expressed in any particular theological terms.
4. The mystical experience is profound yet enjoyable and characterized by positive affect.
5. The mystical experience is paradoxical. It defies logic. Further analyses of reported mystical experiences suggest that the one essential feature of mysticism is an experience of unity (Hood, 1985). The experience of unity involves a process of ego loss and is generally expressed in one of three ways (Hood, 1976a). The ego is absorbed into that which transcends it, or an inward process by which the ego gains pure awareness of self, or a combination of the two.

This latter is described by James, "In mystic states we both become one with the Absolute and we become aware of our oneness" (James, 1902/1990, p.378). Using Stace's criteria of ego loss, unity, inner subjectivity, timelessness, noetic quality, ineffability, positive affect, and the holy, Hood developed an operational measure of mystical experience called the Mysticism Scale (M scale) (Hood, 1975). The M scale is a 32 item paper-and-pencil test that yields two highly correlated factors associated with mysticism which are considered to be two aspects of an overall concept of mysticism:

• Factor I has items dealing with the minimal phenomenological experience, whereas
• Factor II deals with religious interpretation or attributions regarding the experience.

The relationship between church attendance and mysticism is complex. James (1902/1990) contended that religious institutions tend to inhibit people from having mystical experiences. Personally religious people reported more mystical experiences than the equally personal and institutionally religious, and the institutionally religious reported the least (Hood, 1973). However, frequent church attendees and non-attendees report more mystical experiences than infrequent attendees (Hood, 1976b). Similarly, Poloma and Pendleton's (1991) study of prayer experiences showed that rote or mechanical prayers are more likely to be associated with feelings of sadness, loneliness, tension, and fear, whereas, meditative prayer is related positively to feelings of existential well-being and religious satisfaction.

When combined with the data on intrinsic religious orientation and church participation, the results affirm the fact that intense religious experiences such as religious mysticism *occur in the lives of the religiously devout and are not restricted to the non church attendees (Hood, 1976b).* (emphasis added)[9]

Empirical research has yielded common characteristics, which can also be used to define the phenomenon.

In a review of the mystical experience, Lukoff and Lu (1988) acknowledged that the "definition of a mystical experience ranges greatly (p. 163)." Maslow (1969) offered 35 definitions of "transcendence", a term often associated with mystical experiences and used by Alexander et al. to refer to the process of accessing PC [peak consciousness].

Lukoff (1985) identified five common characteristics of mystical experiences, which could be operationalized for assessment purposes. They are:

1. Ecstatic mood, which he identified as the most common feature
2. Sense of newly gained knowledge, which includes a belief that the mysteries of life have been revealed
3. Perceptual alterations, which range from "heightened sensations to auditory and visual hallucinations" (p. 167)
4. Delusions (if present) have themes related to mythology, ...
5. No conceptual disorganization: unlike psychotic persons, those with mystical experiences do NOT suffer from disturbances in language and speech

It can be seen from the explanation of PC earlier that this list of qualities overlaps in part with those delineated by Alexander et al.[10]

It is notable that studies show that speaking in tongues is not a compulsion or a disruption of speech and that there is no link between speaking in tongues and mental problems.

1. Pailin, David. "The Religious A Priori." *The Westminster Dictionary of Christian Theology*. Alan Richardson and John Bowden ed. Philadelphia: Westminster Press, 1983, 498

2. Katz, Steven. *Mysticism and Religious Traditions*, New York: Oxford University Press, 1983

3. Quoted in Gackenback, Jayne. "Transpersonal Childhood Experiences of Higher States of Consciousness: Literature Review and Theoretical Integration" (unpublished paper 1992) http://www.sawka.com/spiritwatch/cehsc/ipure.htm (last accessed summer 2008)

4. Ibid.

5. Anonymous report in James (*Verities of Religious Experience*, 67-68) Quoted by William Alston, *Perceiving God, the Epistemology of Religious Experience*. Ithaca and London: Cornell University Press 1991, 1993, 13.

6. Timothy Breadsworth, *A Sense of Presence* (1977) in Ibid, 17.

7. Pailin, David. "The Religious A Priori." *The Westminster Dictionary of Christian Theology*. Alan Richardson and John Bowden ed. Philadelphia: Westminster Press, 1983, 219-222.

8. Miachael Ramsey "Evelyn Underhill," *Religious Studies*. Cambridge University Press. Volume 12, issue 03, 1976, 273-279: http://journals.cambridge.org/action/displayAbstract?fromPage=online&aid=2409960 published online Oct 2008. Ramsey was later to be Archbishop of Canterbury.

9. Quoted in the Voyle study: Robert J. Voyle, Psy.D.K. *The Impact of Mystical Experiences on Christian Maturity*. Originally published in pdf format: http://www.voyle.com/impact.pdf

10. Lukoff, D. (1985). "The diagnosis of mystical experiences with psychotic features." *The Journal of Transpersonal Psychology,* 17(2), 155-181. Also available on Jayne Gackenback's website *Spirit Watch* and at http://www.spiritualcompetency.com/pdfs/Lukoff1985dxmepf.pdf

1 Decision Making Paradigm

With arguments, the first thing one must understand is what the arguments are intended to prove. Are God arguments meant to be persuasive, to win converts to belief? Are they meant to bolster the belief of believers? Are they meant to prove the existence of God in a way to which all rational beings would give assent? Or, are they merely justifications of belief? The first step is to understand the decision-making paradigm upon which an argument is based. To do that we must know what the argument in question is intended to accomplish. For example, consider atheistic arguments based upon empirical knowledge as a decision-making paradigm. They are often intended to demonstrate the inferior nature of religious belief; that belief in God is groundless if the only valid form of knowledge is scientific empiricism.

Consider Richard Dawkins' major argument in *The God Delusion*. Dawkins argues that God is improbable.[1] This contention is based upon the assumption that God is an object of empirical knowledge, like any other thing in nature. Thus, mathematical probability for God can be calculated based upon the lack of observation of god-like beings. Here the decision-making paradigm is based upon the philosophy of materialism and the methodology of scientific empiricism. The purpose of atheistic arguments might be to show that belief in God is groundless; scientifically empirical knowledge is assumed to be the only valid form of knowledge. If we assume that God is not a proper object of empirical examination, that God is not just another thing in the cosmos, but is, if anything, the *basis* of reality, then this methodology is inapplicable. We need a decision-making paradigm that is not dependent upon empirical knowledge alone. My assertion is that empiricism is an inadequate path to truth. On the other hand, the true path is paved with empirical data; the engine that transports us down that road is powered by reason.

The purpose of God arguments, in my view, should not be to prove the existence of God. Why should believers encumber themselves with a burden that depends upon empirical knowledge when belief in God is not belief in an object of empirical knowledge? God arguments need only engender confidence in the proposition "belief in God is rationally warranted." Arguments can make use of empirical data in proving minor premises, but they can't prove something that is not an object of empirical examination.

Most people do not come to believe in God based only on arguments. I began fashioning arguments to try and either justify my belief to unbelievers, or to demonstrate to myself the rationality of what I believe. Just as the object of religious belief (God) is not analogous to things in the world, neither is religious experience itself like other kinds of belief. Religious belief is not exactly like belief in facts or in principles; it involves an understanding of propositions of fact as constituent parts of a worldview, yet it is not dependent upon many propositions of fact. Religious experience is not established in a scientifically empirical sense, even though it is empirical in the philosophical sense. While some skeptics may see this as an overture to special pleading, the simple fact is that *the nature of belief in God differs from the nature of any other kind of belief.* Its lack of empirical support cannot be construed in and of itself as a drawback since empirical demands made of it can only be valid when religious experience itself overlaps with estimable parts of the world. At its core, religious experience is a realization, a consciousness, a sense of discovery about the nature of one's own being; i.e., it is contingent upon something that is itself the *ground* of being. It's a discovery about being *itself.*

I advance my own God arguments as a means to my own understanding. Skeptics may charge that I'm trying to convince myself, but I do not know why I should have to convince anyone else. The believer needs to justify his beliefs to himself alone, and I am quite sure I was convinced long ago. Justification, therefore, is unnecessary if one is considering one's own sense of certainty. On the other hand, one would like a bit more "kick" to one's constructs. Otherwise, why make arguments of any kind? I have hit upon a *prima facie* case for the proposition: *Religious experience frees the believer from the need to prove.* Implicit in this statement is the idea that freedom from the need to prove means a position is grounded in reason without being entirely demonstrable to the extent that all must give assent.

If one is concerned with convincing others, however, then there must be a decision-making paradigm that would be meaningful to all. Since the existence of God is not given in sense data, the bar cannot be raised to the level of absolute proof, or even of scientifically empirical proof. It is not required that one demonstrate God in order to show that belief is rational or that it is justified to the extent of placing confidence in the proposition: all that is needed is to demonstrate that *belief is more rational and meaningful than unbelief.* I will argue for a set of criteria that will enable us to clarify the concept of "justification." I think the goal of a God argument, at least in terms of how it speaks to skeptics and unbelievers, should be nothing more or less than to demonstrate that one can place *confidence* in the proposition of belief. Placing confidence requires the meeting of a *prima facie* burden. One cannot expect much more than the meeting of a *prima facie* burden. Requiring more than this is unfair and unnecessary. It is unfair because we are dealing with an argument about the framework of reality. There would be no way to demonstrate God as an object in creation alongside egg beaters and swizzle sticks if God is the basis of reality, the ground of being, the foundation upon which things in creation are possible. Therefore, to attempt to treat God as a thing is to reduce the whole concept of God and to insist upon a false notion of the Divine. God is not a big man in the sky; the atheist's demand that we produce evidence on the order of fingerprints and DNA samples is absurd.

One of the major problems in choosing a decision-making paradigm is that there are too many from which to choose. Are we to be Foundationalists? Are we to be Phenomenologists? Evidentialists? Presuppositionalists? Empiricists? There are a couple of dozen others I could name. Which of these, or of however many others one could propose, should one turn to for an understanding of the basic goals of argument? There are many approaches to belief. There are as many reasons for believing as there are believers. My bias is that of phenomenology and existentialism. That doesn't mean all of my ideas and arguments have to square with the works of Jean-Paul Sartre or Gabriel Marcel. One can take a general approach to belief. Individual arguments will have their own basis in one or another paradigm. Belief as a whole rests upon a worldview, upon one's understanding of the interface between one's own individual life and the nature of reality in which one sees oneself embroiled.

Thus, in general, the basic requirement of a religious paradigm should be that it mediate an understanding of the individual's relationship to reality and the role of God in that understanding. Religion would not even exist were it not for the basic religious experiences that have always drawn people to their conclusions about the sense of the numinous. If there were no sense of the numinous, there would be no religion. Why then should the justification for belief do anything more than present a *prima facie* justification for construing such sense as a valid means of understanding one's place in the world? For this reason, I choose as the basic aim of my arguments a general notion of *prima facie* justification based upon Thomas Reid's epistemology. This is because Reid's epistemology was shaped by the same general sense of understanding one's place in the world in relation to phenomena observed in daily living.

An understanding of *prima facie* burden

Consider Mattey's explanation of Reid's notion of prima facie justification:

> ...Far from concluding that our senses are "fallacious," Reid placed them on the same footing as memory and reason, though they are "undervalued" by philosophers because "the informations of sense are common to the philosopher and to the most illiterate . . . Nature likewise forces our belief in those informations, and all the attempts of philosophy to weaken it are fruitless and in vain." Reid pointed out that when we fall into error regarding the objects of sense, we correct our errors "by more accurate attention to the informations we may receive by our senses themselves." So the "original and natural judgments" that are made on the basis of our constitution lose their original justification in the presence of additional information. Contemporary philosophers call this kind of justification "*prima facie,*" a term from law which describes an initially plausible case that could prove to be entirely implausible given further evidence. A belief of common sense, then, is justified "on the face of it."

According to the doctrine of *prima facie* justification, one is justified in accepting that things are the way they appear, when

- it does appear to one that they are that way, and
- there is no reason to think that something has gone wrong.

But if there is such a reason, one's justification is "defeated." Thus *prima facie* justification is "defeasible."

For Reid, our beliefs about physical objects are justified by sense-experience, which he took to be a product of the interaction between the senses and physical objects. Twentieth-century philosophers have been somewhat more cautious, however, and have followed more closely the account of perceptual knowledge given by Reid's predecessors such as Descartes, Locke and Hume: that what justifies our beliefs about physical objects is a mental state such as:

- looking like something is red
- a sensation of red
- seeing red-ly

> For example, what justifies a person in believing that he sees
> something red is that it looks to him as though there is something red.
> The mental state of that person is one in which there is an appearance
> of red, and just being in this mental state is enough to give *prima
> facie* justification to the belief that he really sees something red.... [2]

A set of criteria for a *prima facie* case might include perceptions of the
senses that bear out an assumption, provided there is no alternative
causality that indicates some reason to assume the senses are in error.
This would include the use of reason and logic of both the deductive
and inductive kinds, the latter involving likelihood based upon
comparable knowledge. We need confirmation that is shared by others.
The criteria for shared confirmation would include:

1. Documented perceptual evidence with no counter-causality.
2. Perceptions that are regular and consistent.
3. Perceptions shared or validated by others.
4. Logical inference from both deductive and inductive reasoning.

If a *prima facie* case has been presented, the believer has met the
reasonable burden required of an argument. It then becomes the
skeptic's burden to unseat the *prima facie* status of the case. The
skeptic must prove that more is required to maintain a *prima facie* case.
The grounding assumption is that a *prima facie* case, while not offering
"proof" of God's existence, is an important step on the road to finding
truth. Thus, exhaustive knowledge of truth is not required, but the
assumption is made that one is on the road to truth, and is making
decent strides. The skeptic's burden is in showing that the case has not
been met, or even that a *prima facie* case doesn't tell us enough.
Skeptics often argue that the believer has the burden of proof. After all,
it is the believer who asserts a belief. A skeptic will quickly point out

that the *prima facie* case is an attempt to give the unbeliever the burden of proof. That is valid, but not quite true in an important sense. It is side-stepping the need to prove, and is grounding belief in explication. *Prima facie* burden consists of meeting several criteria, which I will deal with below. Meeting these criteria demonstrates not proof of God's existence, but the viable nature of religious belief as an alternative to proof. Having met this burden, the burden of proof shifts. The aim is not to prove the existence of God, so the believer can't be laden with that burden since it is not the purpose of the argument.

If the *prima facie* burden is overturned with further examination, obviously the believer is again stuck with the burden of meeting it. Obviously, the skeptic will argue that the *prima facie* burden has never been met. One will probably find that no skeptic will ever admit that it has been met. But there has to be a possibility, and the skeptic must admit there are possibilities of meeting it, otherwise dialogue comes to a stop. The basic meaning of the term *prima facie* as used in law means that there is enough evidence to assume that we can continue to dig further, that the case can continue in the legal system. In policy debate such as the National Forensic League (high school debate) or the National Debate Tournament (college debate) it means that a case has been presented which is valid "on the face of it." In other words, if the debate ended after the first speech, there would be enough information for one to consider that the case had adequate grounds to win. In philosophy, *prima facie* means an argument that is complete and able to stand on its own; however, this is considered a bare minimum.

Therefore, we can take the *prima facie* case in God arguments to mean a reason to believe in God is presented which on the face of it appears to be logically sound and valid, the argument is based upon a reason that should hold up under criticism, and that seems to be based upon a sound and valid reasoning. Experience arguments are *prima facie* because they are based upon the same tools upon which we base epistemic judgment. Experiences are not derived from deductive logic, so basing them upon formally valid claims would not go to the heart of the matter. It would be useful to be able to put them into a formally valid format, but they can hardly be based upon that alone. Being "sound" is a trickier matter. Sound in the logical sense means the argument is valid and all of the premises it is based upon are actually true. That is going to be a matter in debate. But if religious experience has the same basis upon which we found our most *prima facie* view of reality, the same "nuts and bolts" that help to shape our epistemic judgment as a whole would seem to offer a *prima facie* case for the validity of such experiences.

Considering Scientific Empiricism vs. Philosophical Empiricism

Atheists dislike the idea of experience because it isn't testable in a scientific sense; it is subjective and violates the paradigm of scientific empiricism. Ironically, this challenge of the scientific paradigm is going to be the major challenge for experience arguments. It is ironic because religious experience is the most attested rationale by empirical scientific evidence of any God argument (see Chapter 3).

The skeptical penchant for scientific empiricism is quite understandable. This is the hallmark of the modern age. Scientific empiricism is what makes the modern world go 'round: it gives us all the fabulous gadgets we love; it "works." Scientific empiricism gives a fingertip control over nature and opens the door to nature's secrets. This form of knowledge has become the umpire of reality. This form of knowledge is the gatekeeper of the real. We judge the real by its testability according to scientific standards.

The problem is that it really only works for certain *aspects* of reality. When it comes to those aspects for which it does not work well, we decide they can't be demonstrated by our modern method of truth keeping, and thus that they are untrue. Even though for major aspects of our thought worlds we take for granted assumptions which are never given through scientific data, we nevertheless privilege those because we must take them for granted, but we privilege no others. For example, no scientific data can guarantee that other minds are not an illusion. Epistemology is more primary than science because science is derived from the struggles of early modern thinkers, such as Descartes, to offer epistemological methods. We have to take other minds for granted; there is no way to empirically prove them. To attempt to prove other minds by scientific means would entail having to violate the most basic canons of epistemology, the epistemologist's fallacy. We cannot step outside of our own perceptions to make sure the data is true, and any data we collect could be an illusion, the same illusion that creates other minds. Rather than finding this debilitating, we simply proceed according to our perceptions because they enable us to navigate the world; they "work." We *assume* the existence of other minds; it seems to get us in trouble when we ignore other minds. Thus, we live as though other minds are real; we do not ignore them as a "default" because they have not been absolutely proven by science.

Many atheistic apologists use a particular decision-making paradigm for deciding about the validity and invalidity of belief; this paradigm is an ideological construct that is based upon an idealization of science and the assumption that science privileges atheism. Let's take this approach at face value as the best reading of their position: empirical scientific data gives us objective facts and faith gives us subjective assertions and wishful thinking. I think this is a fair summation of what most atheist apologists would say, in the most positive light. That in itself is fair enough. But the question here, however, is to decide between *prima facie* justifications as the basis of a God argument versus the demand for empirical scientific data. The problem is that scientific data by itself is not a decision-making paradigm. It's an old argument going back to the 1930's journal wars between two sociologists, Lundberg and Lynd.[3] Lundberg argues in his article "Knowledge for What?" that sociologists don't just collect random files of meaningless data, they don't count the number of bricks in tenement buildings, and economists don't collect dates on coins in the economy. They collect data with a goal in mind. They want to prove something, and that something fits into an overall scheme which is part of a larger worldview. The fact that the "purpose" is often a hypothesis test doesn't mean research is any less pointed toward proving an idea. Moreover, it is unclear that we could even think of hypotheses if they didn't at some point deep down originate in a world view.

Thus, even empirical scientific data is collected with a bias. Of course we would all be ready to spot that bias in dealing with data collected by a creationist, but atheists are naive in their assumption that their research would be any less biased. The empirical scientific paradigm is simply not the objective window on truth as reductionists would wish it to be. To make matters worse, science is inherently ideological, as philosopher of science Thomas S. Kuhn effectively illuminated. Kuhn defined the term paradigm and explained the theory of paradigm shifts in *The Structure of Scientific Revolutions.* According to Kuhn, science is a social construct. It functions by orienting itself around paradigms (theoretical models), and it changes through "paradigm shifts." But the road to paradigm shift is a vast political struggle. Those who are not yet "in the know" and not initiated into the mysteries of the new paradigm, seek to defend the old paradigm in much the same way as a regime in power seeks to defend itself against revolution.[4]

Scientifically oriented skeptics view science as cumulative progress. They want to believe that science is going to stack up each little fact, each point of data, until eventually it spells out the truth of the whole universe. However, this is not the way science works. Science, according to Kuhn, is not cumulative progress. Science (and all human learning) works by an exchange of one paradigm for another. Kuhn developed this theory as an alternative to the former historiographical model, the major inadequacy of which was its tendency to view scientific development as a series of obstacles that are overcome by the accumulation of knowledge, bit by bit, in the face of error and superstition.[5] Kuhn interjected an anthropological method into the history of science; in using the notion of a "paradigm" (not to be confused with decision-making paradigms for arguments), he drew upon Piaget's theory of cognitive childhood development.[6] Kuhn first constructs a description of "normal science," "research firmly based upon one or more past scientific achievements...that some particular scientific community acknowledges for a time as supplying the foundation for its further practice."[7] Scientific achievements constitute a paradigm when they meet two criteria:

1. they must be solid and foundational enough to draw researchers away from other models and other approaches.
2. they must be open-ended enough to allow for further problem-solving to continue.

In this way, paradigms guide research priorities and dictate a set of shared rules within the scientific community.[8] Kuhn likens the development of a paradigm to a judicial decision in common law; it is always open to further elaboration. The procedure of "normal science," then, amounts to what he calls a "mopping up operation," or attempts at fine-tuning.[9]

Meanwhile, the discipline itself grows up around the paradigm. Research priorities are set, new instruments are developed with that viewpoint in mind, the discipline incorporates what fits its needs and weeds out that which does not lend itself to the needs of the paradigm; what Kuhn calls "paradigm-based research"[10]. All fact-gathering operations, experiments and observations, become oriented around that one viewpoint.[11] This fact-oriented nature of paradigm-based research does not assure an unbiased factual approach to "truth," but consists of the attempt to to make the anomalies fit into the regime.[12] Anomalies are not treated as "counter instances," that is, they do not count against

Joseph Hinman

the paradigm, but are treated as mere "puzzles," to be solved through further research. Only a solution within the paradigm is treated as "scientific," only that which is in accord with the theoretical model is presented as a real scientific question worthy of research, and all else is "metaphysics."[13]

In chapters 6 through 8, Kuhn elaborates upon the assumptions of the community with regard to paradigm-based research. Chapter 6 deals with discoveries in particular. Discoveries are made all the time, but it is only when they help to elucidate the paradigm that they are regarded as significant.

Data that is contrary to the paradigm is not, *a priori*, a "discovery," a *fact*, or anything but a mishap, until it is either solved as a puzzle within the perspective of the theoretical model, or the model itself is replaced with a new one.[14] In order to demonstrate this point, Kuhn details the historical problems involved in the "discovery" of oxygen.

Three different researchers may be said to have laid claim to discovering oxygen at different points in time: Scheele, Priestley and Lavoisier. Each found some aspects of oxygen, but no one researcher can be said to have discovered oxygen on a given day (although all three were working in the 1770s).[15] Kuhn's point is that discovery is a cumulative process of conceptual assimilation against the background of the paradigm.[16] But, the actual paradigm shift is not cumulative, it does not just happen after a certain number of new findings pile up. Scientists do not simply record data, and the data does not simply happen to include new discoveries; discoveries are anomalies, and thus, they are only truly known as "discoveries" in retrospect, in relation to the new paradigm.[17] Priestly and Lavoisier made comparable contributions to the discovery of oxygen, but only Lavoisier was able to fully see what had happened in producing oxygen. The major point is that paradigms constitute the scientific world, and the shift from one paradigm to another is a shift, for the researcher, from one world to another. Rigid acceptance and enforcement of the rules is essential, even to the exclusion of new theories. This is not necessarily narrow-minded professional "climate of opinion," but a necessary means of guiding research priorities. It is only against the background of the paradigm that anomaly is known. The more precise the paradigm, the greater the ability to find an anomaly, and fewer are the distractions for researchers.[18]

Anomalies

Chapters 7 and 8 are pivotal chapters because they set up the notion of crisis precedent to Kuhn's discussion of revolutions in science. It is through crisis that new paradigms emerge, when old paradigms fail to solve the growing anomalies. At this point, even though Kuhn does not state it in this manner, one can see a developmental process, or stages of cognitive formation, from discovery, to theory, to paradigms.[19] Anomalies don't just pile up until one day a new paradigm emerges; they are either incorporated into the existing paradigm or dismissed as unscientific, but over time, a sense of crisis emerges when the paradigm fails consistently to solve a "puzzle," or a type of problem. Eventually, new theories emerge from a sense of crisis and a new paradigm is substituted for the old. A classic example is astronomy. The Ptolemaic system lasted for a long time without crisis because it supplied astronomers with sufficient answers to the kinds of problems they were working on. Over time, however, problems solved in one area were often found to show up in another, until it was observed that the complexity of the system was growing much faster than its ability to accurately disclose information about the heavens. Eventually, the Copernican system was offered in its place.[20]

Dilemma in the nature of science

There is a dilemma in the nature of science itself. On the one hand, counter-instances cannot be seen as counting against the paradigm, because they are always turning up, and the paradigm is essential as the basis for shared rules of the community of science. On the other hand, a paradigm without anomalies (counter-instances) fails to produce research questions and ceases to be an important area of scientific work.[21] There is, therefore, a *tension* between anomaly and paradigm, which must be preserved. "Tension" may be a good description because counter-instances must arise, but they cannot count against the paradigm, not until a new paradigm is ready to replace the old one. This is a crucial concept because it constitutes the *nature* of a scientific revolution.[22]

Scientific revolutions: paradigm shifts

To take up this philosophical position, and then to try and justify it through appeal to its "scientific" nature, is to misunderstand the nature of science itself. Science is not a totally objective endeavor capable of yielding 100% truth. Science is a human endeavor and, thus, is limited to human cultural constructs. One of the major culturally constructed positions of science is the notion of the paradigm shift. Science works according to paradigms. One model, the paradigm, explains the nature of the world in a given area. An example of how paradigms have changed is that of the chemical vs. the mechanical model. In the 15th and 16th centuries some investigators thought that the world worked by chemical correspondence, the laws of alchemy. This notion gave way to the view of the universe as a big machine, and that notion has been transformed into the view that the universe is like a giant organism. At each stage along the way, the paradigm shifts and the facts of the old paradigm become anomalies under the new. Conversely, observations which were made before the shift which were viewed as merely anomalous (observations which contradict the paradigm) become "facts" under the new.

Science is *not* cumulative progress

A sense of urgency builds until the paradigm shifts as the old paradigm collapses under the weight of so many anomalies. Kuhn uses the analogy of political revolution precisely because of its sense of urgency and disorder. The notion of an urgent need to change, a great struggle fought on other than a rational basis is the essence of Kuhn's argument. The major conceptual changes which happen in science are not the result of cumulative progress, are not brought about through disinterested and rational discussion of the facts, and they are not predicated upon "scientific proofs." Granted, all of these things are involved, but they function as little more than "regulator concepts" that limit debate. The real change comes through a shift in perception, and thus, its scientific knowledge is not a cumulative endeavor. Kuhn writes:

> ...scientific revolutions are here taken to be those non-cumulative developmental episodes replaced in whole or in part by a new one...[23]
>
> The choice [between paradigms] is not and cannot be determined merely by the evaluative procedures characteristic of normal science, for these depend in part upon a particular paradigm, and that paradigm is at issue. When paradigms enter as they must into a debate about paradigm choice, their role is necessarily circular. Each group uses it's [sic] own paradigm to argue in that paradigm's defense...the status of the circular argument is only that of persuasion.

Joseph Hinman

> It cannot be made logically or even probabilistically compelling for those who refuse to step into the circle...[24]

And again:

> In section X we shall discover how closely the view of science as cumulating is entangled with a dominant epistemology that takes knowledge to be a construction placed directly upon raw sense data by the mind. And in section XI we shall examine the strong support provided to the same historiographic scheme by the techniques of effective science pedagogy. Nevertheless, despite the immense plausibility of that ideal image, there is increasing reason to wonder whether it can possibly be an image of science. After the pre-paradigm period the assimilation of all new theories and of almost all new sorts of phenomena has demanded the destruction of a prior paradigm and a consequent conflict between competing schools of scientific thought. Cumulative anticipation of unanticipated novelties proves to be an almost nonexistent exception to the rule of scientific development. The man who takes historic fact seriously must suspect that science does not tend toward the ideal that our image of its cumulativeness has suggested. Perhaps it is another sort of enterprise.[25]

Kuhn represents the conservative end of a movement that arose out of the 1960s and culminated in the 1990s before being dashed by the rise of the new scientism. The movement is called "social constructivism," or "postmodern social constructivism." At the radical end we had the "hard project" which sought to find epistemological roadblocks to all knowledge. What might be construed as the "conservative end," we find A.E. Burtt (*The Metaphysical Foundations of Early Modern Science*) R.G. Collingwood (*The Idea of Nature.* London, NY: Oxford, 1947), and Richard Westfall (*The Construction of Modern Science*, Cambridge University Press 1971). Herbert Butterfield is credited with kicking off the modern historical study of science. Kuhn was highly

32

regarded in the 60s through the mid 90's. His fortunes have declined since the decline of Postmodernism.

In the 80s and early 90s if you didn't talk about paradigm shifts, you didn't know anything about science. In reality, nothing in the social constructivist movement was disproved. It was all a matter of taste and climate of opinion. People are recovering his work because it was too good to be swept aside with the likes of the hard project.

The major objection that I receive when I use Kuhn in argument is that he poses an attack on science. A serious historian of science should not read Kuhn as attacking science. The problem is that skeptics have tried to *hijack* science. They work upon an assumption that science is somehow an anti-religion mechanism designed to privilege atheism over religious belief. They vest empiricism with sanctity reminiscent of Evangelical fundamentalists promoting Biblical inerrancy.

The fact of the matter is that science is not anti-religious, but rather strives to be neutral and objective. It's not to be monopolized by atheism or turned into an ideological tool for spreading anti-Gospel as Dawkins tries. True science, the way it should work, is as a *cultural construct*. All thought is a social construct because language itself is a construct. Humans do not think in wordless intentions, but in constructs.

A cultural construct is a reference based upon culturally appropriated symbols and signs which is nested in a complex set of ideas, and which is given completely through cultural assimilation, not through genetics or instinct. Cultural constructs are ideas about the world, or about feelings, or about the way we look at things, that are given by culture and that change from culture to culture. Because humans think in cultural constructs, science is made up of cultural constructs. Thus, the skeptic is not really using science in defense of the Dawkinsian ideology, but is using a Dawkinsian construct based upon an ideological filter through which science has been screened. This is the basis of the skeptical decision-making paradigm, but it maintains the *mystique* of science and so projects an image for the skeptics of absolute "objective" proof. This ideology I call "naturalism."

The ideology of naturalism maintains that religion can't have any truth content because it can't have any scientific evidence; any scientific evidence that threatens to crop up in favor of religion can be dismissed *a priori* because it's not part of the naturalistic paradigm, which begs the question. Rather, as an anomaly it is absorbed into the paradigm. This is not the paradigm of naturalistic scientific thinking. I am speaking of the ideological tool employed by skeptics, which is based upon the filtering of real scientific thought into this quasi-scientific, anti-religious ideology. Understandably real science must be done from a naturalistic perspective. I do not advocate mixing magisteria. There are areas where magisteria overlap. In such areas we should be skeptical of supernatural claims, but not in a dismissive way.

We can't expect scientific research to be motivated by an attempt to gain evidence for or against God. To do so would bias the outcome. I have no problem with evolution. I have no problem with using science to study religion, as long as we are clear about where the magisteria are truly divided. We must be clear about where the overlaps are. Hume was not a scientist. He was a philosopher and his anti-religious attitude was ideological and not scientific. Skeptics wave the name of Hume about as though he was a saint in the quasi-scientific anti-church. They try to vest Hume with the sanctity of that calling. However, Hume's views on religion were anything but objective. In fact the passionately religious Bishop Berkeley guided him to embrace skepticism. For modern skeptics, Hume is the champion of their empiricism, but he only furnishes them with circular reasoning and an ideologically-based dismissal of any counter evidence.

Hume's famous argument about miracles goes thusly: "A miracle is a violation of the laws of nature; and as a firm and unalterable experience has established these laws, the proof against a miracle, from the very nature of the fact, is as entire as any argument from experience can be imagined."[26] We see this same sort of thinking used over and over again. Scientists sometimes resort to it. Nobel Prize winning geneticist A.J. Carlson writes, "by supernatural we understand...beliefs...claiming origins other than verifiable experiences...or events contrary to known processes in nature...science and miracles are incompatible."[27]

This thinking is echoed among twentieth century modernists. The great theologian Rudolf Bultmann wrote that "modern science does not believe that the course of nature can be interrupted or, so to speak, perforated by supernatural powers."[28] The context of Bultmann's comment was in proclaiming that the events of the New Testament are mythological because they "contradict" scientific principles (Hume's Argument against Miracles). The nature of this circular reasoning is pointed out by C.S. Lewis, who wrote: "Now of course we must agree with Hume that if there is absolutely uniform experience, if in other words they have never happened, why then they never have. Unfortunately we know the experience against them to be uniform only if we know that all reports of them have been false. And we can know all the reports of them to be false only if we know already that miracles have never occurred. In fact, we are arguing in a circle."[29]

The premise of this circular nature of the reasoning insists that there can be nothing beyond the material realm. Any claims of supernatural effects must be ruled out because they cannot be. And how do we know that they cannot be? Because only that which conforms to the rules of naturalism can be admitted as "fact." Therefore, miracles can never be "fact." The "facts" which prove this rule are the very premises that rule out evidence of miracles *a priori*. While this is understandable as a scientific procedure, to go beyond the confines of explaining natural processes and proclaim that God does not exist and miracles cannot happen far exceed the boundaries of scientific investigation. Only within a particular situation, in the investigation of a particular case, can scientists make such claims. Philosophical naturalism is based upon metaphysical assumptions. Philosophical naturalists go beyond the claims of scientific methodology to take up a metaphysical position.

Metaphysics is the branch of philosophy which seeks answers beyond the confines of the physical realm. Philosophical materialists claim to know that there is no God, or at least to be convinced of it. They rule out miracles from a philosophical basis rather than an empirical one. This position is in fact a metaphysical one. Since metaphysics holds to knowledge of things beyond the material realm, philosophical materialists must count themselves its enemies. But to say that there is no God is to make a metaphysical statement. To claim to know that there is no God is to claim to have knowledge of things beyond the material realm. Philosophical materialists are, in fact, taking up a position contradictory to their stated philosophy. What I am saying should not be construed as an argument against scientific investigation of miracle claims. Science should investigate with all the scientific techniques and assumptions fit for the task of valid investigation and pronounce on those particular cases in which the claims are ruled out. Science should not make blanket assumptions that God does not work miracles. In fact, science itself does not make such claims; scientifically-minded people do, and many atheists do.

It seems that proof or disproof of religious belief depends entirely upon the assumptions one is willing to make. So if one accepts certain methods one can prove God within the nature of that language game. One can reject those language games and choose others that are not quite as cozy with the divine. Neither approach is indicative of one's intelligence or one's morality. On the other hand, belief in God may be just as rational, given the choice of axioms and methodologies. Therefore, what that tells us is that belief in God is rationally warranted; it may not be the only rational conclusion, but it is one rational conclusion. Some atheists agree to this state of affairs, but when push comes to shove they usually insist that the lack of absolute proof leaves the method that yields God arguments in doubt, rather than the other way around. I don't see why either should be privileged. Why can't we simply say that one method is better suited for one kind of question than the other? Science is better suited for study of the natural world. Philosophy is better suited for the question of God's existence. If a scientifically minded skeptic says, 'why should I ask those questions?' I say, 'why shouldn't we leave the choice of questions to the questioner?' Where we have overlap between religion and science would be where religious belief is said to effect some measurable aspect of the world. It is not the case that no scientific data supports belief, it's all a matter of what one expects to get out of the question.

Religious experience is scientifically testable. There is a vast body of data that is the result of empirical scientific studies. The data from this body of work does not tell us the origin of the experiences, whether divine or natural. It does tell us the universality, the uniformity and the effect of such experiences; the origin of the experiences is a logical inference. There is no reason not to allow a *prima facie* standard that includes logical inference as a basis of decision-making, especially when it is backed by empirical scientific data as the informational grounding of the process. Logical inference is still the basis of the interpretation of scientific data. It is no secret in history of science that modern science rose upon metaphysical and logical foundations.[30] I am not suggesting that some other standard be called in to trump scientific data when the two contradict. We can still use scientific data as the guideline where questions of an empirical nature are involved. God is not a question of empirical nature; neither is the question concerning the ultimate nature of reality. Epistemological questions require epistemological thinking. Questions of epistemic judgment require epistemic judgment. We allow methods suited to these types of questions, namely logic, experience, inference where such methods are required. Thus there is no reason why a *prima facie* case should only involve one form of knowledge.

What I am arguing thus far is not just that a rational warrant is only a valid standard of argument, but that it is also a good mark to aim for. We do not have to offer absolute proof of the existence of God. In

Aristotelian logic the assumption is that absolute proof is required. That is to say the logical force of the argument must be such that the opponent has no choice but to submit on pain of being illogical. Stephen Toulmin's theory of warrant offers the innovative position that warrant is permissive rather than obligatory. In other words, we don't need absolute proof that forces the opponent to obey our opinion. The warrant is a permissive tool. The warrant gives permission to accept an argument and can be equated with good reason.[31]

There is nothing magical about the term "rational warrant." The rational aspect just means that the argument is arrived at through reason. Toulmin stresses that warrant is *the statement that authorizes the movement from the data to the claim.* Warrant has a permissive mission in that it is not absolute proof but establishes logical justification for belief.[32]

Keith and Beard tell us that some logicians find Toulmin's concept of warrant confusing. They argue that there is no way to determine when the burden of a warrant has been met or how to recognize one.[33] It seems that what makes for confusion is the permissive nature of a warrant rather than the obligatory version of Aristotelian logic. A rational warrant cannot be construed as irrational, and an argument that is rationally warranted should be taken to be valid. I will deal with the skeptic's standard of scientific empiricism at greater length in Chapter 5 to Chapter 8. The point here is that a *prima facie* standard is a reasonable burden for a God argument, and that experience arguments meet the *prima facie* standard. How to define a "rational warrant?" When the warrant for holding a position is validated to the extent that it can be defended logically, documented through scientific data, or demonstrated according the canons of reason, it is rational to construe a position as warranted. One basic standard that might be valuable is that the warrant seems strong enough to inspire confidence in a proposition. We should not limit the types of evidence that can be used to the exclusion of logic by the imposition of a doubtful standard of "science." That is merely an attempt to move the goal post. The atheist standard of scientific empiricism is a spurious standard, and one based upon an attempt to position the goal post in a self-serving manner. This is illustrated nowhere better than the bromide "extraordinary claims require extraordinary evidence," which was originally advanced by Carl Sagan. It's quoted on message boards and by published academics, yet seldom have I seen atheist apologists deal with it in the valid context in which it was presented.

Do extraordinary claims require extraordinary proof?

While Carl Sagan made this statement popular in its current form, it was originally used by Hume, Laplace and other early theorists. Atheists have since adopted it as a major slogan for their decision-making paradigm.

> In his famous 1748 essay *Of Miracles,* the great skeptic David Hume asserted that "A wise man...proportions his belief to the evidence," and he said of testimony for extraordinary claims that "the evidence, resulting from the testimony, admits of a diminution, greater or less, in proportion as the fact is more unusual." A similar statement was made by Laplace, and many other later writers. I turned it into the now popular phrase "extraordinary claims require extraordinary proof" (which Carl Sagan popularized into what is almost the war cry of some scoffers).[34]

This slogan allows them to raise the bar for any Christian claim, while lowering it for their own purposes.[35] Edward J. Gracely explains the basic logic of the bromide:

> First, it is important to understand that the strength of a conclusion is a function both of the quality of the evidence provided in its support and the a priori probability of the claim being supported. Thus there can never be a single standard of "acceptable evidence" that will suffice to render every claim equally plausible. Suppose, for example, that a reasonably reliable source tells me (a) that President Clinton has vetoed legislation that places restrictions on trade with China and (b) that Newt Gingrich has switched to the Democratic Party. Most people would be much more confident of the truth of the first report than of the second, even though the source is identical. The difference lies in the a priori plausibility of the claims. [36]

A more precise formulation requires us to cast the *a priori* probability of a claim into the form of "odds" in its favor. A proposition with 90% probability of being true has 90 chances of being true for every 10 of being false. Thus the odds are 90 to 10, which reduces to 9 to 1. A proposition with 20% probability of being true has 20 chances of being true for 80 of being false. The odds (in its favor) are 20 to 80 or 0.25 to 1. Note the fractional amount. Stating odds in favor (as opposed to the usually "odds against"), even if it requires fractions, is required by this type of calculation. Pieces of evidence alter the odds in favor of a proposition by a multiplicative factor in proportion to the quality of the evidence.

While it is clear that not all evidence weighs the same, some evidence is better than other evidence. Nothing in this explanation indicates why evidence must be stronger for "extraordinary claims" than for "normal claims." Assuming we can even indicate what "extraordinary evidence" is, what makes it more proven than "ordinary" evidence? It's obvious the extraordinary claim is in the eye of the skeptic. The statement above merely indicates that probability is higher for a proposition backed by more direct evidence, nothing more. If the rationale says that the least likely proposition is less probable, then the assertion that the evidence must be more "extraordinary" (whatever that means) rather than just accurate or valid or to the point is not demonstrated.

Most assumptions about what makes evidence "extraordinary" or "ordinary," or a proposition likely or unlikely is going to be largely a matter of prejudice. Consider the following statement, also by Gracely:

> The principle is clear; the difficulty lies in the application. How likely, for example, is it that homeopathy or therapeutic touch really work?[37] Proponents argue that we need to open our minds to new possibilities and grant these systems a fairly high a priori probability (say, 50-50 odds). Then, even modest-quality evidence would make the claims quite probably true. Skeptics argue that these systems violate known laws of physics and their validity should therefore be considered remotely improbable.[38]

Who decides how likely it is that homeopathy is valid or invalid medicine? One would need a statistical average for cure rates to compare with a control group using orthodox practices to evaluate this. He admits that "modest quality" evidence would be proof if it is granted a high probability. Without proper studies why not so grant? What if one has found such treatments effective already in one's own life? It is nothing more than prejudice to judge something improbable on the basis of guesswork and matters of taste. Why shouldn't the issue be a standard of *evidence adequate for proof* of the issue under consideration? I have yet to find an atheist argument that can tell what extraordinary God evidence is. I've seen attempts on message boards, absurdities such as "Why can't God make all the stars spell out the phrase 'burn pain is the worst pain, Jesus is Lord, convert now?'" Or "God could appear at the UN and hold a press conference." I have yet to see an atheist give me a valid option for "extraordinary evidence." More importantly, we are talking about *God*, not about finding Bigfoot. God is off the scale of empirical investigation. How can the basis of reality be studied as though it's just another "thing" in creation? What could be used as a basis of comparison? How could one ever establish a baseline comparison to determine probability of God? Dawkins tries to, but he merely assumes God would be on a par with any other physical object.[39]

What basis is used to establish the probability of something that is said to be beyond our understanding? Gracely argues:

> An alternative I have heard suggested is to drop the extraordinary proof argument and instead to hold paranormal and alternative medicine claims strictly to the ordinary requirements of replicability and good research. This approach sounds sensible but it has a serious flaw. Skeptics are not willing to accept the plausibility of most paranormal claims unless the evidence is extremely strong. We risk being perceived (correctly) as disingenuous if we call for solid quality research, then revert to the extraordinary claims argument should it in fact appear.[40]

Instead of "ordinary", one term we might use for a sufficient but not extraordinary level of proof would be a *prima facie* case. Gracely may have a point if we are talking about acupuncture or UFOs, but the flaw he sees in it is attitudinal, not logical or methodological. It seems at times that atheists are not willing to accept any level of evidence. The religious experience studies are bona-fide scientific studies; a huge body of work backs them up. These studies, such as Hood's studies validating the M scale, are not on a par with homeopathy or these other matters. They are published by academics in peer-reviewed journals. For all practical purposes, they are "extraordinary evidence" if anything is. Let us not forget there is no set standard any skeptic can offer to define that term. Skeptics are quick to brush aside the experience studies as "subjective" without reading the studies or considering the arguments. Gracely observes that skeptical attitudes are similar even in other areas:

In some areas of paranormal investigation, such as extrasensory perception (ESP), the research is already often better done than much orthodox scientific research, with controls and double-checks most scientists would regard as overkill. Skeptics mostly still feel that the intrinsic implausibility is so great that nothing short of airtight and well-repeated research would be sufficient to support ESP. Little or none of the existing research rises to that level, so we remain skeptical. (Some recent work has been of high quality, see Ray Hyman's article, "The Evidence for Psychic Functioning: Claims vs. Reality", in the March/April 1996 *Skeptical Inquirer*, pp 24-26.) Had skeptics said some 40 years ago that all we wanted was reasonable quality replicated research, we might now be having to eat our words. [41]

When demands for evidence are met, the bar is raised again. The tyranny of "extraordinary evidence," so long as one never defines it, allows for abuse: why should God be subjected to the same standards of proof as empirical objects? Here the skeptic is in the position of arguing "God is improbable because I don't believe in him." Truzzi documents the "Catch 22" designed into the extraordinary proof standard:

> But it is important to remember that the proponent of the paranormal has an uphill battle from the start. The chips are stacked against him, so his assault is not so threatening to the fabric of science as scoffers often characterize it. In a sense, conservative science has "the law" on its side. In law, we find three varieties in the weight of burden of proof:
>
> 1. proof by preponderance of evidence
> 2. clear and convincing proof, and, in criminal law
> 3. proof beyond a reasonable doubt
>
> In conventional science, we usually use (1), but when dealing with extraordinary claims, critics often seem to demand (3) since they demand all alternative explanations must be eliminated before the

maverick claim is acceptable. This demand sometimes becomes unreasonable and may even make the scoffer's position unfalsifiable. Since the anomaly proponent is already saddled with a presumption of "guilt," it would seem to me that (2), clear and convincing proof, might be the best standard, though proponents may reasonably wonder why standard (1) should always be denied them. [42]

But we must also keep in mind that God is not "paranormal." Truzzi and Gracely are speaking in general of any sort of "paranormal" claim, including the claims of alternative medicine. God belief is the status quo for human belief; it is normative. Nor is God a scientific question. It is absurd to expect us to limit evidence to only the scientific when the question about belief is epistemological. More on this aspect of belief and its importance for evidential standards below. But this does raise a further question about the extraordinary evidential standard.

In addition to defining the term "extraordinary evidence" there is also a need to define the term "extraordinary *claim*." Why is God an extraordinary claim? Here the atheist is truly in the position of arguing "God is improbable because I don't believe in him." Atheists make up 3% of the world's population at best. [43] The overwhelming majorities of people alive today, or who have ever lived, believe in some form of God. Our brains are hard-wired to have thoughts of God. Our physical and mental health work better when we believe in God (as will be seen in later chapters). If we are fit for belief, why would belief be extraordinary? Why should the 3% minority define what is normative for humanity? Belief in God is far more than just the average belief; it is *normative as a standard of human understanding*. It forms the basis of our psyches, it forms the basis of our legal system; it is the chief metaphor regulating meaning and morality. Belief in God illustrates all the aspects of a *prima facie* case. This is at least so for RE. Marcelo Truzzi makes the same point:

The central problem however lies in the fact that "extraordinary" must be relative to some things "ordinary." And as our theories change, what was once extraordinary may become ordinary (best seen in now accepted quantum effects that earlier were viewed as "impossible"). Many now extraordinary claims may become more acceptable not when they are replicated but when theoretical contexts change to make them more welcome. [44]

Skeptics have argued that religious experience is not regular or consistent because such experiences are all different. Not only do you have so many different religions, but also even from mystic to mystic things differ. Over the years as one develops a disciplined life of prayer, one does encounter growing diversity and newness, but a certain sense of the familiar as well. Experiences become regular and consistent in that the presence of God is usually found in prayer, the sense of the presence is always of the same quality (although of varying intensity) and the sense of God can become familiar enough that it is always recognized as the same.

This sense of the familiar is communicable and can be recognized from one believer to another. The mystical and devotional literature presents a kind of ordered sameness. One can read accounts as different from one experiencer to another as those between St. Augustine and A.W. Tozer and still find passages that seem to be talking about the same things. This is amplified times millions of believers in the history of the church who have experienced the same things. Even though there is diversification and difference there is still sameness. This sameness in diversity is not even confined to mystics. Conversion accounts exhibit a sameness as well. One can recognize the work of God from one person to another, from one time to the next, from one culture to all cultures. Skeptics may ask, what about the vast array of different religions? These differences are due to cultural constructs. One experiences God beyond words, and when one tries to speak of such experiences one must encode them in a symbolic universe, that is to

Joseph Hinman

say, in culture. These differences in symbolic universes over time have
spelled out the differences in the many religions. There is, however, a
certain unity even among all the differences in religion. The data
presented above on long-term effects represents typologies, which can
be used to compare "peak experience" with that of other phenomena.
Those who experience this "peak experience" can be grouped by the
type of experience. They are not isolated assortments of differing
phenomena. These studies do represent differing cultures and times.
Thus, religious experience is consistent even between cultures.

Archetypal symbolism: universal link to peak experience

"Peak experience" is Maslow's terminology for "mystical experience."
He understands the mystical through a psychological understanding
involving Jungian archetypes:

> Jungian archetypes which can be recovered in several ways. I have
> managed to get it in good introspects simply by asking them directly
> to free associate to a particular symbol. The psychoanalytic literature,
> of course, has many such reports. Practically every deep case history
> will report such symbolic, archaic ways of viewing the woman, both
> in her good aspects and her bad aspects. (Both the Jungians and the
> Kleinians recognize the great and good mother and the witch mother
> as basic archetypes.) Another way of getting at this is in terms of the
> artificial dream that is suggested under hypnosis. It can also probably
> be investigated by spontaneous drawings, as the art therapists have
> pointed out. Still another possibility is the George Klein technique of
> two cards very rapidly succeeding each other so that symbolism can
> be studied. Any person who has been psychoanalyzed can fairly
> easily fall into such symbolic or metaphorical thinking in his dreams
> or free associations or fantasies or reveries. [45]

Maslow and others argue that perhaps all people have some form of mystical experience, or that it is at least accessible to them.

> The literature on peak experiences is sharply divided as to how common these experiences are. Those who have given accounts of these experiences have often described them as once-in-a-lifetime events which were perceived as happening only to a few especially fortunate persons. Yet, countless others may have had such experiences and simply not bothered to leave records of them. Maslow (1962) has suggested, in fact, that nearly everyone probably has them and could describe them if investigators were to ask the right questions.[46]

See Chapter 3 for further examination of mystical experience.

In the meantime, one might ask at this stage, "why does God seem so hidden?" The importance of this question is that the average person doesn't have mystical experiences, at least not all the time. God doesn't seem regular or consistent but hidden. Yet for those who have the sensibility to experience the sense of the numinous or the undifferentiated unity these senses become regular and consistent over time. Moreover, it may be that we are all exposed to God on a very basic level anyway and since we can't understand that exposure without filtering it through cultural constructs, we either explain it through a tradition, ignore it, or explain it away. Scott Gross, a philosopher specializing in religion and theology, explains it this way:

> In terms of process theology, the "communication" of God must be understood as the prehension of God by human beings. A "prehension" is the response of an occasion to the entire past world (both the contiguous past and the remote past.) As God is in every occasion's past actual world, every occasion must "prehend" or take account of God. It should be noted that "prehension" is a generic mode of perception that does not necessarily entail consciousness or

sensory experience. In previous writings I explained that there are two modes of pure perception —"perception in the mode of causal efficacy" and "perception in the mode of presentational immediacy." If God is present to us, then it is in the pre-sensory perceptual mode of causal efficacy as opposed to the sensory and conscious perceptual mode of presentational immediacy. That is why God seems "invisible." The foundation for experience of God lies in the non-sensory non-conscious mode of prehension. So now, there is the further question: Why is there variability in our experience of God? Or, why are some of us atheists, pantheists, theists, etc.? Every prehension has an initial datum derived from God, yet there are a multiplicity of ways in which this datum is prehended from diverse perspectives. [47]

I agree with Hume that sense perception tells us nothing about efficient causation (or final causation for that matter). Hume was actually presupposing causal efficacy in his attempt to deny it (i.e., in his relating of sense impressions to awareness). Causation could be described as an element of experience, but as Whitehead explains, this experience is not sensory experience. From Hume's own analysis Whitehead derives at least two forms of non-sensory perception: the perception of our own body and the non-sensory perception of one's past. Atheists who deny the validity of religious experience often assume that all perception is sense perception. Or, they deny sense perception to theists when they actually presuppose it themselves (Hume is a case in point).

Everyone experiences the reality of God or the "Holy" all the time

The experience of the reality of God or the "Holy" that, I claim, everyone experiences is at an unconscious level. However, in some people, this direct prehension of the "Holy" rises to the level of conscious experience. We generally call these people "mystics". Now, the reason why a few people are conscious of God is not the result of God violating causal principle; some people are just able to conform to God's initial datum in greater degree than other people can. I don't think that God chooses to make Himself consciously known to some and not to others. That would make God an elitist. Now, the question as to why I am a theist as opposed to an atheist does not have to do with me experiencing some exceptional religious or mystical experience. Rather, I believe that these extraordinary experiences of the great religious leaders are genuine and that they do conform to the ultimate nature of things. It's not necessarily a "blind leap" of faith, as my religious beliefs are accepted, in part, on the basis of whether or not they illuminate my experience of reality.[48]

The final proof of a belief is not in the experience of any single witness. The fact that there are millions of witnesses who, in differing levels from the generally intuitive to the mystical, experience much the same thing in terms of general religious belief carries the force of proof. The argument is simply that God interacts on the level of the "human heart" (consciousness at a subliminal level), and that those who have these experiences are strong evidence for that conclusion.

Analogies: on the hiddenness of God

God is "nearer than inmost" as Augustine writes. God is the basic background of the universe, and as such, our situation is like that of a fish in water: we see in light all the time but rarely notice the light.

In other words, belief in God is far from extraordinary, so the basis for comparison that we need to label a claim "extraordinary" has to be taken on a case-by-case basis. We can't just label all religious thinking "extraordinary claims." Clearly belief in God is not extraordinary. "Extraordinary" is a problematic term in science. Kuhn argued that scientific paradigms turn over when there are too many anomalies to explain them all through the orthodox paradigm. The "normal" business of science, according to Kuhn, is that of absorbing anomalies into the paradigm.[49] "Anomalies" are not necessarily extraordinary, but both concepts deal with departures from the expected. Many atheists assert this Saganian imperative about extraordinary experiences in terms of dazzling wonderment. In other words, extraordinary claims are those that they find extremely hard to believe, big amazing claims that require big amazing proof.

Common atheist examples of the extraordinary such as God arranging the stars to spell out messages confirming the truth of Christianity are much more grandiose than Kuhn's anomalies. Dawkins seeks to argue that God is improbable on the basis of uniqueness. There is no other evidence for any sort of thing like God anywhere else in our field of experience as a species, thus God has to be improbable because we have nothing else to compare God to.[50] Again we are dealing with the concept of "the out of the ordinary". We are dealing with ideas of the unique, that which stands out. This is a good indication that scientific thinking seeks an orthodoxy that requires mutually accepted cultural constructs to form a basis of consensus. Of course scientific thinkers will stand staunchly upon the empirical "totally proven" aspects of their views.

Both in normal science and among theorists who attempt to monopolize science, there is a struggle of orthodoxy against revolutionaries, and the struggle revolves around accepted world views, which take on an aura of the sacred. Belief in God comes ready packaged in its own aura of the sacred. The battle between scientifically based skeptical empiricism vs. religious belief is a battle of religions in a sense. It's a party line seeking to secure itself against heretics. Atheists do not have facts that prove their views; they merely have world views that collide with the world views of religious people.

Nor can claiming "extraordinary evidence" make the former world views more cogent. As has been demonstrated, there is no basis for comparison since belief in God is not a scientific question. There is no basis upon which to define "extraordinary evidence" since the term is measured by proximity to orthodoxy. In other words, what is really going to determine the extraordinary nature of a claim for a skeptic of religion is the claim's relation to the paradigm under which the skeptic has formed his worldview. That means that extraordinary evidence must be that evidence which, despite its status as an anomaly under the skeptic's paradigm, and thus its tendency to be explained away, or "absorbed," by the paradigm, the believer would still be expected to have it as means of warrant for the belief. In other words, the atheist demand for extraordinary evidence can never be met because it is a logical contradiction; it is evidence that does something no skeptic can ever admit evidence can do: convince the skeptic that his paradigm is wrong and that he must adopt a new paradigm.

But the skeptic's drive, whether admitted or not, is to defend the paradigm one already works under. The skeptic is asking the impossible since the paradigm shift doesn't result from dazzling or wonderment-evoking evidence, but from constant anomalies, which become so bothersome they cannot be absorbed into the accepted paradigm any longer. But particular anomalies are not going to be seen as "extraordinary" or they would not have their status as "anomaly" in the first place. Such evidence would have to supersede the normal paths that human thought uses to compile world views. In short, the Saganian imperative is wrong. It not only contradicts the way scientific theories come to be accepted in the world of science, but also the way the human mind works in constructing an understanding of the way the world works.

Of course we have to be aware that Kuhn's sense of the term "paradigm" and the sense in which I use it here are not the same. He's talking about the major paradigm, or model, that guides an entire discipline: such as the concept of naturalistic cause and effect. I am talking about the type of case one might make to advance a God argument. Yet the extraordinary claims dictum would seem to violate the Kuhnian sense of paradigm shift. If we think of empirical evidence for religious belief as anomalies (such as the effects of religious experience as long term and positive upon the believer) the data from experience studies might be thought of as an anomaly. Certainly any sort of claim to miracles would be anomalous.

The most frequent application I have seen of the dictum about extraordinary evidence is circular reasoning. The skeptic says, "This is not good evidence, it isn't extraordinary enough." But the believer says, "Ok here's more." That doesn't apply because we know from past experience this isn't extraordinary; it's too much like the other evidence, it wasn't extraordinary either. Therefore this evidence is not extraordinary. For example, say we are arguing about miracles. The Lourdes miracles have 65 examples where the official miracle-finding machine of the church says, "This is an official church miracle." The skeptic says "only 65? That's not extraordinary; these are just anomalies. They are just remission." Then the believer points out that there are also 7,000 remarkable cases which can't be explained —but just missed being tagged as "official" because they lack some perfunctory piece of evidence— where there is enough evidence to say they are "remarkable." They do say of these cases that they are "remarkable." One would think that "extraordinary" would be the same or similar to "remarkable."

But the skeptic replies that they are not extraordinary, they are just like the other 65; the other 65 have been dismissed for not being enough of them therefore the 7000[50] should be dismissed because the original 65 aren't extraordinary so they shouldn't be accepted and the 7000 shouldn't be either because they are no more amazing than the 65. But the effect is that the 65 are being dismissed because there aren't enough of them, but when more are shown they are dismissed for not being amazing enough. Lest one think this is just an anomaly of religion skeptics, there is an example of a major scientist acting this way.

Physicist Louis Frank discusses a theory that oceans on earth were started by very small comets, house-sized comets, which over long periods of time deposited enough water from ice to form huge bodies of water. Frank had evidence from satellite images that the rate of bombardment by such mini-comets is about 20 per minute. Astronomers responded by basically saying "if these existed we would have seen them." In the 1980s Clayne Yeates decided to prove Frank wrong by demonstrating the results of telescopic search. Journal editors told Yeates that the standard requirement for proof was two images photographed from telescope. He had the two images in the paper already. When he pointed this out to the editor of *Geophysical Research Letters,* he was told that he had to obtain three.[51] So the evidence isn't strong enough because it's a new claim that doesn't fall in line with accepted belief, but when more evidence is provided it isn't good enough. The editor didn't say but it appears that the new evidence was dismissed on the basis that, since the old evidence wasn't good so this isn't either, even though more evidence was the requirement. This is perfectly in line with what Kuhn says happens; the old paradigm is challenged and thus is defended by the orthodox who maintain a party line and work to repair damage to the old paradigm. As long as the dictum about extraordinary evidence is waved about as a standard, the bar will always be moved no matter how well the believer meets the requirements.

Marcello Truzzi has a proposal to replace the dictum; it makes a lot more sense. Truzzi proposes:

In addition to recognizing and working through the issues I have raised above, we need scaled terms to deal with levels of evidence for the best of the extraordinary claims put forth by proto-scientists. Scientists might well distinguish between extraordinary claims that are: *suggestive,* meaning interesting and worthy of attention but generally of low priority; *compelling,* meaning the evidence is strongly supportive and argues for assigning a higher scientific priority for greater investigation; and *convincing,* meaning most reasonable scientists examining the evidence would agree at least a preponderance of evidence supports the claim. Using such graded language might help us turn from our present debates, with room only for winners and losers, into dialogues between peers, all of whom should want to see science judiciously progress. We can all be winners.[52]

The upshot of all of this is religious belief is normative for human behavior. It is not merely "normal" but "*normative*" meaning it sets the standard. Belief is basic to human psyche. There is no way belief in God can be thought of as *an extraordinary claim!* We might think of it as extraordinary in the sense of being unique, like no other claim, but in that case it makes no sense to subject it to the regular canons of science as though God's presence is given in daily empirical data. Obviously the more intelligent evidential standard is that the evidence has to be fit for the claim. Fit, not dazzling, not impossible, not amazing, not beyond our ability to produce, but it has to fit the case. It has to be rational, able to bear a *prima facie* burden for the proof attempted.

The difference is that the atheist standard is *ultima facie*, "all things considered" rather than "on the face of it." The atheist demands absolute proof, and that absolute proof must be furnished by just one standard: scientific empiricism.

The *prima facie* standard makes much more sense than does absolute proof, (1) because there cannot be absolute scientific data of questions beyond the empirical realm; (2) because belief is an individual question of a personal existential nature; and (3) because belief deals not merely with facts about things in the universe, but about one's place in the universe. For these reasons it has to be subjective, it has to be private, personal, and by its nature it is not provable in the absolute scientific sense. There's no use pretending that the absolute scientific umpire is the only form of knowledge. I will take this up in later chapters including Chapter 8 (Traditions). The point here is that the *prima facie* case fits the subject matter in a much more rational way. All we can ask of a worldview, after all, is rational warrant. World views take in too much to be demonstrated entirely from empirical data.

Pick a paradigm, any paradigm

Richard Rorty (1931-2007) in his work *Contingency, Irony, and Solidarity* makes the argument against religious beliefs, not that there aren't enough good paradigms of truth available to know what's what, but that there are too many! No one paradigm can gain traction over the others because they are all good. There are so many good descriptions of the world that it is meaningless to have a good description of the world.[53] It would be absurd to try and pick a world just to make an argument for the existence of God. Should one be a Foundationalist? Should one be an Evidentialist? Should one be a Presuppositionsalist? Should one be an Empiricist? Should one be an Existentialist? It would be absurd to choose based upon a God argument, and yet the answer will largely determine how one reacts to various God arguments. I do not believe that it is necessary to be any of these things at any one given time. What would be the point of jumping on a band wagon and waving the flag for one's favorite flavor of misconception? If one must have a label, perhaps "Operationalist," would be the best. There is no reason to pin it down. We can adapt to the question. We can choose criteria that are loose enough to offer a *prima facie* case that conforms to the type of argument being made. According to the argument I just made, the foolhardy nature of empiricism should be apparent. To demand the old, tired refrain about evidence or proof for God has been shown to be off-track. God is beyond the level of empirical proof since God is the foundation of being, not a thing in creation. The believer need not be buffaloed by ideology masquerading as science.

Examining the Criteria

There are three things we need to consider before moving on:

1. What conditions make for a *prima facie* case? How do we know when it has succeeded?
2. What conditions make for overturning a *prima facie* case?
3. How do we know when it is overturned?

The criteria I've listed above dealing with the success of a *prima facie* case include:

1. Documented perceptual evidence
2. Perceptions (or other evidence) that are regular (a form of replicability).
3. Consistency (meaning no internal contradictions).
4. Inter-subjective verification (others can experience similar phenomena, share the data, observe the same kinds of experience).
5. Logical inference from both inductive and deductive reasoning
6. Tangible measurable effects
7. No counter-causality: counter-causes must be defeated, disproved, or rendered less likely
8. Must be falsifiable.

These criteria pertain specifically to an argument based upon experience. Other kinds of arguments, such as cosmological, might require altering the criteria to fit the subject matter. We should set out criteria that govern the presentation of a particular form of argument —not all arguments involve the same type of evidence— being careful to use neutral criteria, not advantaging either side. Obviously, the criteria would also include adequate documentation for any sort of factual evidence. The nature of the question will determine these needs. For example, we would not expect the same sort of questions about reliability of perception in dealing with a cosmological argument as we would in dealing with an experience argument. Since cosmology uses instruments that record data and does not depend upon subjective feelings of the observer, we don't need the same kind of perceptual checks with the former that we do in the latter case.

In answer to 2 and 3, how do we know when it has failed or been overturned? The caveats argued with the skeptic about the conditions under which a *prima facie* case is overturned:

1. Justified until something comes along to take it away
2. Occasional conflicts don't hurt; they are analogous to misperceptions

New evidence coming to light or new aspects of old evidence would be a major recourse for the skeptic. Clearly the use of counter-causality will be a major ploy by the skeptic, especially in dealing with experience arguments. The skeptic will argue that there is no reason to suspect that God is actually causing such experiences because they can be accounted for by everything from stomachaches to insanity to hypnotism. This, we might observe, is basically a paradigm shift argument. Contradictions to the paradigm are absorbed into the model until there are so many that the model no longer hold. But paradigm shifts began as a theory in the realm of child development —Kuhn writes: "...chance led me to the experiments by which Jean Piaget has illuminated both the various worlds of the growing child and the process of transition from one to the next."54— and they probably represent the basic pattern of human learning. We know that the *prima facie* burden has been met when we meet the eight criteria above and demonstrate the logic of a warrant for belief. This amounts to a good logical reason to believe.

1. Richard Dawkins, *The God Delusion*, New York: Houghton Mifflin company, First Mariner books edition,2008, originally 2006, 137.

2. G.J. Mattey, 2002 Lecture notes Lehrers *Theory of Knowledge* Second Edition, Chapter 4 Foundation; fallible foundations." Online http://hume.ucdavis.edu/mattey/phi102kl/tkch4.htm (accessed 11/30/10).

3. Neil J. Smelser, Sociology Spanning Two Centuries, *The American Sociologist*. Springer New York (vol 34, no. 3, September 2003), 5-19.

4. Thomas S. Kuhn. *The Structure of Scientific Revolutions*, Chicago: University of Chicago Press, 1962, 1-2.

5. *Ibid.*, 2.

6. *Ibid.*, vi.

7. *Ibid.*, 10.

8. *Ibid.*, 10.

9. *Ibid.*, 23-24

10. *Ibid.*, 25.

11. *Ibid.*, 27.

12. *Ibid.*, 35.

13. *Ibid.*, 37.

14. *Ibid.*, 53.

15. *Ibid.*, 54.

16. *Ibid.*, 55.

17. *Ibid.*, 56.

18. *Ibid.*, 65.

19. *Ibid.*, 67.

20. *Ibid.*, 68-69.

21. *Ibid.*, 79.

22. *Ibid.*, 90.

23. *Ibid.*, 92.

24. *Ibid.*, 94.

25. *Ibid.*, 96.

26. David Hume, *An Essay Concerning Human Understanding,* Chicago, Illinois: Open Court Publishing Company 1958, 126-27

27. A. J. Carlson, *Science Magazine,* Science and The supernatural. Feb. 27, 1937, 5.

28. Rodolf Bultmann, *Jesus Christ and Mythology,* New York: Scribner and Sons, 1958, 15.

29. C.S. Lewis, *Miracles: a Preliminary Study*. New York: MacMillian, 1947, 105.

30. A.E. Burtt, *The Metaphysical Foundations of Early Modern Science*. Garden City, New York: Doubleday 1954, 10.

31. William Keith and David Beard, "Toulmin's Rhetorical Logic: What is the Warrant for Warrants?" *Philosophy and Rhetoric*, Vol. 41, No. 1, 2008, 22.

32. Stephen E. Toulmin, *The Uses of Argument*, Cambridge Mass.: Cambridge University Press, Updated edition, 2003, originally 1958, 89-91.

33. Keith and Beard, *op. cit.,* 22.,

34. Marcelo Truzzi, "On Some Unfair Practices Toward Claims of the Paranormal." *Skeptical Investigations:* http://www.skepticalinvestigations.org/Anomali/practices.html (visited 10/21/10). *This article was published in slightly edited form in: Edward* Binkowski, editor, Oxymoron: Annual Thematic Anthology of the Arts and Sciences, Vol.2: The Fringe, New York: Oxymoron Media, Inc., 1998.

35. Edward J. Gracely. "Why Extraordinary Claims Demand Extraordinary Proof." Quackwatch, blog, July 24, 2003, http://www.quackwatch.org/01QuackeryRelatedTopics/extraproof.html (accessed 5/3/13). Originally published December 1998 issue of *Phactum*, the newsletter of the *Philadelphia Association for Critical Thinking (PhACT)*. Dr. Gracely is Associate Professor of Community and Preventive Medicine at the MCP*Hahnemann School of Medicine in Philadelphia.

36. *Ibid.*

37. See, for instance, *homeopathy* (http://www.quackwatch.org/01QuackeryRelatedTopics/homeo.html) and therapeutic touch (http://www.quackwatch.org/01QuackeryRelatedTopics/tt.html) on QuackWatch.com (accessed 10/21/10).

38. Gracely, *op. cit.*

39. Gracely, *op. cit.*, 137-140

40. Gracely, *Ibid.*

41. *Ibid.*

42. Truzzi, Op. Cit.

43. Adherents.com, "Major Religions of the World Ranked by Number of Adherents, http://www.adherents.com/Religions_By_Adherents.html (accessed 5/1/2013), 16% are in the category "non-religious"; it says in that section that "half of this group is theistic but non-religious." That means 8% believe in God. Of the other 8% they list atheist, agnostic, and

humanist. I assume about half of those are atheist. This means that atheism could be as high as almost 8%.

44. Truzzi, *op. cit.*

45. Abraham Maslow, *Religions, Values, and Peak-Experiences.* New York: The Viking Press. Published by Penguin Books Limited, 1970, Appendix I. An Example of B-Analysis.

46. Robert Wuthnow, "Peak Experiences: Some Empirical Tests." *Journal of Humanistic Psychology,* 18 (3), (1978). 60.

47. Scott Gross, "Why does God Remain so Hidden? Summary on Prehension in J.L.Hinman, Doxa: Christian Thought in the 21st Century, Website, Thomas Reid Argument, http://www.doxa.ws/Reid2.html (accessed 5/2/13).

48. *Ibid.*

49. Kuhn, *op. cit.* 67-69.

50. bytrentsacred.co.uk. "The Protestant Atheism of Richard Dawkins," Comment 1, blog, http://www.bytrentsacred.co.uk/index.php/dawkins-protestant-atheism/the-god-delusion-comment-1 (accessed 5/1/2013). My statement was hypothetical but this example of Dawkins fits it. The blogger gives the example of Dawkins going to Lourdes and saying there are only 66 miracles while ignoring the millions of others who have faith in the miracles. As a personal aside, in the official literature of Lourdes there are 7,000 remarkable cases, and he only looks at the official Church-endorsed 66. The actual remarkable cases are only rejected for technical problems related to formalities of documentation, not because they can't be proved to be beyond our explanation.

51. Patrick Huyghe, "Extraordinary Claim? Move the Goal Post," Archive commentary, reprinted from *The Anomalist 3* winter 1995/6, online, *http://www.anomalist.com/commentaries/claim.html* (accessed 7/9/08). For Franks theory see *The Big Splash* by Louis A. Franks with Patrick Huyghe. (Avon books, 1991).

52. Marcelo Truzzi *op. cit.*

53. Richard Rorty, *Contingency, Irony, and Solidarity.* Cambridge Mass: Cambridge University Press, 1989. 7-10.

2 Arguments

Overview

In this chapter I will focus more explicitly upon the arguments laid out in the introduction, in a more detailed version. I will answer certain skeptical objections (but save certain major objections for their own chapters). I will also examine other arguments made from religious experience and show either how mine hold advantages or how they differ. Arguments about brain chemistry (the so called "God part of the brain"), drugs, and Placebo effects will receive their own chapters.

In this chapter I make two basic arguments:

1. **Argument from co-determinate:** The historical association between the object of mystical experience and a human understanding of the divine goes all way back to the beginnings of humanity as we know it. Moreover, the content of modern experiences also indicate form of the "holy" the "sacred," "the divine." For this reason we can understand these experiences as "the trace" or the track, the signature of God upon humanity. It gives us an empirically based understanding that warrants belief.

2. **Argument from epistemic judgement:**
   The nature of the experiences fits the criteria that we use to determine the reality of our experiences. Therefore we should be able to trust it as indicative of reality. This criteria centers around the fact that assuming the reality of such experience "works" in that it enables us to navigate through life.

Joseph Hinman

Having provided a set of "thumbnail" arguments to lay out the territory to be covered, a deeper structure will be developed for each part.

Co-determinate argument: the logic of the lamp post

The term "co-determinate" refers to what I call "the trace of God:" the effects of the divine upon human experience. The former concept is from Schleiermacher; the latter is a Derridian expression of it. In Derrida's terminology "trace" means footprint, or like tracks in the snow, something that leads us to an object we seek but cannot see. We follow the signs of its egress, just as we follow tracks in the snow. The Derridian terminology refers to the meaning pointed to by linguistic signifiers —for instance, road signs and markers in language itself. The meaning is never present in a signifier —it's always being shunted off to another signifier that implies meaning— but by the time we get there the meaning has moved on. So it is with experiences of God. The experience itself is the trace of God: this is analogous the Derridian concept of trace. Even though God is not given in a sense data, and God is not an empirical question, the trace of God is empirical. The problem with this argument is that it assumes we know about God up front; otherwise how can we know the trace of God when we see it? The answer to this problem is phenomenological. We must construe this conclusion logically from the facts. This is why it has to be done on a *prima facie* basis, because we don't have the luxury of absolute knowledge. We need only offer a *prima facie* case as to why we should understand the phenomena as the trace of God. I should say the trace of "the divine." This is distinct from "God" in that there are many conceptions of the divine, but they all imply God as a reasonable surmise. "Divine" can be polytheistic, it can be pantheistic, it can be pneumatic ("spiritual"), but all of these options point to a single organizing principle which we call "God." There are two sub-arguments: argument from the co-determinate and argument from epistemic judgment. The co-determinate is the thing that goes along with something as its signature or trace; footprints in the snow signify a footfall, fingerprints on a table tell us that fingers were there. Epistemic judgment deals with judgment-calls we must make on an epistemological level. The two are really concerned with the same things, but from two different angles. Thus I present this as one big argument with two major sections. The arguments self-evidently indicate the justification for the construal:

1. **Co-determinate argument**: We can construe religious experience (RE) as the co-determinate (the "trace," the footprint) of God upon the human heart for three reasons:

   1. Historical association

      1. Pre-historic sense of the numinous
      2. Origin of all religion in the sense of the numinous
      3. Origin not found in functionalism

         1. Antiquated hypothesis
         2. Not failed primitive attempt at explanations

      4. Content

         1. Draws subject to the divine
         2. Instills sense of the Holy
         3. Unity and meaning speak of divine

      5. Effects

         1. Life transforming

            1. Self Actualization
            2. Mental health
            3. Physical health

         2. What we should expect from the Divine
            The purpose of religion is to mediate the transformative power of the divine. Religions do this all over the world.

They define the problem of being human and resolve that problem with a transformation experience . They mediate this experience through ceremony or religious experience (either derived from ceremony or not). In Christian life, the Fall (when the first man and woman went from innocent obedience to God to a state of guilty disobedience) and sin nature are the nature of the human problematic, the born-again experience and/or baptism of the Holy Spirit are the examples of transformative experience. In Hinduism, the problem is re-birth while the transformative power comes through meditation. In Buddhism, it comes through enlightenment that stems from giving up desire. In Shinto, the problematic is lack of balance with nature and the transformation comes through re-establishing balance. In all of these examples the ultimate point of having a religion is to mediate this transformation. In all religious traditions around the world, mystical experience communicates transformative power; the studies I will discuss demonstrate this.

3. The effects are real so we can infer the cause is real because:

   1. We can logically infer God as cause (based upon content)
   2. Alternate causes can be refuted

2. **Argument from Epistemic Judgment**

   1. Meets criteria of epistemic judgment

      1. Criteria

         1. Regular
         2. Consistent
         3. Shared (inter-subjective)

      2. Works for navigation in the world

3. **Normative nature of religion provides freedom from need to prove**

    1. Special sense ("religious *a priori*")
    2. Existential Self Authenticating

        1. Object of ultimate concern
        2. Life Transformation

    3. Works = Normative
    4. Normative = Rational

4. **How the Arguments meet their *Prima Facie* Burden**

    1. Criteria

        1. Documented perceptual evidence
        2. Regular perceptions
        3. Consistency (no internal contradiction)
        4. Inter-subjective verification
        5. Logical inference from both inductive and deductive
        6. Tangible measurable effect
        7. No counter causality: counter causes defeated or demonstrated to be less likely
        8. Must be falsifiable

    2. Rationally Warranted

Logic of the lamp post

Experience of the sense of the numinous, the sense of divine presence and love which offers a meaning to life and sense of Holiness and a special quality which we associate with the divine, is at the heart of all religious belief and all organized religions. It is also the basis of the kind of religious experience we are talking about. It is the foundation of religious belief. If we were going to argue for God it would behoove us

Joseph Hinman

to examine the nature of this sense. God is not a case of the empirical; God is not given in sense data. Thus, we must use the logic of the lamp post: we can't find our keys in the dark, therefore, we look under the streetlight because that is where they will be visible; if we are to find them, even if we did not drop them there, that is where they will be found. God is not the object of objective sense data as if the divine is a solid object. The sense of the numinous is not sense data, it's a qualitative experience based upon a heightened state of consciousness; it's not something we see with our eyes, or hear with our ears, or touch with our hands. So we look in a place we will find it: personal experience. Since this is the basis of religious belief it makes sense to look there.

The co-determinate is like the Derridian trace, or a fingerprint. The trace is the sign that always accompanies the thing itself. In other words, you can't see the invisible man, but you can see his footprints, and wherever he is in the snow his prints will always follow. We cannot directly observe God, but we can find the "trace," the co-determinate, the effect of God in the world. Now how does one identify the co-determinate with God? Schleiermacher saw it as the feeling of utter dependence. Just as feelings of sublimity imply that one encounters the sublime, and feelings of love imply that there is a beloved, so feelings of utter dependence imply that there is a universal necessity upon which all that is, is supremely utterly dependent. We can also include mystical experience and life transformation because these are part and parcel of what is meant by the idea of religion and the divine. As far back as the Upper Paleolithic we find what seems to be some form of the mystical experience that is at the heart of all organized religion. The studies that we will be discussing shortly tell us that life transformation always accompanies dramatic experiences which are understood as and which evoke a strong sense of the Holy. So we can conclude that God, religion and life transformation always go hand in hand.

How do we know what the trace of God is? How do we know what it looks like? As I said above, it should correlate with what we expect religion to accomplish on an experiential level. It would be circular reasoning to assert that we know the trace of God and then use the trace of God to prove that God exists. If we already know that God is real, why not just use that knowledge and not bother with the trace? As stated several times before, our understanding of the trace is based upon the construal. This is not merely guessing because the reasons for the construal are bound up in the very origins of religion. We are getting to the core of the basic reason for all religious belief. The reasons for understanding the phenomena of religious experience as the trace of God are basic to the very reason we talk about God in the first place, the very reasons the first humans even came up with the notion. Now, of course, skeptics have always tried to impugn religious origins. They try to chalk it up to ignorance, fear of nature, the need to explain in the primitive unscientific past. Some skeptical explanations throw in some hints of mental illness and stupidity. None of those reasons are sufficient. They are out of date, out of fashion —nineteenth century horse-and-buggy thinking. Modern anthropologists and psychologists realize that religious belief is much more deeply based in the way humans react to their own sense of what it means to be. Based upon this sense of being and the way it has produced religion, we have good reasons for associating the sense of the numinous with the divine. These mystical experiences contain in their core the basic components that have always led to belief in God; people who experience these things are sometimes led to their belief through these experiences. Historically the association between the sense of the numinous and the presence of the divine is thousands of years old and universal to all cultures.

Historical Association

One of the major reasons to construe the trace as the trace of the divine is the historical association between the sense of the numinous and the divine. This association goes back as far as prehistoric times. The case is mainly conjectural but becomes stronger and more concrete as we approach the Bronze Age. Some scholarly work interprets evolutionary development of religion among hunter gatherer societies at 35,000 years ago and probably much further back.[1] Rosano finds that "...Many items recovered from the late, Lower, and Middle Paleolithic sites (from 300,000 to 35,000 years ago) contain what appear to be intentional zigzagging, parallel, or radiating markings that may represent the 'entoptic experiences of altered states of Consciousness.'" He also finds evidence of Neanderthal ritual that he has also linked to mystical experience. Earlier he has found that mystical experiences (defined as ineffability, noetic quality and undifferentiated unity) are linked to religion at an early stage. "Religious rituals that bring about ecstatic states such as those involving rhythmic dancing, stressful initiations, and the ingestion of intoxicants are commonly used to establish social bonds among hunter gatherers."[2]

In addition to this we have the Venus figures of northern Europe from the last ice age. These are figurines of fat women with big breasts. Anthropologists have suggested that these figures were totems or fertility charms of some kind. Some paintings in caves show a gallery of animals not on the Neanderthal or early human menu, which means they weren't drawing them to teach hunting.

> The Cro-Magnon people of Europe regularly decorated their tools and sculpted small pieces of stone, bone, antler, and tusks. Necklaces, bracelets, and decorative pendants were made of bone, teeth, and shell. Cave walls were often painted with naturalistic scenes of animals. Clay was also modeled occasionally. From our culture's perspective, these symbolic and naturalistic representations would be referred to as art. However, that is an ethnocentric projection. For the Cro-Magnon who made this art, it was very likely thought of as being something different, or at least much more, than we think of as art. For instance, it may have had magical and/or religious functions...[3]

Although they might have drawn them to teach hunters about dangers they face, the late Neolithic rock paintings of southern Spain suggest cults of spirits and ancestors among early farmers of Europe.[4] The standard interpretation says that around this time the early farmer was personifying nature, and that these aspects upon which he so truly depended, the sun, the earth, and so forth became gods.[5] We do know that early religion was oriented around nature worship. That would be a good indication of mystical consciousness because the extroverted form of mysticism is usually connected with nature. It might indicate that early humans had a strong connection to the natural world and sensed in that world the transcendence of religious experience triggered by nature. None of that is overtly mystical in the sense in which I am using that term. On the other hand, one might surmise that these things are indicative of it since one can see a link between the sense of power in nature and extroverted mystical consciousness that is often triggered by contact with nature. Or one may see a link between belief in spirits, a sense that a presence is near, and the feeling of divine presence in mystical experience. There is a strong link that connects mythology and expression of folk religion and the artifacts of early humanity such as Venus figures and cave paintings, spirit cults, and so on with mystical consciousness. Human beings seem to have always identified some aspect of being that they see as transcendent, as "the divine." There is a good possibility that these artifacts and folk religions are expressions of mystical consciousness and that, as a form of consciousness, is the basis of all religious belief.

Some atheists and skeptics reduce everything that they criticize and then lose the phenomena in the reduction. Thus, they only see the explanatory aspects of ancient religion and never try to think beyond the simple assumption that people were doing this merely to explain things. If we imagine our stone age ancestor (lets call him "Og"), he might feel fear and wonder at the thunder, so he explains the noise as "angry chief in sky." Hence the idea that primitive people without science try to explain simple things they don't understand by making up religion. But —even though I am sure skeptics will argue that we are projecting our assumptions about mystical consciousness into the scenario when we link the development of religion with the sense of the numinous— those who appreciate mystical consciousness can see more to the situation.

Maslow interpreted everyday psychology as laced with the trace of the supernatural, because for him "supernatural" just meant *a deeper level of consciousness about ordinary things*. His views of human psychology were laced with Jungian notions of archetypes. He equated archetypes with "supernatural." In speaking of the relationship between men and women and their relation to psychological archetypes, he finds that the same symbols are always used for the same meanings; Maslow tells us that these meanings and symbols are linked in psychological studies across the board. Maslow provides examples as he marks archetypical thinking, he labels these kinds of thinking "B" and "D" forms of analysis. "B analysis" is found where symbols reflect ideas having to do with the higher good, the ideal, the abstract. "D" has to do with the earthy human aspects of our existence. An example of B analysis would be symbolism that reflects the idea of the woman as an angel, a saint, a nurturer. D analysis would be symbols that links the woman to the whore, the bitch the shrew. These are roughly equivalent to St. Augustine's terms: *height and depth*. An example of what he's talking about is the male tendency to seek two forms of womanhood: the "goddess" and the "witch," "whore," "bad girl." Maslow says that psychology tells us that we need a bit of both. A woman put on a pedestal and seen only as a goddess is unapproachable and cannot be pleased. A woman seen only as the "other" can't be respected and won't make a good partner. Of course this goes vice-versa for the way women view men: the "good guy" *vs.* the "outlaw," "rebel," "bad boy."

Materialists are going to find that this point is trivial and just a part of daily living, and that's the point. The reason ancients have a tendency to sacralize these kinds of ordinary relationships is because they sense a connection between them and the transcendent, that is the *sense of the numinous*. The same symbols turn up again and again, according to Maslow, in all kinds of psychological studies. Psychologically, there is a link between the use of certain symbols (in mythology and religion) and the transcendent. Maslow makes this connection himself in speaking of the dichotomy of most religious life between the "mystical" or "inner personal" to the organizational (which he calls "doctrinal"): "The profoundly and authentically religious person integrates these trends easily and automatically. The forms, rituals, ceremonials, and verbal formulae in which he was reared remain for him experimentally rooted, symbolically meaningful, archetypal, unitive."[7] He is revealing a link between the rituals of the primitives, mythology and religious experience (especially "peak experience" or Mystical consciousness). That link is in archetypes, the psychological symbols that ground us in a sense of what life is about and give us a connection with these concepts of height and depth, or the ideal and practical. In "An example of B analysis" he states:

> This can also be seen operationally in terms of the Jungian archetypes which can be recovered in several ways. I have managed to get it in good introspectors simply by asking them directly to free associate to a particular symbol. The psychoanalytic literature, of course, has many such reports. Practically every deep case history will report such symbolic, archaic ways of viewing the woman, both in her good aspects and her bad aspects. (Both the Jungians and the Kleinians recognize the great and good mother and the witch mother as basic archetypes.) Another way of getting at this is in terms of the artificial dream that is suggested under hypnosis. It can also probably be investigated by spontaneous drawings, as the art therapists have pointed out. Still another possibility is the George Klein technique of two cards very rapidly succeeding each other so that symbolism can be studied. Any person who has been psychoanalyzed can fairly easily fall into such symbolic or metaphorical thinking in his dreams or free associations or fantasies or reveries.[8]

He is relating this to the mythological symbols, for women, of the
Great Mother, the Goddess, the Witch, the Demon, and one might also
think of Lilith; for men, the Sky Father *vs.* the Demon, the Trickster.
The link between mythological symbols and mystical consciousness is
further borne out by another psychologist, David Lukoff, who made the
link between the high-incidence rate in the general population found by
the Greeley study and the use of archetypes. Lukoff framed
schizophrenic delusions as private mythology.

> This method derives from the discipline of comparative mythology
> but goes beyond to decipher the psychological truths embodied in the
> symbol-laden stories. Campbell's (1949) work *The Hero With a
> Thousand Faces* is the premier example of this method. Lukoff
> (1985) treated the account of a psychotic episode as a symbol-laden
> personal myth and attempted to uncover themes that parallel the
> structure and content of classic mystical experiences."[9]

Other studies, such as one by Buckley and Galanter (1979) have
observed individuals in the midst of mystical experience when exposed
to religious ceremonies.[10] Some might see this as undermining my
argument because skeptics do argue that religious experience is a form
of mental illness. But there is a distinction between some mentally ill
people having religious experiences and all mystical experience being
mental illness. Many studies disprove this assertion (see Chapter 3 on
studies). But as Lukoff shows, this does not mean that some mentally
people can't have mystical experiences.

Maslow talks about the psychological necessity of being able to
maintain a transformative symbology. He is not merely saying that we
should do this, but that this is what we do; it is universal. Through
many different techniques and psychological schools of thought he
shows that this transformative symbology has been gleaned over and
over again. What Jung called Archetypes are universal symbols of
transformation, which we understand in the unconscious , and we must

be able to hold them in proper relation to the mundane (the Sacred and the Profane) in order to enjoy healthy growth, or we stagnate and become pathological. It is crucial to human psychology to maintain this balance. Far from merely being stupid and —not understanding science— striving to explain a pre-Newtonian world, the primitives understood this balance and held it better than we do. Religious belief is crucial to our psychological well-being, and this fact, far more than the need for social order or the need to explain thunder, explains the origins of religion.

As Maslow says:

> For practically all primitives, these matters that I have spoken about are seen in a more pious, sacred way, as Eliade has stressed, i.e., as rituals, ceremonies, and mysteries. The ceremony of puberty, which we make nothing of, is extremely important for most primitive cultures. When the girl menstruates for the first time and becomes a woman, it is truly a great event and a great ceremony; and it is truly, in the profound and naturalistic and human sense, a great religious moment in the life not only of the girl herself but also of the whole tribe. She steps into the realm of those who can carry on life and those who can produce life; so also for the boy's puberty; so also for the ceremonies of death, of old age, of marriage, of the mysteries of women, the mysteries of men. I think that an examination of primitive or preliterate cultures would show that they often manage the unitive life better than we do, at least as far as relations between the sexes are concerned and also as between adults and children. They combine better than we do the B and the D, as Eliade has pointed out. He defined primitive cultures as different from industrial cultures because they have kept their sense of the sacred about the basic biological things of life.
>
> We must remember, after all, that all these happenings are, in truth, mysteries. Even though they happen a million times, they are still mysteries. If we lose our sense of the mysterious, or the numinous, if we lose our sense of awe, of humility, of being struck

dumb, if we lose our sense of good fortune, then we have lost a very
real and basic human capacity and are diminished thereby.

Now that may be taken as a frank admission of a naturalistic
psychological origin, except that it involves a universal symbology,
which is not explicable through merely naturalistic means. How is it
that all humans come to hold these same archetypical symbols? The
"primitives" viewed and understood a sense of transformation, which
gave them integration into the universe. This is crucial for human
development. They sensed a power in the numinous, that is the origin
of religion.[11]

Ceremonies and rituals about ordinary things —such as puberty, sex,
marriage, birth, death— are attempts at mediating the ultimate
transformative experiences that religions take as the resolution of what
they identify as the *human problematic*. Prehistoric man says, "I see a
connection between my place in the universe, and this sense that I get
when I reflect upon nature as a whole. I sense that I am one small part
in a great unity, and I sense this in everything in life: falling in love,
having children, death. I have a place in the universe in relation to
whatever it is I sense beyond the stars…" The skeptic reduces this to
"the clueless primitive" making rituals about sex and relationships to
ward off the evil spirits that make him nervous. But it's clear, while
prehistoric man probably wasn't an existentialist and perhaps wasn't
that sophisticated about it all, he did sense a connection between life
and the numinous. Of course this doesn't mean that primitive humans
had any special insight into relationships that we need to follow. There
is strong evidence that people have had a sense of the numinous as far
back as we know. This is an indication of some form of this sense
because it clearly shows a connection between ordinary aspects of life
and the transcendent. It also means that the typical skeptical
explanation for the origin of religion amounts to reducing the
phenomena; taking out the real indications of a form of consciousness
and reducing what they find to nothing more than an over-simplified
explanation for things.

In the early part of the twentieth century there was a strong movement toward mystical consciousness and interest in mystical writings among middle and upper-class English and Europeans. The emphasis at that time was upon unity. Thinkers like Dean Inge and Baron von Hügel and popularizers such as Evelyn Underhill focused upon the similarities between all mystics. In the late twentieth century the emphasis was upon differences. A counter movement, led by Steven Katz, set about trying to break up the connections between all mystics. While it is true that many of these connections were read in by eager expositors trying to feed a movement, it is equally true that their critics worked overtime at denying connections. And the same commonalities emerge time and time again. Throughout history, in every religious tradition, we find mystics and they show the same characteristics, no matter how their contexts vary, and no matter how different their understanding in relation to their own traditions. Even though skeptics have tried to focus on differences, and there are many, the studies consistently show the same commonalities emerge among all mystical traditions. [12] The very reason we are talking about something called "God" in the first place is because people have this sense of the numinous that forms the basis of all religion.

The origin of all religions stems from the sense of the numinous.

All religious traditions from prehistory to now have mystical traditions within them. [13] Any indication of the mystical in the Hebrew scriptures could be from the exile period. What we have in the "OT" comes to us from that era. No doubt the Hebrews were working with older traditions, but they did redact them. We can also find mystical traditions at a much earlier phase of human endeavor.

Joseph Hinman

Rudolf Otto's (1869-1937) notion of the religious *a priori* was based upon the experience of the numinous or the Holy. It "combines both rational and non-rational elements." In his book, *The Idea of The Holy,* "Otto saw the origin of religion in what he called the *mysterium tremendum et fascinans...* some particular experience, usually for primitive people some confrontation with natural forces, but for the more sophisticated some depth of personal relationship, where simultaneously one is both attracted and repelled by a sense of awe..."[14] Many researchers have viewed mystical experience as the core of religious faith:

> The experience of pure consciousness is typically called "mystical". The essence of the mystical experience has been debated for years (Horne, 1982). It is often held that "mysticism is a manifestation of something which is at the root of all religions (p. 16; Happold, 1963)." The empirical assessment of the mystical experience in psychology has occurred to a limited extent.[15] [16]

Hardy developed a most detailed phenomenological classification system to evaluate 4,000 personal accounts of mystical experiences that were sent to him when he placed a newspaper ad requesting such accounts. A follow up questionnaire was also sent. Hardy concluded, after evaluating the responses, that feelings for a transcendental reality are at the base the human religious sense.[17] Thomas A. Idinopulos wrote:

> It is the experience of the transcendent, including the human response to that experience that creates faith, or more precisely the life of faith. Wilfred Cantwell Smith seems to regard human beings as having a propensity for faith, so that one speaks of their faith as "innate." In his analysis, faith and transcendence are more accurate descriptions of the lives of religious human beings than conventional uses of the word, religion. The reason for this has to do with the distinction

between participant and observer. This is a fundamental distinction for Smith, separating religious people (the participants) from the detached, so-called objective students of religious people (the observers). Smith's argument is that religious persons do not ordinarily have "a religion." The word, religion, comes into usage not as the participant's word but as the observer's word, one that focuses on observable doctrines, institutions, ceremonies, and other practices. By contrast, faith is about the non-observable, life-shaping vision of transcendence held by a participant. [18]

In speaking of Smith's view, Indinopulos says, "Smith considers transcendence to be the one dimension common to all peoples of the religious faith: what they have in common lies not in the tradition that introduces them to transcendence, not in their faith by what they personally respond, but in that to which they respond, the transcendent itself. [19] Smith distinguished between the formal lines of a religious tradition, with doctrine and theology, and the everyday experience of faith that guides one in living. The real core of faith is found in the daily practice of faith as one confronts life. In that sense, RE in general, and even mystical consciousness in particular, is at the core of all faith. Brother David Steindl-Rast, O.S.B., is a monk of Mount Savior Monastery in the Finger Lake Region of New York State and a member of the board of the Council on Spiritual Practices. He holds a Ph.D. from the Psychological Institute at the University of Vienna and has practiced Zen with Buddhist masters. He is the author of *Gratefulness, The Heart of Prayer* and *Music of Silence: A Sacred Journey Through the Hours of the Day*. He wrote:

> If the religious pursuit is essentially the human quest for meaning, then these most meaningful moments of human existence must certainly be called "religious." They are, in fact, quickly recognized as the very heart of religion, especially by people who have the good fortune of feeling at home in a religious tradition. And yet, the body

of religion doesn't always accept its heart. This can happen in any
religious tradition, Eastern or Western.[20]

The organized aspect can often set formal religion against true faith. In
the Catholic tradition the mystics usually wind up as saints, but along
the way they are shunned and controlled. Mysticism itself is
downplayed and even snubbed, and often mystics themselves deny
being mystics and speak with only the gravest sense of risk in
discussing their experiences. Yet there are currents and eddies of
mystical tradition lacing all Christianity. Mystical consciousness is not
only found among the monastics shut up in monasteries or convents,
but throughout the Christian world. Jonathan Law, in England during
the time of Newton, was a major voice of mystical consciousness in the
Protestant tradition. Even scientists such as Sir Isaac Newton and
Robert Boyle had their mystical sides. Boyle, who discovered air
pressure, underwent conversion due to a mystical experience that was
brought on by a thunderstorm. Mystics can be found in all times and
places.

Skeptics and atheists usually tend to think of "religion" in terms of
the formal structures, membership in a group and the like. Atheists
often include in their ranks, and pollsters also include, those who
actually do believe there may be some sort of "higher power" but who
reject organized religion.[21] It may be difficult therefore, for them to
think of "religious experience" in terms of the way people understand
being in the world, the way we grasp our place in the universe in
relation to the vast array of sense data and the organized patterns it
seems to form. It may be difficult for skeptics to understand that belief
is largely a matter of construing our relationship to the universe, the
place we understand ourselves to occupy in it, and our relationship to
the transcendent meaning derived from the experiences that point to
that place in the universe. Skeptics too often explain religion in terms
of its formal structures. When they try to explain the more "hands on"
side of faith, they explain it in terms of their interests, primitive failed

science, the need to explain the physical workings of the universe. This explanation is inadequate to anyone who really experiences the sense of the numinous.

The origin of religion is not found in functionalism; this is an antiquated hypothesis

Structural functionalism was the major explanation for all social structures given by sociologists in the nineteenth century. It survived as the dominant branch of the two main sociological camps to the late twentieth century, and still holds a major position. The theory was the brainchild of the founder of sociology, French thinker Auguste Compte. The theory says that anything found in the social structure serves a function in the social structure. Thus, religion exists because it serves a function in the social structure. This has been the dominant way to look at religion for sociologists for the last two centuries. Within this framework, people chalked up religion to an array of disparate but related activities that serve a function, or are thought to have served a function for primitive man. These include: a means of ensuring the growth of crops, a means of ensuring a good hunt, a means of placating fears of the unknown, a means of explanation in the face of terrifying social ignorance of the natural world. Today social scientists have grown rather impatient with that sort of patronizing answer. The reason for this disquietude is that not only does it completely fail to explain the reason why people believe today but it also completely ignores aspects of belief that we know were important to the ancients. Of course, if they didn't have science, and if they were afraid of storms and that their crops would not grow, if they wanted to explain things and if they needed to believe they were protected, of course they would draw upon the beliefs they already held for answers. However, that assumes they already held them; it does not tell us why they held such beliefs.

Joseph Hinman

Religion is not a failed primitive attempt at explanation

Religious beliefs do not function as scientific explanations or as hypotheses. Philosopher Norman Lillegard wrote:

> ...Scientific explanations get started generally with hypotheses (at least on a Popperian account) which are then put to various tests in attempts to get independent evidence for the explicans. Now there surely is something quite odd in the suggestion that such a religious belief as that God created the universe, or guides its development, is in any way a hypothesis. This belief is normally acquired in "dogmatic" contexts, it is not held in a tentative fashion, and its function in a believer's life is, arguably, quite distinct from the function of hypotheses, and thus of explanations, in the lives of scientists. Does this show that religion and science simply bypass one another? Perhaps. It will no doubt be argued that even if religious beliefs are not hypotheses they still have a definite cognitive content, are true or false, and thus are capable of contradicting scientific claims. To deny this would seem to be tantamount to endorsing some kind of emotivism with respect to religious belief, and in fact suspicions of emotivism have undoubtedly contributed to what I think are premature dismissal of Wittgensteinian approaches in the philosophy of religion. ... I will argue that the dynamics of belief change in the sciences and in religion are distinct in ways that support the idea that religious beliefs do not generally function as hypotheses or indeed function as explanations at all. [22]

It makes sense to see primitive humanity as striving to understand the physical world. Our natural intellectual curiosity would lead our prehistoric ancestors to define and explain the natural world, and to do so in terms of the thought categories they understood. Thus, the explanations of thunder, lightening, drought, disease and so forth would naturally draw upon their sense of the numinous in framing an explanation. Thus, is it not unlikely that they did explain such things in religious terms, and that may be an origin of superstition. This in no way means that religion grew out of superstition, or that it has to lead to it. It does not mean that the origin of religion is found in the need to explain the physical world. The sense of meaning and integration into the universe that can derive from RE is an indication that belief is based upon something much deeper than just the need to explain the physical world. Religious beliefs do not function as scientific hypotheses to be tested, but as guides to navigate through life. We can logically construe these experiences as a sense of the divine given the nature of their content.

Religious experience most often contains an inherent sense of the divine. This includes a presence of God, a personal sense of love, even a sense of identity. This is not always the case. Often the experience itself draws the subject to the divine.

Content

Even when one is not led to a conventional sense of "God" through mystical consciousness, there is still an aspect of the divine that marks the experience. There are mystical experiences in which one has no sense of a personal deity or a presence, and even in such cases there are senses that mark it as "divine." Sri Aurobindo (1872 – 1951), Indian scholar, thinker and revolutionary, was drawn to a form of Hindu philosophy and mysticism called *Advaita Vedanta*. This is a form of monism which says that there is only one thing ("God" or *Braman*). All else that we perceive, besides God, is an illusion. Aurobindo found that a certain kind of meditation gave him a sense of mystical ecstasy. *Advaita Vedanta* is the belief that all is God, our individuality is illusory, and in us is the atman (equivalent to "soul" in Western understanding) and this is actually identical to Braman, which is equivalent to "God" but not personal. So all is God and we are God. Aurobindo's experience confirmed this for him. At the same time he derived even more from the experience.

> Now to reach Nirvana was the first radical result of my own Yoga. It threw me suddenly into a condition above and without thought, unstained by any mental or vital movement; there was no ego, no real world —only when one looked through the immobile senses, something perceived or bore upon its sheer silence a world of empty forms, materialized shadows without true substance. There was no One or many... (only) featureless, relationless, sheer, indescribable, unthinkable, absolute, yet supremely real and solely real. This was no mental realization —it was positive, the only positive reality— although not a spatial physical world, pervading, occupying or rather flooding and drowning this semblance of a physical world, leaving no room or space for any reality but itself, allowing nothing else to seem at all actual, positive or substantial. I cannot say there was anything exhilarating or rapturous in the experience as it then came to me —the ineffable Ananda I had years afterwards— but what it brought was an inexpressible Peace, a stupendous silence, an infinite of release and freedom.[23]

This is a good example of the kind of thing I'm talking about in these experiences. But over the course of several months he began to feel "more."

> ...In the end it began to disappear into a greater Superconciousness from above. But meanwhile, realization added itself to realization and fused itself with this original experience. At any early stage the aspect of an illusory world gave place to one in which illusion is only a small surface phenomenon with an immense Divine Reality behind it in the heart of everything that had seemed at first only a cinematic shape or shadow. Amid this was no reimprisonment in the senses, no diminution or fall from supreme experience, it came rather as a

constant heightening and widening of the Truth; it was the spirit that saw objects, not the senses, and the Peace, the Silence, the freedom in Infinity remained always with the world or all worlds only as a continuous incident in the timeless eternity of the Divine.[24]

The examples quoted in the introduction could also suffice to provide examples of the sense of the Holy and the sense of unity which makes up the content of mystical experiences. Not all such experiences are about God but most of them are. The sense of the numinous is about a sense of presence of love and holiness. Whether a loving sense of the personal or an impersonal void there is a sense of a higher divine reality.

Richard Bucke was a young man of 36 when, in 1874, he had a strange experience. He had been to some sort of poetry colloquy (poetry can be a trigger of mystical experience) when on his way home he saw a strange sort of light as though everything around him was on fire. The resulting mystical experience led him to study mental illness and he wound up making a significant contribution to the care of mental patients. He himself never showed any signs of mental illness. His experience is described as follows:

> I saw and knew that the cosmos is not dead matter but a living Presence, that the soul of man is immortal that the universe is so ordered that without any peradventure all things work together for the good of each and all, that the foundation principle of the world is what we call love and that the happiness of everyone in the long run is absolutely certain.[25]

His life after that point exhibits the classical effects of one who has been touched by the divine; he devoted himself to tireless reform of the conditions of and for the mentally ill. I am going to ask the Christian readers to bracket doctrinal objections to these ideas and follow the argument. All will be resolved in the final chapter.

Effects

Life Transforming

The effects of these experiences are dramatic, positive, and long-term. Such experiences totally change the lives of those who have them. While skeptics often try to downplay or reduce the effects, they have no data to back them up. I've seen them assert that they get the same kind of "charge" out of becoming atheists, but it's pretty clear they don't even understand the ramifications. Not all of these effects are as dramatic as stories such as *The Cross and the Switchblade*, but there is data to suggest that religious experience has enabled addicts to get off of heroin, alcoholics to stop drinking and even helps people quit smoking. More on this sort of thing is found in the next chapter where I discuss the studies in detail. The major effects are just a clear feeling of meaning in life. Many speak of losing their fear of death.

Self-Actualizing

Self-actualization is a term that emerges out of the work of Abraham Maslow and his transactional school, or "third force" psychology. Dr. Michael Nielson, Ph.D. explains:

> What makes someone psychologically healthy? This was the question that guided Maslow's work. He saw too much emphasis in psychology on negative behavior and thought, and wanted to supplant it with a psychology of mental health. To this end, he developed a hierarchy of needs, ranging from lower level physiological needs, through love and belonging, to self- actualization. Self-actualized people are those who have reached their potential for self-

development. Maslow claimed that mystics are more likely to be self-actualized than are other people. Mystics also are more likely to have had "peak experiences," experiences in which the person feels a sense of ecstasy and oneness with the universe. Although his hierarchy of needs sounds appealing, researchers have had difficulty finding support for his theory.[26]

This is the finding of a vast body of work. Some studies show that "peakers" (those who experience "mystical experiences:" what I'm calling "religious experience" in this essay) are more self actualized than those who do not have these experiences. But there are also studies that show that any inkling of religious experience carries some degree of the same advantages. Four hundred studies show that participation (as well as the nominal experiences) produces many benefits, among them less depression and better mental health. Savage, et al. in 1995 found clinical evidence that "peakers" have greater feelings of self-confidence and a deep sense of meaning and purpose in life.[27] The Mathes Study in 1982 validates Maslow's findings. [28] The Kass study (91) found that spiritual experience equates to life purpose.[29] Studies that investigate well-being measure spiritual experience.

In fact researchers are of the view that a positive relation between positive affect and mystical experiences may not be surprising given that intense positive affect is often considered to be one of the defining characteristics of these experiences (Noble, 1985; Spilka, Hood & Gorsuch, 1985). The few studies that investigated well-being measures, spirituality and spiritual experience have found that people who have had spiritual experiences are in the normal range of well-being and have a tendency to report more extreme positive feelings than others (Kennedy, Kanthamani & Palmer, 1994; Kennedy & Kanthamani, 1995).[30]

Joseph Hinman

The "new atheists" put forth the notion that all of religion itself is a form of mental illness. There is no basis whatsoever for this notion in the data. The effects are varied but over the entire range of research they spell out a healthy well-adjusted whole person. The qualities mentioned over and over again in the research on religious experience include: less dogmatic, less authoritarian, more socially conscious, are about people, happy, healthy, successful, self-aware, self-assured, find life meaningful, enjoy their work, strong ego, strong sense of self, more self-actualized. All the studies mentioned to this point back this up such as the Mathes study as well as Maslow:

> In terms of psychological correlates, well-being and happiness has been associated with mystical experiences (Mathes, Zevon, Roter, Joerger, 1982; Hay & Morisy, 1978; Greeley, 1975; Alexander, Boyer, & Alexander, 1987) as well as self-actualization (Hood, 1977; Alexander, 1992). Regarding the latter, the developer of self-actualization believed that even one spontaneous peak or transcendental experience could promote self-actualization. Correlational research has supported this relationship. In a recent statistical meta-analysis of causal designs with Transcendental Meditation (TM) controlling for length of treatment and strength of study design, it was found that: TM enhances self-actualization on standard inventories significantly more than recent clinically devised relaxation/meditation procedures not explicitly directed toward transcendence mystical experience] (p. 1; Alexander, 1992) Lester Grinsppon and James Bakalar (1983). "Psychedelic Drugs in Psychiatry" In *Psychedelic Drugs Reconsidered*, New York: Basic Books.[31]

Religious experience produces long-term positive effects. Below are lists of findings from two of the major studies.

Robert Wuthnow conducted an early major study —the first scientifically systematic attempt at a double-blind study— "Peak

Experiences: Some Empirical Tests" (published in the *Journal of Humanistic Psychology*) in 1979. The subjects in Wuthnow's Study:

- Say their lives are more meaningful
- Think about meaning and purpose
- Know what purpose of life is
- Meditate more
- Score higher on self-rated personal talents and capabilities
- Are less likely to value material possessions, high pay, job security, fame, and having lots of friends
- Give greater value on work for social change, solving social problems, helping needy
- Are reflective, inner-directed, self-aware, self-confident life style[32]

Kathleen D. Nobel, "Psychological Health and the Experience of Transcendence," (Published in *the Counseling Psychologist,* 1987) found subjects:

- Experience more predictive of psychological health than illness
- Are less authoritarian and dogmatic
- Are more assertive, imaginative, self-sufficient
- Are more intelligent, relaxed
- Have high ego strength
- Exhibit integration, allocentrism
- Exhibit psychological maturity
- Show self-acceptance, self-worth
- Exhibit autonomy, authenticity, need for solitude
- Experience increased love and compassion[33]

Short-Term Effects, usually on people who did not previously know of these experiences, included:

- Experience temporarily disorienting, alarming, disruptive
- Likely changes in self and the world

- Space and time, emotional attitudes, cognitive styles, personalities, doubt sanity and reluctance to communicate, feel ordinary language is inadequate
- Some individuals report psychic capacities and visionary experience destabilizing relationships with family and friends, withdrawal, isolation, confusion, insecurity, self-doubt, depression, anxiety, panic, restlessness, grandiose religious delusions

Studies dealing with mystical experience (peak experience or "RE") itself find that this kind of experience is also a major factor in well-being. According to Greeley (1974), and Hay and Morisy (1978) "people who reported having intense religious experiences were significantly more likely to report a high level of psychological well being than those who did not experience transcendence. Greeley's 'mystics' were also more likely to be optimistic than were his "non-mystics" and less likely to be authoritarian or racist."[34] Furthermore, Greeley found no evidence to support the orthodox belief that frequent mystic experiences or psychic experiences stem from deprivation or psychopathology. He did find "mystics" were generally better educated, more successful economically, less racist and rated substantially happier on measures of psychological well-being.[35] "Transcendent experience may well lead toward a permanent transformation of the psyche in the direction of wholeness and health (Maslow 1970; Owens 1972; Wapnick 1972).[36]

Mental health

Believers: less depression, less mental illness, lower divorce rate

The study by Gartner and Allen indicates that religious belief is associated with good mental health, less depression and so on:

> The Reviews identified 10 areas of clinical status in which research has demonstrated benefits of religious commitment: (1) Depression, (2) Suicide, (3) Delinquency, (4) Mortality, (5) Alcohol use (6) Drug use, (7) Well-being, (8) Divorce and marital satisfaction, (9) Physical Health Status, and (10) Mental health outcome studies...The authors underscored the need for additional longitudinal studies featuring health outcomes. Although there were few, such studies tended to show mental health benefit. Similarly, in the case of the few longevity or mortality outcome studies, the benefit was in favor of those who attended church...at least 70% of the time, increased religious commitment was associated with improved coping and protection from problems.[38]

This finding was based upon a review of social science studies. These were regular projects by social scientists published in the scholarly literature. All the researchers did was to read the literature and report the findings of these studies. In the past, psychiatry has tended to assume what Freud assumed —that religion is pathology. This is no longer the case. The basic assumption in the mental health field today is that religion is positive, healthy and a sign of functionality.

In the 1990s several studies found the majority of practicing psychologists, even if not religious themselves, consider religious involvement and experience important to their clinical work: Allman (1992)[38] Elkins (1995)[39] Glick (1986)[40], Shafranske and Malony (1990).[41] The Sullivan study in 1993, which used a large quantitative base of former mental patients and those who cared for them, found that 48% identified spiritual practices as crucial to their healing. This was a two-year exploratory group study on spiritual healing practices.[41]

Joseph Hinman

Religion is positive factor in physical health

Many studies confirm that religion is a powerful force in physical
health. This is important because it seems that we are *constructed* as
organisms to be religious. Religion seems good for us on many levels. I
resist the urge to make a design argument, tempting though it is. Yet,
the point is that religious experience is as trustworthy as other forms of
experience, in a general sense. One indication of that trustworthy nature
is its healthy effect upon our bodies. Much has been said in the popular
mainstream press, such as this Knight Ridder news release of 1998:

> Some suspect that the benefits of faith and churchgoing largely boil
> down to having social support a factor that, by itself, has been shown
> to improve health. But the health effects of religion can't wholly be
> explained by social support. If, for example, you compare people
> who aren't religious with people who gather regularly for more
> secular reasons, the religious group is healthier. In Israel, studies
> comparing religious with secular kibbutzim showed the religious
> communes were healthier." Is this all a social effect you could get
> from going to the bridge club? It doesn't seem that way," said
> Koenig, who directs Duke's Center for the Study of Religion/
> Spirituality and Health. Another popular explanation for the link
> between religion and health is sin avoidance.
>
> The religious might be healthier because they are less likely to
> smoke, drink and engage in risky sex and more likely to wear seat
> belts. But when studies control for those factors, say by comparing
> religious nonsmokers with nonreligious nonsmokers, the religious
> factors still stand out. Compare smokers who are religious with those
> who are not and the churchgoing smokers have blood pressure as low
> as nonsmokers. "If you're a smoker, make sure you get your butt in
> church," said Larson, who conducted the smoking study.[43]

Even when we control for smoking, religious belief still comes out ahead.[44] Lukoff and Lu's report (1988) covered a study (by Richards) showing that mystical experience is helpful in aiding the patient in fighting cancer:

> **Method:** Twenty-Eight terminal cancer patients were administered the Psychedelic Experience Questionnaire (PEQ) on the day following a drug assisted therapy session. The PEQ contains 43 items rated on a 0-5 scale of intensity designed by Pahnke (see Pahnke & Richards 1969 abstract…) in Transpersonal psychology (aka "The Good Friday Experiment") to measure the presence of six categories of mystical consciousness. The Personal Orientation Inventory was administered at screening and one week after the DPT-assisted therapy and was considered a measure of therapeutic improvement.
>
> **Findings:** The 13 "subjects deemed to have experienced mystical consciousness" based on the results for the PEQ regarding their DPT-experience showed significant gains on 9 of the 12 subscales of the POI. The 15 "subjects deemed not to have experienced mystical consciousness" showed no significant improvements: "the cluster of significant results for the group that experienced mystical consciousness…suggests a different response to the therapeutic procedure.[45]

The scale mentioned above, "PEQ" is a means of measuring, by comparison, the experience with those who did not have them. Its connection with the Good Friday Experiment is that it was developed and used by Pahnke & Richards in that experiment.

This is what we should expect from the Divine

These effects fulfill what could be a prediction about the results; this is a good indication that we are dealing with experience of the divine. The reason we can link these experiences and their effects with the divine is because they fulfill the basic nature and purpose of religion itself. All religions identify a *human problematic*, the complex of problems at the heart of being human. For some this is seen as imbalance with nature, for some it is seen as re-birth into a world of woe, for others as desire. Still other religions understand the problematic as estrangement from God through sin. But all religions understand that there is a basic problem with being human.

In addition to identifying a form of human problematic, all religions seek to resolve such a problematic by mediating a sense of ultimate transformative experience through the use of ritual. Religions do not identify the same problematic. For Christianity it's sin, for Buddhism it's desire, and so on. All the problematics relate to and revolve around humanity's place in being: imbalance, re-birth or fall from the grace in which we were created. The ultimate transformative experience is essentially mystical experience and it's found in all religions and as I said above, it's at the base of the origin of all religion. This experience is mediated through ritual, although most such rituals may seem boring and rarely produce any sort of "big experience." Nevertheless, religious rituals have psychological value and can mediate mystical experiences. We can expand the definition of ritual to include things like private prayer, the "sinner's prayer," meditation, and even drug taking, in which case the incidence of religious experience during meditation goes way up. Even the Catholic mass has been known to produce mystical experience. In the "Good Friday experiment," a control group was asked to attend a mass, and an experimental group attended the same mass on a hallucinogenic drug such as LSD. Members of both groups underwent mystical experience, but the experimental group had a much higher rate of mystical experience. Now one might conclude that the drug caused the experiences. The fact is both groups had experiencers in them; even the Mass alone triggered the experiences in some people. This fact that some in both groups had the experience indicates that these experiences are more than just some drug-induced form of delusion. I will deal with this at greater length in a later chapter.

My point in dealing with this now is that we should consider these experiences to be fallout from the divine/human encounter, for the simple reason that this is what we should expect from the divine, given the nature of all religions and their ultimate goals and aims. I can't attest to traditions to which I do not belong, but at least the Christian tradition seems to be about infusing human nature with divine love. A major focus of Christian piety in the New Testament is about human nature being renovated by divine nature. Romans 5:1 says, "love is poured into our hearts by the Holy Spirit."

The effects are real...

The effects are real, so we can assume the cause is real if:

1. We can logically infer God as cause (based upon content)
2. Alternate causes are eliminated

Construing causes from effects is a problem; the result could be argument from sign—merely argument from correlation without providing understanding of the true cause. This is not necessarily a fallacy but the situation has to be handled carefully. On the other hand, such an approach is largely what we do with cause and effect anyway. Go back to Hume's billiard balls, which were an example instrumental in establishing empiricism and that eventually led to scientific inductive methods. We do not see a cause happening when one ball hits another. What we really see is one ball stop and the other starts up. So argues Hume. We do not see causality happening, we infer the cause from the effects. If someone comes to work one morning in a neck brace and says "I am sorry I missed work yesterday but I was in a terrible car wreck and am suffering from whiplash" the immediate reaction is going to be "Well he has a neck brace, maybe he's telling the truth." If the same guy comes in with no neck brace, not a scratch on him, and on his lunch hour he goes to the jogging track and runs, the reaction is going to be "How could he have been in a bad wreck?" We do infer causes from effects. Sometimes this methodology is fallacious. It's easy to mistake the cause. For this reason we have to be careful and make sure that counter causal explanations are either much less likely or that they have been eliminated completely. But if there are no counter-explanations standing, and if the divine is the only theoretically logical explanation left, and if the effects fit what we should expect to see as the trace of God, then it would be logical to make the construal. All of these conditions are met above, except the dispensing with counter causality. That will be dealt with in other chapters. Some counter causes pose serious questions. These are assigned their own chapters, such as Chapter 5 (Proudfoot) and the chapter on "God Pods." This is one of the major aspects critics harp upon; that we cannot demonstrate the true cause of the experiences or prove that it is beyond the human mind. This is a serious problem but it is not insurmountable. We have fine evidence in the nature of the experiences themselves and the accounts of the experiences to the effect that the experience is about the divine; that is the content of it. We have good reason to assume it is an experience of God's presence. That is the ambiance of the experience.

Now we come to the second argument. We have already considered the first argument, the co-determinate, now the second: epistemic judgment.

Argument from Epistemic Judgment

Epistemic judgment is a necessary means of determining reality. We make epistemic judgments all the time, and it is necessary to do so. That is to say, few things can be proven by science or by empirical means, except matters given in sense data. But there are many more items of consideration in reality than just matters of sense data. Anything requiring the word *ought*, anything that relates to a higher meaning, anything on the level of epistemology, requires a judgment because we cannot directly observe it. Philosophers have concerned themselves with what is real. Some have feigned doubt about their own existence in order to make a point (to the ire of non-philosophically minded people). There is a real point to be made here. We cannot prove that we exist, we cannot prove that the world is real and no scientific data tells us that the world is not an illusion or that we are not butterflies dreaming we are human. We do not find this state of affairs debilitating because we construe reality based upon our perceptions of it. It is surprising that skeptics (including atheists) refuse to trust experiences, and yet the only true fail-safe we have against solipsism (the belief that there are no other minds and that the world is an illusion) is experience. This is how we know the world. Moreover, we take it for granted. As Thomas Reid argued, the solider on the battlefield does not stop to ask if the bayonet of the encroaching enemy is real, he just assumes that he needs to act as though it is.[46] No scientific data can help us because any such data could easily be part of the illusion. We assume that scientific data is useful for understanding the world, because it works to use it. Science is not giving us absolute empirical proof in the sense in which atheists demand proof of God. It is only giving a level of confidence in proportion to the extent that we rule the data in by means of a judgment. In other words, we have no absolute scientific guarantee of the reality of the world. We make a judgment by means of the constant nature of our perceptions; we judge

Joseph Hinman

that the world is real and that science is telling us about it because it works to do so. Bridges get built, products get made, disasters happen when things go wrong and get cleaned up when we make the right assumptions about cleaning them up. What drives all of these instances of epistemic acuity is the epistemic judgments we make that allow us to take for granted that our perceptions are giving us reality.

The means by which we make these judgments can be very complex. Philosophers love to argue about them. I will merely deal with a simplified and very straightforward argument that makes use of some of the most basic criteria of judgment: Regular, consistent and shared (inter-subjective—or validation):

> **Regular:** We deem that which is regular as a valid product of perception, and that which is not regular as anomalous. We deem the anomalous to be a mistake. This tendency is borne out in many ways but none better than in Thomas Kuhn's theory. Kuhn says that when a bit of data is opposed to the paradigm it is absorbed into the paradigm as an "anomaly." What's really being said? That which doesn't fit the paradigm is a mistake, it stands out from what? The norm. It does not fit the expected form as prescribed by the paradigm, so we call it an "anomaly," which means basically a mistake, a one-time happening. We think of "freaks" as things to avoid because they are unique; they are departures from what we expect, from that which conforms to our expectations. Thus, we think of odd happenings we can't explain as "flukes." It's a one-time deal. So we value the regular—that which conforms to what we have observed in the past—as valid.
>
> **Consistent:** We value consistency. Consistency, the lack of contradiction, the likeness of multiple examples, gives us a sense of order, we can depend upon what can be expected. Thus, contradictions are invalid. When a system does not contradict itself we value it as "stable" or "consistent." We judge perceptual matters partly by their consistency. Thus, we find episodes of the *Twilight Zone* most disturbing where one is displaced in the familiar. The one where everyone a certain man knows forgets who a certain man is, and he has to prove to people that he was part of their past even

though they don't remember him. Or the one where the man returns to his childhood but of course his parents don't know him because he's middle-aged in his own time, but only a boy in theirs. Because reality is consistent we find it predictable and to that extent we trust our perceptions when they are consistent.

Shared: When people see a strange sight, the first thing they do is say is, "Did you see that?" We value the confirmation of others. Among the major aspects of science that makes it work are validation and replication. This is merely the application of the consistency criteria and shared experience. Of course by "shared" I don't mean we have the very same experiences, but that our experiences are judged accurate when they are confirmed by the experiences of others. One of the major reasons skeptics discount personal experience is its subjective nature. Yet there is "subjective" and there is "inter-subjective." By inter-subjective I mean subjective experiences stack up as very similar across the board, and when they do, we consider them more reliable. An example of this would be medicines. When many people experience the same effects we conclude that they all took the same medicine, so this medicine tends to have this effect upon people. If there were no validity to inter-subjectivity there would be no basis for scientific disciplines such as psychology.

Religious experience tends to meet these criteria. Religious Experience (RE) tends to be regular to the extent that the incidence rate of mystical experience or peak experience is very high. Some researchers have determined that as many as one in four people have some form of RE. [47] Moreover, RE tends to have a consistency within the experiences themselves. The Presence of God might feel the same way every time (with some reasonable variations as one grows in the experience). Although there are counter examples, RE tends not to contradict itself. Thus, what seems joyful, peaceful, loving, on one occasion will tend to feel that way every time in varying degrees. As for "shared" or inter-subjective experiences, the studies show that for the same sets of experiences, the same qualities tend to crop up time after time. Mystics all over the world, in all times and all cultures, have the same kinds of experiences. It's true that mystical experiences tend to reinforce the mystic's view of his own tradition, and that each mystic defines them by means of their own tradition. Nevertheless, the characteristics themselves, when the specifics of the traditions are removed, are the same, as Gackenback tells us:

> In a recent review of the mystical experience Lukoff and Lu (1988) acknowledged that the "definition of a mystical experience ranges greatly (p. 163)." Maslow (1969) offered 35 definitions of "transcendence", a term often associated with mystical experiences and used by Alexander et al. to refer to the process of accessing PC.

She also quotes Lukoff (1985), who identified five common characteristics of mystical experiences, which could be operationalized for assessment purposes. They are:

1. Ecstatic mood, which he identified as the most common feature;
2. Sense of newly gained knowledge, which includes a belief that the mysteries of life have been revealed;
3. Perceptual alterations, which range from "heightened sensations to auditory and visual hallucinations (footnote 50)";
4. Delusions (if present) have themes related to mythology, which includes an incredible diversity and range;
5. No conceptual disorganization; unlike psychotic persons, those with mystical experiences do NOT suffer from disturbances in language and speech. [48]

It can be seen from the explanation of PC earlier that this list of qualities overlaps those delineated by Alexander et al.

Navigation in life

By "navigation" I mean not physically finding our way in the world, such as sailing the ocean to Jamaica; nor do I mean prognostication, prophecy or using divine knowledge to get around on a daily basis. Rather, I mean finding our way emotionally in life. Mystical experience, religious experience, enables us to know who we are and where we are going, fills us with purpose and gives us a sense that our lives are on track and there is a purpose in living. It also enables us to face life's material trammels and bitter experiences. The upshot of the argument is that RE works for navigation in the world. I am thinking of something more metaphorical, but just as important. The five senses enable us to navigate physically; certain regions of the brain enable us to remember not to try and walk through walls but use the door. This is analogous to the way that RE enables us to navigate. It doesn't help us walk down the street, it helps us live and make choices and keep going in a complex world in which we long for a clue about higher meaning. These experiences give us a sense of self-actualization, which is the basis of self-authentication. We understand who we are in relation to the whole. This is the basis of mythology; it's the basis of what religion was always about: integration into the universe and understanding what life is about and how we fit into the bigger picture. These experiences fit the same kinds of criteria that we use already to make judgments about reality. There is no scientific data that give us ultimate truth. There is no open door to ultimate truth and complete understanding of reality through any scientific or natural means. All we can do is make judgments about epistemology (and we do make them), and the extent to which they give us navigation is the extent to which we deem a set of phenomena real. Thus, since RE gives us that same kind of judgment-making ability, and for the same reasons (it works), we should construe it as an avenue to truth about the divine.

What is said above about self-authentication and mental health is evidenced by Allman (1992),[49] Elkins (1995),[50] Shafranske and Malony (1990).[51] It is also documented by the Sullivan study (1993), which shows therapeutic value in mystical experience, and the Richards study (mentioned above) about mystical experience and surviving cancer. Several other studies show therapeutic value in spiritual, religious and mystical experience. Pargament (1996) finds five studies suggesting that religious forms of coping are especially helpful to people in uncontrollable or extremely difficult circumstances.[52] Elliot (1994) found that female survivors of childhood sexual abuse who displayed religious belief systems (namely Christian) were less likely to display the symptoms of other females so abused.[53] Himelein and McElrath (1996) find that female survivors of childhood sexual violence who scored high on adjustment scales indicated, among positive change brought about by the experience, their discovery of religious faith.[54] Survivors of childhood sexual abuse found that their religion "was important in assisting them in making sense of the experience in a manner that served to free them of blame and guilt for the abuse... and gave them the faith to hold on to life and find meaning in their lives (Valentine and Feinauer 1993 (220)."[56]

There are two problems with using this material. First, Elliot, Himelein and Valentine are not necessarily talking about mystical experience per se (although some are as indicated above). They talk about "religious beliefs" and "religious forms of coping." It will be seen in chapters Five and Six that there is a continuum of experience. All believers probably encounter some aspect of mystical experience even though they don't necessarily have the full-blown mystical union. Nevertheless, if a belief system is an effective means of coping then surely we can infer from that that the actual transformative power of that belief system will also be an effective means of coping. This leads to a discussion of the second problem, that survivors (especially female) of sexual trauma and violence often reject religion and often experience negative aspects associated with religion. These effects are not the result of religious experience such as peak experience, but are associated with the religion of the abuser, especially if the abuser put a religious justification on his/her abuse.[56] This is also where mystical experience enters the picture again. An alternative to rejecting religion as whole is to change religious views, sometimes change religions altogether and to take a more private and spiritualized practice. This often takes the form of mystical experience. Some researchers, according to Ryan, find that the violence itself is an occasion for mystical experience and it is theorized that violence can be a trigger.[57] Non-religious women who have not been forced to associate their abuse with a particular religious tradition often turn to religion and spiritual practice as solace.[58] Irwin found that the more likely a child was to have traumatic events in childhood the more likely the child was to experience paranormal events latter in life.[59] Moreover, it has also been found that as people reach middle age they are more likely to broaden their religious perspective to a point that they see more of a transcendent form of spirituality. Many abuse victims come to view God in more cosmic and impersonal terms, which would be compatible with some forms of mystical experience. Survivors of childhood trauma and abuse often report that they felt the abuser was trying to destroy their soul but that this was the one inviolable core that the abuser could not reach.[60] This finding should certainly link survival to spiritual experience.

Loretta Do Rozario's hermeneutic phenomenological study of disabled people indicates the value of peak experience or self-transcendence, and the transformative power of religious experience.[61] The study was conducted as series of interviews with respondents chosen for disabilities and hardships that they faced (more about the methodology in Chapter 3, on Studies). The study proceeded based upon two major procedures: analysis of interviews done with respondents and of autobiographies the respondents wrote.[62] The findings indicate a set of overall strategies and paradigms that people use to enable them to move forward, survive and deal with their conditions. The major results show that the states of hardship and joy can coexist in the same life at the same time but that these results depend upon strategies. Mystical experience is not a panacea through which all problems vanish just because one has this experience. But the study does show that the transformative power of religious experience as a whole (and mystical experience in particular) is a vital and integral part of making the strategies work. The sense of spiritual unity involves transcendence of the self, thus making suffering bearable. Spiritual awareness (which is clearly an aspect of experience) fosters hope through belief in some greater aspect —such as the divine or a cosmic force, religious assurance as a value of traditional beliefs, religious experience— and, along with rituals, provides order and meaning, adds to the sense of an existential journey in which the sufferer is growing and progressing. The idea of purgatory enables one to separate oneself from suffering.[63] De Rozario wrote:

> The findings of this study put the experience of having an illness or disability into an overall context of a person's universal search for meaning and self-transcendence. This can be likened to Victor Frankl's belief, based upon his experience of living in a Nazi concentration camp, that "suffering ceases to be suffering in some way at the moment it finds a meaning…and that through suffering one is given a last chance to actualize the highest value to fulfill the deepest meaning…" People in this study concurred with this personal and contextual interpretation of illness and disability by reaffirming that the process of meaning-making was similar to that of the mythology of the hero and heroine's journey, which depicts a universal journey from a separation of self to a return to "true self." The inner-awareness of wholeness despite all the odds points to an implicit experience of life which can transcend form and matter. This experience of wholeness or consciousness extends and challenges the view of disability and illness as only a meaning-making and revaluing opportunity in the lives of people. Instead, the model of wholeness and reconstitution point to the possibility of an implicit order of consciousness or wholeness in which people who have

undergone some crisis or critical incident in their lives may be able to access and experience a "deeper reality" or "flow" in life...similar to the insights of the great religions.[64]

Thus the "shared" aspect of the experience is not in terms of physical navigation of the world nor the shared perception of objective phenomena, but in terms of the "inter-subjective" similarities of navigation in life. Religious experience is an integral aspect of the spiritual and psychological wherewithal that we all need to "make it," to bear up under the material trammels and horrific disappointments and tragedies that life brings our way. Just as the same kinds of experiences, the same emotional and para-sensory features, are aspects of experience that impair enjoyment of life, so the same coping ability and meaning and journey to wholeness is also part of religious experience.

Now we turn to the third argument, which is actually not an argument but an insight, the insight that, due to what has already been said, RE frees us from the need to prove. We are freed from the need to prove the existence of God and we are freed from the need to prove the validity of the experiences because their validity is proved by their very nature.

Normative nature of religion equals freedom from need to prove

Special sense ("religious a priori")

As pointed out in the introduction, the "religious a priori" is a special sense of the divine that transcends words, thoughts, and images. It's something one must experience to understand. Based upon this concept, thinkers such as Schleiermacher, Otto and Tillich argue that religion is its own discipline and cannot be critiqued or judged by science. I don't necessarily agree that religion is totally impervious to critique. There are areas where it overlaps with science, and none of those thinkers were creationists. They did not have in mind support for the historical validity of the creation myth in contradiction to Darwin. That issue would just simply be of no importance to them. But I do agree with them that religion as a whole cannot be judged by the standards of science as though it were a scientific discipline. I deal with this issue in more depth in the chapter on "Normative Nature of Religion." I have a problem with the phrase "religious a priori" and substitute the normative concept. *Normative* does not mean "normal" or "popular"; it means the standard by which things are judged. So normative ethics would the standard set for ethical decision-making. The normative nature of religious experience means that it sets the standard for human being, for our sense of what it means to be in the world; it gives us a sense of meaning and coordination with the ultimate goals and ends of the universe. The normative nature of RE is the basis of self-authentication.

Existential self-authenticating

The basis upon which one decides that one is living consistently with what one's life is about is called self-authentication. It is the sense that one has a place in the world, that one's life has meaning in relation to other lives and the whole of the universe in so far as one can understand it. In the 1960's, a common expression was, "we are looking for significance." People used to say that something "relates," meaning it makes sense to them where they are in their life situation. Theologians do talk about "theological significance." The normative nature of religion gives us that sense of theological significance to our lives.

Object of ultimate concern

The "object of ultimate concern" is Tillich's term for God. By this designation I mean, referring to his reason for using it, our ultimate concern is death. The sense of having a relationship with God enables to face to death with courage, dignity, and a sense that our lives have had meaning.

Life transformation

In argument one, I talked about life transformation. Religious experience is life transforming across the board: mental health, physical health, self-actualization and general happiness. In an argument, the purpose of discussing life transformation is to show that since the effects are real, so we can assume the content is real as well. Since the contents are about the divine, we can construe the effects as indicative of the divine. The ultimate purpose of religion as a whole is to resolve the human problematic by means of ultimate transformative experience. So RE does what religion is supposed to do. By way of demonstrating this, I return to the concept of transformative power. The purpose here will be to argue that this is the normative nature of religion, and since it is normative for human being, the sense of what it means to be in the world as a human, then it cannot be irrational to make the assumption that it is the logical conclusion to the basis upon which we find our sense of fulfillment as humans. I begin by demonstrating that religious experience is therapeutic.

Therapeutic

The life-transforming effects are well-documented above. In addition to what has been said about physical health, mental illness, and self-actualization, it is also important at this point to acknowledge that clinicians and psychologists recognize the therapeutic effects of religious experience.

Gackenbach refers to studies by Alexander and others:

> These states of being also result in behavioral and health changes. Ludwig (1985) found that 14% of people claiming spontaneous remission from alcoholism was due to mystical experiences while Richards (1978) found with cancer patients treated in a hallucinogenic drug-assisted therapy who reported mystical experiences improved significantly more on a measure of self-actualization than those who also had the drug but did not have a mystical experience. In terms of the Vedic Psychology group they report a wide range of positive behavioral results from the practice of meditation and as outlined above go to great pains to show that it is the transcendence aspect of that practice that is primarily responsible for the changes. Thus improved performance in many areas of society have been reported including education and business as well as personal health states (reviewed and summarized in Alexander et al., 1990). Specifically, the Vedic Psychology group found that mystical experiences were associated with "refined sensory threshold and enhanced mind-body coordination (p. 115; Alexander et al., 1987).[66]

Studies have shown that religious satisfaction was the most powerful predictor of general happiness and acceptance of life. Prayer was also an important contributing factor. As Paloma and Pendelton wrote, "As a result of their study the authors concluded that it would be important to look at a combination of religious items, including prayer, relationship with God, and other measures of religious experience to begin to adequately clarify the associations of religious commitment with general well-being."[67] As Abraham Maslow tells us:

The question has to be differentiated still further. There is no doubt that great insights and revelations are profoundly felt in mystic or peak-experiences, and certainly some of these are, ipso facto, intrinsically valid as experiences. That is, one can and does learn from such experiences that, e.g., joy, ecstasy and rapture do in fact exist and that they are in principle available for the experiencer, even if they never have been before. Thus the peaker learns surely and certainly that life can be worthwhile, that it can be beautiful and valuable. There are ends in life, i.e., experiences which are so precious in themselves as to prove that not everything is a means to some end other than itself... Another kind of self-validating insight is the experience of being a real identity, a real self, of feeling what it is like to feel really oneself, what in fact one is—not a phony, a fake, a striver, an impersonator. Here again, the experiencing itself is the revelation of a truth. [68]

Object of Ultimate Concern = Self Authentication

On this matter Maslow said:

> ...My feeling is that if it were never to happen again, the power of the experience could permanently affect the attitude toward life. A single glimpse of heaven is enough to confirm its existence even if it is never experienced again. It is my strong suspicion that even one such experience might be able to prevent suicide, for instance, and perhaps many varieties of slow self-destruction, e.g., alcoholism, drug-addiction, addiction to violence, etc. I would guess also, on theoretical grounds, that peak-experiences might very well abort "existential meaninglessness," states of valuelessness, etc., at least occasionally. (These deductions from the nature of intense peak-experiences are given some support by general experience with LSD and psilocybin. Of course these preliminary reports also await confirmation)... This then is one kind of peak-knowledge of whose

validity and usefulness there can be no doubt, any more than there could be with discovering for the first time that the color "red" exists and is wonderful. Joy exists, can be experienced and feels very good indeed, and one can always hope that it will be experienced again....

Perhaps I should add here the paradoxical result—for some—that death may lose its dread aspect. Ecstasy is somehow close to death-experience, at least in the simple, empirical sense that death is often mentioned during reports of peaks, sweet death that is. After the acme, only less is possible. In any case, I have occasionally been told, "I felt that I could willingly die," or, "No one can ever again tell me death is bad," etc. Experiencing a kind of "sweet death" may remove its frightening aspect. This observation should, of course, be studied far more carefully than I have been able to. But the point is that the experience itself is a kind of knowledge gained (or attitude changed) which is self-validating. Other such experiences, coming for the first time, are true simply because experienced, e.g., greater integration of the organism, experiencing physiognomic perception, fusing primary-and secondary-process, fusing knowing and valuing, transcending dichotomies, experiencing knowing as being, etc., etc. The widening and enriching of consciousness through new perceptual experiences, many of which leave a lasting effect, is a little like improving the perceiver himself.... [69]

It works is normative

By "works" I mean RE works to give us self-authentication (actualization) and to enable us to be well adjusted and navigate in the world with a sense of meaning and purpose. Since this means that our lives work better, that our needs are met at the highest level of Maslow's hierarchy, we can consider RE to be normative for human experience. Dr. Jorge W.F. Amaro, Ph.D., head of the Department of Psychology at the University of Sao Paulo, says that the unbeliever is the Sick Soul:

A non spiritualized person is a sick person, even if she doesn't show any symptom described by traditional medicine. The supernatural and the sacredness result from an elaboration on the function of omnipotence by the mind and can be found both in atheist and religious people. It is an existential function in humankind and the uses each one makes of it will be the measure for one's understanding...." "Nowadays there are many who do not agree with the notion that religious behavior a priori implies a neurotic state to be decoded and eliminated by analysis (exorcism). That reductionism based on the first works by Freud is currently under review. The psychotherapist should be limited to observing the uses their clients make of the representations of the image of God in their subjective world, that is, the uses of the function of omnipotence. Among the several authors that subscribe to this position are Odilon de Mello Franco (12).... W. R. Bion (2), one of the most notable contemporary psychoanalysts.[70]

This relationship is so strong it led to the creation of a whole discipline in psychology, transactional psychology. The transactional school is based upon the work of Abraham Maslow, who was the first modern researcher (since William James at the turn of the twentieth century) to subject the outcomes of religious experience to modern social science research methods (late 60s to early 80s). Professor Neilson writes:

One outgrowth of Maslow's work is what has become known as Transpersonal Psychology, in which the focus is on the spiritual well-being of individuals, and values are advocated steadfastly. Transpersonal psychologists seek to blend Eastern religion (Buddhism, Hinduism, etc.) or Western (Christian, Jewish or Moslem) mysticism with a form of modern psychology. Frequently, the transpersonal psychologist rejects psychology's adoption of various scientific methods used in the natural sciences.

The influence of the transpersonal movement remains small, but there is evidence that it is growing. I suspect that most psychologists would agree with Maslow that much of psychology —including the psychology of religion— needs an improved theoretical foundation.[71]

There is a vast array of studies on other areas besides RE, studies that demonstrate the validity and advantage of participation in a religious tradition, or of religious belief. This is not best evidence for the arguments because it's not so much the trace of the divine in human lives, but a demonstration of the advantages of a belief. Nevertheless, because there is a link between belief, participation, and experience, especially if Maslow, et al. are right that we all experience God to some degree, we can assume that participation is a response to some degree of experience. So these studies are important for the religious *a priori* argument, and they serve as secondary back up for the co-determinate and Thomas Reid arguments.

Normative is rational

It is rational to follow the normative. Normative does not mean "moral" or "popular;" it means something that sets the standard. RE is the standard setting for human orientation to a sense of direction in life. The sense of direction is "transformative" in that it radically changes our lives in a positive way. It is rational to follow something that works to make our lives better and give us purpose. There is no need to prove the truth claims involved; belief is rationally warranted on the assumption that if it was false it would not overhaul our lives and give us direction.

How Arguments meet their *Prima Facie* Burden

1. Documented perceptual evidence

2. Regular perceptions
3. Consistency (no internal contradiction)
4. Inter-subjective verification
5. Logical inference from both inductive and deductive
6. Tangible measurable effect (Hood scale—see next chapter)
7. Counter causes defeated or demonstrated to be less likely (see subsequent chapters)
8. Must be falsifiable

If the studies and self-actualization tests could show that the long-term positive effects don't obtain then the argument would be falsified. They don't show that because it's not false.

Rationally warranted: the logical conclusion, the case is *prima facie* so belief is rationally warranted.

The major arguments against the view I just laid out are going to be counter causality arguments making use of new scientific data on neurology. Those arguments will be presented and dealt with in their own chapters. Here I want to go into just a few additional classic arguments that skeptics commonly offer.

Counter-arguments

Other things can make for transformational experiences

Atheists have argued that everything from football to a good night's sleep can be life-transforming. This argument is a variant of trying to minimize transformational experiences. Football will not do this for you. In fact, in numerous arguments, I have yet to see a single scrap of data or documentation or a single study backing them up on any of it. I am not arguing that God is the only thing that will fix up your life. In that sense, this rejoinder is totally irrelevant, because it does not demonstrate that RE is not a rational warrant for belief. So what if there are other things that are good for you? The argument is not that there are not other things that are good for you. To attribute transformational powers to something trivial like football is just a reduction of the value of transformational aspects in the first place. We are talking about getting off drugs, self authentication, being a better person, losing fear of death; a total life transformation.

Emotions and feelings are not real

The argument doesn't turn on the validity of the experience itself but upon the effects of having had it. Of course we must deal with what is meant by "not real." The assertion that feelings don't pertain to real events in our lives is clearly foolish. The assertion that feelings don't mark profound events in our lives is clearly foolish. The idea that the mystic is seeing visions and hearing voices but these should be disregarded because they are not real, or that a feeling of God's presence doesn't prove anything because it's an illusion is just a misunderstanding of the argument. Mystical experience is not about visions and voices. They can be included but they don't really constitute actual mystical experience, which is beyond word, thought and image. Most mystics have advised discounting visions and voices. The skeptics have a bad habit of assuming that the argument turns upon the miraculous nature of the experience itself. Thus, they imagine that the religious person who has an experience is saying "I felt a presence so that proves there's a presence." The real argument turns upon saying "this experience changed my life" not because the experience itself imparted such amazing material, but because the assumption about having it and the effects of having had it upon one's outlook and ability to cope with life means that it is rational to construe it as the trace of God. Moreover, the effects of having had it are very real. Therefore, we can assume the experience itself is a real experience of something. This is the logic of the co-determinate: two things that go together logically and practically, but only one of them can be spotted; the other is the trace or the track, or the indication of the other. A foot on snow leaves an impression called "a footprint." The foot is gone but the impression is there. The impression clearly shows us a foot was there because of its shape. Even if the footprint is hoaxed (as some tracks of "bigfoot" have been) the fact of the impression shows us someone was there, whether it be bigfoot or Ray Wallace. The impression in the snow fits the contour of the thing that made it. Thus, its absence, marked by the former presence, is a demonstration of that presence even though now absent.

RE is mental illness or emotional instability

It will be seen in the next chapter that there is no basis for this claim. Many studies show that there are no commonalities between mental illness and mystical experiences, and those who have them tend to have a better handle on their emotions than do skeptics.

Reduction to mere happiness

I once presented the study findings to a group of skeptics who said, "This is just a bunch of pastors emailing their flock and telling them to send in emails about how they 'get happy.'" One will see in the next chapter how unsupported that is. These are real social scientists and real empirical studies and the transformative effects are more than just

Joseph Hinman

"getting happy." But the skeptics will make a concerted effect to reduce and minimize the advantage of RE.

Atheists can have mystical experiences

Maslow talks about atheists having mystical experiences, and since he reduced it to the level of ordinary psychology it's clear he himself, as an atheist, has had such experiences. Nevertheless, Maslow also intimates that the atheist and theist alike are finding something that is unique and amazing and hidden about the nature of being. And that one chooses to understand that in a religious way while the other does not. In other words, the atheist could choose to take it in that direction, but as we have free will, the atheist chooses not to take it in that direction. The atheist is just choosing not to adopt a religious attitude. Above, I discussed the experience of Bucke in which he did not have a sense of God per se, but adopted a religious attitude toward the phenomena nonetheless. There is an argument that God uses receptors in the brain, just as God speaking to Moses must vibrate the air to make Moses hear, and he must give Moses ears to hear with; thus God must also use brain chemistry to make us feel this presence because that's how we feel things, through brain chemistry. Thus there are receptors and they can be triggered.

I don't blame an atheist for arguing that there must be some difference that will indicate the experience is more than just the ordinary working of nature by itself with no divine influences. This must be the case, otherwise it's hardly a "trace of God." There are several ways to demonstrate this —tiebreakers— of which I will present five in subsequent chapters. Atheists posit a void in place of God or the numinous. But this void functions ontologically in the same way that the transcendental signifier functions in theist experience. This will be demonstrated empirically in the next chapter with the "M Scale."

114

Reprise on logic of the co-determinate

The "co-determinate" is a term used in connection with Schleiermacher's notion of the feeling of utter dependence. In his book *Schleiermacher The Theologian,* Roy Williams [72] uses this antiquated term for "correlate." The argument is that we can't demonstrate God's existence directly because God is not given in sense data. We can point to and discuss the *feeling of utter dependence* (which is actually a form of mystical experience) of which Schleiermacher spoke. In in this context, Williams states that God is the co-determinate of the feeling. What he is saying is that God correlates with the feeling of utter dependence, which in context is actually a feeling of ontological contingency —or dependence upon God, ontologically speaking. Atheists approach this relatively. It is unmanageable and that's a fallacy in and and of itself. I expect the skeptic to question the argument, but to actually question it in a way that implies that there's some big logical problem with correlations is baffling.

Before going into specifics, let me draw a couple of analogies: first the idea of smoking as a cause of cancer. In 1964 the Surgeon General ruled that smoking might be the cause of cancer and thus a warning was printed on cigarette packs. That ruling was made not because they had direct scientific proof. For almost a quarter of a century after that ruling, the whole campaign and war against smoking rested totally upon statistical correlation. I use this fact to indicate that science really has no other alternative but to construe correlation as proof of causality, if the correlation is tight enough. It's not illogical to assume that if a correlation is tight enough, causality is a reasonable inference. The atheist response has been "but the link has been proved." [73] It is true that the link has now been proven, but only recently (in this first decade of the twenty-first century, the ban ruling was imposed over forty years ago when all they had to go by was a correlation). The fact that the link was proven and a mechanism found over forty years later doesn't in the least blunt the fact that for almost half a century science was willing to assume something was a fact based upon statistical correlation.

Clearly, science respects a good correlation; we may treat correlations as causality if (and only if) the correlation is tight enough. There's also a mechanism that must be provided, yet ultimately even proving the relationship to a mechanism will depend upon correlation. Another analogy is that of the neutrino. Before I go into that, let me point out that I am not arguing from analogy. I understand that the similarity to cases in these analogies is not proof of the existence of God. The function of an analogy is only to illustrate an idea. That is exactly what I'm about here, nothing more. Atheists treat the correlation of God to religious experiences as though there is no implication of God's reality in the experiences because, they think, there is no proof of causality in a correlation. But, the fact is, scientists are willing to assume strong *correlation as rational warrant for a causal relationship.*

For the neutrino example, I quote the Fermi National Accelerator Laboratory:

> Neutrinos didn't emerge onto the particle physics scene until 1930, when Wolfgang Pauli invented the neutrino to "save" conservation of energy, which was under threat from observations of beta decay in radioactive materials. Scientists such as Henri Bequerel and Marie and Pierre Curie performed the first studies into radiation starting in 1898. In the years that followed radiation was classified into 3 categories: alpha, beta and gamma. In studying beta radiation, scientists discovered a disturbing phenomenon. It seemed that when a nucleus underwent beta decay, which consisted of the emission by a neutron of an electron to create a proton, conservation of energy was violated. There was a missing amount of energy that could not be accounted for by their measurements or calculations. In 1930 Pauli made his hypothesis....

It was not until 1933 that Pauli admitted the possibility of a zero mass neutrino (the discovery of the neutron in 1932 by James Chadwick forced him to change the hypothesized particle's name to neutrino). Today we know that neutrinos have some unknown mass and that they move close to the speed of light. The first detection of neutrinos occurred in 1956 by Clyde Cowan and Fredrick Reines who found a convenient source of neutrinos —nuclear power plants. Power is created in nuclear plants when atoms undergo nuclear fission, a process of which the neutrino is a byproduct. Cowan and Reines employed a 400 L tank of cadmium chloride as their target. The neutrinos struck a proton inside the target, producing a positron and a neutron. That positron encountered an electron; the two annihilated each other, producing two gamma rays The neutron was absorbed by a cadmium chloride atom, producing a photon at a 15-microsecond delay from the emission from the positron. Using this knowledge of the photon emission, Cowan and Reines were able to detect the electron neutrino.

Leon Lederman, Mel Schwartz and Jack Steinberger followed with the detection of the muon neutrino in 1962. They fired a GeV beam of protons through a target creating pions, which decayed into muons and muon neutrinos. Thick shielding halted the muons but the neutrinos continued until they entered a detector where they produced muons, decaying into electrons and a photon that were observed in the spark chambers. [74]

Pauli describes his reasoning in asserting an unproven hypothesis (the neutrino):

I have hit upon a desperate remedy to save the ''exchange theorem' of statistics and the law of conservation of energy. Namely, the possibility that there could exist in the nuclei electrically neutral particles, that I wish to call neutrons, which have spin 1/2 and obey the exclusion principle and which further differ from light quanta in that they do not travel with the velocity of light. The mass of the neutrons should be of the same order of magnitude as the electron mass and in any event not larger than 0.01 proton masses. The continuous beta spectrum would then become understandable by the assumption that in beta decay a neutron is emitted in addition to the electron such that the sum of the energies of the neutron and the electron is constant...[75]

A probable response by atheist apologists is "That's just the way science works. State a hypothesis and test it." However, the problem is this is pretty much what has been done in regard to mystical experience. While religious believers have been more definite about their hypothesis, Pauli and religious believers have taken comparable approaches and achieved very similar results. The only real difference is the scientist can eventually get "absolute" proof (in a scientific sense) when the question is an empirical one, but we can't get this kind of certainty of God. Nevertheless, we can be as certain, thanks to the M scale, as were the physicists in their discussion of neutrinos at the time that Mel Schwartz and Jack Steinberger did their work. Of course, I'm not advocating understanding religious belief as scientific hypothesis, but the basic logic of the co-determinate is the same. One can clearly see that the logic of the co-determinate is not a fallacy, formal or informal; it is not the same as saying "I believe it, so that proves it." It is not a radical move that I invented. It's the normal way correlations have been used to assume causality since modern science began. It's the use of the term "co-determinate" that gives atheist the idea that this is some new brand of logic I invented. If I called it "the correlate" they would probably not be so dismissive. In that case they would turn around and say, "Correlations are not proof of causality." No, they are not, but I did not claim to prove it. I only claimed that *it's reasonable to draw a conclusion from the association!*

Here's an even more interesting twist: Since the work in 1962, science assumed that neutrinos were proven, but they didn't have direct proof until much latter:

An international collaboration of scientists at the Department of
Energy's Fermi National Accelerator Laboratory announced on July
21, 2000 the first direct evidence for the subatomic particle called the
tau neutrino, the third kind of neutrino known to particle physicists.
They reported four instances of a neutrino interacting with an atomic
nucleus to produce a charged particle called a tau lepton, the
signature of a tau neutrino. [77]

The "detection" of the muon was in 1962, and yet the first direct
evidence of the subatomic particles called tau neutrinos wasn't until
2000. These are different particles that are coming out of a different
stage in the process. But the fact remains, the original hypothesis was
merely an attempt to explain the actions of certain particles in a certain
context; theory was manufactured to fit the apparent case. The theory
was born out later with empirical proof. The point is that the theory was
deduced from the action of particles around the neutrino, not from
direct evidence of the thing itself. The neutrino is the co-determinate of
those reactions, it goes with them logically and is implied by them, just
as the foot that makes the impression in the snow is logically deduced
from the impression and is thus implied by it and inseparable from it.

A similar scenario is seen with respect to the scientific study of
religious experience. First, people have had such experiences for
thousands of years. They developed an explanation for them (God, the
divine, the supernatural). With that explication there evolved a
complicated economics of metaphor that emerged as a means to try to
comprehend that which is beyond understanding. Then, after all that
fuss, the hypothesis is partially corroborated with empirical scientific
techniques (such as the M scale). What has been corroborated is that
the process works, as we would expect it to in living up to the
exceptions derived from our teachings on the divine. Real experiences
that are truly affecting the brain produce real, measurable, concrete
change in life and a valuable way of life that revolutionizes the lives of
those having these experiences in a dramatic and positive way. Thus,

the scientific findings corroborate that the experiences conform to what the divine is supposed to do. But we should not be surprised since that understanding is derived from the experiences themselves, and now that process is validated through science.

Atheists may object "This explanation does not prove the origin." I never said it was "proof" (except in the practical sense: close enough to proof to place confidence in the hypothesis). Why is it not reasonable to assume that the origin is the divine, since it conforms to our ideas of what it is supposed to be? After all, that is literally exactly what the supernatural actually was in its original conception. [77, 78] Thus it is a reasonable *construal.* In response to this, some atheists have launched an old, familiar tactic from message boards: ridicule of a hypothesis by use of reduction to absurdity. So they will say there's a high correlation between global warming and pirates, therefore, global warming causes piracy. This is supposed to prove the fallacy and unreasonableness of asserting a "co-determinate." *Reductio Ad Absurdum* is not necessarily the best-advised course for an argument. It is fallacious to maintain that just because one can construct a false association based upon absurdities that a valid association is illogical. The logic of the argument within the argument is what must determine whether or not an association is logical. Again, this is a concern about the soundness of an argument. All they are saying at this point is "that's not sound," although their only justification for the assertion is that they don't like the conclusion I'm drawing. *They cannot tell me why the argument is unsound without elevating my claims to the level of proof. But I don't claim proof.*

The Trace

If any of the alternate explanations were sufficient we should able to find some examples of them providing the same affect as mystical experiences. But since comparisons of people with mystical experiences (ME) with those who don't have it show that ME people have higher self actualization and cope better with life, it stands to reason that these things (coping, serotonin, etc) are not capable of producing the same effects. The basic correlation is in the experience itself. Just like the footprint in the snow is one half of the correlation between a foot and a print, the presence of the print demonstrates the former presence of the foot in the snow— the foot is gone, but it left an impression. So even though we don't have the foot, it's a good assertion to make that a foot was there because the foot is what goes with the impression, its co-determinate. So too the nature of the experience and its power to draw one to religious life, to "turn one on" to God, and the historical association that has always been made between the experience and God going back to the dawn of the concept of the divine, gives reason to suppose that the experience itself is the impression in the snow, the thing that made the impression is God, because that's the shape of the impression, just as the footprint is foot-shaped.

Some atheists have said that the use of historical association of primitive humans with sense of the numinous is a case of either begging the question or assuming God in the premise of the argument (which is really the same thing). Some even say it's an assertion that "If I believe it, that makes it so." This is not the case. The concept of "God" wouldn't exist and religion would not be part of our vocabulary were it not for these experiences. The association formed is the underpinning of the basic ideas of God and religion to begin with. The conclusion is merely the working out of an inductive form of reasoning. This is the basis of the co-determinate; the content of the experience is identified such that we use the term "God" to designate the thing that has always been sensed as belonging to these experiences as their object. It's the co-determinate. The shape marked out by the trace is a God-shaped trace. This is what people have always found as the corollary to the experience. Even when they call it different things, even when the details show it as a "void" rather than a "father" it is still a transcendental signifier. It is still the organizing principle of the metaphysical hierarchy, it is still the basis of reality, and it is still the object of the experiences.

Objections to Argument from Epistemic Judgment

Types of perception are different

One of the major arguments that skeptics make is that the kinds of perception or epistemic judgment we make by the normal five senses and those we might make based upon religious experience are not the same. The waking experience of the world is right in front of us. We can't deny it. We can't walk through walls or fly off the top of the roof, we can't deny that. But there is room for interpreting the experiences we have that draw us to God. And RE does give us a kind of "navigation" that I've already mentioned; through it we can "navigate" in the living world in the sense of bearing up under hardships, dealing with depression and disappointment, understanding a sense of purpose, and feeling as though our lives are meaningful. These things are just as important as being able to see, hear, touch and smell as we walk down the street. The epistemic criteria of regular, consistent and shared (or inter-subjective) are just as operative for this kind of "navigation" as they are for walking down the street. The sources of emotional strength and the solace of feeling that our lives are meaningful and have a valid relation to the whole of reality can be measured by their regularity and consistency. If they never gave us this sense more than once or twice, if these aspects that result from the experience could not be recognized from time to time they would mean nothing. If no one else ever experienced such things and could not relate to the need to feel that life is meaningful and has purpose, that might be thought of as a symptom of dysfunction and we would not have this sense that clearly gets us by in hard times. The skeptic will no doubt argue that the intensity of the two types of perception is different. The desk in front of me is solid. I can bang my hand on it; I have stubbed my toe on it more than once. It's much harder to deny its reality than a skeptic would imagine it is to deny the reality of RE. But that just suggests a skeptic who has not had RE, or one who has had faint RE. This just depends upon the quality of one's experiences. I admit they are of a different sort; in that sense, waking reality and RE are very different. But I cannot question or deny the experiences I've had. When I have been tempted to deny the interpretation I gave them, I still could not deny the experience itself. Based upon this, I can well imagine that for Saint Teresa of Avila or a similar mystic, RE would be as real as anything.

This point flows out of the logic of criteria effects (listed above). The effects of RE allow navigation in the world, both the world of daily life and the world of religious belief. Navigation is allowed because one can make decisions based upon the values born out of RE, and one can more clearly think about the consequences of these decisions, and one can use RE as an indicator for sense data as an approach to life. In terms of religious belief, one trusts the outcome for the same reasons that one trusts ordinary experience: because it works. In living daily life, we do not stop to access causality in all of our actions. When we see an accident we do not say, "Now I didn't really see the car actually cause the pedestrian to go flying. If I am honest with myself, all I really saw was the car stop, and the pedestrian fly, but I did not see a causal implication that proves that the car made the pedestrian fly several feet in the air. Therefore I do not know that being hit by a car actually makes one fly, or indeed that playing on the freeway actually causes one to be hit by a car. I need further data, therefore, I shall play on the freeway and observe." We stay off the freeway because we know at least as much as a good surmise that it is not healthy. We don't continually try to walk through solid walls on the premise that reality might have changed. We know solid objects can't be traversed without some displacement of matter, so we look for the openings. We don't worry every night when we go to bed that we might wake up in the morning and be someone else. We don't worry that the route to work might have changed in the night or that we might somehow work somewhere else, be someone else, and so on. The experience we have of the world on a daily basis is regular and consistent and inter-subjective to the extent that we can all pretty much agree upon the general outlines of it, so we assume it is stable even though we don't know everything about it.

Thomas Reid, who was a later contemporary of Hume's, claimed that our beliefs in the external world are justified. "I shall take it for granted that the evidence of sense, when the proper circumstances concur, is good evidence, and a just ground of belief" *(Essay on the Intellectual Powers of Man,* Essay IV, Chapter XX). This evidence is different from that of reasoning from premises to a conclusion, however.

> That the evidence of sense is of a different kind, needs little proof. No man seeks a reason for believing what he sees or feels; and, if he did, it would be difficult to find one. But, though he can give no reason for believing his senses, his belief remains as firm as if it were grounded on demonstration. Many eminent philosophers, thinking it unreasonable to believe when they could not show a reason, have labored to furnish us with reasons for believing our senses; but their reasons are very insufficient, and will not bear examination. Other philosophers have shown very clearly the fallacy of these reasons, and have, as they imagine, discovered invincible reasons against this belief; but they have never been able either to shake it themselves or to convince others. The statesman continues to plod, the soldier to fight, and the merchant to export and import, without being in the least moved by the demonstrations that have been offered of the non-existence of those things about which they are so seriously employed. And a man may as soon by reasoning, pull the moon out of her orbit, as destroy the belief of the objects of sense. [79]

Here Reid shows himself to have foundationalist tendencies, in the sense that our beliefs about physical objects are not justified by appeal to other beliefs. On the other hand, all he has established at this point is what Hume had already observed, that beliefs about physical objects are very hard to shake off. Hume himself admitted only to lose his faith in the senses when he was deeply immersed in skeptical reflections. But why should Reid think these deeply-held beliefs are based on "good evidence" or "a just ground?" One particularly telling observation is that a philosopher's "knowledge of what really exists, or did exist, comes by another channel than reason], which is open to those who cannot reason. He is led to it in the dark, and knows not how he came by it" (Essay on the Intellectual Powers of Man, Essay IV, Chapter XX). Philosophers "cannot account for" this knowledge and must humbly accept it's a gift of heaven.

If there is no philosophical account of justification of beliefs about the physical world, how could Reid claim that they are justified at all? The answer is the way in which they support common sense.

> Such original and natural judgments based on sense-experience are, therefore, a part of that furniture which Nature hath given to the human understanding. They are the inspiration of the Almighty, no less than our notions or simple apprehensions. They serve to direct us in the common affairs of life, where our reasoning faculty would leave us in the dark. They are part of our constitution; and all the discoveries of our reason are grounded upon them. They make up what is called the common sense of mankind; and, what is manifestly contrary to any of those first principles is what we call absurd. [80]

One might say that judgments from sense-experience are justified insofar as they justify other beliefs we have, or perhaps because they are the output of a perceptual system designed by God to convey the truth. (Of course, if the latter is what gives these beliefs their justification, the claim that we are designed in this way needs to be justified as well.)[81]

No scientific data can provide proof of cause and effect; we have to piece that together out of data, correlations and consistency. No scientific observation can prove that life is real or the world is as we perceive it, because any scientific data we could gather could be part of the illusion. We do not find this state of affairs debilitating, however. We operate in the world according to our perceptions and we only doubt them or seek re-examination of them when something stands out, doesn't work or doesn't conform to the basic assumptions we take for granted, such as regularity, consistency or inter-subjective nature of the real. When we do find something that stands out, we check the shared nature of the perceptions, "Did you see that?" "Do you find it hot in here too?" We take for granted that as long as we all see relatively the same things, and as long as our perceptions stay within acceptable bounds of regularity and consistence, they are truth-worthy. The same is also true of RE. The studies show, as will be seen in Chapter 3, that RE is regular, consistent and, even though the actual experiences themselves are not shared, the type of experience is shared across the board; the same commonalities, indicated above, continue to crop up. RE transforms our lives, gives us a long-term positive sense of meaning, purpose, well being and a connection to the infinite. It is regular and consistent for those who seek to cultivate it and these experiences contain commonalities and that indicates verification. It works for navigation in the world so that one can live by the beliefs fostered through these experiences and one can live well in this manner (some studies show it's the major factor in a sense of well being and happiness). Thus one is rationally warranted by RE to place confidence in the God hypothesis.

The idea of navigating by religious experiences might conjure up images of the lunatic who hears a voice saying "put your baby in the oven." As already pointed out, "peak" experience does not involve voices or visions or direct guidance from on high. This is not the kind of "navigation" intended. Rather, "navigation" means accepting a belief system based upon RE as a warrant for belief. This does not mean one should follow such experiences as any sort of direct guidance. The studies show RE is indicative of good mental health, so we can rule out putting the baby in the oven *a priori*. Confidence in a proposition fostered by RE will probably culminate in acceptance of a religious tradition. This is not always the case, but it is a likely outcome. By "navigation" I mean as a source of inspiration for coping with the material trammels of life. The effects of enabling coping skills and mechanisms form the basis for warrant because they work. Belief fostered by RE works for successful daily living and coping with problems.

I think these two arguments —specifically the argument from co-determinate, and the argument from epistemic judgment— form the basis of a realization that we are freed from the need to prove the existence of God. We have all we need in the experience and its long-term effects to demonstrate that belief is rationally warranted.

1   Matt J. Rossano, "The Religious Mind and the Evolution of Religion." Department of Psychology, Southeastern Louisiana University, 17-18. http://www2.southeastern.edu/Academics/Faculty/mrossano/recentpubs/ EvolOfReligionFinal.pdf (accessed 3/27/13). Rossano has Ph.D. in Cognitive Psychology, University of California Riverside. He is Professor of Psychology at Southeastern Louisiana University at Hommand.

2   *Ibid,* 12.

3   Dennis O'Neil, "Early Modern Human Culture," *Evolution of Modern Humans, a Survey of Biological and Cultural Evolution of Archaic and Modern Homo Sapiens*. Anthropology Tutorials by Behavioral Science Department, Palomar College, San Marcos, California. http://anthro.palomar.edu/homo2/mod_homo_5.htm. O'Neil is at Palomar College San Marcos California. Some of the animals depicted in the caves were predators rather than prey. This may have been a way of obtaining

protection from these creatures or of taking on their ferociousness and skill.

4 Mary Ilford, *The God's of pre-Historic Man*. New York: Sterling Publishing Company, Inc., Johannes Maringer, trans., 2003, 198. Johannes Maringer was professor of Prehistoric archeology at Mission seminary.

5 *Ibid.*

6 Abraham H. Maslow, "Preface," *Religions, Values and Peak-Experiences*, New York: Penguin Books, 1970. vii.

7 *Ibid.*, appendix I." An Example of B Analysis."

8 *Ibid.*, appendix I." An Example of B Analysis."

9 David Lukoff," the Diagnosis of Mystical Experiences With Psychotic Features," *Journal of Transpersonal Psychology*, (1985) 17, (2) 155-81 in Lukoff and Lu, *Journal of Transpersonal Psychology*, (1988) 20, (2) 182.

10 Ibid

11 Abraham H. Maslow, Op.Cit., Appendix I. An Example of B-Analysis

12 Lukoff in Jayne Gackenback Spiritwatch, http://www.sawka.com/spiritwatch/cehsc/ipure.htm (accessed 10/4/08)

13 Ralph Hood Jr.," The Common Core Thesis in The Study of Mysticism," in *Where God and Science Meet vol. III: How Brain Evolution Studies Alter our Understanding of Religion: Psychology of Religion* Patrick McNamara, ed., Westport, CN: Praeger, 2004. 120.

14 R. Jones "Numinous," *Westminster Dictionary of Christian Theology*. Philadelphia, Pennsylvania: Westminster Press, Alan Richardson, John Bowden, eds., 1983,405.

15 Jayne Gackenback, website: "Trans personal Childhood Experiences of Higher States of Consciousness: Literature Review and Theoretical Integration" (unpublished paper 1992) Website "Spirit watch," http://www.sawka.com/spiritwatch/cehsc/ipure.htm (accessed 3/27/13).

16 A. Hardy, *The Spiritual Nature of Man*, Oxford, Clarendon Press, 1979, 131-140.

17 ibid

18 Thomas A. Idinopulos, "What is Religion?" Cross Currents, Fall (1998), Vol. 48 Issue 3. See also online version of "Cross Currents" http://www.crosscurrents.org/whatisreligion.htm (accessed 10/10/08). Idinopulos is professor of religion at Miami University of Ohio.

19 *Ibid.*, Idinopulos cites work of Wilfred Cantwell Smith, work *The Meaning and End of Religion*, 119, and 173.

20   David Steindl-Rast "The Mystical Core of Organized Religion" *ReVision,* Summer (1989) 12(1):11-14. also used on website for Council on Spiritual Practices, http://www.csp.org/experience/docs/steindl-mystical.html (accessed 10/10/08).

21   J.L. Hinman, " How Many Atheists Are There?" Doxa: Christian Thought in the Twenty-first Century, http://www.doxa.ws/social/percentage.html In this article I draw upon many sources. See also Pew Forum, "On Religion and Public Life: US Religious Landscape" http://religions.pewforum.org/affiliations (accessed 05/27/2009).

22   Norman Lillegard: "On Some Differences Between Religious and Scientific Beliefs" Website at University of Tennessee Martin http://www.utexas.edu/cola/depts/philosophy/faculty/koons/ntse/papers/Lillegar.txt (accessed 10/10/08)

23   Sri Aurobindo Ghose. *On Himself.* Pondicherry: Sri Aurobindo Ashram, 1972., 101

24   *Ibid.,* 102

25   R. Bucke Cosmic Consciousness: "A Study In The Evolution of the Human Mind." New York: Dutton, 1968, (originally 1901). Quoted in Andrew Newberg, *Why We Believe What we Believe: Uncovering Our Biological Need for Meaning, Spirituality, and Truth.* New York, London: Free Press, (2006), 168.

26   Michael Neilsen, Ph.D. psychology of religion: website: *Psychology and Religion,* http://www.psywww.com/psyrelig/ukraine/index.htm (accessed 10/10/08)

27   Faidman C. Savage,, J., Mogar, R. & Allen, M. (1966). "The effects of psychedelic therapy on values, personality, and behaviour." *International Journal of Neuropsychiatry, 2,* 241-254.Scheier, M.P., & Carver, C.S. (1987). "Dispositional optimism and physical well-being: The influence of generalized outcome expectancies on health". *Journal of Personality, 55,* 169-210

28   Eugene W. Mathes, "Peak Experience Tendencies." Journal *of Humanistic Psychology* vol 22, no 3(1982) 92-108.

29   J.D. Kass, R. Friedman, J. Lescrman, P.C., Zuttermeister,, and H. Benson, . "Health outcomes and a new index of spiritual experience". *Journal for Scientific Study of Religion,(1991) 30,* 203-211

30   K Krishna Mohan, "Spirituality and Well Being: an Overview" presentation at conference on Second International Conference on Integral Psychology," Pondicherry India jan 4-7, 2001.Text published in

Consciousness and its Transformation, M. Cornelissen (ed.)
Pondicherry:SAICE 2001. http://ipi.org.in/texts/ip2/ip2-4.5-.htm (accessed
3/25/13)

31   Gackenbach, Jayne. "Pure Consciousness/Mystical Experience"from
      Spiritwatch website: Childhood Transpersonal Childhood Experiences of
      Higher States of Consciousness: Literature Review and Theoretical
      Integration, http://www.spiritwatch.ca/cehsc/ipure.htm (accessed 6/20/
      2010).

32   Robert Wuthnow, (1978). "Peak Experiences: Some Empirical Tests."
      Journal of Humanistic Psychology, 18 (3), 59-75.

33   Kathleen D. Noble, Kathleen D. (1987). "Psychological Health and the
      Experience of Transcendence." *The Counseling Psychologist*, 15 (4),
      601-614. this list and the one on Wuthnow, both long term and short term
      effects are summarized on the website of the Counsel on Spiritual
      Practices: "States of Unitive Consciousness" (http://www.csp.org/
      experience/docs/unitive_consciousness.html) (accessed 3/25/13).

34   Noble, *Ibid.,* 606

35   Charles T. Tart, *Psi: Scientific Studies of the Psychic Realm*, Bloomington
      Indiana: IUniverse inc. 2001.p. 19

36   *Ibid.,* 607

37   J. Gartner, D.B. Allen, *The Faith Factor: An Annotated Bibliography of
      Systematic Reviews And Clinical Research on Spiritual Subjects Vol. II*,
      David B. Larson M.D., ed., Bethesda, Maryland: National Institute for
      Health Research Dec. 1993, p. 3090

38   L.S. Allman, L.S., Dela, R.O., Elins, D.N., & Weathers, R.S..
      Psychotherapists Attitude Towards Mystical Experiences. Psychotherapy,
      (1992) 29, 564-569.

39   D.N. Elkins, "Psychotherapy and spirituality: Toward a theory of the
      soul". *Journal of Humanistic Psychology, 35,* (1995), 78-98.

40   E.P. Shafranske and H.N. Malony, "Clinical Psychologists Religious and
      Spiritual Orientations And Their Practice of Psychotherapy."
      Psychotherapy, 7, 72-78

41   W. Sullivan, "It helps Me to Be a Whole Person: The Role of Spirituality
      Among the Mentally Challenged." *Psychological Rehabilitation Journal,*
      (1993) 16, 125-134.

42   D. Glik, "Psychosocial Wellness Among Spiritual Healing Participants".
      Social Science and Medicine, 22, (1986). 579-586.

43 Usha Lee McFarling, "Doctors Find Power of Faith Hard to Ignore," Knight Ridder News Service (Dec. 23, 1998), http://www.tennessean.com/health/stories/98/trends1223.htm (accessed 3/27/09)

44 J Gartner, *op. cit.*

45 Lukoff and Lu *op. cit.*, 177, Discuss original Research in W. Richards, "Mystical and Archetypal Experiences of Terminal Patients in DPT Assisted Psychotherapy." *Journal of Religion and Health* 17 (2) 117-26.

46 J.G. Matty, " Op. Cit. (see chapter one).

47 Wuthnow, *op. cit.* Wuthnow Theorizes that all people experience mystical consciousness at some level, this is why I argue it on a continuum.

48 Lukoff in Jayne Gackenback Spiritwatch, http://www.sawka.com/spiritwatch/cehsc/ipure.htm (accessed 10/4/08).

49 L.S. Allman, L.S., Dela, R.O., Elins, D.N., & Weathers, R.S. . "Psychotherapists attitude towards mystical experiences." *Psychotherapy,*(1992) 29, 564-569.

50 Elkins, D.N. "Psychotherapy and Spirituality: Toward a Theory of the Soul". *Journal of Humanistic Psychology, (1995).35,* 78-98.

51 E.P. Shafranske and H.N. Malony, "Clinical Psychologists Religious and Spiritual Orientations And Their Practice of Psychotherapy." *Psychotherapy*, 7, 72-78

52 K.I. Pargament, in Patricia L. Ryan, "Spirituality Among Adult Survivors of Childhood Violence A Literature Review." *Journal of Transpersonal Psychology,* Vol. 30, no. 1 (1998) 41.

53 D.M. Elliot, "The Impact of Christian Faith on the Prevalence and Sequelae of Sexual Abuse." *Journal of Interpersonal Violence*, 9(1) (1994) 95-108.

54 M.J. Heimelein and McElrath, "Childhood Sexual Survivors, Cognitive Coping and Illusion." *Child Abuse and Neglect,* 20 (8), (1996) 747-758.

55 L Valentine and LL. Feninuer. "Resistance Factors Associated With Female Survivors of Childhood Sexual Abuse." *The American Journal of Family Therapy,* 21 (3) (1993) 216-224.

56 Ryan, 41-46.

57 *Ibid.,* 47

58 *Ibid.,* 42

59 H.J. Irwin, "Childhood Trauma and the Origin of Paranormal Belief: A Constructive Replication." *Psychological Reports.* 74 (1) (1994) 107.

60 Patricia L.Ryan, "Spirituality Among Adult Survivors of Childhood Violence: A Literature Review," *The Journal of Transpersonal Psychology*, Vol. 30, no. 1, (1998) 43, Ryan cites Gamje-Fling and McCarthy.

61 Loretta Do Rozario, "Spirituality in the Lives of People With Disability and Chronic Illness: A Creative Paradigm of Wholeness and Reconstitution." *Disability and Rehabilitation: An International and Multidisciplinary Journal.* Vol 19, no 10 (1997) 427

62 *Ibid.,* 428

63 *Ibid.,* 430-431

64 *Ibid.,* 433

65 *Ibid.,* 433

66 Alexander et al, quoted in "Transpersonal Childhood Experiences of Higher States of Consciousness: Literature Review and Theoretical Integration." Unpublished paper by Jayne Gackenback, (1992) http://www.sawka.com/spiritwatch/cehsc/ipure.htm (accessed 3/20/13)

67 Poloma and Pendelton *The Faith Factor: An Annotated Bibliography of Systematic Reviews And Clinical Research on Spiritual Subjects,* Vol. II, David B. Larson M.D., National Institute for Health Research Dec. 1993, p. 3290.

68 Abraham Maslow, *Op.Cit.*"D Analysis."

69 Maslow,*Ibid., op. cit.*Appendix D, "what is the Values Gained in Peak Experience?"

70 Jorge Amaro, "Psychology, Psychoanalysis, and Religious Faith," Published by Michael Nielsen, on his *Psychology of Religion Homepage*, http://www.psywww.com/psyrelig/amaro.html (accessed 3/27/13). The article was written in 1998.

71 Michael Nielsen, "Notable people in Psychology of Religion: Abraham Maslow," Psychology of Religion Homepage: http://www.psywww.com/psyrelig/psyrelpr.htm (accessed 3/27/13). Nielsen

72 Robert R. Williams, *Schleiermacher the Theologian.* Philadelphia: Fortress Press, 1978, 35.

73 Website, "Smoking and Cancer," Cancer Research UK: http://info.cancerresearchuk.org/healthyliving/smokingandtobacco/ (accessed 3/24/2009).

74   Fermi National Accelerator Laboratory, Donut Home, "Neutrinos What are they? http://www-donut.fnal.gov/web_pages/neutrinospg/ Neutrinos.html (accessed 03/24/2009).

75   *Ibid.*

76   Fermilab "Inquiring minds, Physics at Fermilab," http://www.fnal.gov/ pub/inquiring/physics/neutrino/discovery/index.html (accessed 3/24/ 2009).

77   "What is the Supernatural," *Doxa.* http://www.doxa.ws/meta_crock/ Supernature.html On line resource, (accessed 3/24/2009).

78   Eugene R. Fairwairweather, "Christianity and the Supernatural," *New Theology No. 1* edited Martin E. Marty and Dean G. Peerman,. 1964, 235-256. My recommendation to the reader for a real understanding of the concept of the supernatural would be to read: Matthias Joseph Scheeben, *Nature and Grace*, Wipf and Stock Publishers, 2009 (paperback) originally unpublished 1856.

79   Thomas Reid, *Essays on the Intellectual Powers of Man,* Essay IV, Chapter XX, 1785. Standard text.

80   Thomas Reid, *An Inquiry Into the Human Mind on the Principles of Common Sense,* Chapter VII, Section 4. 1764.

81   G.J. Mattey, Thomas Reid,*Theory of Knowledge lecture notes.* Philosophy, UC Davis, http://-philosophy.ucdavis.edu/phil02/tkch4.htm prior to the Revision of May 22,2008. Now located at http://www-philosophy.ucdavis.edu/mattey/mattey/phi022/reidlec.html

3 Studies: A Closer Look at Findings and Methodology

A vast array of scientific data demonstrates the value of religious experience for the individual. Those who experience mystical consciousness score higher on measures of self-actualization. They prove to be happier, better-adjusted, more confident, more successful, find life more meaningful and are more content in their work than those who do not experience these phenomena. My argument is that these effects, which are long-term and can last a lifetime after only one experience (according to Maslow), are indicative of some sort of contact with the divine. The major argument that I am making is comprised of three sub-arguments:

1. Argument from co-determinate
2. The Thomas Reid argument
3. The argument from religious *a priori*

These are three constituent parts of one major argument. That major point that I make is founded upon the bedrock of "RE" (religious experience) or "mystical experience." There is a great deal of prejudice about RE. Skeptics are constantly assuming that religious experience includes visions and voices *a priori*, that it is about explaining the nature of the natural world, that it results from mental illness or from some form of pressure or mental breakdown, etc. There is a debate about the possibility of studying RE through empirical means. Some mystics have seen visions and heard voices, but mystical experience is not about visions and voices. The whole concept of "the mystical" is that the experience is beyond word, thought or image.[1] Mystics have at times been insane, but a vast body of work has been done over the last forty years giving a strong indication that RE is not born of mental illness. Nor is the point of RE the explanation of the natural world. It is true that explanations of ancient man drew upon religious thinking since that was the major tool they had to draw upon. The idea that God or the gods created the world offered itself as the logical, ultimate explanation for things, but that in no way means that religion came to exist solely for that reason. Religious belief came to exist because people had a sense of the numinous. The sense of mystical consciousness is at the heart of religion. The ability to study RE is the ability to study the effects of such experiences upon the recipient. We cannot go inside their heads and understand what they are feeling as they experience it, but we can understand and quantify the effect of such experiences upon people. When this is done, the evidence that RE is not the product of mental illness, but is somehow in line with our basic endowment as humans is overwhelming.

As has been pointed out, we can assume that RE is the trace of God because of its effects upon those who perceive such experiences. We can assume that they are experiences of the divine because of the way they affect us —they produce belief, they transform lives for the better— and nothing else works that way. There would be no point in even discussing religion were it not for the effects of RE upon the believer. The content of the experience itself is primarily religious.

Defining characteristics of mystical experience

In a recent review of the mystical experience, Lukoff and Lu acknowledged that the "definition of a mystical experience ranges greatly."[2] Maslow (1969) offered 35 definitions of "transcendence", a term often associated with mystical experiences and used by Alexander *et al.* to refer to the process of accessing RE. Lukoff (1985) identified

five common characteristics of mystical experiences, which could be
defined in an operational sense for assessment purposes. They are:

1. Ecstatic mood (which he identified as the most common feature)
2. Sense of newly gained knowledge, which includes a belief that the
   mysteries of life have been revealed
3. Perceptual alterations, which range from "heightened sensations to
   auditory and visual hallucinations
4. Delusions (if present) have themes related to mythology, which
   include an incredible diversity and range
5. No conceptual disorganization; those with mystical experiences
   (unlike psychotic persons) do *not* suffer from disturbances in
   language and speech

It can be seen from the explanation of RE earlier that this list of
qualities overlaps in part those delineated by Alexander et al.[3]

The Voyle study sets out defining characteristics that are very
similar and based upon Stace (1960). Stace's work was a watershed; it
influenced Hood and has continued to influence many. The
contemporary interest in the empirical research of mysticism can be
traced to Stace's (1960) demarcation of the phenomenological
characteristics of mystical experiences (Hood, 1975). In Stace's
conceptualization, mystical experiences had five characteristics (Hood,
1985, p.176):

1. The mystical experience is noetic. The person having the experience
   perceives it as a valid source of knowledge and not just a subjective
   experience.
2. The mystical experience is ineffable; it cannot simply be described in
   words.
3. The mystical experience is holy. While this is the religious aspect of
   the experience, it is not necessarily expressed in any particular
   theological terms.
4. The mystical experience is profound yet enjoyable and characterized
   by positive affect.

5. The mystical experience is paradoxical. It defies logic. Further analysis of reported mystical experiences suggests that the one essential feature of mysticism is an experience of unity (Hood, 1985). The experience of unity involves a process of ego loss and is generally expressed in one of three ways (Hood, 1 976a): The ego is absorbed into that which transcends it, or through an inward process the ego gains pure awareness of self, or a combination of the two. [4]

Religious Experience can be studied empirically

While it is probably impossible to study the actual experiences as people have them, it is certainly possible to gather empirical data about RE and ME. A vast body of work has grown up around this phenomenon. Statistical scales and psychological instruments have been developed to study the authenticity of RE. It is possible to understand if one's experiences do fall within the range of what is understood as ME. In essence, the basic idea is to construct a typology of the "peaker" by collecting data from surveys about experiences and then compare with standardized psychological personality-theory instruments. Three major instruments have been developed for determining the authenticity of ME: Greeley's questionnaire (1974), the "M" scale ("M" for mysticism) by Hood (1975), and the State of Consciousness Inventory (SCI) by Alexander and Boyer (1987). Greeley asked the question "Have you ever felt as though you were very close to a powerful, spiritual force that seemed to lift you out of yourself?" He used this in several national opinion surveys. Thomas and Cooper (1980) demonstrated that Greeley's answers were general and varied considerably. Subjecting Greeley's data to their own criteria, they found that only 1% of his "yes" responses were genuine mystical experience. Thus Hood's scale is more widely favored. Holm and Caird validated the "M" scale with cross-cultural data in 1982 and 1988. [5]

The SCI by Alexander and Boyer is the most researched. As the authors tell us, "the SCI was designed for quantitative assessment of frequency of experiences of higher states of consciousness as defined in Vedic Psychology".[6] The SCI is more focused upon meditation practices and their results. Items are constructed based upon first person accounts, but also drawn from authoritative literature. Subscales are added to differentiate experiences from normal waking experience and with neurotic and schizophrenic experiences. The authors assume that the core state of consciousness is pure consciousness and out of that emerges higher states of consciousness.

> Whereas most researchers on mystical experiences study them as isolated or infrequent experiences with little if any theoretical "goal" for them, this group contextualizes them in a general model of development (Alexander et al., 1990) with their permanent establishment in an individual as a sign of the first higher state of consciousness. They point out that "during any developmental period, when awareness momentarily settles down to its least excited state, pure consciousness [mystical states] can be experienced (p. 310)." Virtually all of researchers using the SCI are very careful to distinguish the practice of meditation from the experience of pure consciousness, explaining that the former merely facilitates the latter. They also go to great pains to show that their multiple correlations of health and well-being are strongest to the transcendent experience rather than to the entire practice of meditation (for psychophysiological review see Wallace, 1987; for individual difference review see Alexander et al., 1987[7]

How common are such experiences? Skeptics used to suggest that these experiences were confined to "strange people" who just had "that sort of temperament." While estimates vary as to incidence rate, all the major finds show that the rate is so high that this is one of the major reasons to rule out mental illness as a cause of RE. We can determine that ME is quite common, and RE to some degree may be almost universal.

Incidence

Several studies have charted the incidence rate of RE or ME. Greeley (1974) found it to be 35%, whereas in 1970 Back and Bourque had reported increases in frequency of such incidence from 20% in 1962 to 41% in 1967.[8] Researchers once treated them as rare events limited to a small group of the fortunate. They were dealing mainly with regular experiences as a way of life. Alexander quotes Maslow: "In terms of incidence Maslow felt that in the population at large less than one in 1,000 have frequent 'peak' experiences so that the 'full stabilization of a higher stage of consciousness appears to be an event of all but historic significance' (p. 310)."[9] On the other hand, Maslow also suggested that everyone probably has them to some degree. While most research focuses upon the dramatic and constant events, Maslow felt that everyone experiences some degree of transcendence at some point.[10] In his 1978 study, Wuthnow asked three different questions designed to reflect a general sense of the commonality of "peak" experience.[11] The first question was "Have you ever had the feeling that you were in contact with something holy or sacred?" This was designed to reflect a religious dimension to the experience. The second question was "Have you experienced the beauty of nature in a deeply moving way?" The third question was "Have you had the feeling that you were in harmony with the universe?" For those who answered affirmatively for any of these three questions they were asked if it had a lasting and deep influence upon their lives. The findings show that one in two has experienced contact with the sacred. Eight in ten have been moved deeply by the beauty of nature. Four in ten have experienced harmony with the universe. Wuthnow concludes that Maslow was right, and the right kind of probing would show that virtually everyone has had some degree of experience of this kind. "This data clearly demonstrates that peak experiences are not just the domain of mystics or artists or people with unusual talents for having such experiences..."[12] Noble found in her 1984 study that 100% of her 120 subjects drawn from Seattle area colleges experienced transcendence, measured by both Hood's "M scale" and Mathes' *et al.* "Peak scale."[13]

Incidence rate suggests no pathology

A group of professional psychiatrists, the Group for the Advancement of Psychiatry, has made the statement:

> Numerous studies assessing the incidence of mystical experience (Back and Bourque, 1970; Greeley, 1974, 1987; Hay and Morisy, 1978; Hood, 1974, 1975, 1977; Thomas and Cooper, 1980) all support the conclusion that 30-40% of the population does have such experiences, suggesting that they are normal rather than pathological phenomena. In addition, a recent survey (Allman et al., 1992) has demonstrated that the number of patients who bring mystical experiences into treatment is not insignificant. Psychologists in full-time practice were asked to estimate the percentage of their clients over the past 12 months who had reported a mystical experience. The 285 respondents indicated that of the 20,670 clients seen during the past year, the incidence of mystical experience was 4.5%. This clearly challenges the GAP Report on Mysticism, which claims that "mystical experiences are rarely observed in psychotherapeutic practice"[14]

There have been a few studies with negative findings. When I say no skeptic has been able to supply the data, that is true: Wuthnow (who is not a skeptic, although not a believer either) supplies it in his own article. Prince in 1966 found that ME "may be associated with pathological regression." However, Adler in 1972 found that such people were antinomian personalities who couldn't cope with their problems.[15] These seem more like judgments imposed by the researcher rather than the result of data. Wuthnow's study (1978) is much more systematic and rigorous, and most of the positive studies come later and are better done. He finds that "peakers" have more confidence, are more self assured, and are more apt to find life meaningful. These experiences do make a big difference for those who have had them versus those who have not. Peakers are more apt to be analytical, to feel that their lives are meaningful, and that there is meaning to life. A reported 68% of those who had had such experiences in the past year said their lives were meaningful, compared with 46% of those who had had such experiences (but not in the past year), while 39% of those who had not had them but wanted to have them, and 36% of those who neither had them nor wanted them, said the same.[16] Noble found that negative effects were only temporary and amounted to short-term disorientation.[17]

Religious experience is not a form of mental illness

Often skeptics assume that RE is the product of mental illness. A vast body of data, however, shows that there is no correlation between mental illness and religious experience. Part of the reason they think that is because they think RE is about visions and voices. Images of people sacrificing their children to a voice in the head come to mind. The data tells a much different story. Some mentally ill people have laced their delusional worlds with religious motivations, but no data demonstrates how these people would score on the M scale, or that their experiences are valid mystical ones. Gartner, Allen and Larsen indicate that their data shows that those with psychotic ideation are not necessarily preoccupied with religious concerns, nor do they frequently attend religious services; rather they are less frequent attendees than those in the general population..."[18] There is no correlation between RE and neuroticism. Spanos and Moretti (1988) found no relationship between a measure of mystical experience and psychopathology.[19]

> The experience of pure consciousness is typically called "mystical". The essence of the mystical experience has been debated for years (Horne, 1982). It is often held that "mysticism is a manifestation of something which is at the root of all religions (p. 16; Happold, 1963)." The empirical assessment of the mystical experience in psychology has occurred to a limited extent. Scientific interest in the mystical experience was broadened with the research on psychoactive drugs. The popular belief was that such drugs mimicked either mystical states and/or schizophrenic ones (reviewed in Lukoff, Zanger & Lu, 1990). Although there is likely some physiological similarity as well, phenomenological recent work has shown clear differences. For instance, Oxman, Rosenberg, Schnurr, Tucker and Gala (1988) analyzed 66 autobiographical accounts of schizophrenia, hallucinogenic drug experiences, and mystical ecstasy as well as 28 control accounts of important personal experiences. They concluded that the "subjective experiences of schizophrenia, hallucinogenic drug-induced states, and mystical ecstasy are more different from one another than alike."[20]

Most of the time people who are mentally ill get worse. They can stabilize with medication and treatment, but there is no data to indicate that mentally ill people can find their mental illness as a source of vast and dramatic positive changes that make their lives better forever. Such change is what we find with mystical experience. The burden is on the skeptic to offer data to the contrary. RE builds a sense of self-actualization in the "peaker"—mental illness does not.

RE is a much fuller, richer and more textured experience than mental illness. Consider the fact that, sometimes, mentally ill people take medication and their delusions go away, but rarely does anyone take medication and belief in God goes away. Mental illness might be as complex as religious experience, but when I say "full, rich and textured" I mean in a positive, life-affirming way. Many studies have found no relationship between mental illness and religious experience; one such example is the Nobel study.[21] While Freud thought that RE was pathological, most psychiatrists today see it as positive and not as pathological. "Offsetting the clinical literature that views mystical experiences as pathological, many theorists (Bucke, 1961; Hood, 1974, 1976; James, 1961; Jung, 1973; Laski, 1968; Maslow, 1962, 1971; Stace, 1960; Underhill, 1955) have viewed mystical experiences as a sign of health and a powerful agent of transformation."[22] Allman, et al. (1992) suggest that most clinicians do not view ME as pathology. Several studies show that mystical experiencers score lower on psychopathology scales and higher on well-being scales than do non-experiencers.[23] There is an old assumption, a myth that mystical experience stems from deprivation—that the mystic is missing something in life, or is trying to cope with some loss or some lack, and thus the mind manufactures such experiences. As pointed out earlier, Greeley found that his mystics were generally better educated, more economically successful, less racist, and rated substantially happier on psychological well-being scales, than did non-experiencers.[24] Mystical experience offers therapeutic insights. As Roger Walsh says:

> ...Within the Western model we recognize and define psychosis as a suboptimal state of consciousness that views reality in a distorted way and does not recognize that distortion. It is therefore important to note that from the mystical perspective our usual state fits all the criteria of psychosis, being suboptimal, having a distorted view of reality, yet not recognizing that distortion. Indeed from the ultimate mystical perspective, psychosis can be defined as being trapped in, or attached to, any one state of consciousness, each of which by itself is necessarily limited and only relatively real.[25]

McDowell et al (1996) studied 101 mental patients and found that both their attendants and the staff that treated them found spirituality to be a vital part of their recovery.[26]

Mystical experience is not epilepsy

Because one of the characters in *The Possessed* by Fyodor Dostoyevsky thought that mystical experience was epilepsy, many people make this assumption. Both phenomena do produce some sense of unity of the world and understanding of the world. But the Sensky study (1983) demonstrates there is a sharp distinction:

> The author developed a self-administered questionnaire incorporating 51 items which elicited religious and mystical experience characteristics as well as the relationship of these experiences to epileptic seizures. They surveyed 46 outpatients attending the Maudsley Epilepsy Clinic.Their findings: Contrary to previous reports based upon case studies, patients with temporal lobe epilepsy and generalized epilepsy did not have a higher rate of religiosity or mystical experiences compared to a control population.[27]

Religious experience indicative of good mental health

Many "new atheists" put forth the notion that religion itself is a form of mental illness. This is the impression many tend to cultivate but there is no basis for it in the data. The effects are varied, but the entire range of research indicates that religious and mystical experiences result in a healthy, well-adjusted, whole person. The research finds over and over that such people are less dogmatic authoritarian; that they are more socially conscious, happy, healthy, successful, self-aware, self-assured; and that they find life meaningful, enjoying their work more, are strong in ego, strong in sense of self and more self actualized. All the studies mentioned to this point back this up: Mathes, Maslow, Wuthnow, Greeley, Luckoff and Lu, Noble, Hood, Glick and others. In the 1990's, several studies found the majority of practicing psychologists, even if not religious themselves, consider religious involvement and experience important to their clinical work: Allman (92),[28] Elkins (95),[29] Glick (86)32 and Shafranske and Malony (90).[30] The Sullivan study in 1993, which used a large quantitative base of former mental patients and those who cared for them, found that 48% identified spiritual practices as crucial to their healing. This was a two-year exploratory group study on spiritual healing practices.[31]

Not the result of technique alone

Some have argued that such religious and mystical experiences are just the result of years of training or the practice of Transcendental Meditation, psychological states and/or imagination due to self-hypnosis and the like. However, 43% of mystical experiences are in children. It is highly unlikely that many children would have spent years practicing transcendental meditation, have elaborately developed ideologies of the world or have been exposed to any hypnotic techniques (although mystical experience is also developed over the long-term through such techniques as Transcendental Meditation).

Data on experiences in childhood are obtained from adult recollections and children's reports, or studies on children using techniques proposed to get near or attain peak experience. Both Millar (1990) and Hunt, Gervais, Shearing-Johns & Travis (1991) asked their adult subjects about mystical experience incidence in childhood. (Hunt et al. defined it as, "During waking you may experience a sense of oneness and unity in all things, along with experiences of awe, bliss and/or wonder. Sometimes this involves a sensation of melting or fusing with one's surroundings, feelings of being overwhelmed by a sense of love or compassion. Some of these experiences can be very hard to put into words." Millar defined it as, "This is often a profound and deeply moving sense of communication, unity and oneness; a transcendental experience of higher consciousness or love, too beautiful to fully express in words. It can also be an experience of the void."). A large percent (45%) of Millar's sample of self-identified psychics reported mystical experiences in childhood.[33]

In Hunt *et al.,* people doing meditation reported significantly more mystical experiences in childhood than the those not meditating.

Finally, Robinson (1977) found that 15% of his adult respondents spoke of childhood mystical experiences. This from a 40-year-old female:

> When I was eleven years old I spent part of a summer holiday in the Wye Valley. Waking up very early one bright morning, before any of the household was about, I left my bed and went to kneel on the window seat, to look out over the curve which the river took just below the house... The scene was very beautiful, and quite suddenly I felt myself on the verge of a great revelation. It was as if I had stumbled unwittingly on a place where I was not expected, and was about to be initiated into some wonderful mystery, something of indescribable significance. Then, just as suddenly, the feeling faded. But for the brief seconds while it lasted I had known that in some strange way I, the essential "me", was a part of the trees, of the sunshine, and the river, that we all belonged to some great unity. I was left filled with exhilaration and exultation of spirit. This is one of the most memorable experiences of my life, of a quite different quality and greater intensity than the sudden lift of the spirit one may often feel when confronted with beauty in Nature.[34]

The long-term positive effects of having had these experiences are demonstrated in the previous chapter. A vast array of data shows that

every area from self-authentication to physical health is demonstrated
to follow as a result of RE.

- Self-Authentication
- Mental health

  ◦ Positive therapeutic effects
  ◦ Major factor in well-being

- Physical health (including healing from cancer).

Methodology: Cross-cultural and Longitudinal

One of the major limitations on current studies, as pointed out by Nobel
in her 1987 article, is the need for studies from beyond Western Anglo
culture, as well as for longitudinal studies. Krishna Moham, an Indian
psychologist, answers the need for studies from non-Anglo cultures in
large part. In his article "Spirituality and Well-being: An Overview"[35]
Mohan discusses many studies done in India, mostly involving Hindus.
These studies come to the same conclusions as the studies previously
discussed above. The basic difficulty is the difference in the way
Western culture understands "well-being" and the way Hindu or Indian
culture understands it. Mohan discusses the vast tradition of
understanding on this point described in Hindu literature, which
stretches back though Hindu history. Essentially, the difference is this:
in the West, well-being is the absence of material trammels. The studies
that show an increased sense of well-being due to religious experience
deal with an increased sense of well-being —the perception of well-
being— not with the reality of it. These studies do not determine the
financial situation of the experiencer. They determine to what extent the
experiencing one feels a sense of well-being. In short, the Indian
concept is not the absence of problems but the ability to cope with
problems.

Psychological well-being to the Hindu means (1) integration of emotions with the help of an integrated teacher (a spiritual master, Guru), (2) acquiring a higher philosophy of life which helps to resolve inner tensions, (3) channelizing basal passion directing the emotions to ultimate reality, (4) developing an attitude whereby everything is viewed as a manifestation of ultimate reality (5) cultivation of higher qualities which replace negative qualities, and (6) the practice of concentration (Sinha, 1965).

The ultimate goal in Indian thought goes beyond self-realization or transcendence and seeks for a spiritual pursuit leading to the highest state of everlasting happiness, "*nirvana*" or supreme bliss. The ultimate motive is spiritual pursuit with the aim of attaining union with the universal self or *moksha* or *nirvana*. The concept of well-being has also been elaborately given in *Charaka Samhita* the ancient treatise on the Indian systems of medicine which is called Ayurveda (the treatise on life). In this treatise, the characteristics of happy and unhappy life have been elaborated. According to the *sankhya* philosophy, human personality is a product of the interaction between the spirit (*purusha*) and matter (*prakriti*). The influence of *prakriti* on behavior is emphasized in terms of the three Gunas or qualities called *sattva* or the element of knowledge, *rajas* or the principle of activity, which on the affective side is the cause of all painful experiences, and *tamas* or the principle of passivity that clouds our intellect thereby producing ignorance. It is said that the state of *samyavastha* or equilibrium of the three Gunas is that which holds the secret to an individual's well-being.[36]

Another major concept of the Indian view comes from the *Bhagavad-Gita*, one of the ancient and traditional works of Hindu religious writing. The emphasis here is upon moderation. The suppliant is given the ability to control his desires and passions, to keep the self in check. Balance or equilibrium is the most desirable state for well-being. This concept includes steadying of mind, self-control and the realization of the interconnectedness of all things.

Joseph Hinman

William James, as a western observer, perceived the great importance in such deliberate ways of relating self to what lies beyond the self. "William James (1842-1910) was one of the first to talk about various levels of self: he defines the level of the *personal* as the creativeness of our own choices and the level *beyond the personal* as a surrender to a spiritual or "higher" self(s). This self is in his view connected to the personal yet beyond it and greater/more."[37] This aspect is shared among most descriptions of "peak experience." Maslow's "Peakers" speak of it, as do subjects of many other studies. Gackenbach lists it among the standard characteristics. Mohan sums up the difference in this way:

> From the above account it is clear that there exist differences about the concept of well-being in the West and the East, in that the conceptualizations made in the West revolve around the ability to satisfy one's needs, avoidance of frustrations and stress, and exercising certain amounts of control on the environment such that it enhances the satisfaction of personal and social needs. In the Indian tradition control over the senses is thought to be essential to well-being. Emphasis is on the maintenance of balance between extremes of satisfaction and denial (implying that needs need not be totally denied) and adoption of a path of moderation. Further, since frustrations, failure, successes and joys are considered inevitable in one's life, the essence of well-being lies in not being overwhelmed by either. While in the West the idea is to have control or exploit the environment since it is thought that environment provides the inputs that lead to need satisfaction, in Hindu spiritual thought the concept of "being in tune" with the environment is encouraged to be able to experience well-being.[38]

What seems clear is that in both cultures RE leads to the ability to cope with stress and offers the subject a greater sense of well-being, however that is construed in the culture. Despite a vast deluge of spiritual writing from India, little empirical research has been done on RE relative to that done in the West. Yet there are a number of good studies cited by Mohan such as Naidu and Panda (1990).

Naidu and Panda's study (1990) on 465 Hindu adults aged 30-50 years, found that those who scored low on understanding and practicing the Hindu concepts of non-attachment (*anasakti*) had higher levels of stress than those who grasped the concept. Their conclusion was that non-attachment reduces stress. Mohan himself did a study in 1999 on the "spiritual experiences of 200 respondents aged 20-70 years, belonging to 13 various spiritual organizations based on Hindu Philosophy."[39]

> The subjects were administered the Life Experience Questionnaire (LEQ), Index of Changes Resulting from Experience (ICRE) and Checklist of Effects of Experiences (CEE). The findings revealed that after the spiritual experiences they were generally happy, cheerful and at peace most of the time, and rarely downhearted or depressed. Among the values and motivations which give them meaning in life, they reported that the need to achieve personal growth and maintaining close relationships with loved ones who are important gave them a purpose in life. The majority of the respondents reported having excellent health, and were satisfied with the meaning and purpose they found in their lives. A significant number of respondents said that the spiritual experiences they had were valuable or beneficial to them. It was also found that most of the experiences contained references to the spiritual leader, God and a "Higher power." Further they have reported an increase in areas reflecting humanistic and spiritual concerns and a decrease in negative feelings and beliefs.[40]

Laboratory, experimental and quasi-experimental studies

Examples of this type include Hood (1977).[41] Hood administered his M scale to students involved in outdoor, high-stress activities such as a canoe trip. Students taking part in the high-stress activity scored high on the mysticism scale (M scale), significantly higher than students not taking part. This section includes the famous Pahnke "Good Friday" study (1962) where the experimental group was issued a "psychedelic drug" and the control group was not. Both groups attended a mass on Good Friday. The drug group had much higher incidence of mystical experiences. This study will be discussed in-depth in the Chapter 7 (Placebo and drugs).[42] The meaning of "experimental design" refers to a control group and an experimental group. There are several studies mentioned that employ a double blind technique and control group and experimental group. I'm only giving a few examples of each type of study—there are many more studies of each type.

Studies Using a Survey Instrument

In this kind of study a survey is designed to measure mystical experience, and the respondents are questioned about their experiences. Atheists will make light of such a method, but this is a widely used and valid method in social science research. Many different types of scales have been designed to measure attitudes and beliefs, and the methodologies are well-proven. This section includes Gallup polls that tried to ascertain the incidence rate of mystical experiences by asking, "Would you say that you have ever had a religious or mystical experience—a moment of sudden religious awakening or insight?" The findings included affirmative responses by 20.5% in 1962 (measure of the whole American population) and 31.8% in 1966 and 41.2% in 1967.[43] The Greeley study (1974) used a representative survey of 1468 respondents conducted by the National Opinion Research Center. Greeley included the question, "Have you ever felt that you were very close to a powerful spiritual force that seemed to lift you out of yourself?" About 35% answered affirmatively and half of those reported experiencing this several times. The five most frequent triggers were: music, prayer, observing nature, quiet reflection, and attending a church service. In 1987 the author re-administered the study under the title "Mysticism goes Mainstream." In the intervening 14 years a major change took place. This time 42% reported contact with the dead! In 1973 this had been 23%. This time 43% reported an unusual mystical experience.[44]

Studies using questionnaires

The difference between a survey and a questionnaire is that a survey is usually administered —someone asks the questions— whereas questionnaires are filled out by the respondents directly. The technical difference is often not observed and questionnaires are called "surveys." Questionnaires tend to be shorter and more concise. That can make a big difference. In the way the question is asked, an adept interviewer can draw out the respondent, but a questionnaire would miss a lot of what a good interviewer can solicit. Questionnaires are shorter, not as complex and thus do not use the same kinds of scales. Greeley in 1975 undertook the study "The Sociology of the Paranormal" using a questionnaire and the Bradburn well-being scale. This standardized scale used in social sciences measures a sense of the respondents' sense of well-being. Such methodologies are fairly standard for many mystical experience studies; the purpose is to compare the findings of those who rate as "peakers" with their scores on scales that measure self-actualization or well-being. Another self-actualization scale is the Personal Orientation Inventory (aka "Shortstorm" or POI). The correlation between mystical type experiences and well-being is very high. Just because the questionnaire is self-administered and less complex does not mean that the findings are any less valid. Some major studies are done this way. The researchers choose the scales and the methods that are appropriate to the subject group and the answers sought.

The Wuthnow study was an example of a study using questionnaires. Wuthnow collected questionnaires from a systematic, random sample of 1000 people in the San Francisco-Oakland area. He asked them about transcendent experiences, revealing contact with the sacred, beauty of nature, harmony with the universe; whether it was within the last year or before and whether it made a lasting difference in their lives. For those who said they had had contact with the sacred: 68% of those experiencing within one year said life is very meaningful, while 46% of those (contact with sacred) having such experiences more than one year before answered this way. Forty-six percent of those (contact with sacred not in the last year) said yes but it was not lasting, and 39% and 36% respectively said they had not had such an experience or they did not want to have such an experience. "Knowing the purpose of life" applied to 82% of those experiencing within one year and 72% of those whose experiences were further back than that, compared with 18% and 21% for those who had not had or did not want an experience. The figures for the other categories (sensing beauty of nature, harmony with the universe, etc.) were similar. One of the more compelling findings was that 41% of past-year experiencers and 39% of those whose experiences were further back than one year felt greater self-assurance, compared with just 22% and 31% of the no-experience groups.[45]

There is not one standard methodological approach for these studies. A variety of methodologies have been used to establish the long-term positive effects of mystical experiences. In their 1988 literature search, David Lukoff and Francis Lu[46] summarized the methods they found in use.

Studies Using Interviews

The difference between a survey and an interview is that in the latter, an interviewer is present and the questioning attains greater depth. The interview, with a one-on-one setting, allows the interviewer to go in-depth on any loose ends and to define or qualify answers in ways that set scales do not. Examples of this type include a 1973 study, "Religious Orientation and the Report of Religious Experience." Hood used a pool of 123 subjects; from this, the 25 scoring the highest on the Extrinsic and Intrinsic subscales of Allport's Religious Orientation Scale were interviewed. The interview concerned their "most significant personal experiences." Five categories of transcendence were allotted and the interviews placed accordingly within these categories. The findings: "These data clearly support the hypothesis that intrinsically oriented persons are more likely to have transcendent experiences than are extrinsically oriented persons."[47] Another example would be Ludwig's 1985 interview of recovering alcoholics. Interviews were conducted with 29 alcoholics who claimed a "spontaneous remission" from alcoholism. No reliability co-efficient was reported. Four of the 29, the findings show, credited mystical experience with their recovery.[48] The Richard study that found that cancer patients are aided in recovery due to mystical experience (1978) is another example of this sort of study.[49]

Studies Using Self-Administered Surveys

Shafranske and Malony used a self-administered instrument they refer to as a "survey." It was mailed out to one thousand clinical psychologists and psychiatrists chosen at random, all of whom were members of the American Psychiatric Association. A total of 409 surveys were completed and returned (41%). The respondents were 107 females (26%) and 299 males (73%). Part of the survey included a set of statements which represented a belief system such as "There is a personal God of transcendent existence and power whose purpose will ultimately be worked out in human history" or "The notions of God or transcendence are illusory products of human imagination, therefore they are irrelevant to the real world." There were several gradations in between: there is a transcendent aspect but it is removed from life and understanding, any divine or transcendent aspect is related to the human self, transcendence or the divine is found in all nature, notions of God are illusory but meaningful to human existence (my paraphrases).

Forty percent valued orientation toward a personal God, 30% valued regard for a divine dimension in all nature, and 26% that all ideologies are illusory but meaningful. The number that endorsed the statement that all ideologies are illusory and irrelevant was 2%, while 53% said that religious beliefs are desirable for people in general. "The data suggested that psychologists in general value the religious or spiritual dimension." Of the respondents 97% were raised in religious backgrounds and 71% maintained current affiliation, while only 41% had regular participation. By faith there were 13% Catholic, 15% Jewish, 5% Methodist and other Protestant denominations equally as low, 29% no religion, and 10% "Other."[50]

Allman, et al. mailed surveys to 650 clinical psychologists who were members of the APA. A total of 285 returned the surveys, or 45%. Of those 69% were male and 31% female. The respondents worked full time delivering client services and 90% had doctoral degrees. They derived their definition of mystical experience by synthesizing Hood, Lukoff, Stace and Conger. They defined mystical experience as "a transient extraordinary psychological event marked by feelings of being in unity and harmonious relationship to the divine and everything in existence plus one of the following effects: noesis, religiosity, loss of ego, time and space alternations, ineffability, affect change during the event, transformation effect, passivity" (no control over the event). Noesis is a modern English derivative of the Greek Gnosis (knowledge), the idea that some form of transcendent knowledge is communicated in the event. Religiosity means they tend to become more religious as a result of the experience. During time and place alternations, the event might last 30 minutes yet it seems like hours or vice versa. Transformation effect means it changes one's life dramatically for the better.[51] The non-participating respondents were sent a short form asking about their reasons for non-participation. Those returning the short form and those answering all the questions had similar findings as to the number of their patents who had mystical experiences: 5% for the non-participants and 4.5% for the participants. This does not mean that in those 5% mental illness caused the mystical experience: 21% of non responders and 50% of responders reported they themselves had had mystical experiences.[52] The relatively small group of psychologists represented 20,670 clients, 4.5% of whom had had mystical experiences at least once.

The respondents were tested for their exposure to mystical experience literature as a means of determining their attitudes. A seven point Likert-scale was used, with "1" indicating no exposure and "7" indicating a lot of exposure. Spearman rank order correlations were used to access the relationship between the degree of exposure and scores on the attitude on the diagnosis scale. Religious affiliations were also measured to assess their role in the attitude toward mystical experience. The professional orientation was also assessed with appropriate statistical and methodological procedures. There was also assessment of the personal spiritual orientation of the therapist. The results show that the higher regard the therapist places upon his/her own spirituality and mystical experiences, the less likely that therapist is to see the patient's experiences as a symptom of mental illness or problems related to therapy. The greater the degree of spirituality of the therapist, the less likely that therapist is to see mystical experience as pathological.[53]

Psychodynamic and behavioral psychologists were more likely humanistic existential therapists to view the client's mystical experience as pathological. This study, along with several others, shows that the majority of therapists view spirituality as very important, and while most psychotherapists are not active in traditional religion, they do view personal spirituality as valuable and as a positive force in their work —66% rated spirituality as important in their private lives.[54]

Content Analysis

This methodology is concerned with analyzing the content of previously written materials. Take "R. Bucke (1901-1961)." The date does not mean he started the study as a baby and finished it as an old man. The book, *Cosmic Consciousness*, Secaus, NJ, Citadel Press, was written in 1901 and republished in 1961.The book compiled biographies of 43 individuals, from Moses to Whitman and including some people the book's author knew personally who had experienced a state of what he called "cosmic consciousness." He coded various parameters about the subjects such as age at the time of illumination, sex, time of year the experience occurred and age at death. He sought to understand commonalities, and his understanding was aided by a systemic approach. His findings: commonalities include "subjective light, moral elevation, intellectual illumination, sense of immortality, loss of the fear of death and sin, the suddenness of the awakening. Median age was 35 and most were men." He calculated that the ratio would be one person in several million. Of course, these findings on incidence rate were contradicted later by more scientific studies which find a much more common incidence rate (see earlier in this chapter).[55] The Hardy study (1979), which will be used again in Chapter 5 (Proudfoot), put appeals in newspapers and collected 4,000 accounts of mystical experiences. The accounts were coded phenomenologically. A follow-up questionnaire was sent. The most detailed phenomenological classification system in the literature was devised to code the responses. The author states: "It seems to me that the main characteristics of man's religious and spiritual experiences are shown in his feeling for a transcendental reality which frequently manifest themselves in early childhood; a feeling that something other than the self can actually be sensed; a desire to personalize this presence into a deity and to have a private I-thou relationship with it, communicating through prayer."[56]

The Rozario Study: Spirituality in the lives of people with disability and chronic illness

Basic assumptions and method

This study uses both interviews and biographical essays.[57] This study methodology is known as "hermeneutic phenomenology." It aims to understand the phenomenology of inner transcendental experience. While this sort of thing is bound to be dismissed by "hard science" purists and religion skeptics, this is a valid methodology in the social sciences. "This type of research has been gaining recognition within many fields such as the health domain, as a methodology that can provide an approach and a process that describes and represents human experience as it is lived."[58] Rozario uses Carter's five assumptions of hermeneutic phenomenology:[59]

1. Humans are born into a social and cultural situation that becomes an integral part of what Heidegger calls "their world."
2. The understanding of being and selfhood are integrally embodied in the fabric and practices of cultural and social meaning.
3. People's integration with life self-interprets being and selfhood.

Joseph Hinman

4. Language is an important factor in determining and influencing the development of culture and selfhood.
5. Meanings are created from inner and outer processes, and are essentially transactional interpretations of a world of interrelationships.

Sample size and diversity

The study had a sample population of 35 participants, and in addition to this there were 14 autobiographers, all of whom had chronic conditions (disabilities or illnesses that lasted more than 6 months). Subjects were gathered by word-of-mouth, newspaper advertisements and community organizations. The autobiographers represented a wide range of individuals and a wide a range of problems. Critics might be tempted to think this is a pathetically small sample size. Actually, it's a large sample. The nature of the size of sample is relative to the study design, and the type of questions asked and the type of answers sought. Analyzing autobiographies is very complex. "This large sample size was chosen to reveal a broad range of people's life experiences and to include a broad range of diagnostic categories…"[60] These categories included age, gender and socioeconomic backgrounds, while diagnoses included cancer, AIDS, diabetes, polio, congenital blindness, dislocated hips, cerebral palsy and other such medical problems.

Data collection

The study used taped in-depth interviews, analysis of autobiographies, phenomenologist logs, and focus group interviews. The 14 autobiographies by people with disabilities were selected from among published sources and analyzed into clusters of meaning, codes and emerging themes. Data from autobiographies and interviews were reviewed by Benner's striates of analysis of identifying paradigm cases.[61]

160

Results

The study demonstrated that religious experience is an integral part of coping strategies. Self transcendence and the transformative power of religious experience are essential to not only survival but growth and progress paradigms, meaning and wellness. Religious experience gives these people the strength to keep going and the ability to progress and grow as people in spite of their situations. It's essential for fostering meaning in their lives. For more on results, see the previous chapter (Arguments).

Qualitative Research

Qualitative methods make a tradeoff with the quantitative, losing the ability to generalize and validate for a deeper understanding of the phenomena within a single context. There are also *hermeneutical studies* and *mythical analysis.* An example of the latter is Lukoff's 1985 study (mentioned in the chapter on arguments) that compared psychotic episodes to private mythology based upon Campbell's *Hero With a Thousand Faces* (1946). A lot of people may take this approach as an interesting waste of time, but that study appears to have produced some important findings in that the archetypes show up and seem to be functioning in the way Maslow predicts they would.[62]

Some of these studies are more useful than others, but there are hundreds and they span the gamut of methodologies. Not in the case of every single study, but in the case of every methodology, we find positive effects resulting from mystical experience. This lends a validating effect across the board. It would be a hard but useful task to find exactly how many studies there are. During my own research —including primary studies referred to by Mohan, Gackenbach, Lukoff, Hood and Voyle as well as primary studies recommended by advisers— I have counted about 200 (perhaps 220) that show positive effects of mystical experience. Lukoff lists Silverman's 1983 study of 292 references to scales devised for such studies and 170 references to questionnaires. This was back in 1983. In 2004, Mohan lists over 100 studies that actually show positive effects — many long-term. But Mohan is limited to studies in the 1990s and early twenty-first century. This kind of research and these kinds of findings have been going on for four decades. If we include all studies about mystical experience, church attendance and participation that indicate positive effects, the number could well be in the thousands. The overwhelming preponderance of the evidence is that religion is good for you. There are a few studies that show some problems among various religious people and some that find negative effects, but not one study that I've ever come across (and no skeptic has ever able to bring one up in debate) shows findings opposite to the general sort of affirmations about self-authentication and religious experience.

There just are no studies, so it seems, showing that "peakers" are very screwed up, that religion is linked to mental illness, that those who experience mystical consciousness feel guilty, that they can't face life, or that religious people are less well-educated, have lower IQs or anything of the kind. No studies link religious experience or mystical experience to any of these negative qualities. Of course, this does not include a study of cults or of groups that place inordinate demands upon their followers. That is another question and I have not studied it. Such groups are not represented in these studies, and indeed I would think such groups would be opposed by many people who have transformative experiences. Those who experience the undifferentiated unity and who sense the numinous and whose lives are transformed by those experiences apparently do not need to join cults.

The M Scale

The "M Scale" (Mysticism scale) was developed by Ralph Hood, Jr., at the University of Tennessee at Chattanooga. It has become the standard study instrument to *empirically* validate mystical experience. Hood's instrument has been cross-culturally validated and represents the cutting edge of research in this field of psychology of religion and empirical study of religious experience. The scale is a series of questions and a scoring technique which has been worked out according to standard social scientific assumptions. The scale has been so successful its use has become the standard procedure[63] and replaces the former practice whereby each researcher tried to develop her own scale, a practice that led to as many scales as there were studies. It is based on the phenomenological categories of mystical study by W.T. Stace and makes certain assumptions similar to those of William James. Hood's original measuring instrument, the REEM, was based upon the categories of James. The scale uses 32 items (these are questions that are asked of the subject). The items are organized with 16 positive and 16 negatively worded questions. Independent studies supported Hood's original design (Caird, 1988, Reinert and Stifler, 1993).[64] Originally, the M scale measured two factors: (1) Assessed items indicating an experienced unity (introvertive or extrovertive), (2) Assessed items of an experience of religious or non-religious and knowledge claims —knowledge derived from mystical experience that is positive and can be understood, as opposed to transcendent knowledge that is only experiential and thus beyond words.This method is consistent with Stace's concept that mystical experience can be interpreted in many ways. Reinert and Stifler suggested that religious items and knowledge items might emerge as separate factors. This separation would split the interpretative factors between religious and non-religious factors. That result would not contradict Stace. There is a distinction between "spiritual" and "religious." Mystical experience can be interpreted (as we have seen already) as "spiritual" without being thought religious, or as "mystical" without involving God. The two-item approach allows greater interpretation. But the interpretive factor was religious in nature. The assumptions made in the study and used in answering the questions tended to be religious.[65]

Hood changed his strategy from two analytic factors to three ("the three-factor solution"). The three-factor solution sets up three factors, or categories, which more closely follow the predictions of Stace based upon his reading of mysticism and personal experience ("phenomenological"). The three categories for Stace included introvertive and extrovertive mysticism emerging as two separate factors. The third factor is an interpretive dimension where the respondent relates the experiences to knowledge claims ("God is love" or some such). *Introvertive* means the mystical experience is beyond word, thought or image; it is inward-directed and not related to any outside phenomenon, and is supposed to be beyond description. This dimension will also be discussed more in Chapter 4 (Religious A Priori). *Extrovertive* means the subject's experience is related to nature or to some external image in the immediate environment, a sense of the numinous, the harmony underlying all of nature or something on that order. The tables below demonstrate the basic structure of Stace's theory and the three-factor test. They demonstrate the closeness with which the latter validates the former.

Stace Model of Mystical Experience (phenomenologically derived)

Introvertive Mysticism	Extrovertive Mysticism
a. Contentless Unity	a. A Unity in Diversity
b. Timeless/Spaceless	b. Inner Subjectivity

Interpretation

a. Noetic

b. Religious

c. Positive Affective

d. Paradoxicality (not measured in M scale)

e. Ineffability (alleged)

Hood Model of Mystical Experience (Empirically Derived): (triple solution)

Introvertive Mysticism (12 items)   Extrovertive Mysticism (8 items)

a. Contentless Unity items	a. Unity in Diversity items
b. Time/Space items	b. Religious items
c. Ineffability items	c. Positive Affective items

Interpretation

a. Noetic

b. Religious

c. Positive Affective

This chart is from the Spilka/Hood book.[66]

One thing that will become important in Chapter 7 (Drugs) is the fact that Hood's M Scale is designed to measure mystical experience related to Stace's theorizing, not the wide variety of experiences labeled "peak" experiences that may not even relate to mystical experience. Such is the case with Panhke, who did the "Good Friday" experiment (drug-induced mystical experiences).[67] This will also be important in Chapter 7 (Drugs).

Several different versions of the M scale were made, and they were designed to reflect cross-cultural validation. Rather than just measuring two factors, they measured three-factors or "general categories" that more closely mirrored Stace's reading of mystical accounts and experiences. The important thing is that the empirical studies demonstrate findings that corroborate Staces's theory of mystical experience. This demonstrates the basis for a body of work confirming the common core theory: the idea that mystical experiences are the same, minus the details of individual traditions. That is a good indication that the same basic reality stands behind all of these experiences, regardless of the religious tradition. They tailored the questions to treat the overall ontological structure of a belief system. So "God" is treated not as a specific personality but as the transcendental signifier (although Hood does not use that term). This means atheist mystics who sense a void and Christian mystics who sense Christ are talking about the same things, because whether they call it "a void" or "Jesus," both function the same way in the overall economy of an ontological system. That means that mystics the world over are probably experiencing the same thing, but they load that into different cultural constructs in order to explain it.

The M scale follows Stace's phenomenological accounts of mystical experience. It also reflects, therefore, Stace's theoretical concerns. His major concern is known as "the common core" hypothesis. The common core assumption is a universalistic approach, whereby it is assumed that a variety of different interpretations and descriptions match the same experiences. A corollary might be that one reality stands beyond the many different mystical traditions. One of the major critics of this view, whom we will meet again in discussing Proudfoot (Chapter 5) is Steven Katz (1977), who wrote and edited an anthology against Stace's work. He assumes that the common core thesis is asserting that mystical experience is unmediated (that is to say that it's a direct experience of the divine with no principle of mediation to filter us from the divine). Thus he argues that extreme language is used not just to describe mystical experience, but that language itself is experience. Language used in description constitutes the experience itself rather than merely describing it. This position will be critically examined in Chapter 4 and Chapter 5 (a priori and Proudfoot)[68] But Stace doesn't argue that the experience is unmediated. Hood points out that Stace only says there are degrees of interpretation, and descriptions can mark similar but not identical experiences. Hood also points out that Foreman marshals opponents against Katz. He argues that since the introvertive form of ME is devoid of descriptive language, it can't really play a role in constituting it (again, see Chapters 4 and 5).

Hood and Spilka point out three major assumptions of the common core theory that flow out of Stace's work:

1. Mystical experience is universal and identical in phenomenological terms.
2. Core categories are not always essential in every experience; there are borderline cases.
3. Introvertive and extrovertive are distinct forms: the former is an experience of unity devoid of content, the latter is unity in diversity with content.

The M scale reflects these observations and, in so doing, validates Stace's findings. Hood and Spilka et al. then go on to argue that empirical research supports a common core/perinnialist conceptualization of mysticism and its interpretation.

The three-factor solution, stated above, allows a greater range of interpretation of experience, either religious or not religious. This greater range supports Stace's finding that a single experience may be interpreted in different ways.[69] The three-factor solution thus fits Stace's common core theory. One of the persistent problems of the M scale is the neutrality of language, especially with respect to religious language. For example, the scale asks about union with "ultimate reality" not "union with God." Thus there's a problem in understanding that ultimate reality really means God, or ultimate reality or something, thus unifying two different descriptions: one about God and one about reality.[70] There is really no such thing as "neutral" language; the attempt to be neutral may offend non-neutral people. On the one hand, the common core idea will be seen as "new age," yet on the other hand, identification with a particular tradition will be off-putting for people of other traditions and secularists. Measurement scales must sort out the distinctions. Individuals demand interpretation of experiences, so the issue will be forced despite the best attempts to avoid it. In dealing with

William James and his interpreters, it seems clear that some form of transformation will be reflected in the discussion of experiences. In other words, the experiences have to be filtered, through cultural constructs and human assumptions of religious and other kinds of thought traditions in order to communicate them to people. Nevertheless, experiences may share the same functionality in description. Christians may want the experiences they have that would otherwise be termed "ultimate reality" to be identified with Christ, while Muslims identify with Allah and atheists with the "void." Each expression is important as the "social construction of experience," but differently expressed experiences can have similar structures. Hood and Williamson (2000) designed the three-factor analysis to avoid these problems of language:

> Each paralleled the original M scale, but where appropriate, made reference to either God or to Christ. Both the original M Scale and either the God-language version or the Christ-language version were given to relevant Christ-committed samples. The scales were then factor analyzed to see whether similar structures would emerge. Basically, whether the M scale items were phrased in terms of God, Christ or more neutral terms, the structures were identical. The structures for all three versions of Stace's phenomenologically derived models did quite well. For all versions of the scale, clear introvertive, extrovertive, and interpretative factors emerged.[71]

M scale and Cross Cultural Validation

In a series of empirical measurement-based studies employing the Mysticism scale, introvertive mysticism emerges both as a distinct factor in exploratory analytic studies[72] and also as a confirming factor analysis in cultures as diverse as the United States and Iran; not only in exploratory factor analytic studies (Hood & Williamson, 2000) but also in confirmatory factor analyses (Hood, Ghornbani, Watson, Ghramaleki, Bing, Davison, Morris, & Williamson. (2001).[73] In other words, the form of mysticism that is usually said to be beyond description and beyond images, as opposed to that found in connection with images of the natural world, is seen through reflection of data derived from the M scale and as supporting factors in other relations. Scholars supporting the unity thesis (the mystical sense of undifferentiated unity—everything is "one") have conducted interviews with mystics in other traditions about the nature of their introvertive mystical experiences. These discussions reveal that differences in expression that might be taken as linguistics, or as culturally constructed, are essentially indicative of the same experiences. The mystics recognize their experiences even in the expression of other traditions and other cultures. These parishioners represent different forms of Zen and Yoga.[74] Scholars conducting literature searches independently of other studies, who sought common experience between different traditions, have found commonalities. Brainaid found commonality between cultures as diverse as Advaita-Vendanta Hinduism, Madyhamika Buddhism and Nicene Christianity. Brainaid's work supports conclusions by Loy with respect to the types of Hinduism and Buddhism.[75]

The M scale developed by Hood has been validated by many studies in cross-cultural context, while Greeley's Gallop Poll questions have been used both cross-culturally and longitudinally.

> The two major exceptions to the lack of shared instrumentation are the mysticism scale by Hood (1975), which has been used in quite a number of studies by Hood and others, and the repeated use of certain questions in survey research by Greeley and the Gallop Organization over a sixteen-year period.[76]

Holm's (1982) "mysticism and intense experiences" demonstrates another level of cross-cultural validation:

Method: The author translated into Swedish several Hood scales designed to measure mystical experiences. The items describing religious experiences were drawn from William James, on Hood's (1970) Religious Episode Experience Measure (REEM) with narratives taken from Nordic anthologies. Eighteen teachers of religion and psychology each administered the scales to 6-9 persons.

Findings: The study replicated most of Hood's findings with the same instruments. 'The results of our empirical study of mysticism in a Finnish-Swedish environment largely coincide with Hood's results in an American environment…The cross-cultural testing that some of Hood's methods have received as a result of our research on another continuant and in another linguistic area means that the results have received a wider range of applications.'[77]

Holm (1982) presented a Swedish M scale administered to 122 Swedish "informants". Factor I correlated best to non-Christian profiles, while factor II worked best with those who had Christian assumptions. Holm accounts for a general mysticism factor and a general religious factor. This finding parallels earlier research in Sweden (Solderblom—see Holm 82, 275-76) .[78]

Wood and colleagues (2001) found the M-Scale held up as well with Muslims in Iran:

In a mostly Christian American sample (N = 1,379), confirmatory factor analysis of Hood's (1975) Mysticism Scale verified the existence of Stace's (1960) introvertive and extrovertive dimensions of mystical phenomenology, along with a separate interpretation factor. A second study confirmed the presence of these three-factors in not only another group of Americans (N = 188), but also a sample of Iranian Muslims (N = 185). Relationships of the introvertive and extrovertive factors with the interpretation factor were essentially identical across these two cultures, but the Americans displayed a stronger association between the two phenomenology factors. In both samples, the interpretation factor correlated positively with an intrinsic, and negatively with an extrinsic, religious orientation, and the introvertive factor predicted psychological dysfunction. Associations of the interpretation factor with relative mental health appeared only in the Iranians. These data offered general support for Stace's phenomenology of mysticism, although the ineffability he linked with interpretation proved to be as much or even more a feature of the introvertive experience, as hypothesized by Hood. [79]

The M Scale in relation to other measurement scores.

The overall result demonstrates the superiority of Hood's model (and Stace's categories) over other models. "Thus empirically there is strong support to claim that as operationalized from Stace's criteria mystical experience is identical as measured across diverse samples, whether expressed in 'neutral language' or with either 'God' or 'Christ' references." [80] The M Scale has been correlated to scores on standardized personality measures in two studies. In 1985, Hood found that the Minnesota Multiphasic Personality Inventory (MMPI) "...did not correlate with the M Scale. Different correlations of factors between factors I and II were compatible with non-pathological interpretations of mysticism." [81] The score for the MMPI applies to people who are apt to lie or present themselves in a favorable light to their own advantage. But Hood argues that high scores on factor II (religious) may be due to the fact that traditional religious people are less likely to engage in deviant behavior. Thus the score doesn't apply to them.

Spanos and Moretti (1988) directly correlated M scale scores with the Tellegen and Atkinson absorption scale and found no correlation between religion and psychopathology:

A sample of 124 female university students was administered measures of mystical experience, diabolical experience, absorption, hypnotizability and psychopathology. The mystical experience scale correlated significantly with measures of absorption and hypnotizability but failed to correlate significantly with indexes of psychopathology. However, the diabolical experiences scale correlated significantly with indexes of neuroticism and psychosomatic symptoms as well as with hypnotizability and absorption. Subjects who reported out-of-body experiences scored higher than those who did not on all measures of hypnotizability, but these groups failed to differ from one another on absorption, mystical or diabolical experiences, or on most indexes of psychopathology.[82]

The scale correlated positively on all measures. Absorption proved to be the single most important variable in regression analysis, with 29% variance. None of the other hypnosis scales added predictive power. John Kilstron's writes:

By any standard, the most frequently studied correlate of hypnotizability is *absorption*, or 'openness to absorbing and self-altering experiences' (Tellegen & Atkinson, 1974). A series of studies from our laboratory by Martha Glisky and her colleagues offered a close examination of the relationship between absorption, hypnotizability, and a broader trait of *openness to experience* identified by Costa and McCrae as one of the "Big Five" traits of personality measured by various versions of the *NEO Personality Inventory*. The first of these studies (Glisky et al., 1991) confirmed the basic absorption-hypnotizability relation, and showed that absorption was related to those facts of Openness having to do with imaginative involvement (i.e., Fantasy, Aesthetics, and Feelings), but not with those facets having to do with sociopolitical liberalism (i.e., Actions, Ideas, and Values). The second study (Glisky & Kihlstrom, 1993) showed that hypnotizability was related to Absorption, but not to either Sociopolitical Liberalism or Intellectance (an alternative construal of Openness).[83]

Spanos and Moretti concluded that "although Mystical experience can
occur among distraught and troubled individuals, it is as frequent
among psychologically untroubled people."[84] In other words,
hypnotizability is a standard of other traits that can indicate mental
instability. From this scale there is no indication that those who have
mystical experiences tend to be any more unstable than the average
person. Research by Hood and Morris in 1981 shows that mysticism is
better known than previously thought, and that while the full, advanced
form of intervertive experience may be somewhat rare, there is a
continuum of experience, and most people have had some experience.
This research further shows that mystical experience is not the result of
mental illness, it is normal among healthy individuals, but it is not
confined to healthy individuals alone.[85] Thus the M Scale remains the
state-of-the-art standard for research and measurement of religious
experience in terms of that which is known as "mystical." This is very
important, as we will see in Chapter 6 (God Pod) and Chapter 7 (Drugs
and Placebo).

1   Jayne Gackenbach, "Childhood: Transpersonal Childhood Experiences of
     Higher States of Consciousness: Literature Review and Theoretical
     Integration" (unpublished paper 1992 by Jayne Gackenbach),
     "Spiritwatch," http://www.sawka.com/spiritwatch/cehsc/ipure.htm
     (accessed 1/2/11)

2   D. Lukoff and F.G. Lu, "Transpersonal Psychology Research, Mystical
     Experience," *The Journal of Transpersonal Psychology*, 20 (2) (1988)
     162-184, 163.

3   *Ibid.*

4   Hood and Stace quoted in Robert J. Voyle, "The Impact of Mystical
     Experiences Upon Christian Maturity." originally published in pdf format:
     http://www.voyle.com/impact.pdf (accessed 2/1/07)

5   Dale Caird, "The structure of Hood's Mysticism Scale, a Factor Analytic Study." *Journal for the Scientific Study of Religion*, (1988): 27 (1), 122-126

6   Charles N. Alexander, Robert W. Boyer, and Victoria K.Alexander, "Higher states of consciousness in the Vedic Psychology of Maharishi Mahesh Yogi: A theoretical introduction and research review." *Journal of Modern Science and Vedic Science,* Vol. 1, no. 1 (1987), 89-126, 100.

7   C.N. Alexander, J.L. Davies, C.A. Dixon, et al., "Growth of higher stages of consciousness: Maharishi's Vedic psychology of human development." In C.N. Alexander and E.J. Langer, *Higher Stages of Human Development*, Oxford University Press, 1990, 286-387.

8   Alexander, *Ibid.,* 286. The increase might be explained by the growth of he counter culture in those years, practices such as transcendental meditation, yoga, and greater general awareness of the spiritual. This is my own speculation.

9   C. N. Alexander, K. Chandler, & R.W. Boyer, "Experience and understanding of pure consciousness in the Vedic Science of Maharishi Mahesh Yogi." In Gackenbach, J.I. & Hunt, H. (Eds.). Higher states of consciousness: Theoretical and experimental perspectives, N.Y.: Plenum Publishing. No date listed. 310.

10   Abraham Maslow, *Toward a psychology of Being*, Princeton, NJ: D. Van Nostrand company, 1962 in Wuthnow, Robert, "Peak Experiences: Some Empirical Tests." *Journal Humanistic Psychology* Vol. 18, no. 3 summer (1978), 60

11   "Peak experience" is Maslow's term. It is often used by sociological and psychological researchers, and is not highly distinctive from "mystical" experience. "Peak" is used because "mystical" has religious and metaphysical overtones which my not apply to the one doing the experiencing.

12   Wuthnow, "Peak Experiences: Some Empirical Tests." *Journal of Humanistic Psychology*, 18 (3), 59-75. (1978).61-62.

13   Katheleen D. Noble, ``Psychological Health and the Experience of Transcendence.'' *The Counseling Psychologist*, vol. 15, no. 4, Oct. (1987), 602.

14   Lorraine Allman, Olivia De La Rocha, et al., "Psychotherapist's Attitudes Toward Clients Reporting Mystical Experiences," *Psychotherapy*, vol. 29, no 4, (1992), 564-569.

15   Wuthnow, *op. cit.,* 64.

16   *Ibid.,* 65.

17   Kathleen D Noble, *op. cit.,* 601-614.

18   J. Gartner, D.B. Allen, *The Faith Factor: An Annotated Bibliography of Systematic Reviews And Clinical Research on Spiritual Subjects Vol. II,* David B. Larson M.D. (ed), National Institute for Health Research, Dec. 1993, 3090.

19   J.I. Gackenbach, quoting Caird, op. cit. (fn. 1) "found no relationship between reported mystical experience and neuroticism, psychoticism and lying while Spanos and Moretti (1988) found no relationship between a measure of mystical experience and psychopathology." See N.P. Spanos and P. Moretti, "Correlates of Mystical and Diabolical Experiences in A sample of Female University Students." Journal of the Scientific Study of Religion. 27, (1988) 105-16.

20   Gackenback, *op. cit.,* 401.

21   Kathleen D. Noble, *op. cit.,* 602.

22   Spiritual Competency Resource Center: "Treatment: types of Spiritual emergency," http: //www.virtualcs.com/se/dxtx/types/ mysticalexperience.html (accessed 2/08/11), Spiritual Competency Resource Center is affiliated with David Lukoff, who is one of the major researchers of mystical experience. He and Dr. Francis G. Lu did a major literature search which I have used heavily in this chapter, and his name figures in several sources.

23   Spiritual Competency, *Ibid.,* the studies referred to are: Caird, *op. cit.* 1978; Hood's studies of, 1976, 1977, 1979; Spanos and Moretti, *op. cit.,*1988.

24   Council on Spiritual Practices, *State of Unitive Consciousness Research summary,* http://www.csp.org/experience/docs/ unitive_consciousness.html. (accessed 2/25/10)

25   Roger Walsh, "The consciousness disciplines and the behavioral sciences: Questions of comparison and assessment." *American Journal of Psychiatry,* 137(6), (1980), 663-673.

26   D. McDowell, M. Galanter, L. Goldfab, H. Lifshutz, "Spirituality and the treatment of the dually diagnosed: An investigation of patient and staff attitudes". *Journal of Addictive Diseases.(1996) 15,* 55-68.

27   T. Sensky, Religiosity Mystical Experience," summary of research in David Lukoff, Francis G. Lu, "Transpersonal Psychology Research Review Topic: Mystical Experience," *The Journal of Transpersonal Psychology* vol. 20, no 2 (1988) 161-183, 175.

28 L.S. Allman, L.S., Dela, R.O., Elins, D.N., & Weathers, R.S. (1992). *Psychotherapists attitude towards mystical experiences*. Psychotherapy, 29, 564-569.

29 , D.N. Elkins, "Psychotherapy and spirituality: Toward a theory of the soul". *Journal of Humanistic Psychology, 35,* (1995),78-98.

30 E.P. Shafranske, H.N. Malony, "Clinical Psychologist's Religious and Spiritual Orientations and Their Practice of Psychotherapy." *Psychotherapy*, Volume 27, no. 1 (Spring 1990) 72-78.

31 W. Sullivan, "It helps me to be a Whole Person: The Role Spirituality Among the Mentally Challenged." *Psychological Rehabilitation Journal,* (1993) 16, 125-134.

32 D.Glik, "Psychosocial wellness among spiritual healing participants". *Social Science and Medicine, 22,* (1986). 579-586

33 C. Millar, A descriptive analysis of psychic opening. Dissertation Abstracts International, (1990). 51/05, 2629B. (University Microfilms No. 9027841)

34 Edward Robinson, *The original vision: A study of the religious experience of childhood*. New York: The Seabury Press. 1983, 37.

35 Mohan, *op. cit.*

36 Mohan, *Ibid.,* see subsection labeled "Well being Indian perspective."

37 *Ibid.*

38 *Ibid.*

39 Ibid

40 Ibid

41 Ralph Hood, "Eliciting Mystical States of Consciousness With Simistructured Nature Experiences." Journal for the Scientific Study of Religion, 16, (1977) 155-163.

42 Ibid

43 K. Back, L. Bourque, "Can Feelings be Enumerated?" *Behavioral Science*, 15, (1970), 487-496 in David Lukoff, Francis G. Lu, "Transpersonal Psychology Research Review Topic: Mystical Experience," *The Journal of Transpersonal Psychology* vol. 20, no 2 (1988) 161-183,171.

44 A. Greeley, "Ecstasy: A Way of Knowing," in Lukoff, Lu, "Transpersonal Psychology Research," Op. Cit. *Ibid.,* 172.

45 Wuthow, *op. cit.,* Table 2 Personal correlates of Peak Experiences, 66.

46 Lukoff, Lu, *op. cit.,* they used a variety of data bases including Medline, PSYCINFO, and the Religion Index.

47 Ibid 176

48 *Ibid.,* 176-77

49 Richards, *op. cit.*

50 Edward P. Shafranske, H. Newton Malony, *op. cit.,* 73-74.

51 Lorranine S. Allman, Olivia De LA Rocha, David N. Elkins, and Robert Weathers, "Psychotherapists Attitudes Toward Clients Reporting Mystical Experiences." *Psychotherapy.* Vol. 29, no. 4, (winter 1992). 564-569.

52 *Ibid.,* 566

53 *Ibid.,* 568

54 *Ibid.*

55 Lukoff, *op. cit.,* 178

56 *Ibid.*

57 Rozario, Loretta Do "Spirituality in the Lives of People with Disability and Chronic Illness: A Creative Paradigm of Wholeness and Reconstitution." Disability and Rehabilitation: An International and Multidisciplinary Journal. Vol 19, no 10 (1997) 427-433.

58 *Ibid.,* 428

59 Carter, B. *A phenomenological Study of Survivors of Adult Cancer.* Doctoral Dissertation University of California, San Francisco 1989. in Rozario, "Spirituality in the Lives of People with Disability and Chronic Illness." *op. cit.*

60 Rozario, *op. cit.,* 430.

61 Benner, P. *Stress and Satisfaction on the Job: work meanings and coping of mid career men.* in Rozario, *op. cit.*

62 Abraham Maslow, *Religions, Values, and Peak-Experiences,* Appendix I. An Example of B-Analysis, *op. cit.*

63 Bernard Spilka, Ralph Hood Jr., Bruce Hunsberger, Richard Gorwuch. *The Psychology of Religion: An Empirical Approach.* New York, London: the Guildford Press, 2003, 323.

64 *Ibid.,* 323

65 *Ibid.,* 323

66 *Ibid.,* 325

67 *Ibid.,* 321

68 *Ibid.,* 321

69   *Ibid.*, 323

70   *Ibid.*, 323

71   *Ibid.*, 324

72   Ralph Hood Jr., W.P. Williamson. "An empirical test of the unity thesis: The structure of mystical descriptors in various faith samples." *Journal of Christianity and Psychology*, 19, (2000) 222-244.

73   Ralph. W. Hood, Jr., N. Ghorbani, P.J. Waston, et al "Dimensions of the Mysticism Scale: Confirming the three-factor Structure in the United States and Iran." *Journal for the Scientific Study of Religion*, 40 (2001) 691-705.

74   R.K.C. Forman, *Mysticism, Mind, Consciousness*. Albany: State University of New York Press, 1999, 20-30.

75   F.S. Brainard, *Reality and Mystical Experience*, University Park: Pennsylvania State University Press. (2000). See also D.Loy, Nonduality: A Study in Comparative Philosophy. Amherst, New York: Humanities Press.

76   David Lukoff and Francis G. Lu. *op. cit.*, (1988), 161.

77   *Ibid.*

78   Spilka et al, *op. cit.*, 326.

79   Ralph W. Hood Jr., Ghorbani, Nima, P. J. Watson, et al. *op. cit.*, 691-705.

80   Spilka and Hood, *op. cit.*, 324.

81   *Ibid.*, 327.

82   Nicholas P. Spanos, Patricia Moretti, "study Abstract" "Correlates of Mystical and Diabolical Experiences in a Sample of Female University Students." *Journal For the Scientific Study of Religion* 1988. 105-116, 105. see also Spilka et al,op cit 327on JSTOR: http://www.jstor.org/pss/1387405

83   Website of John Kilstron, Professor of psychology, University of Berkeley: http://socrates.berkeley.edu/~kihlstrm/TAS.htm, (accessed 06/07/2009)

84   Nicholas P. Spanos and Patricia Morretti, *op. cit.*, 105.

85   Spilka and Hood, *op. cit.*, 326.

4 The Religious *A Priori:* Believer's Default?

Put simply, this is the argument that I am making in this essay:

1. We can construe religious experience (RE) as the co-determinate (the "trace," the footprint) of God upon the human heart for three reasons:

   1. Historical association
   2. Content
   3. Effects

2. RE can be trusted in the same way, if not to the same extent, as our daily waking experience, because it works for navigation in the world (with all necessary caveats: see Chapter 3, "Studies").

3. Therefore: Belief is rationally warranted as the religious *a priori,* apart from the need to empirically prove the existence of God.

The religious *a priori* is (as seen in Chapter 1):

> ...used by philosophers of religion to express the view that the sense of the divine is due to a special form of awareness which exists alongside the cognitive, moral and aesthetic forms of awareness and is not explicable by reference to them. The concept of religion as concerned with the awareness of and response to the divine is accordingly a simple notion which cannot be defined by reference other than itself.[1]

The term itself, religious *a priori*, seems like a misnomer, because its experiential basis requires empirical —not *a priori*— reasoning.

However, the actual concept itself is that the value of religion does not require explanation by reference to other subjects; that religion is, in and of itself, its own form of knowledge. The larger epistemological question that emerges from the framework of RE and its God arguments, forms the basis of a larger argument itself, but it is really more than just an argument. It is a worldview that argues for belief as the only rational approach to the world of sense data. This approach, *the religious a priori*, demands epistemic judgment rather than absolute proof. One need not prove the existence of God. The supposed lack of scientific or logical proof (if we grant the atheists' assertion for the sake of argument) is no barrier to belief and casts no shame upon devotion. Religion is not reduced to science; it is not a scientific matter. It is not the rhetorical duty of the believer to prove God's existence. This is why the experience arguments are put over as "rational warrant" rather than "proof." Few things in this world are really provable. As William Abraham says, "we know more than we can say or prove."[2] Religion must be understood and judged upon its own merits. It is not failed science or jumped-up ethics, it is its own discipline – its own *epistemic approach to judgment about the nature of being.*

The *a priori*

God is not given directly in sense data, as God transcends the threshold of human understanding and thus is not subject to empirical, scientific proof. Religion is not a scientific question. There are other methodologies that must be used to understand religion, since the topic is essentially inter-subjective (while science centers on objective data). There are overlapping areas where scientific data is very useful, such as the *results* of religious experience —but those methods can't get at the texture of the experience itself. We can study religious behavior through empirical means, and we can compile all sorts of statistical realizations through comparisons of differing religious experiences, behaviors and options. But we cannot produce a trace of God in the universe through direct, "objective" scientific means. Here I have been using the term "trace" in the Derridian sense: the "track," the "footprint," the thing to follow to put us on the scent. As I have stated in previous chapters (including Chapter 1), what we must do is find the "co-determinate," the thing that is left by God like footprints in the snow. The trace of God can be found in God's effects upon the human heart, and that shows up objectively or inter-subjectively in changed behavior, changed attitudes, and life transformations. But here I wish to detail another view of the trace of God. This could be seen as a co-determinate, perhaps, but more importantly, it frees religion from the structures of having to measure up to a scientific standard of proof: the *religious a priori.*

The *religious a priori* deals with the special nature of religion as non-derivative from any other discipline. It also deals with the special religious faculty of understanding, which transcends ordinary means of understanding. Atheists since the enlightenment have sought to explain away religion by placing it in relative terms so that it can be discarded. The major tactic for accomplishing this strategy has been the use of the sociological theory of structural functionalism. According to this assumption, religion arose to fulfill some relative and passing social function, such as promoting loyalty to the tribe, or teaching morality for the sake of social cohesion. In this way, religion was explained naturalistically, and in relative terms, because these functions in society, while still viable (since religion is still around), could always pass away. But this viewpoint assumes that religion is derivative from some other discipline; that it is primitive failed science concocted to explain thunder, for example. Religion is also simplified into merely an emotional solace to get people through hard times and make sense of death and destruction. But the *a priori* does away with such motivation for naturalizing religion. The *a priori* says religion is its own thing —it is not a failed primitive science, nor is it merely a help in surviving or making sense of the world (although it can be that). Religion is also its

Joseph Hinman

own discipline; the major impetus for religion is the sense of the numinous, not the need for explanations of the natural world. Anthropologists are coming more and more to discard that nineteenth-century approach anyway.

Thomas A. Indianopolus, Professor of Religion at the Miami University of Ohio, tells us:

> It is the experience of the transcendent, including the human response to that experience, that creates faith, or more precisely the life of faith. [In *The Meaning and End of Religion,* Wilfred Cantwell] Smith seems to regard human beings as having a propensity for faith, so that one speaks of their faith as "innate." In his analysis, faith and transcendence are more accurate descriptions of the lives of religious human beings than conventional uses of the word, religion. The reason for this has to do with the distinction between participant and observer. This is a fundamental distinction for Smith, separating religious people (the participants) from the detached, so-called objective students of religious people (the observers). Smith's argument is that religious persons do not ordinarily have "a religion." The word, religion, comes into usage not as the participant's word but as the observer's word, one that focuses on observable doctrines, institutions, ceremonies, and other practices. By contrast, faith is about the non-observable, life-shaping vision of transcendence held by a participant...[3]

The skeptic might argue, "If religion is this unique form of consciousness that sets it apart from other forms of understanding, then why does it have to be taught?" If hunting and killing is part of our genetic makeup, then why do armies need war games? If birth is a natural part of life, then why do we need Lamaze classes? Obviously religious belief is taught through culture, and there is a good reason for that, because religion is a cultural construct. We have to distinguish between religious experience and our understanding of religious experience. We can experience things without talking about them. We can experience things that we do not understand and cannot put into words. But in order to talk about these experiences, we have to put them into words. To put experiences into words, we must filter them through cultural constructs, because that is what words are. But that does not diminish the reality of God. Culture teaches religion but people know God in the heart. This comes through a variety of ways: direct experience, miraculous signs, intuitive sense or a sense of the numinous. The *Westminster's Dictionary of Christian Theology* defines "numinous" as "the sense of awe in attracting and repelling people to the Holy." The background assumption I make is that we apprehend God mystically – beyond word, thought, or image – and that we must encode that understanding by filtering it through our cultural constructs, which creates religious differences and religious problems.

The culturally constructed nature of religion does not negate the *a priori*. Pailin states that "even though the forms by which religion is expressed are culturally conditioned, religion itself is *sui generis*. Religion is essentially irreducible to and unperceivable from the non-religious" (Pailin). Nor can the *a priori* be reduced to some other form of endeavor. It cannot be summed up by the use of ethics or any other field; it cannot be reduced to an explanation of the world or to other fields, or to physiological counter causality. To propose such scientific analysis, except in terms of measuring or documenting effects upon behavior, would yield fruitless results. Such results might be taken as proof of no validity, but this would be a mistake. No scientific control can ever be established, because any study would only be studying the culturally constructed bits (by definition since language and social sciences are cultural constructs as well); thus, all that the social sciences would end up doing would be to reify the phenomena and reduce the experience. In other words, this idea can never be verified in a social sciences sense. All that the social sciences can do is redefine the phenomena until they are no longer discussing the actual experiences of the religious believer, but merely the ideology of the social scientist (see my comments on Kuhn in Chapter 2). However, the effects of the experience upon the believer can be studied.

The attempt of skeptics to apply counter causality —that is, to show that *a priori* phenomena are the result of naturalistic forces, not ones that are miraculous or divine— not only misses the point in its assumptions about the nature of the argument, but it also loses the phenomenon by reducing it to some other phenomenon. It "misses the boat" because it assumes that the reason for the phenomenon is the claim of miraculous origin, e.g. "I feel the presence of God because God is miraculously giving me this sense of his presence." While some may say that, it need not be the believer's argument. The real argument is simply that the co-determinates are signs of the trace of God in the universe; not that we can't understand them being produced naturalistically, but that they evoke the sense of the numinous and draw us to God. The numinous implies something beyond the natural, but it need not be "a miracle." The sense of the numinous is actually a natural thing, as it is part of our apprehension of the world, but it points to the sublime, which in turn points to transcendence. In other words, the attribution of counter causality does not, in and of itself, destroy the argument; it is the life transformation through the experience that is truly the argument, not the phenomenon itself. It is the effects upon the believer of the sense of God's presence and not the sense of God's presence *itself* that truly gives evidence of the trace of God.

Moreover, the attempts to reduce the causality to something less than the miraculous also lose the phenomenon in reification. William James says:

> Medical materialism seems indeed a good appellation for the too simple-minded system of thought which we are considering. Medical materialism finishes up Saint Paul by calling his vision on the road to Damascus a discharging lesion of the occipital cortex, he being an epileptic. It snuffs out Saint Teresa as an hysteric, Saint Francis of Assisi as an hereditary degenerate. George Fox's discontent with the

shams of his age, and his pining for spiritual veracity, it treats as a
symptom of a disordered colon. Carlyle's organ-tones of misery it
accounts for by a gastro-duodenal catarrh. All such mental over-
tensions, it says, are, when you come to the bottom of the matter,
mere affairs of diathesis (auto-intoxications most probably), due to
the perverted action of various glands which physiology will yet
discover. And medical materialism then thinks that the spiritual
authority of all such personages is successfully undermined.[4]

This does not mean that the mere claim of religious experience as God
consciousness is proof in and of itself, but it means that it must be
taken on its own terms. It clearly answers the question about why God
doesn't reveal himself to everyone: He has. Further, he has provided
everyone with a means of knowing Him. He doesn't get any more
explicit because faith is a major requirement for belief. Faith is not an
arbitrary requirement, but the rational and logical result of a world
made up of moral choices. God reveals himself, but on His own terms.
We must seek God on those terms, in the human heart and the basic
sense of the numinous and in the nature of religious encounter. There
are many aspects and versions of this sense, since it is not standardized
and can be described in many ways.

Forms of the *a priori*

Frederick Schleiermacher, (1768-1834) "Feeling of Utter Dependence."

In his major works, *On Religion: Speeches to Its Cultured Despisers*,
and *The Christian Faith*, Schleiermacher sets forth the view that
religion is not reducible to knowledge or ethical systems. It is primarily
a phenomenological apprehension of God consciousness through means

Joseph Hinman

of religious affections. The term "affections" is not used much anymore, and is easily confused with mere emotion. Schleiermacher is sometimes understood as saying that "I become emotional when I pray and thus there must be an object of my emotional feelings." Though he does venture close to this position in one form of the argument, this is not exactly what he is saying. Schleiermacher is saying that there is a special intuitive sense that everyone can grasp, of this whole, this unity, of being bound up with a higher reality, of being dependent upon a higher unity. In other words, the "feeling" can be understood as an intuitive sense of "radical contingency" (in the sense of the above ontological arguments). He goes on to say that the feeling is based upon the ontological principle as its theoretical background, but doesn't depend on the argument because it precedes the argument as the *pre-given, pre-theoretical and pre-cognitive realization* of what Anselm sat down and thought about and turned into a rational argument: why has the fool said in his heart "there is no God?" The famous Psalm does not say that anyone who fails to believe in God is a fool, but the one who says *in his heart* there is no God. Why in the heart? The heart is the basic ground of belief. The heart is actually the mind, the deepest part of consciousness where we understand intuitively. To deny God in the heart is to shut off the basic, intuitive sense of God consciousness.

In the earlier form of his argument he was saying that affections were indicative of a sense of God, but in *The Christian Faith* he argues that there is a greater sense of unity in the life world and a sense of the dependence of all things in the life world upon something higher. What is this *feeling of utter dependence*? It is the sense of the unity in the life world and its greater reliance upon a higher reality. It is not to be confused with the stray "sky at night in the desert" feeling, but is akin to it. I like to think about the feeling of being in my backyard late on a summer night, listening to the sounds of the freeway dying out and realizing a certain harmony in the life world and the sense that all of this exists because it stems from a higher thing. That is just shorthand for those of us to whom this is a new concept, to get some sort of handle on it. Nor does "feeling" mean "emotion" here, but it is connected to the religious "affections." In the early version, Schleiermacher thought there was a correlate between the religious affections and God; God must be there because I can feel love for Him when I pray to him. But that is not what it is saying in the later, improved version.

Platonic background

The basic assumptions that Schleiermacher is making are Platonic. He believes that the feeling of utter dependence is the backdrop, the pre-given, pre-cognitive notion behind the ontological argument. In other words, everyone feels what Anselm tried to capture in his logical argument, if they were honest, in a pre-cognitive way. In other words, before one thinks about it, there is this "feeling" of utter dependence. After one ponders it and makes it into a logical argument, it is the ontological argument.

Unity in the Life world

"Life world," or *Labeinswelt*, is a term used in German philosophy. It implies the world of one's culturally constructed life, the "world" we "live in" —life as we experience it on a daily basis. The unity one senses in the life world is intuitive and unites the experiences and aspirations of the individual in a sense of integration and belonging in the world (as Heidegger says "a being in the world.").

Now, do not think by any stretch of the imagination that I believe this proves the existence of God! No, it is not "proof." Rather, it is *freedom from the need to prove.* As Robert R. Williams puts it:

> There is a "co-determinate" to the Feeling of Utter Dependence. It is the original pre-theoretical consciousness... Schleiermacher believes

Joseph Hinman

that theoretical cognition is founded upon pre-theoretical inter
subjective cognition and its life world. The latter cannot be dismissed
as non-cognitive for if the life world praxis is non-cognitive and
invalid so is theoretical cognition... [Schleiermacher] contends that
belief in God is pre-theoretical, it is not the result of proofs and
demonstration, but is conditioned solely by the modification of
feeling of utter dependence. Belief in God is not acquired through
intellectual acts of which the traditional proofs are examples, but
rather from the thing itself, the object of religious experience... If as
Schleiermacher... says God is given to feeling in an original way, this
means that the feeling of utter dependence is in some sense an
apparition of divine being and reality. This is not meant as an appeal
to revelation but rather as a naturalistic eidetic or *a priori.* The
feeling of utter dependence is structured by a correlation with its
whence.[5]

Rudolf Otto's *The Idea of the Holy* (1868-1937)

The Idea of the Holy is the sense of power in the numinous which
people find when confronted by the sacred: the special sense of
presence or of Holiness, which is intuitive and observed in all religious
experience around the world. Otto's *Idea of the Holy* is a complex
concept (as well as the title of the book), consisting of several aspects,
comprising the notion of the non-rational side of religion that must be
given credence because it plays a vital role in religious experience. By
"non-rational" is meant not something fatuous, but something beyond
our understanding. The Holy (synonymous with the sacred) is the
numinous (the spiritual aspect) apart from its moral and rational
foundation. The sense of the numinous is part of the Holy as is the
creature-feeling of being dependent upon an overwhelming and
incomprehensible higher power.[6]

Let us consider the deepest and most fundamental element in all
strong and sincerely felt religious emotion... it is to be found in
strong, sudden ebullitions of personal piety, ... in the fixed and
ordered solemnities of rites and liturgies, and again in the atmosphere
that clings to old religious monuments and buildings, to temples and
to churches. It may be peaceful and come sweeping like a gentle tide,
pervading the mind with a tranquil mood of deepest worship or faster
moving thrillingly vibrant and resonant, until at last it dies away and
the soul resumes its 'profane', non-religious mood of everyday
experience even violent, erupting from the depths of the soul with
spasms and convulsions and leading to the strangest excitements, to
intoxicated frenzy, to transport, and to ecstasy [7]

Paul Tillich: Object of Ultimate Concern

Tillich observes that the surface elements by which people describe
religion are immediately recognizable through membership,
institutions, rituals and the like. The true basis of religious belief,
however, is much deeper than these things. It is marked by a concern
about the meaning of one's life and one's being. It may also appear in a
form not immediately recognizable as "religious" such as art or
literature or music. [8] "If the word 'God' does not have much meaning
for you, translate it, speak of the depths of your life, of the source of
your being, of your ultimate concern, of what you take seriously
without any reservation."[9]

Think back to the quotation from Williams above about the
original pre-theoretical consciousness and its life world
(Schleiermacher). "The latter cannot be dismissed as non-cognitive for
if the life world praxis is non-cognitive and invalid so is theoretical
cognition..."[10] What does all this talk of "pre theoretical" "pre-
cognitive" amount to? Belief in God is prior to any theories we make
about God. Belief is not the result of proofs and demonstration, but is
conditioned solely by the modification of the feeling of utter

dependence. Belief in God is not acquired through intellectual acts of which the traditional proofs are examples, but rather from the thing itself, the object of religious experience. Williams goes on to state, "If as Schleiermacher... says God is given to feeling in an original way, this means that the feeling of utter dependence is in some sense an apparition of divine being and reality. This is not meant as an appeal to revelation but rather as a naturalistic eidetic" or *a priori*. "The feeling of utter dependence is structured by a correlation with its whence."[11] God is the co-determinate of the feeling. The feeling is the trace; God is that which is traced. The believer is thus justified in assuming that his/ her experiences are experiences of a reality: that is to say, that God is real.

Religious experience: freedom from the need to prove

Schleiermacher came up with his notion of the feeling when wrestling with Kantian Dualism. Kant had said that the world is divided into two aspects of reality: the noumenal (spirit —the unseen, the transcendent) and the phenomenal (that which we can see and account for by natural observation). The numinous (the all-pervasive sense of divine presence and love that mystics often feel in their mystical experiences) is not experienced through sense data, it is "prehension": a generic mode of perception that does not necessarily entail consciousness or sensory experience. If that seems incredible, think of the subliminal (the difference being subliminal does require sense data). Since God is not experienced through sense data, God belongs only to the numinous. The problem is that this robs us of an object of theological discourse. We cannot talk about God because we cannot experience God in sense data. Schleiermacher found a way to "do an end run" and get around the sense data. Experience of God is given directly in the "feeling of utter dependence" apart from sense data. This frees us from the need to prove the existence of God to others, because we know that God exists in a deep way that cannot be dismissed as mere cultural construct, by reductionism, empirical data or deified phenomena. This restores the object of theological discourse. Once having regained its object, theological discourse can proceed to make the logical deduction that there must be a co-determinate to the feeling, and that the co-determinate is God. In that sense Schleiermacher is saying "If I have affections about God, He must exist as an object of my affections" because of the logic of the co-determinate. That is, if there is a sense of radical contingency, then there must be an object upon which we are radically contingent.

What is the relationship between the feeling of utter dependence and Maslow's Peak experience? Abraham Maslow is discussed in Chapter 2 as one of the early researchers who studied "peak experience." The former feeling deals with mystical consciousness, the latter with feeling-related phenomena. They are not exactly the same thing. Schleiermacher's feeling is not Maslow's peak experience. It is clear there may be a link between the two. Maslow believed that there is a continuum of religious experience that extends from the most ordinary, daily flash of insight about God's existence, to the most advanced level of mystical union. Most people fall somewhere near the former pole and closer to the middle. The feeling of utter dependence would be closer to the end of that daily experience pole, and Maslow's Peak experience would fall more towards the other pole. I am not advancing the religious *a priori* as a third, independent proof of the existence of God. I am advancing it only as a further illustration of the consequence of accepting the first two arguments. These could be three independent arguments, but here I put them together as one argument, in three parts, the conclusion of which is that *the believer is freed from the need to prove, due to the rational nature of belief based upon RE.* The co-determinate argument is grounded in the assumptions of the *a priori.* Both Schleiermacher's feeling and Maslow's peak experience can be taken as co-determinates, or as aspects of the *trace of God.*

Schleiermacher has been attacked many times throughout the years. Many times his arguments have been assumed to be laid waste.

But his ideas keep coming back. Recently, the most devastating attack is by a philosopher named Wayne Proudfoot. Proudfoot also criticizes William James and the basic concepts of Religious Experience set forth in the *Varieties*. In so far as I have adapted my "religious *a priori*" argument to turn upon the idea of the co-determinate (which I take from Schleiermacher), and inasmuch as Proudfoot attacks the basis upon which James conceives of RE, his attacks are also applicable to my arguments.

Proudfoot's Criticisms of Schleiermacher

Since it behooves me to deal with Proudfoot's attacks, a brief overview is in order. Proudfoot observes that Schleiermacher's "program" requires two moves:

1. The experience is independent of concepts and beliefs. This is to show it is original and not artificial.
2. The experience must be identified under the label of feeling the absolute or sense of the infinite. This is to show that the object (the thing felt) and authority (God) are given in the experience (one is experiencing God because one is experiencing the infinite). [12]

This (2) is very close to my content in Chapter 3. Proudfoot says this is a contradiction! The experience cannot be independent of concepts if it is said to be a sense of the infinite or "absolute infinite" (as opposed to the limited infinite?). The "infinite" is a concept, so if the experience is beyond concepts then it can't be said to be a feeling of anything, let alone the infinite. The idea that Schleiermacher's *feeling* is independent of culture cannot be carried off. As Proudfoot puts it, "Most contemporary philosophers of religion would agree that religious experience assumes concepts, grammatical rules and linguistic practices. Those influenced by Wittgenstein and by recent representatives of the hermeneutic tradition emphasize the impossibility of transcending language in order to discover some aspect of experience, which is innocent of conceptual assumptions or grammatical practices."[13] He goes on to assert that many argue a distinction between experience itself, and a description of it. To this he argues: "Our examination under which people ascribe emotions to themselves and others and under which they identify certain moments of experience as 'religious' has shown that these conditions include not only background concepts and rules but also tacit judgments about the causes of their experience. The label a person adopts in order to explain what is happening to him determines what he experiences."[14] That's a neat trick for those who did not try to describe or explain what was happening until after the experience was long over. That would mean they contaminated their own experience and determined its outcome after having already had it. He is arguing that the experience is reformed in our minds ex post facto as we re-describe what happened. Thus, our memory of the experience is conditioned by our beliefs, practices, and words concerning religious matters. If taken literally this would mean we can never perceive anything in an objective sense. Perhaps we can't make most of the assumptions we make about being rational that we assume that we can.

How many actually wait to try and explain? While data doesn't exist on that point (to my knowledge) we might suppose that a large percentage wait to explain what happened. In some samples, as many as 45% of subjects were children when they had their experiences.[15] It seems unlikely that children would already have well-thought-out doctrinal biases. I was not a child when I had my first "peak" experiences, but I know that I did not have pre-conceived notions about religious experiences. I barely had an idea that there were such experiences. I did not know of their content at all. I was totally surprised when I had my first ones, and had to ask other Christians later "have you ever had anything like this?" When I had what I think of as "my true mystical experience," I had already learned to associate a certain feeling with the presence of God, but I had not read any

Christian mystical literature and I had no pre-conceived notions about undifferentiated unity or anything like that. When I read Stace[16] for the first time, I remember thinking, "Hey, that's what I experienced that time in the Sandia foothills." But this sense of association between words and feelings is just what Proudfoot uses to try to convince us that we do not have experiences and that we do not have feelings. To be more accurate, he argues that we do not have private mental states that are isolated from linguistic description. That would be a devastating blow to Schleiermacher's project, if it were true. Just because something is filtered or encoded doesn't mean there's no core meaning in the code.

Schleiermacher's insistence upon the purity of experience, apart from words, was motivated by an attempt to guard RE from the Enlightenment criticism, so argues Proudfoot. "Schleiermacher's insistence on the immediacy of religious experience is descriptively accurate, but it is theoretically inadequate."[17] Experience is not independent of concepts, beliefs and practices. Proudfoot charges Schleiermacher with confusing the distinction between phenomenological and theoretical senses of the immediate, and considers this failure central to Schleiermacher's entire project.

Kant is the starting point. Schleiermacher was mainly trying to come to terms with Kant's reading of understanding gained from experience, as his argument that God is not given in sense data removes the object of theological discourse from religious thought. "Objects can be apprehended," Proudfoot explains, "only through the forms of sense and the categories that structure the judgments we make...we have no access to any uninterrupted given. All the data to which we appeal are informed and categorized by antecedent judgments and interpretations."[18] There is no data apart from these sources. Those categories cannot be used to yield knowledge that transcends our experience. Much religious doctrine and metaphysical speculation derives from the attempt to do just that, to gain knowledge from transcending the categories and judgments "beyond the limits of experience," as Proudfoot puts it. Whether he is right or wrong, doesn't Proudfoot simply assume everything must start with sense data? Doesn't he basically start with a distinct and incompatible *a priori* assumption? According to him, Schleiermacher tries to do an "end run" to get around sense data by making RE the product of something not given in sense data. He tries to isolate religion in its own special domain, sequestered from criticism and impervious to critique from other disciplines:

> The religious is governed by its own rules and ought not to be assimilated to scientific or moral paradigms. This claim for the autonomy of religious experience, religious language, and religious judgments has become prominent in the world of contemporary religious thinkers and philosophers of religion. It has become the chief strategy for protecting religious beliefs and practices from the possibility of conflict with the conclusions of science or with the assumptions that inform our perceptual and moral experience. [19]

Schleiermacher rejects the Kantian assertion that religion is jumped-up ethics. Religion is its own thing; it is not failed science or elevated ethics. Kant reduced religion to morality so that certain categories of thought could be primary in understanding. Moral judgment is one of the basic forms of judgment that pre-structure our understanding.

In seeking to free religion from the onus of reduction to moral judgment, àla Kant, Schleiermacher hits upon religious affections as the key to pure religious sense. "In doing so, he contributed to a tradition in which religious experience, concatenated chiefly as affective experience and differentiated from both intellect and will, has been regarded as the original characteristic form of religion." [20] This tradition, according to Proudfoot, includes Jonathan Edwards, William James, and Rudolf Otto, among others. They differ in particulars but basically all push the line that religious experience is typified by a pure moment of pre-cognitive understanding, transcending words, images

and cultural constructs. James argued that feeling is the deeper source
of religion and that affections transcend philosophical formulations,
which are secondary.[21] Piety becomes the expression of religion that
sets it apart. Proudfoot characterizes Schleiermacher's *Speeches on
Religion to Its Cultured Despisers*, as a "sustained argument against
reductionism."[22] He contrasts his analysis with what the affections
crowd is doing with "reductionism." This is because what Proudfoot is
doing goes beyond methodological reductionism and takes on an
ideological or doctrinal air. He is using reductionism to lose the
phenomena, to reduce RE out of existence. By the time he is through
reducing the experience, it will not be an experience anymore; there
will be nothing to study; it is merely nothing more than a suggestion
one tricks oneself into believing. This form of ideological reductionism
is not science but a strategy. It is a way of using the scientific mystique
to privilege one's own reading and one's own doctrine.

While Proudfoot presents a fine summary of the developments
from Kant to Otto, he continually moves the reading along in the
direction of a bait and switch. He starts with the criticism that
Schleiermacher's view is contradictory because it both demands
experience and understanding beyond words, and uses words that
express that understanding. Proudfoot fails to distinguish between
experience itself and the difficulties in describing an experience. But he
then begins contrasting reductionism with affections as a defense
against reductionism, as though Schleiermacher knew about twentieth
and twenty-first century science, and as though Enlightenment criticism
of religion revolved around modern scientific reductionism rather than
anti-clericalism. In other words, Proudfoot simply argues against
Schleiermacher anachronistically, from the assumptions contained
within Proudfoot's own worldview.

He moves into an analysis of Schleiermacher's language in order
to show that the terms he uses are actually evocative terms, which they
should not be if Schleiermacher is right and RE is beyond words and
beyond understanding. Schleiermacher makes some moves, later

influential in phenomenological circles, designed to get around subject-object dichotomy. A moment of RE must be unstructured by and prior to any distinction of that dichotomy. Proudfoot describes this prior moment as, "a unity that precedes the differentiation that is present in perception, thought or feeling."[23] Focus upon a particular thought or object loses the moment.

> The belief that a particular moment of consciousness is immediate and prior to all concepts and beliefs may well be constitutive of the experience. In that case, Schleiermacher's account would be theoretically inaccurate because the experience would be dependent upon a rather sophisticated set of concepts and beliefs (e.g., infinite, whole, the belief that the experience is prior to concepts), but it would be effective as rhetoric that serves to evoke such an experience. Schleiermacher is convinced that piety is an original and underived moment of consciousness, and that the study of religion and of religious thought ought to be approached as the attempt to describe and experience through an examination of its expression. [24]

But wait, what did he just say? He said "the *belief* that a particular moment of consciousness is immediate" —not if a moment is immediate, but if we *believe* that it is— then the belief is constitutive. In other words, the belief is made out of a complex set of beliefs and assumptions. If that is the case, then the account (which is the understanding of the moment and what happens in such moments) would be wrong. Why? "[Because] the *experience* would be *dependent* upon a rather sophisticated set of concepts and beliefs..." In other words, what we believe about an experience determines the experience. Now this can only be true if all ideas of experience are back-read; thus he is saying that we cannot make a theory about an experience without changing our memory of the experience; this is *ex post facto* back-reading into the memory of the experience. He doesn't explicitly say it, but he is actually saying there are no true memories. If he is not saying this, he must define when this belief/back-reading thing happens and when it does not. Why would it happen with experiences involving a belief we form about the experience later, and not with memories of childhood, people we know, things we learn in school, and in fact everything we ever experience? We know from personal experience this is the case to some extent, but does it mean that we did not really live our lives? So we never really experienced love, joy, fear, the challenge of learning, the sense of triumph when we finally made that grade we wanted —none of this ever happened because if we believe anything about it, then we are forever tainting the memory of what really went on? Maybe it is just me, but I am betting that I really was present in my own life.

Yet Proudfoot takes another path to understanding. He assumes that since any belief would taint the experience after the fact, then Schleiermacher's descriptions of the experience are just rhetoric (see the quote above). Moreover, it is rhetoric used to evoke a feeling that approximates what he believed should have been happening. Apparently, there is no such thing as an honest attempt to remember a past feeling or event. This doesn't seem to taint his own critique of the *a priori*. We can privilege that as a true, standing observation.

I may not be so inclined to go along with Schleiermacher on the idea that piety is nothing more than an original and underived moment of consciousness, nor would I agree that the study of religion should be entirely caught up in the consideration of such moments. There are a lot of other ways to study religion. It also seems to me that piety is more a response to several different kinds of feelings, rather than the feeling itself. I do agree with Schleiemacher that there is such a moment, and that we can experience and know it beyond words. But we do not have to accept the entire account. There is a distinction between the experience and the description of it. Any description will contains words, and those words will always be both inadequate and tainted with conceptual frameworks that make any sort of description inadequate.

Concepts are language; we cannot have concepts apart from language. Thus, any attempt to describe such a pure moment will have to come off sounding like rhetoric, because the description will have to be created out of the pure stuff of rhetoric: words. This fact really should not be debilitating, however, because the point of religious experience is not to describe it, but to have it. We need to have some idea about what is going on, so it has some relevance to something, but we do not need to expect to derive any doctrinal language from it. We don't need to expect that these experiences will give us an understanding of propositional truth. All we really need to derive is more experience.

Piety is the religious moment in consciousness. Schleiermacher offers distinguishing marks to enable one to identify the appropriate feeling.[25] Proudfoot complains that the most fundamental distinguishing marks are the concepts. From this point on he is going to direct the reader to Schleiermacher's activities with a view toward "exposing" his apologetic intent in the rhetoric of experience in order to direct his reader towards "God," "the infinite," or "the whole." These references are required; otherwise there is no description. If that is what one feels the experience is about, then how could the description not include these words? Let us not forget that the concept of mysticism openly includes the necessity and insufficiency of language. The whole concept is that we are doomed not to be able to communicate to others, or even to fully understand, our own experiences. Yet according to Proudfoot, it seems that we should not be able to even have an idea of anything in relation to the experience; and that is a perfect example of losing the phenomenon. It seems as though Proudfoot is not willing to accept the concept of analogical language. He cannot seem to accept metaphors, which point beyond their signification to something else. He continues along lines that illustrate this one point: that the memory of the experience is tainted by the attempt to understand it. Piety is the target, since that houses the affections that are the hallmark of the *a priori*. Proudfoot must lose the phenomenon (which is the object of ideological reductionism) and toward that end he must apply many coats of varnish, painting the attempt at description as conditioning that controls the experience *ex post facto*. He seeks to get under the basic process of linking experiences with God. He charges Schleiermacher with seeking to use a circular formula as a hallmark; that the experience is caused by God. He quotes Schleiermacher: "[Y]our feeling is piety insofar as it expresses in the manner described, the being and life common to you and to the All. Your feeling is piety insofar is it is the result of the operation of God in you by means of the operation of the world in you." Proudfoot misses the importance of the link between the world and God, which is part of the quotation. That is the crucial part. Schleiermacher is not saying anything so fatuous as "the sign that the experience is from God is that it is caused by God."[26] Schleiermacher is alluding to the larger Platonic background that is part of the assumptions that he makes about co-determinates and the sense of radical contingency, which is the essence of the feeling of *utter dependence*. Late twentieth-century thinkers tended to understand Schleiermacher as speaking of emotions —feeling helpless in the wake of a higher power— but the original concept is as much about the nature of contingency (as in the terms of logic, "necessity" versus "contingency") as it is "dependence" in the sense of poor on the rich, or children upon parents. Schleiermacher has a whole world of understanding that makes up the framework in which the feeling is understood, and that framework involves things Proudfoot does not begin to talk about: Platonic assumptions, the cosmological argument, and nineteen hundred years of Christian thought.

Proudfoot takes this link between piety and the assumptions about God and turns them into an occasion for understanding an apologetic purpose underlying the entire project. In other words, he's charging Schleiermacher with doing apologetics which would make his reading of the experiences propagandistic. He identifies the criteria for understanding the identification of an experience with the divine, with specific beliefs that condition the experience. He then chides

Schleiermacher for contradicting his insistence that religious ideas be restricted to descriptions of religious affections, and his claim that explanation has nothing to do with "the childlike intuition that informs those affections."[27]

In summarizing, Proudfoot says that the account of piety contains two components: (1) Religion is not about ideas, principles or beliefs, it is a state of consciousness, a matter of taste, sense or feeling, and (2) God is the object of feeling (what I call co-determinate); "a judgment that this feeling is the result of divine operation." Which is very different from the circular reasoning he tries to stick this with above. "Piety cannot be independent of concepts and beliefs and at the same time an intentional state that can only be specified by reference to objects of thought and explanatory claims."[28] Of course this is only true if piety is the feeling itself, and not a response to the feeling.

Now Schleiermacher may have so considered it as the feeling itself; this does not mean that we have to consider it so, even those of us who understand ourselves to be moving in his wake. Proudfoot does not distinguish between the experience itself and the attempts to describe it. For him, memories of experiences are not just conditioned by the language used to describe them, they are deconstructed by that language —and thus all that was experienced is lost in the words of description. This is nothing more than so much Derridian invention.

Proudfoot moves from *On Religion* to *The Christian Faith*, Schleiermacher's magnum opus. With that he focuses his sights upon the feeling of utter dependence, Schleiermacher's core concept. First, Proudfoot situates Schleiermacher's overall project with respect to the eighteenth century and the world of letters. The project is romantic, and it borrows from Pietism in asserting that religion is feeling with an anthropology – in light of Spinoza and Kant. *The Christian Faith* was written twenty-two years after *On Religion*, and it is the product of a professor who is now ready to answer questions about theology left unanswered in the previous work. *The Christian Faith* represents an innovation in theology: the development of a systematic theology. "It is not the product of metaphysical speculation," Proudfoot tells us, "it is the science that systematizes the doctrine prevalent in a particular community."[29] Here Schleiermacher unveils one of his major principles: doctrines are not codified revelation, they are verbalizations of the feeling of absolute dependence. "Christian doctrines are accounts of religious affections set forth in speech"[30] Thus, questions about the accuracy of doctrine in terms of revelation do not come into it, because that is not what doctrines are about. They are attempts by the community to codify in its own unique language the essence of their religious affections. The major innovation, as Proudfoot tells us, is that the original notion of a taste or a sense for the infinite has been replaced with the *feeling of utter dependence*; it is a sense of total dependence upon a source of power that is distinct from the world. "The edifying language of *On Religion* has been supplanted by a careful analysis of the religious self-consciousness."[31] Whereas formerly the religious sense was defined chiefly in terms of the object, now it is defined in terms of the feeling of utter dependence. Religion is specifically defined not as a matter of knowledge or action ("neither a knowing, nor a doing") but in terms of the feeling. According to Proudfoot, Schleiermacher assumes that thought enters into emotion only in explicitly reflexive moments. Schleiermacher exploits an ambiguity in his conception of immediacy. Feelings such as joy and sorrow involve complex concepts. These feelings may be immediate in a phenomenological sense (we experience them in the now); when one is involved in the feelings one is not aware of the concepts that go into them. "Confusion is caused by the employment of an account of how an emotion or experience seems to be subject as an account of what must be assumed in order to have such an experience."[32] In other words, you do not know your own feelings.

The feeling of utter dependence becomes, for Schleiermacher, the core of religious experience. For Proudfoot this is critical, because it means that his arguments of reduction (enabling the loss of phenomena) can become crucial in invalidating all religious experience.

The reduction process works by denying that the subject of experiences knows her own mind. Feelings can be reified by later memories of them and the memories can be conditioned by conceptions, which form assumptions about what "must have been felt." We can then replace the content of an experience with a preconceived assumption that it must not have been as it seems. Thus, the phenomena are hidden in the hermeneutic of suspicion, and we are no longer dealing with the experiences themselves, but with the suspicion of how they must have been reified. "Despite Schleiermacher's claims to the contrary, to attribute to a person the consciousness of absolute dependence is to ascribe to him or her a concept of dependence as well as that of some source on which one is totally dependent. In Chapter 3 we shall examine how even apparently simple feelings of joy and sorrow assume particular concepts and beliefs."[33] Proudfoot has already argued that the feeling of utter dependence is biased in favor of theistic belief.[34] At the end of the first chapter of his book we can see him setting in place his basic reductionist assumptions, in order to connect the deconstructing of Schleiermacherian language with the moves that enable the switch from a discussion of the kinds of feelings one has in RE, to feelings in general, then to his ideas about the nature of emotions. In the end, he winds up critiquing the idea of private emotions itself, and that is supposed to simultaneously devastate the idea of private emotions revealing encounters with the divine. At the end of chapter one he says:

> Whatever the reader focuses on is, according to Schleiermacher, not the moment under discussion. The moment is by definition one that underlies and precedes our reflective consciousness. The passage appears to be pure description, but it actually serves to direct one's attention and to form one's judgments in such a way as to support the inference that there is an undifferentiated moment that cannot be given a determinate characterization. The use of the empty term *whence* as a place holder for that indeterminate source of power that is the object of the feeling of absolute dependence plays an important

role in this process. Religious language is not only the expressive, receptive medium Schleiermacher believed it to be. It also plays a very active and formative role in religious experience.[35]

That last sentence is important. It says point-blank: "religious language plays a very crucial role in religious experience." According to Proudfoot it certainly does, as it re-shapes the experience in our minds through reification. He is just about to make the switch that will "prove" this, by replacing attempts at describing what people felt in an experience that is said to surpass all ability to describe, with a critique of ordinary language and ordinary feelings —in an effort to then make us think he is disproving religious experience because it must fall to the same process of reification that negates all our private feelings. In the ideology of pure reductionism, there is no place for private feelings; we are merely organisms waiting to be told the inner secrets of the illusion we call "our own minds."

What he has done so far is to set up a hermeneutic of suspicion to which he subjects all Schleiermacher's statements and infects them with the notion that there is no simple, honest attempt to describe what went on in a given experience. We are to believe, any time Schleiermacher tries to describe the nature of the experience, or the process that goes into it, that he is spinning an apologetic ploy. Thus, the problems that manifest in trying to describe an experience that is essentially beyond language, become paramount in debunking the entire experience, because the difficulties in description offer much fuel for suspicion. When he says "serves to direct one's attention and to form one's judgments in such a way as to support the inference that there is an undifferentiated moment that cannot be given a determinate characterization," it appears that he is actually giving analytical commentary on the strategies of Schleiermacherian rhetoric. What he is really doing is merely injecting the suspicion that the ideology of reduction demands, in order to cast a pall over the whole enterprise of religious experience. It is supposed to detract from the fact that millions of people actually do experience a sense of *an undifferentiated moment that cannot be given a determinate characterization.* What if there is such a moment? Then any time someone tries to describe it, we are supposed to automatically suspect that she is just re-shaping the moment in her mind, because she has been led to do that so by the nature of the kind of language that one is supposed to use in describing such experiences. If such a moment does exist, then it can only exist because people experience it. The very idea of such a moment implies that someone has experienced it at some time, but we can never say that —because it's always got to be reified by the use of the dreaded "religious language." Now let us move on and observe the great switch.

1   David Pailin, "The Religious *a priori*," *Westminster Dictionary of Christian Theology*, Louisville, Kentucky: Westminster John Knox Press, Alan Richardson and John Bowden ed., 1983, 498.

2   See William Abraham, *Canon and Criterion,* London: Oxford University Press, >1992, 1.

3   Thomas A. Idinopulos, "the Creation of Human Behavior: Reconciling Durkheim and the Study of religion," in *Cross Currents,*" What is Religion" vol 48, issue 3 fall 1998. see on line version http://www.crosscurrents.org/whatisreligion.htm (accessed 1/2/11). The quote refers to Wilfred Cantwell Smith, *The Meaning and End of Religion* (New York: Mentor Books, 1962), 74

4   William James, *the Varieties of Religious Experience.* New York: Modern Library 1994, 16.

5   Robert Williams, *Schleiermacher the Theologian: The Construction of the Doctrine of God.* Philadelphia: Fortress Press, 1978, 4.

6   John C. Durham, "Understanding the Sacred." Aberdeen University Sociology Society, 2001. http://www.bytrent.demon.co.uk/otto1.html (accessed 4/25/13).

7   Rudolf Otto, *The Idea of the Holy.* London: Oxford University Press, Trans. John W. Harvey, 1923 (first imprint), 12-13 in the standard English version.

Joseph Hinman

8 D. Mackenzie Brown, *Tillich in Dialogue*. New York: Harper and Row, 1965, 10.

9 Paul Tillich, *The Shaking of The Foundations*. New York: Scribner and Sons 1948.

10 Robert Williams, *op. cit.*, 4.

11 *Ibid.*, 4

12 Wayne Proudfoot, *Religious Experience*. Berkeley: University of California Press, 228.

13 *Ibid.*, 228-29

14 *Ibid.*, 229

15 C. Millar, "Developmental Characteristics of Psychic Opening," Paper Presented at the Annual Meeting of the Lucidity Association, University of California Santa Cruze, June, 1992, referenced in J. I. Gackenback, "Pure Consciousness, Mystical Experience," published on Spirit Watch website, http://www.sawka.com/spiritwatch/cehsc/ipure.htm (accessed 2/4/11).

16 W.T. Stace, *Mysticism and Philosophy*, New York: Palgrave Macmillan, 3d ed. June 1960. Stace is one of the major philosophers sited in defining mysticism. He was a major influence upon Ralph Hood, Jr. in creation of the M scale. Stace was an English philosopher (Princeton 32-55) who turned to the study of mysticism after his retirement. He wrote a more popular book *The Teaching of the Mystics.*

17 Proudfoot, *op. cit.*, 3.

18 *Ibid.*, 3

19 *Ibid.*, 6

20 *Ibid.*, 7

21 *Ibid.*, 7

22 *Ibid.*, 10

23 *Ibid.*, 12

24 *Ibid.*, 13

25 *Ibid.*, 13

26 *Ibid.*, 14. Quoting Schleiermacher from *On Religion*, 45.

27 *Ibid.*, alluding to *On Religion*, 127.

28 *Ibid.*, 15

29 *Ibid.*, 16

30   from *Christian Faith*, 15, quoted in Proudfoot 16 (quotations given by paragraph and section numbers quoted from Schleiermacher, 1928).

31   Proudfoot, 17

32   *Ibid.,* 19

33   *Ibid.,* 21

34   *Ibid.,* 19-20

35   *Ibid.,* 40

5   Proudfoot Loses the Phenomena: the "Bait and Switch"

Chapter Three ("Emotions") of Proudfoot's *Religious Experience* (1987) begins with the observation that religious experience has come to be associated with a set of experiences that, according to "some quarters", transcend the verbal. He offers two reasons why this is so. One reason is "descriptive," the other is "apologetic." The descriptive reason is the need to find commonality among religions (or "different experiences we call religious" which is a very revealing way of putting it); the second reason is to distinguish "religious" experience from other kinds of experience. This latter reason he dubs "apologetic." He uses Schleiermacher (and rightly so, I think) to say that religion is more deeply entrenched in the lives and communities of people than are doctrines. Feelings are more basic and more entrenched in life than words on paper. This probably seems pretty reasonable to most people, but to Proudfoot it is an apologetic ploy. In calling one reason "descriptive" and the other "apologetic," he is trying to cast a pall over the whole process of distinguishing religious experience from other kinds of experiences. This is important for his strategy because it will enable the switch from religious experience feelings to all feelings.[1] If we can describe commonalities between religions, does that not automatically imply that we can distinguish between religious and non-religious feelings? If not, how then can we find commonalities? If so, why is number two (2) apologetic? It seems that each reason is equally required to support the other and both equally apologetic and equally descriptive. Of course, even if there is an apologetic argument, it does not mean there are no religious experiences. However, setting up that possibility is part of the hermeneutic of suspicion that he tries to cast over the whole concept of "religious experience" and it sets up the reductionist ploy of "losing the phenomena." After page 78, he slides into a critique of all feelings in general.

Proudfoot cites Hume as a major source of the modern view: that passions (which underlie feelings) are simple and cannot be captured fully in words. Humean examples include: the taste of honey, the smell of camphor, a certain shade of blue. Proudfoot points out that we can discuss comparisons and contrasts —that is his answer to the argument that some experiences of ordinary things are beyond words. Of course, you can only compare and contrast when you have something you know to compare to. We can hardly compare and contrast Krishna to Christ with regard to feelings of presence. He acknowledges there is no way to be sure we are talking about the same things.[2] The view he attacks is that words represent emotions, but they are merely names for feelings, they do not describe what goes on in a feeling —feelings do not rest on concepts. Proudfoot believes that feelings are illusions that are conditioned by concepts, and through those concepts we talk ourselves into believing that we have had such feelings.[3] According to Hume passions are prior to thought and are simple impressions that cannot enter into logical relations. The relation between object and emotion is causal, and emotions give no information. For example, love could involve the desire to make the beloved miserable, and hate could involve the desire to make the hated happy. The feelings are separate from logical relations. At this point, after laying out Hume's views on passions, Proudfoot brings in modern viewpoints that seem to argue against Hume's reading. Hume connects feelings to memory. However, memory requires comparisons to the past, and that requires more than a simple reading. Thinking of feelings as resemblance to things remembered requires understanding contrasts between resemblances in several respects. Emotions, according to Proudfoot, require prior concepts. The passionate reaction to the feeling of having been slighted, for example: this requires a concept of self-worth or dignity, of the idea of an insult, of linguistic concepts related to cultural constructs that would enable one to recognize the idea of being slighted. He then moves into a discussion of William James' view, which is different from Hume's but shares the assumption that emotions are directly perceived or intuited and thus are unscathed by conceptual presuppositions and interpretations.[4] James' view is a translation of empiricism into the physicalist's view. James locates emotions in the body, not the soul. He then points out that the view that emotions are internal events that are directly known is a recent view. He brings in Aristotle to contrast with Hume's view. Aristotle's view is that emotions are identified by thoughts. They are aligned with a ground of emotion. Specific cognitive structures and capacities for judgment must be presumed for certain kinds of emotions to be possible. An emotion, according to Aristotle, is not a simple impression that is prior to, or unstructured by, concepts.[5]

Instead of discussing the specifics of religious experience, Proudfoot is analyzing the general topic of emotions. He is assuming that religious experience would be like any other experience and would follow the same developmental path as any other kind. Why so much attention to emotion? What is it about emotions that makes or breaks religious experience? If a religious experience is just made up of feelings, then for Proudfoot, if you eliminate one then you eliminate the other. But why should we think that religious experience would be the same as any other experience? Imagine a terrorist attack; 9/11 for example. Would the experience of 9/11 be like the experience of a stroll in the park? Should we expect it to be? If one is confronted by a bewildering experience that one has never had before, which assumes some circumstance or event is really there, one is not just convincing oneself that 9/11 must have happened because my religious doctrines tell me it did. Such an event evokes a kind of feeling very much out of the ordinary. Our ordinary feeling capacity would come into the process of emotional response. But why should we think that the usual methods of formulating passions and passionate responses would be the same as we take for any ordinary event? Proudfoot's argument is much like saying: "you do not really find sunsets beautiful, you just think you should because people have told you so, so you convince yourself that you have felt enjoyment at the sight of a sunset, but you really do not really like them and you have never really felt enjoyment." Or the old saw: "you think that you are happy, but you really do not know how miserable you are." Proudfoot is actually arguing that religious people cannot know their own minds.

Do we really need Schleiermacher's reading of the feeling of utter dependence to say that there is such a feeling? Schleiermacher was trying to describe something he experienced. If he got the description wrong, does that really mean he did not have the experience? Suppose he did "spin" the description for apologetic purposes, why would that mean there was no experience in the first place? Could it not as easily mean that he is trying to convey something he felt by the way he writes about it? The overall effect of Proudfoot's strategy is that now the "switch" is complete. He has managed to take us away from religious experience to ordinary experience; now his critique will demolish ordinary feelings and emotions. He will argue, however, that the outcome falls upon religious experience.

Proudfoot proceeds with what he calls "a philosophical critique of the traditional view." However, not the traditional view of religious experience, rather the traditional view of feelings and emotions in general. "Theories in which emotions are thought to be directly or intuitively known and independent of cognitive assumptions have been challenged by recent work in philosophy and psychology."[6] The views under attack are those based upon both Hume and James. This does not mean that he is dealing with religious experience *per se*. He assumes that religious experience needs to be the same as all feelings and emotions, regardless of how "special" or "different" the reports make it seem. This is partly James' fault, because he made the same assumption. This does not mean *we* have to make that assumption.

There is, however, a lot more to James' view than Proudfoot is willing to bring out. Of course, he first turns to Wittgenstein, even though the Wittgenstein of *Philosophical Reflections* seems a lot more like a mystic than the Wittgenstein of the *Tractatus*. But he does not use Wittgenstein directly; he uses Errol Bedford's arguments based upon Wittgenstein.[7] "Emotion-words" are not names for feelings, nor are they names at all. Here is an excellent sleight-of-hand within the grand "bait and switch": according to his reading of Bedford, if emotion-words are feelings of inner states, he tells us: "Are they somatic experiences or even experiences of any kind?" "The confusion arises, according to Bedford, with the assumption that emotion words are names. This leads to a misconception of their function and a search for the states, events, or processes that are being named."[8] What we see here is the payoff to the switch: he has just denied the reality of internal states. You do not have feelings; you do not know your own mind. That this is what he actually means, is clearly stated:

> Two considerations render implausible the classification of emotion words as nominative. First, we have no evidence to suggest the existence of a multitude of different internal states corresponding to the varied and subtle linguistic differentiation that is available for discussing emotions. The postulation of such subtle differences in inner states becomes even less plausible if one accepts James' identification of emotions with the perception of bodily changes. Are we ready to posit physiological differences, or even different states or events, to correspond to the subtle differentiation between the various forms of despair described by Kierkegaard in the *The Sickness Unto Death*, or even to correspond to the difference between pride and joy, or annoyance or indignation, and between various modifications of each? Is it plausible, as Hume suggests, to think we identify these emotions by direct inspection of the qualitative difference in feeling which marks one off from the other? Psychologists have not been able to discover particular physiological states that are correlated

with each of the emotions. An emotion cannot be identified at that level. [9]

But let us remember now, this is supposed to give us a critique of religious experience, yet it only pertains to ordinary emotions in general. We should be able to assume that the feelings and experiences which seem to have a "religious" quality or which seem to be the trace of the divine would be different than "run of the mill" emotion, since the outcome is so different, tangible and measurable. What if psychologists have not been able to discover particular physiological states that correspond to every emotion? Does that mean no one experiences these religious experiences? Does it mean that we do not have the outcome that study after study says we do have? It would only mean William James was wrong about one thing; it does not affect or debunk James' overall viewpoint. "An emotion cannot be identified at that level." But, why would it have to be identified before we could say that religious experience is beyond our ability to really pin down in words?

But there is something more incredible about the statement by Proudfoot just quoted. First of all, he says that we have no evidence for internal states that correspond to all the emotions. He does not cite a study except an article by Bedford that is not an empirical study and is 50 years old. He has no data to back up his claim. But aside from this, he says, "First, we have no evidence to suggest the existence of a multitude of different internal states corresponding to the varied and subtle linguistic differentiation that is available for discussing emotions," and then he gives examples of feelings that we cannot pin down by precise correspondence of one-word-to-one-feeling, such as the difference between types of despair. But wait, what he actually said looks pretty good as a defense of religious experiences being beyond words! He is actually arguing against his own position from the first part of the book. To be fair, this argument has a place in the grand scheme of things, and where he presents it, the argument makes sense.

But one could as easily use the same "facts" (if they are facts) to argue for religious experience as transcending words. Just because there are no correspondences between all the words and all the inner states does not prove that there are no mental states. That is more likely a proof that there may not be enough words!

James then moves into an argument that emotion terms are not names for private experiences. For example, how could we explain the expression "feels angry?" He invokes the problem of the inverted spectrum; we cannot be sure that we are all seeing the same colors and not just seeing different colors and calling them by the same name. Of course, one wonders how we know about all those 'color blind' people if colors are not discernible. In a social situation someone is bound to notice if we go around calling red "gray" all the time. That does not mean that we know exactly what a given color looks like to that person, but we do know that we are seeing roughly the same colors. Here he shifts from color to understanding emotions. There's an old term in psychology "role talking" concerning how we understand the other person's feelings that he/she is communicating to us. Now from this argument he goes along with Bedford that we do not need to know the exact feelings in order to take a role and understand when someone is angry.[10] Again, this argument could be turned around and be made to support the "mystical experience thesis" as easily as Proudfoot's dismissal of it. We do not need to be totally bereft of words to describe our feelings in order to understand the inadequacy of words in describing certain experiences.

Proudfoot continues to insist that we do not know our own minds, that we have to take role to know our feelings, and that we have to use bodily changes:

> I don't appeal to private inner states in ascribing emotions to myself anymore than I do in ascribing them to others. I often come to know what I am feeling by interpreting psychological changes or my behavior in exactly the same way in which another might interpret

them if the data were available to him. Suppose I'm involved in a
heated discussion. Someone tells me I'm angry and I deny it, but then
I notice my fists are clenched and my pulse is racing. If the context is
one in which I think I have been unjustifiably slighted, and thus in
which there are grounds for anger, I conclude I am angry.... no
specific feeling by itself is sufficient to justify the ascription of a
particular emotion... [11]

What is Proudfoot arguing? That we cannot just feel an internal state
and know what it is? Yet we do. I think the fact that we do feel our
emotions, even separately from bodily reactions, is demonstration
enough that we have them and that we know what our emotional
reactions are. Just because Proudfoot is in denial about feelings does
not mean that the rest of us do not have them. That a particular feeling
by itself is not sufficient to justify the ascription of a particular emotion
is almost a contradiction in terms. That is basically the same as saying
"just feeling X is not enough to tell us that we feel X." That there may
or may not be other aspects that clue us in, such as bodily changes, is
entirely beside the point. He says that he does not appeal to inner states
to know his feelings but that he assesses them in the same way that he
does for others. That statement means he knows he has feelings, and he
knows he can understand what they are.

Proudfoot's overall point is: that words for emotions are not
merely names for inner states. He is arguing that feelings are not
merely bodily changes, but bodily changes help us clue in to feelings.
He also denies that feelings are inner states, impressions or sensations.
Emotions like fear and pride can be justified and related to their
objects, but that means that they are connected to complex ideas. Thus,
he is going to argue that ascribing a feeling to an experience is really
more a matter of reshaping what we think we should have felt based
upon our beliefs and ideas. To back this up he presents a couple of
studies that supposedly prove that bodily changes are not part of
emotion, and this is supposed to disprove internal states.

Social psychologist Stanley Schachter did several experiments (1971) and thus advances such a theory of emotions.[12] Schachter is following up on studies by Walter Canon from 1927 and 1929. These studies supposedly show that emotional behavior is not altered by total separation of the visceral from the central nervous system. The same changes occur in very different and non-emotional states.[13] Schachter theorizes that the specific character of emotional states may be determined by "cognitive factors." But is this the same as proving that emotional states are reified afterward based upon constructs and beliefs about what one should have felt? All this really proves, is that bodily changes are not necessarily coterminous with particular feelings. Again, this has nothing to do with RE and frankly could just as easily prove that something really happens in RE (that such emotional reactions are really justified and really about something that happens). Since that is what Newberg claims his studies prove (see next chapter) this might be a good point. Maranon (1924) injected subjects with adrenaline to excite the central nervous system and discovered that this sympath-mimetic arousal was not enough to produce emotion. Now Schachter's theory has two parts: (1) general and diffuse arousal in the sympathetic nervous system is part of what emotion consists of; (2) a cognitive label or "an explanation by which the subject understands this arousal." The label would be what determines how the arousal was experienced. In other words, the label or the construct that explains the feeling to the subject is what determines whether the feeling is one of joy, sorrow, anger, or what have you. Proudfoot reflects the crucial point of all of this research for our purposes in this summation: "this theory of the dual determinations of an emotional state led Schachter to predict that if a person were to find himself in a state of arousal for which no explanation or appropriate cognition were immediately available he would feel pressured to understand and to label his feelings."[14] This is just what Proudfoot is saying that people do in religious experience: They seek to define it in terms they can understand, according to the cultural constructs they think in and know.

This is also what mystics are saying, but somehow Proudfoot thinks it really proves something when he says it. This is no mystery; it is what many thinkers have been saying all along.

Schachter devised an experiment to support his claim. He made the radical hypothesis that a confused person having an experience for which he could not account would label his experience in terms available to him and, of course, Proudfoot will argue that those would be coined religious terms (that is what is available for understanding the unexplained). Schachter also hypothesized that the same state of arousal might elicit any number of labels. The experiment consisted of giving adrenalin to subjects; some knew about the mixture and some did not. The researchers then manipulated the cognitive context in order to evoke emotions. The expectation was that those who did not have a clue would draw upon the cognitive stimulus provided to explain what was happening. These were subtle cues manipulated by the researchers and not explicitly explained to the subjects. There was a confederate in the study who was used to stimulate certain moods in the subjects. Those who were told about the adrenalin were much less likely to share the mood of the confederate. Those not in the know were in need of explanations and were willing to draw upon cues in the environment to explain what was happening. This is exactly the process Proudfoot uses to explain away religious experience. RE is merely what happens when those who do not understand a certain arousal try to explain it by reifying it in a "religious" context.

This matter is by no means settled in the field of psychology. There are opposing studies and opposing voices. For example, from *MetaPsychology* 2005:

> *Gut Reactions: A Perceptual Theory of the Emotion*, Jesse Prinz
> challenges this trend for cognitive theories of emotion via a re-
> examination and consideration of the notion of emotion as connected
> to the body. Prinz concludes that emotion is connected to the body far
> more than most cognitive theories allow or recognize. For Prinz,

emotions are somatic (they are perceptions conscious or unconscious) of patterned changes in the body even though they are also fundamentally semantic.[15]

Proudfoot depends upon two separate sources for discussion of Schachter's theory. One of those sources is Robert Plutchik. But Plutchik's actual theory, the one for which he uses Schachter as a background source, is much more complex than the "labeling idea" that Proudfoot uses. Plutchik has a well-developed and complex theory based upon another theory about emotions and how they evolved. An abstract for his article in *ScienceWeek* summarizes his view:

1) The author (Plutchik) points out that what we call "cognition" —the activity of knowing, learning, and thinking, of which emotion is a part— evolved over millions of years. Charles Darwin (1809-1882) recognized that the process of evolution by natural selection applied not only to anatomic structures but also to the "mind" of an animal and to expressive behavior, a conclusion that led him to write a treatise on emotional expression (*The Expression of Emotion in Man and Animals*, 1872). Those who have followed Darwin in studying the evolutionary origins of emotions have sought to understand how emotions increase evolutionary fitness for the individual.

2) The author (Plutchik) points out that an emotion is not simply a feeling state: emotion is a complex chain of loosely connected events, the chain beginning with a stimulus and including feelings, psychological changes, impulses to action, and specific goal-directed behavior. In other words, feelings do not happen in isolation. They are responses to significant situations in the life of an individual, and often they motivate actions. The author suggests this definition of emotions allows the concept to be generalized to lower animals without difficulty. From his studies of animals, human infants, and human adults, Darwin concluded that expressive behaviors communicate information from one animal to another about what is likely to happen, and emotions therefore affect the chances of

survival of the individual demonstrating the behavior. Darwin stated:
"Even insects express anger, terror, jealousy, and love by their
stridulations."

3) The author (Plutchik) proposes that in general emotions are
activated in an individual when issues of survival are raised in fact or
by implication. Such situations include threats, attacks, poisonous
substances, or the sighting of a potential mate. The effect of the
emotional state is to create an interaction between the individual and
the event or stimulus that precipitated the emotion. The interaction
usually takes the form of an attempt to reduce the disequilibrium and
reestablish a state of comparative rest.[16]

This leaves a lot more room for a view that is sympathetic to James
without being entirely neglectful of some salient points made by
Proudfoot. In other words, it appears the real situation is more complex
than a narrow choice between the two. Would not the idea that
emotions are survival-oriented (the summary does not mention
Schachter's theory of labeling) and are responses to major events, fit
with what we would call contact with the trace of God? Is this not what
we should expect from some form of encounter with the divine?
Moreover, there is no firm consensus in the field. Neural connections to
emotions have been found, but most textbooks on neural science do not
include any discussion of emotions. Even though this is changing and
we know much more now than we did fifty years ago, emotions have
been left as the providence of psychology and we still do not know
enough to settle the issue.[17]

Proudfoot debunks a conversion experience

Proudfoot uses an example from William James' *The Varieties of
Religious Experience* in order to illustrate his argument about how

inner states (and RE) are merely the work of our minds explaining unknown affects. He argues that the bodily changes and the need to explain them forces us to make explanations from emotional clues in the constructs we inherit from culture. The example is the testimony of Stephen Bradley who had just returned from a revival. He returned home from the meeting as an unbeliever and not emotionally affected at all. "At first I began to feel my heart beat very quickly and all of a sudden..." He feared he was getting physically sick and laid down to rest.

> ...My heart increased in its beating, which soon convinced me that it was the Holy Spirit from the effect it had on me. I began to feel exceedingly happy and humble, and such a sense of unworthiness as I never felt before... My heart seemed as if it would burst, but it did not stop until I felt as if I was unutterably full of the love and grace of God. In the mean time while thus exercised, a thought arose in my mind, what can it mean? And all at once, as if to answer it, my memory became exceedingly clear, and it appeared to me just as if the New Testament was placed open before me, eighth chapter of Romans, and as light as if some candle lighted was held for me to read the 26th and 27th verses for that chapter, and I read these words: 'The Spirit helpeth our infirmities with groaning which cannot be uttered.' And all the time that my heart was a-beating, it made me groan like a person in distress, which was not very easy to stop, though I was in no pain at all, my brother being in bed in another room came and opened the door, and asked me if I had got a toothache...[18]

Apparently Bradley was having a heart attack (perhaps) and concluded it was the Holy Spirit. If I were dying, or feared that I was, I might consider that a good time to be contacted by the Holy Spirit, and an excellent time to "get saved." Proudfoot sees this as proof of his thesis, but clearly he had mined the data for an example that fitted his needs. Most mystical experiences do not involve such overt physical elements.

In fact, I do not think this even qualifies as the sort of RE or ME that I am talking about in my argument. It does not seem to be a mystical experience at all. To really prove his argument Proudfoot should show that the vast majority of religious experiences involve some form of overt physical distress. The example I give of RE in Chapter 1 (quoted by Gackenback) reveals no trace of such a physical clue. Proudfoot states, "Bradley's testimony reads like a textbook example designed to illustrate Schachter's theory."[19] Indeed, but "designed?" or *mined* to illustrate it? It is not typical. But even if we accept the testimony (after all it is a "religious experience" even if it is not a *mystical experience*) there is still an epistemic gap between the description and the explanation that Proudfoot offers. That gap is indicated where the subject speaks of suddenly being filled with the joy and grace of God. Now if it was a heart attack, how normal is it to suddenly stop in the middle of a heart attack and feel a flood of love and grace? Did he also leave out feelings of peace and assurance he could have spoken about? If so, then this does seem a departure from the norm. Thus, this abnormal sense of joy and grace would be the key to the experience and would indicate why Bradley felt that he had experienced the touch of God and not a heart attack. I grant that, coming from a revival meeting, he would be thinking in religious terms and perhaps struggling with conversion even though he claims not to have been aware of such a struggle. That would stand in favor of Schachter's thesis. At the same time, it seems that the reductionists cannot account for this difference in attitude. They must instead ignore it or explain it away as merely something that he talked himself into. But clearly there is something about the incident that for the subject warranted belief; more so than just regurgitating the things that he had heard at the meeting. Proudfoot will not be able to traverse the epistemological gap. And, in an approach taken by many atheists, he will insist that the possibility of an alternate explanation is enough, yet at the same time ignore the fact that there is rational warrant for a possibility that the incident is more than just an example of how reductionism can eliminate a phenomenon.

There is a problem in dealing with this epistemic gap that really gets to the heart of the matter. One side will try to minimize any sense of warrant for a belief in an experience and play up the alternate causes even if they are only theoretical. The other side, of course, the believer's side, will do the opposite. Proudfoot states: "Bradley, like so many prospective devotees before and since, could not understand his feelings in naturalistic terms. Religious symbols offered him an explanation that was compatible both with his experience and with his antecedent beliefs."[20] One problem with this is that his antecedent beliefs were not religious. He even says "had any person told me prior to this that I could have experienced the power of the Holy Spirit in the manner in which I did I could not have believed it."[21] This was a *conversion* experience. Now, granted he just got back from a revival and it is likely that he was favorably disposed to the message and probably thinking in religious categories. However, that does not remove the fact that there was something more than just a rapid heartbeat that makes the event noteworthy and gives it a "religious" dimension. The reductionist strategy whereby one "loses the phenomena" turns largely upon re-description. The skeptic does not buy the idea that the believer could really be convinced by some aspect of an experience, nor is she/he willing to accept that there is an unexplained dimension. In the skeptic's view, everything must be explained whether we understand how it is explained or not. That attitude accounts for the idea upon which Proudfoot ends the chapter, and it really amounts to the brunt of his argument. It is a question-begging assumption that says, "there cannot be anything other than the natural realm, therefore, there must be nothing but naturalistic causes even if we do not understand them." If a religious person made a similar statement it would be ridiculed as faith. But, when the "reductionist" makes it, it is supposedly backed by "science." Proudfoot will argue that the religious person's explanations leave no room for the naturalistic, but in so arguing he reveals just the opposite about his own strategy. Rebutting the "experience" argument will come down entirely to a matter of deflecting alternate causalities.

Proudfoot reveals the ideologically conditioned nature of his strategy: he is going to make the case for that of which I just spoke, and in giving examples to back this up he will demonstrate that he leaves no room for the actual data of the experience but loses the data and redefines the experience. This he calls: "leaving room for a naturalistic explanation." He goes through much speculation about Bradley and his state of mind. But he ignores the one aspect of Bradley's experience that marks it as a departure from the norm —the warrant for belief was the sudden burst of joy and grace. He is assuming that is just the effect of Bradley talking himself into belief. Then he follows this up with a reflection upon the "Good Friday experiment." This is a very famous experiment done in 1970 by Pahnke. It involved exposing the control group to Good Friday services at a church, and the experimental group was exposed to the same services but they had also taken psilocybin. When skeptics read about the Good Friday experiment they always assume that Pahnke has disproved mystical experience because it was induced by psilocybin more so than by the church service. But Pahnke himself never agreed to that reading; skeptics always ignore this fact. The author of the experience concluded that psilocybin *facilitated*, not *caused*, the experiences.[22] Of course, for the "reductionist", facilitation is as good as a cause; it is just a matter of re-describing facilitation as a form of suggestion. "The results show that the subjects who received the hallucinogen labeled their experiences in religious terms to a significantly greater extent then did those who received the placebo."[23] Ah, now here we have a very significant and revealing statement. First of all, the subjects were not given a "placebo" —they were either given a Church service, or service *and* the drug. Who is labeling now? Why does he say "the subjects labeled their experiences in religious terms to a significantly greater degree?" This is not the language of the study. Pahnke never said this. All other commentators mentioning this study that I have seen (and I found, in researching this book, that is a considerable number) have said "the experimental group experienced a higher degree of mystical experience..." or some such formulation. But Proudfoot re-describes the event to lose the idea that there is an experience here, and makes it just a matter of "labeling" because that is the theory he advocates. Experience is just labeling in an *ex post facto* descriptive process through which the subject, ignorant of his/her own mind, merely explains in terms of his/her own beliefs, or in terms of some cultural construct that is familiar. So because Proudfoot's ideology demands that RE is nothing more than re-describing after the fact, he re-describes and loses the phenomenon and casts it in light of his theory. The re-description puts the event in terms not of an experience, but of a labeling process. They did not have RE, they "labeled" things in religious terms. But of course he leaves out the major fact that it was on Good Friday, they were in a church service, and the point of the experiment was to see what happened when psilocybin takers were influenced to think religious thoughts. This is supposed to disprove "the average" religious experience that happens out in the world at random. That is to say Pahnke's purpose was not to disprove religious experience, but according to Proudfoot it is supposed to disprove it. Perhaps Proudfoot might say "see they have all these religious icons and symbols to evoke that label," but by the same token (there's that epistemic gap again) how can he ever know that these religious proceedings did not evoke the emotional triggers that induce a real religious inner state?[24] The reductionist cannot assume that the one experiencing knows anything, and cannot take the experience on its own terms. He must re-describe it in the terms he wishes and then he calls the actual dimension (that is religious and that warrants belief) in the experience "labeling." The tactic is clearly a "bait and switch", i.e. lose the phenomenon, re-describe it in naturalistic terms and then proclaim that the original phenomenon has been "explained."

Proudfoot makes much of the fact that one person in the Good Friday experimental group did not experience the religious aspects. This person was skeptical to begin with and did not have the experiences. Proudfoot concludes that since this person did not share the others' beliefs, he did not label the experiences in religious terms, and Proudfoot takes this to prove his point. "The subject was unwilling or unable to adopt the attributions suggested by context and so the effects of the psychedelic drug were not experienced as mystical or religious."[25] Proudfoot is assuming that the drug evokes the experiences, not merely that the drug enhances the working of psychological triggers that would be there anyway. For his theory those triggers cannot exist, but he offers no real proof. The possibility that the triggers were not operative for this person because they were skeptical of religion in the first place does not enter into Proudfoot's analysis. He assumes that an automatic process involving drugs caused the phenomena labeled as RE. I cannot find what he is talking about in the study itself. Most of the control group did not have religious experiences (only two did); I assume that he means the experimental group but every member of that group did. I surmise Proudfoot may be referring to the one who had a "bad trip", who "freaked out." I do not think that one really counts. The participant did not just fail to label the experience because he was skeptical; he completely "freaked out" because he was afraid.[26]

Proudfoot's take on feelings seems to be somewhat contradictory. He refutes Hume's idea that emotion-words are names for feelings, and that the content is beyond real description. He argues that emotions are triggered by concepts and ideas, thus descriptions are more than merely names. At the same time he asserts that those who have religious experiences are merely labeling the experiences with words that denote implied religious concepts and doctrines. The labeling process is done after the experience and in an attempt to understand it; the attempt is made in light of pre-conceived notions that are imposed upon the experience. But if this is true, then the mystic is using the descriptive terms as labels, and what is a label but a name? Thus, the mystic is making an association between an experience, a certain kind of feeling, and some idea that this feeling seems to evoke, or a chord that seems to be strictly reminding one of religious ideas. This would seem to be an inherent feature of the process of trying to describe something. All we can do is relate what we do not understand to what we do understand. In either case the descriptive words seem to be functioning as names for feelings that are never fully grasped because we cannot talk about them except in terms of comparison to things we already know about. Thus, labeling is a name for a feeling; the feeling is the content of an experience that evokes something that can only be described analogically. This seems to be a real contradiction, because Proudfoot wants us to believe that words used to denote emotions are not merely names for feelings that we cannot describe, and yet in terms of religious experience that seems to be what they are. What Proudfoot leaves out is the idea that the mystic can relate the feeling to an idea, at least in some sense. Proudfoot takes this to mean that having the idea pre-conditions the reminiscence of the experience; but what is he really talking about besides the problem that we can only relate experiences to ideas that we know and not to things beyond our understanding? We have to think in cultural constructs in order to be able to talk about our thoughts. This does not imply that there is nothing beyond our cultural constructs. Meaning in language arises from context. The evocation of a religious idea seems to indicate that the feeling is more closely related to a construct that is historically understood in a religious context, thus the experience is dubbed "religious experience." Proudfoot sees this as proof of his theory; however, it seems far more logical to understand it as an inherent feature of the process of trying to communicate.

Proudfoot critiques mysticism: losing the phenomena

Proudfoot brings together the elements of the strategy worked out to this point and applies them to a general critique of mystical experience. But he also tries to argue that the mystic is losing the phenomena in the

Joseph Hinman

labeling process. In making this argument he is once again pretending to know the mind of the subject better than the subject herself. But rather than the mystic losing the phenomena, it is the labeling theory itself that loses it. The loss of phenomena in the mystic's description is just the necessary product of missed understanding; after all, "mystical" experience is supposed to be "beyond understanding." But the loss of phenomena in Proudfoot's re-description is a true strategic attempt to lose the phenomena: in an attempt to cast doubt upon its veracity he re-describes an experience he did not have. He accuses the mystic of losing the phenomena in relation to the search for a mystical core, the concept of a true experience beyond words at the heart of one's experiences. "Attempts to differentiate a core from its interpretations may cause the theorist to lose the very experience he is trying to analyze. The terms in which the subject understands what is happening to him are constitutive..."[27] There is a clear statement of what Proudfoot argues. But notice his question-begging tactics. He has eliminated any possibility that something in the experience itself (for Bradley it was the inexplicable sense of joy and grace) would mark the experience as "religious" and something out of the ordinary. For Proudfoot, it is totally a matter of assuming that RE must be a matter of labeling and re-defining, it cannot be a matter of actually experiencing something. Thus, anything that could mark the experience becomes a subject of re-describing and the evocation of labeling. This means that nothing can count against the theory of labeling that Proudfoot argues because everything can be a source of evocation of labeling. In effect, his theory rules out anything that would count against the theory and in favor of experience. He is losing the phenomena, and constructing a theory that cannot be falsified.

One aspect that is used as a major mark of the 'core' of mysticism, is the commonality shared by most mystics mentioned in Chapter 1: the "undifferentiated unity." Proudfoot makes the argument that not all mystical experiences are the same. Some mystical experiences are different, and *that* he thinks counts in favor of his theory; for in his mind different traditions label experiences according to their own understanding. While it is true that mystics are different, each with their own experience, there are commonalities, and unity is one of them. All that is needed is commonality. They need not have identical experiences for us to take their experiences seriously, or as valid. Apparently Proudfoot thinks so, but there is no logical reason to do so. Moreover, I have already said that we must draw upon constructs in order to use language, and thus any attempt at examination must automatically involve labeling and drawing upon constructs. How can we think about falsification in either case, whether different or similar, diverse or unified? Not by assuming that any time an explanation involves a belief it must be false. The best way would be to deal with the effects of the belief in the life of the person being analyzed. If the effect is transformative —a concept Proudfoot does not even consider— we can assume there is validity to the experience. Instead he cites sources that attempt to indicate that undifferentiated unity is not a true commonality among all mystics. He cites Steven Katz (1978) who "recognizes that the mystic's experience is conditioned by the complex pre-experiential pattern of beliefs, attitudes and expectations."[28] Katz compares a Jewish mystic's sense of non-absorption with a Christian mystic's concept of undifferentiated unity. This is important because one would think that the commonality of unitive sense would be present in all mystical experiences. Just because the unitive concept is not one of the commonalities does not invalidate all mystical experience. But, Katz' mistake is in thinking that the Jewish experience is completely bereft of the experience of undifferentiated unity. Jewish mystics emphasize the sense of distinction between creature and creator (as Katz says) but they also maintain a coincidence of opposites, which means that in the final analysis there is a sense of unity in Jewish Mysticism, contrary to Katz' understanding. According to Sanford L. Drob:

In this paper I explore the use of *coincidentia oppositorum* in Jewish mysticism, and its singular significance for the theology of one prominent Jewish mystical school, Chabad (or Lubavitch) Chasidism. It is the achievement of Elior and other modern scholars of Jewish mysticism to have brought the Chasidic use of the *coincidentia* doctrine to our attention. In this essay I hope to move beyond mere explication by introducing two models through which we can begin to understand the Kabbalistic and Chasidic conception of the coincidence of opposites rationally, in philosophical and theological terms. These models each rest upon, and develop, the Kabbalistic/ Chasidic view that language (or representation in general) sunders a primordial divine unity and is thus the origin of finitude and difference. The first, *cartographic* model, draws upon the idea that seemingly contradictory but actually complementary cartographic representations are necessary in order to provide an accurate two-dimensional representation (or map) of a spherical world. The second, *linguistic* model draws upon Kabbalistic and postmodern views on the relationship between language and the world, and in particular the necessity of regarding the linguistic sign as *both identical to and distinct from* the thing (signified) it is said to represent. In the course of my discussion, I hope to provide some insights into the relevance of *coincidentia oppositorum* to contemporary philosophical, psychological, and especially, theological concerns.[29]

We might view this as a sort of "reverse labeling" whereby the mystic has experienced unity and is trying to explain it theoretically because it does not fit in with his preconceived doctrine. This would be a counter to Katz and Proudfoot (it is also the case in my own experience). Daniel C. Matt describes the sense of undifferentiated unity in Jewish Mysticism:

> The Essence of Divinity is found in every single thing. Nothing but it exists. Since it causes everything to be, nothing can live by anything else... If you suppose that *Ein Sof* emanates until a certain point, and

that from that point on is outside of it, you have dualized. Realize, rather, that *Ein Sof* exists in each existent.[30]

Katz argues for a labeling process:

> That is to say, the entire life of the Jewish mystic is permeated from childhood up by images, concepts, symbols, and ideological values, and ritual behavior, which there is no reason to believe he leaves behind in his experience. Rather, these images, beliefs, symbols and ritual define, *in advance*, what the experience *he wants to have*, and which he then does have, will be like."[31]

Proudfoot goes into a long discussion documenting the fact that many mystical traditions work on this same principle, which seems so shocking to modern people, that the mystic predetermines the course of the experience. To Proudfoot this is proof that his theory "hits the nail on the head." This tendency must seem very suggestive to a modern reader who is not well acquainted with the mystical tradition of Christianity, but to one who has read Underhill, or studied Augustine or St. Symeon the New Theologian, it is nothing new or alarming. Nor does it bode ill for the RE argument, nor does it bolster Proudfoot's argument at all. It is not as though the mystic says "today I shall experience a feeling of overwhelming love, tomorrow I shall experience dread in the presence of the Holy, and next, the dark night of the soul."

Instead, it works as follows: There are guides who have trodden the way before, and they exist within all religious traditions. The purpose of a tradition is to provide one with a vocabulary (which is also needed for labeling; so again, everything counts for Proudfoot's theory, and therefore, nothing counts against it). These guides set out a general course to mark the path upon which they have trodden, and the mystic follows that path; and the extent to which his experiences stack up is his theology. In the days before modern concepts of autonomy (beginning with St. Thomas Aquinas), theology was not an original set of intellectual ideas that the mystic offered in the vein of a theologian; instead, one's theology was the set of experiences one had while moving along the path. I can well understand why Proudfoot and Katz would see this as proof that experiences are just pre-conditioned labeling. But for several reasons this should not derail the argument from RE.

First, Proudfoot is assuming that all mystics are experienced ones and that they have already been raised in their traditions when they first try to describe their experiences, or that they are at least steeped in knowledge of the theory of mystical experience. Such is by no means the case. There are converts who had no prior knowledge of any religious tradition, or who had no concept of the mystical aspects of such a tradition. High rates of first-time mystical experiences come from children as well. One would expect that children would not be steeped in mysticism, especially if they did not grow up in mystical households. Certain research has shown that mystical experiences "frequently manifest themselves in early childhood."[32] Robinson found as high as 15% of his sample had mystical experiences in childhood; several other studies found similar results, such as Millar (1990) and Hunt, Gervais, Shearing-Johns and Travis (1991).[33] Hardy's analysis of the accounts of 4000 people prompted him to conclude that mystical experience "frequently" happens in childhood.[34] The literature on childhood and spirituality is unfortunately not immense. Too little work has been done in this field. Chris J. Boyatzis provides an excellent summary of the field.[35] Many studies focus on developmental processes of the child's cognition of spiritual concepts. The first wave of study lasted from the 1960's to 70's. The major findings seemed to indicate that children developed ideas of religiosity in relation to their parents and conventional society. This wave of research was dominated by previous thinking which saw childhood development in terms of stages. A second wave of research in the 1980's was led by rebellions against this view, and childhood development was understood in terms of "domain-specificity" and the child as "builder of naïve theories in specific domains" (Carey 85).[36] Sound familiar? This is a fancy way of saying first of all, that children believe what we tell them, and secondly, that children make up their own crazy ideas. Does it sound familiar to find that the results move in relation to the predominate theories? Does it seem that they are *labeling* things according to preset assumptions? In the 1990's and in the past decade another wave of research has gone full circle and finds that "children are not all that different from adults in their thinking." These moves represent the relation of the field to the theories of Piagert. It seems that future research will revolve around whether the market favors Piagert in a decade, or rebels against him.[37]

Most research on children and religious thinking centers on their concept of God. Much research has been done on children of different cultures and different traditions. A great deal of that research demonstrates that children are influenced by the tradition in which they are raised. The research shows that children have a system of mystery relating to the divine, that they can feel awe and that they do have mystical experiences. None of that research seems to indicate that children who have these experiences have preconceived notions of the ineffable or a sense of the numinous or undifferentiated unity. Although the author does not point this out directly, he presents no research that would indicate that they do. They tend to be influenced by the parent's tradition.[38]

Secondly, many "peakers" (mystics, those who have the experience) find that their initial experiences contradict their religious viewpoints. Proudfoot's theory suggests that those experiencing RE label unknown experiences with their preconceived doctrinal ideas in order to explain them. This is how he analyzed the Bradley case. But then how does one explain the fact that for some, their experiences contradicted cherished notions? Why would one label an unknown

Joseph Hinman

experience with a viewpoint that contradicts what they take to be divine truth? St. Teresa tells us:

> There was one thing that I was ignorant of at the beginning. I did not really know that God is present in all things; and when he seemed to me so near, I thought that it was impossible. Yet I could not cease believing that he was there, since I seemed to almost certainly to have been conscious of His very presence. Unlearned persons told me that he was there only in his grace. But I could not believe this, because as I have said, he seemed to be really present. [39]

Why allow the experience to indicate a contradiction to what one accepts as true teaching? Why allow this, even to the point of accepting what seems impossible, when all one really has to do —according to Proudfoot— is to label the experience in line with one's doctrine? G. William Barnard discusses a second example of a mystic or religious experiencer whose experiences contradicted his religious belief. The case, found in James' *The Varieties of Religious Experience*, concerns a man named Ratisboone. He was a Jew; his brother had converted to Catholicism and become a priest. Ratisboone was very angry about this. One day while traveling with a friend he found himself in a small church waiting on his friend to finish paying respects. He then had a vision, which completely removed his awareness of the world around him. In this vision the Virgin Mary appeared to him. Ratisboone also converted and became a priest. Proudfoot assumes that the image in the vision was modeled after a painting he had seen. Thus, Proudfoot argues that the image is a conscious creation in the mind re-labeled as a vision. But as Barnard points out there is no indication that the vision had anything to do with any known artistic production of the image of the Virgin. Ratisboone says nothing about a painting and does not even describes the image in any detail. The experience itself included a sense of presence, and was a shattering, life-changing encounter. Proudfoot loses all the phenomena that marked it as a distinct event. "In the bottom of my soul I felt the most ardent joy," Ratisboone says, and he also speaks of an abyss of darkness, or not knowing where he was, all of which Proudfoot neglects to mention. Ratisboone also claimed he knew very little about religion.[40] One can add the experience of the Muslim philosopher Aurobindo, who after his first encounter with meditation wound up reversing his views and taking a theological position he had previously opposed because of the nature of the experiences:

> The first result was a series of tremendously powerful experiences and radical changes of consciousness which he (Lele) had never intended —for they were Adwaitic and Vedantic and he was against Adwaita Vedanta— and which was quite contrary to my own ideas, for they made me see with a stupendous intensity the world as a cinematographic play of vacant forms in the impersonal universality of the Absolute Brahman.[41]

Another example is that of Richard Bucke, documented by Andrew Newberg.[42] In the year 1874 Bucke (who was 36 at the time) had a vision accompanied by a mystical experience. This experience shaped the rest of his life. He went on to study mental illness and became a major contributor to clinical psychology, but he never abandoned belief in the experience he had that day when he was 36. Newberg states: "Bucke was a social Darwinist, in his biography he wrote that even as a child he wrote that he 'never accepted the doctrines of the Christian Church.' Yet he never doubted the transcendent truth of what was presented to his mind."[43]

Furthermore, not to compare my own meager experiences with those of a real mystic such as St. Teresa, but in my experiences I also felt a total contradiction between what was happening and what I thought was the gospel truth. I had no knowledge of mysticism prior to that day. I did know the names of some mystics, but I had no idea what mysticism was about. This was the early 1980's, I was in my early 20's, and I was a charismatic. I had ideas about the baptism of the Holy Spirit, His gifts, and I had felt the presence of God before. Yet it came as a shock to me when I felt it. I had little idea about the concept of undifferentiated unity, because what I knew of that concept (which was not much) I tagged as "evil Catholic false doctrine that leads to Pantheism." If anything, prior to this time I had tried to force the few mystics I knew a bit about, such as Augustine, into the Charismatic category, and denied any of their experiences that contradicted what I understood. I lived in Albuquerque at the time. One day alone in the foothills of the Sandia Mountains I was praying. I felt the presence of God around me in a strong way and prayed for over an hour. But I had not felt anything like what happened next. My heart was not beating rapidly; I had no bodily changes for which I could not account. Suddenly it seemed as though a door opened in reality. I do not know how to describe this, but it was the sense that a door was opening in front of me. A presence emerged from that door, and that presence I immediately recognized as Christ, distinct from the general presence of God I had already felt.

Suddenly this presence of Christ, which I clearly recognized in a strong way, sort of expanded to fill the entire world. It merged with the general presence of God so that I could not sense a distinction; then I realized I sensed this presence radiating from all things. God was radiating from the rocks, the trees, the sticks on the ground; the air was made of God, and the whole world was made out of God. I did not describe this later on, and I said to myself at the time "this can't be true, it's a contradiction to sound doctrine." I clearly and distinctly felt that all things are made of God and that there is no real distinction between God and these things. That experience evolved into a sense that I understood everything. In a flash I realized I knew why there is pain and suffering, why God created the universe, why I had gone through all my problems, everything seemed so clear and logical to me. The specific reasons that seemed obvious in that moment went away, like one forgets the content of a dream. But what has stuck with me to this very day is a deep-seated realization that it all does make sense and that there are higher reasons that we cannot guess at but are "darn good ones." In that moment everything I was experiencing totally blew away my whole Charismatic Protestant framework. Now, I did not just abandon my beliefs to become a Pantheist. I am not, nor have I ever been, a Pantheist. But I was well aware in that moment that what I was experiencing seemed to validate Pantheism (which I regarded as a Satanic counterfeit) and blew away my Charismatic understanding. What I took away from that experience (aside from a deep-seated satisfaction that everything really does make sense) is a tendency to be less hasty in dismissing what I had called "Satanic counterfeit." I did not try to describe the experience in a way that fit my beliefs because I knew that it did not. But neither do I take that experience as the ultimate means of theological understanding. I put it all into a rational framework, and I try to explain it in light of church doctrine and theological thought but informed by actual experience. It would have been a lot easier just to say, "I didn't really experience that, I really experienced the distinction between creator and creation." There is something in the quality of the experience that will not let me do that. [44]

Now let us be clear about what was just said. I argued that Proudfoot's claim that the mystic loses the phenomena is ridiculous because it is he who loses the phenomena. I argued that the so-called "labeling process" that he finds mystics perform is just the normal pitfalls of trying to describe an experience. I found that Proudfoot is not making a distinction between an experience and the describing of that experience. His loss of phenomena is a conscious strategy that hides the aspects of the experience that really mark it as distinct, so that he can bring in the labeling argument. To illustrate this point I demarcated three arguments that disprove labeling: (1) children have RE; (2) RE can contradict the mystic's cherished doctrine; (3) the vast body of empirical data disproves the label aspect. (It would be absurd to think that all this labeling produces long-term positive effects that are consistently associated with such experiences —the same psychological trick does not work for other kinds of social support or psychological enhancement.)

Now, I want to return to the argument that the labeling approach loses or even hides the phenomena of RE. I will argue that Proudfoot's labeling theory actually goes against the basic experiences we find in all epistemic judgment. I will turn to William P. Alston who sets up the argument. Alston points out the distinction between the content and the description of an experience; his criticism of Proudfoot includes a demonstration that Proudfoot confuses this distinction. Alston argues that he confuses identifying a type of experience and what the experience consists of. He finds that this is a total non sequitur:

> From the fact that we use concepts to identify something as of a certain type (how else?!), it does *not* follow that *what* we are identifying 'involves' concepts and judgments. If it did we would be unable to classify anything but cognitive psychological states. From the fact that we use concepts to pick out cabbages and vegetables, it does not follow that cabbages are, have or use judgments. Close to home, pick your favorite case of conscious state that does not involve concepts and judgments in its own nature —a pain or a throb. But to identify a state as a pain I must employ a concept, the concept of pain, naturally. But then, we see that we are mistaken in supposing that pains are non-conceptual!!! I can't see that this argument is any better than the one about cabbages, and the same applies to Proudfoot's assault on Schleiermacher. To be sure, it may well be that Schleiermacher cannot, consistently with his other key views, maintain that "piety" or the "sense of the infinite" or the "feeling of absolute dependence" is free of concept, so it may be that he does so characterize these states that they do involve one or more beliefs, for example, that everything depends upon God for its existence. But if so, this will be because of his *characterization* of the states, not because he uses concepts to classify them in a certain way. [emphasis his][45]

It is precisely because Proudfoot confuses the content with the description that he loses the content. This is because he has already presumed that the content cannot be real and overlooks the subject's actual memory of the experience. Thus the aspects that make the experience different from all others and mark it as religious are simply ignored because they do not fit the theory of how the labeling works.

Barnard argues that we should stay true to the phenomenology of the experience, rather than reading into the process a preconceived idea of what happened. Even though he does not say it, what he is really arguing, even if he does not mean to, is that Proudfoot is doing his own labeling. Barnard says:

> This experience [Ratisboone's] is not devoid of intellectual content but according to the phenomenology of the account; that content comes with the experience itself, it is not added on by Ratisboone. It seems philosophically imprudent, then, to claim that this experience emerged as the result of the superimposition of Ratisboone's previous religious beliefs onto the neutral template of some physiological or psychological shift in equilibrium. Even if we indulge our skeptical academic propensities and question whether Ratisboone was as innocent of previous religious beliefs as he claims, we would still have difficulty explaining how Ratisboone's fragments of religious knowledge managed to transform themselves into the living, immediate, earthshaking apprehensions that characterized his experience in the church.[46]

This basically amounts to a labeling process whereby Proudfoot loses phenomena, ignores crucial elements and on the basis of re-described data reads into the process the necessary elements to argue for the labeling theory. Barnard demonstrates in more than one example that Proudfoot leaves out about half the contents of every example he deals with. This is seen in the Bradley case, the Ratisboone case, and the case of the man who felt a presence in his room in college: leaving out about

Joseph Hinman

half of what the subject says in describing the experience, literally losing the phenomena. [47]

Proudfoot does not refer to any of the studies

Proudfoot uses his own studies. Proudfoot draws conclusions from his own outdated studies, conclusions that simply can't be supported. He does provide studies on some matters, as I have already mentioned. Yet he makes absolutely no reference at all to any study that deals with the material surrounding the long-term positive effects of RE. It is a bit much to assume that all mystics pre-determine their experiences by re-describing them in light of their beliefs, which then "psych" them into totally changing their lives in ways that transform them into self-actualization. If this were the case, then one would think that secular processes could duplicate the effect, but they do not. There is no data to support the idea that secular thinking can copy the labeling process and give people self-actualization without introducing them to some form of religious thinking or experience. There is a great deal of data to suggest that having RE has more transformative effects than any secular process has produced. [48] If religious thinking in and of itself has this effect, it might suggest truth-content. Moreover we should expect to find some form of labeling based upon beliefs; the primary function and reason for the development of a religious tradition is to serve as a spiritual guide and to help people understand this experience by reflecting on the experiences of those who went before. The outcome should be what we view as the real acid-test of validity. Proudfoot and Katz merely beg the question. Transformative power is not about words on paper. It is not meant to be the kind of theoretical construct that can be measured mathematically and demonstrated through double blind tests. It is meant to be experienced. It is not about words, it is about doing something. It does not matter if our

240

understanding of it is off-base, or if we cannot manipulate people like an engineer; it is not engineering, is not mere words on paper, it is life. It is living a life in the presence of God.

Is it really so devastating to Schleiermacher's project, or to the co-determinate argument, to find that RE is not totally beyond words? If RE was not totally beyond words, would that mean that RE does not exist? William P. Alston makes an argument based upon RE, which he regards as an apprehension of knowledge. He does not accept the idea that RE is isolated from language and transcends meaning. Yet, he does not discard RE as some conditioned nonsense that we trick ourselves into believing because language fools us into thinking we have feelings. Perhaps we might need a Schleiermacher with minor repairs. Perhaps we might abandon him altogether — although I think not — but this does not mean that the argument from the co-determinate does not "fly," nor does it undermine the religious *a priori*. First of all, experience is not undermined even if it is gotten at by language. Linguistic utterances can be meaningful and refer to feelings in meaningful ways without describing them totally. We do actually experience the sight of color. We see the color we identify as blue, we actually do see something. Now we may be seeing different colors. Perhaps what I call "blue" is what others call "green." I see a color, yet I cannot describe it. The best we can do in description of color is light and dark. But we cannot describe colors. Proudfoot wants us to believe that we are fooling ourselves into thinking that we have these experiences of something we refer to as "God." In reality, he thinks, we are merely conditioning ourselves to remember what we felt in a certain way because we connected it to religious belief. Of course, he wants us to think that this is some sort of empirical philosophy, but in reality it is just as much an example of an ideology conditioning a critique.

There seems to be a continuum between two poles: understanding on one end, and transcendence on the other. It is not the case that everything connected with RE is beyond words and beyond understanding. Some things experienced can be put into words; not much, and probably not exhaustively, but those limitations obtain in any case where emotions come into play, simply because it is hard to pin them down in the moment. One aspect that we use to identify "mystical experience" is that it is "beyond words." That does not mean, however, that all aspects of those experiences are beyond words. One might experience "love" or "presence" or "peace" in some sense that cannot be fully gotten at by anything we can say about it. So there is a range from the known to the unknown and each experience may contain part of the known and part of the unknown.

Proudfoot wants to undermine a stable understanding by suggesting that language tricks us into thinking that we experienced something that is merely conditioned by later descriptions of the experience. He confuses the difficulty in talking about transcendence with evidence that WE never had an experience or a feeling. While it is possible that we are reifying our experiences by talking about them, it seems that is a good reason for not trying to say too much about them. Yet why does it really matter if our feelings are pristine and isolated from descriptions, or if words cannot describe them? If it is purely a matter of wanting doctrine, then Proudfoot is free to make up some doctrines. Either way, what difference does it make? It only matters if we assume that there is crucial information to be derived from the experience and that the information can be put on paper in the form of words, and that it is terribly important to do so. Proudfoot gives us no reason to believe any of this. The value of RE *is* the experience. It does not matter if we understand it; it does not matter if we *can* describe it. What matters is that we *have* it. There is a vast body of scientific, empirical data that proves the long-term positive and transformational effects of RE. It behooves us, therefore, to seek the object that leads us down the path that includes this experience. It may not be important whether or not we derive words on paper that give us propositional truth. In saying this, I am not suggesting that propositional truth is not important. What I am suggesting is that it does not have to be derived from RE alone.

1   Proudfoot, *op. cit.* 75,76.

2   *Ibid.,* 80.

3   *Ibid.,* 81.

4   *Ibid.,* 82.

5   *Ibid.,* 84.

6   *Ibid.,* 89.

7   *Ibid.,* 90 (Proundfoot cites Bedford, "Emotions", *Proceedings of the American Society,* 1957, n.s. 57:281-304).

8   *Ibid.,* 90. "Role talking" is a psychology term that refers to understanding the feelings others communicate to us.

9   *Ibid.,* 90-91.

10   *Ibid.,* 91.

11   *Ibid.,* 93.

12   *Ibid.,* 98.

13   *Ibid.,*98.

14   *Ibid.,* 99.

15   Adele Tomlin, Review of Prinz, Jesse J., "Gut Reactions," *Metapsychology: Online Reviews,* 2005, http://metapsychology.mentalhelp.net/poc/ view_doc.php?type=book&id=2596&cn=396, (accessed 9/10/08).

16   Abstract summary of Robert Plutchik, "The Nature of Human Emotions" in *Scienceweek,* 3 August 2001, http://cogweb.ucla.edu/ep/Emotions.html (accessed 9/10/08). Original: *American Scientist* 89 (2001): 344.

17   *Ibid.,* 344.

18   Proudfoot, *op. cit.,* 103, quoting William James (The *Varieties...*1902, 190-193).

19   *Ibid.,* 103.

20   *Ibid.,* 104

21   *Ibid.,* 104.

22   see my discussion of "Good Friday" and follow up in chapter eight.

23   Proudfoot, 107.

24   see my chapter on placebo and drugs for a description of the Good Friday and analysis that disproves Proudfoot's assertions about it: (1) the study itself involved people who had had religious experiences before; (2) other

studies do not involve church service but the drug takers had religious
experiences anyway from listening to classical music.

25 Proudfoot, *op. cit.* 106.

26 see discussion in chapter 8.

27 *Ibid.,* 121.

28 *Ibid.,* 122.

29 Sanford L. Drob, *The New Kabbalah:* website:
http://www.newkabbalah.com/home.html (accessed 7/24/13). The New
Kabbalah is a philosophy and Jewish theology grounded in the union
between traditional Jewish mysticism and modern rational thought.
Rooted in the visionary mythos of Rabbi Isaac Luria (1534-72), and
interpreted through such modern and postmodern thinkers as Freud, Jung,
Hegel, Wittgenstein and Derrida.

30 Daniel C. Matt, *The Essential Kabbalah: the Heart of Jewish Mysticism.*
New York: HarperCollins, 1995, 24.

31 Steven Katz, quoted in Proudfoot, *op. cit.* 122.

32 Hardy. A. in Lukoff, *op. cit.,* 178. Original research: Hardy *The Spiritual
Nature of Man* Oxford: Clarendon Press, 1979. Hardy collected 4000
accounts of RE by placing ads in the newspapers; these were coded for
phenomenological features and a follow up questionnaire was
administered.

33 See Chapter 3 (Studies) section "not the result of technique alone."

34 A. Hardy, *op. cit.*

35 Chris J. Boyatzis, "Religious and Spiritual Development in Childhood,"
Handbook of The Psychology of Religion and Spirituality. New York,
London: Guildford Press, Raymond F. Paloutzian, Crystal L. Park ed.,
2005, 123-143.

36 *Ibid.,* 125.

37 *Ibid.,* 125.

38 *Ibid.,* 127-128.

39 St. Teresa of Avila, *The Life of St. Teresa of Avila by Herself,* trans. J.M.
Cohen., London: Penguin, 1957, 127.

40 G. William Barnard, *Exploring Unseen worlds: William James and The
Philosophy of Mysticism,* Albany: NY SUNY press, 1997, 104.

41 Sri Aurobindo Ghose. *On Himself.* Pondicherry: Sri Aurobindo Ashram,
1972. 79.

42 Andrew Newberg, Mark Robert Waldman. *Why We Believe What we Believe*, New York, London, Toronto: Free Press, 2006, 167.

43 *Ibid.,* 171.

44 Just how I rationalize that experience with traditional orthodox theology without resorting to Pantheism; well I have to save something for the next book, however, I do recognize a disparity between phenomena and doctrine. In Chapter 8 of this work I discuss my view that mystical experience should not be used to base doctrine upon, at least not entirely.

45 William P. Alston, *Perceiving God: The Epistemology of Religious Experience*. Ithaca and London: Cornell University Press, 1991, 40-41.

46 Barnard, *op. cit.* 106.

47 *Ibid.,* 106-7.

48 Studies cited in Chapter o studies indicate that religious experiencers have much less depression, incidence of mental illness, better health and so forth.

6 God on the Brain: Are Mystical Experiences Caused by Brain Chemistry, a "God Gene" or Some Other Naturalistic Mechanism?

Neurology of the spirit

The skeptical argument maintains that RE is not the trace of the divine because it is merely a side-effect or by-product of our genetic endowment; it contributed to survival and that's the only reason we still have it. RE could be the product of a gene, but in either case the skeptic will argue that it is totally naturalistic. There are many indications that religion has a genetic basis, there may even be a part of the brain associated with religious belief, and drugs can duplicate RE. The response to this argument is: Genetic endowments, either as adaptations (which would include some genetic basis, either as a "religious gene," the "God module," (or "God pod" as I call it) or RE as a Spandrel (side-effect of other adaptations) are merely indicative of God's creation. God created flesh and blood beings and this is how flesh and blood beings work. We access the divine through the neural net that God created, the same neural net that allows us to understand the physical world around us. Drug inducement of RE is misunderstood and overrated. The argument is not that RE is so amazing and unexplainable that it must be a miracle. Naturalistic processes may account for it, but that is only half the story. The argument is that it can be rationally construed as the trace because it is what we should expect of the divine, because the trace hypothesis explains the outcome, and because it is the basis of all religious belief.

We have made great strides in the last two decades understanding the relation between consciousness and brain chemistry. As a consequence of their reductionist mentality, atheists assume that any relation between brain and mind sums up all relations between brain and mind. Atheists tend to side with the functionalists, assuming that all consciousness is mere epiphenomena related to brain function. Thus, they are quick to argue that RE is nothing more than some sort of misfire of the synapse, or a heritable trait of evolution produced by the need of the tribe for unity. This viewpoint is disproved, however, by none other than Andrew Newberg, one of the major researchers on the "God Pod." Researchers have discovered that there are parts of the brain that react to God-Talk. "The God part of the brain" as well as "God module" (and also "God Pod") are misnomers because several areas react in this way. Newberg demonstrates that the existence of a "God pod" is not proof that RE can be reduced to brain chemistry, rather, not only is it the only way sentient flesh and blood beings could think or communicate, but it is also a pretty good indication that there is more to reality that just atoms in the void. Newberg himself is a believer in some form of Buddhist-like theory about reality; he does not try to present a full-blown God argument. What he does present is a clear indication that consciousness cannot be easily reduced to brain chemistry and nothing more. Newberg actually does make the argument that what he has discovered could well bolster belief in some notion of the undifferentiated unity of which the mystics speak.[1] What Newberg claims he has proven is that religious experience is real. It is not merely a trick of the mind, but something that really happens in the brain and can be studied and understood:

A skeptic might suggest that a biological origin to all spiritual longings and experiences, including the universal human yearning to connect with something divine, could be explained as a delusion caused by the chemical misfiring of a bundle of nerve cells. But... after years of scientific study, and careful consideration of the neurological process that has evolved to allow us humans to transcend material existence and acknowledge and connect with a deeper, more spiritual part of ourselves perceived of as an absolute, universal reality that connects us to all that is.[2]

Newberg and his colleague Eugene D'Aquili[3] have been involved in this research for many years. They use a SPECT camera, which stands for *single photon emission computed topography.* They trace a radioactive dye through the bloodstream. The dye collects in brain cells, and they know that these are the cells most in use at the time because that's where the blood is going. They find unusual activity in the *posterior superior parietal lobe* (PSPL) of subjects who are meditating. This area helps us discern up from down, judge angles and distances, and negotiate landscape. In order to perform these functions the PSPL must keep strict tabs upon the distinction between what is "me" and what is "not-me." How could it negotiate landscape if it could not distinguish us from the things around us? For this reason Newberg and D'Aquili rename the area the OAA (orientation association area). The two researchers find that this area (OAA or PSPL), which otherwise never rests, is strangely inactive while the meditation is in progress. After examining the descriptions "mystics" and those meditating reported, researchers concluded that the area was working, but it wasn't getting any data. That would explain the sense mystics make of their experiences when they describe feeling *an undifferentiated unity of all things.* While skeptics might read this and think "Ah ha! There's the trick of the mind that makes it seem there is some spiritual reality," Newberg sees much more to the issue than that.[4] Praying Franciscan nuns had similar findings, but their experience was describes as "closeness to God" rather than

Joseph Hinman

undifferentiated unity. Newberg argues that the research proves that
these experiences are not merely tricks of the mind, wishful thinking or
some form of "psychology," but are instead "observable neurological
events... mystical experience is biologically, observably and
scientifically real."[5]

Skeptics are quick to argue that the RE is clearly the product of
brain chemistry and results from the PSPL malfunctioning, thus it is
clearly an accident or epiphenomenal; after all, all of consciousness
itself is epiphenomenal. This is a misbegotten assumption that Newberg
disproves. While skeptics try to ground the origin of religion in this
"misfiring," their argument is merely begging the question. Newberg
points out that the use of brain chemistry is really the only way God
could communicate with sentient flesh-and-blood creatures. Our
consciousness is transmitted through brain chemistry; this is the way
we work. The argument is like saying the function of car antenna (or
for television, a digital converter box) is a mechanism which makes the
instrument function; therefore, it is the rabbit ears or converter box that
produces the programming. This is my analogy, not Newberg's. But he
does say:

> ...Tracing spiritual experience to neurological behavior does not
> disprove its realness. If God does exist, for example, and if He
> appeared to you in some incarnation, you would have no way of
> experiencing His presence, except as part of a neurologically
> generated rendition of reality. You would need auditory processing to
> hear his voice, visual processing to see His face, and cognitive
> processing to make sense of his message. Even if he spoke to you
> mystically, without words, you would need cognitive functions to
> comprehend his meaning, and input from the brain's emotional
> centers to fill you with rapture and awe. Neurology makes it clear:
> there is no other way for God to get into your head except through the
> brain's neural pathways. Correspondingly, God cannot exist as a
> concept or as reality anyplace else but in your mind. In this sense,
> both spiritual experiences and experiences of a more ordinary

material nature are made real to the mind in the very same way
—through the processing powers of the brain and the cognitive
functions of the mind. Whatever the ultimate nature of spiritual
experience might be —whether it is in fact an actual perception of
spiritual reality or merely an interpretation of sheer neurological
function— all that is meaningful in human spirituality happens in the
mind. In other words, the mind is mystical by default.[6]

Newberg is not saying that there can't be a God, nor is he saying that
we understand all reality and can rule out the spiritual. He is saying that
all we know of reality is mediated; what we take to be the unvarnished
world is just a rendition of the unvarnished and that's all it can be.
Where I take issue with him is in his assertion that even mystical
experience itself is mediated. In my view the actual experience at the
mystical level is direct experience of the divine. But any attempt to
understand it or put it into words is mediated by our brain's rendition of
the world. Thus the only way we can ever empirically comprehend the
real is through the mystical; to discuss it we must use analogical
language and cast our experience into the realm of metaphor. Trusting
metaphor to interpret the world might make many people nervous, as
many are skeptical of the subjective. But this is the nature of the case
for all knowledge, and moreover, metaphor is basically how we explain
everything. We are separated from the things in themselves by our
understanding and perceptions of the world.

Atheists tend to scoff at religious experience anyway because they
dichotomize between perceptions gained through scientific means and
perceptions "off the cuff." The latter are to be scoffed at and rejected as
"subjective," the former are to be sought as somehow guaranteed to be
valid even though they are still filtered through the "construct" created
by the brain. The reaction of naturalistic thinkers to all manner of
phenomenological apprehension has been to write it off as the
subjective (thus untrustworthy) residue of outmoded misconceptions.
One such misconception is the concept of the spiritual. Naturalists tend

to write off consciousness as a whole, content to allow their reductionism to saw off anything they can't study through their methods. A common atheist assertion is that brain creates mind; this is evident since any sort of brain injury changes the nature of mind, thus mind is just a trick of the light, and brain is all there is. Thus experience is a side-effect of the autonomic system and other systems of the brain. Daniel Dennett argued that consciousness is a side-effect of brain function.[7] Newberg demonstrates the foolishness of this view. He does not speak of "holism" but what he says about the brain/mind dichotomy would fit in with that viewpoint. Yes, brain creates mind, but that does not mean that mind reduces to brain. The two are inseparable, but they are no more the same thing than are hardware and software. He uses the analogy of waves. We can no more separate brain from mind than we can separate wave from the energy that produces it. Without the energy, the wave would lie flat; without the energy the wave would have no expression.[8] In my own view spirit = mind, mind = consciousness. The soul is symbolic of the overall life of the individual in relation to God. In other words, "soul" is a symbolic term; it is something we are, and not something we have. "He is a lost soul," "seventeen souls were lost that day," and other such phrases exemplify what I mean. I make the case that the Bible more often than not employs the phrase in this way. The soul is a way of speaking about the overall direction of a person's life in relation to its final destiny in God. It is not a little ghost in the machine. I do not blame atheists for their assertion that such notions are outmoded and unscientific. They are. We need not maintain the notion of a Casper the Friendly Ghost inside us that lives on after we are gone. We need not think of spirit as some special substance that is just too special for science to discover. These are outmoded concepts; they are unnecessary to maintain a concept of life after death.

We do not know what consciousness is per se; science has not come close to pinning it down. Nevertheless, most science rules out the *ghost in the machine* as a philosophical fallacy. I agree with them. Mind is spirit, and spirit is mind. If there is spiritual force or power or

substance in this life, it could as easily be the force of God's mind
rather than a discreet substance. Spirit, or mind, in biological organisms
is created by the brain; that does not make it reducible to the brain nor
does it mean it has nothing more than epiphenomenal status. The fact
that the two are inseparable does not mean the two are the same thing.
Just as the wave and the energy that makes the wave are inseparable
they are still not the same thing. What of life after death? If we have to
think of life after death as the survival of an independent agent that can
move around under its own power then one can hardly see how
consciousness could survive apart from brain. But if we think of it as
not a "place" where one lives, but a larger framework of consciousness
which one joins, "God himself," then it might be more intelligible. It is
beyond the scope of this essay to speculate about the nature of heaven.
The only point I wish to make here, and not to belabor it, is that
accepting a neurological basis for spirituality need not eliminate or
"disprove" anything generic to the Christian faith. No biblical passage
says that the spirit is a Casper the Friendly Ghost-type agent floating
around out of the body. My view is not an abandonment of the spirit.
We are spiritual beings, but the spirit is consciousness, the mind. I
accept the idea that consciousness is a basic property of nature because
it is irreducible. Thus consciousness in humans may be the result of
brain chemistry, but it is not identical or reducible to brain chemistry
and nothing more. It is the intangible dimension that Newberg proves is
necessary for one to understand reality or think. Perhaps it is
complexity that produces consciousness. If consciousness is a basic
property of nature, than when a certain level of complexity is achieved
consciousness is born. Maybe there are different levels of
consciousness. Thus rocks have their own rocky consciousness that
doesn't do much by our estimation. Trees have a bit more
consciousness but still can't write a poem or go to the moon, and then
we have a high level of consciousness but still not divine. This is not
the venue for this discussion. I only mention these as hypothetical
possibilities. For the sake of my experience arguments, I will assume

that consciousness emerges at a certain level of complexity just as heat results at a certain degree of friction.

What is this intangible dimension that Newberg proves is necessary for one to understand reality? How does he prove this? By the nature of the way in which the brain understands the world, as seen in what he calls "brain architecture." By overviewing this structure of brain interaction with world, he shows that the naïve empiricist view of "objective" observation of the world is outmoded and inaccurate. Our raw observations of the world around are not "plain, unvarnished," "literal" views of the world.

> The medieval German mystic Meister Eckhart lived hundreds of years before the science of neurology was born. Yet it seems he had intuitively grasped one of the fundamental principles of the discipline: What we think of as reality is only a rendition of reality that is created by the brain. Our modern understanding of the brain's perceptual powers bears him out. Nothing enters consciousness whole. There is no direct, objective experience of reality. All the things the mind perceives —all thoughts, feelings, hunches, memories, insights, desires, and revelations— have been assembled piece by piece by the processing powers of the brain from the swirl of neural blimps. The idea that our experiences of reality —all our experiences, for that matter— are only "secondhand" depictions of what may or may not be objectively real, raises some profound questions about the most basic truths of human existence and the neurological nature of spiritual experience. For example our experiment with Tibetan meditators and Franciscan nuns showed that the events they considered spiritual were, in fact, associated with observable neurological activity. In a reductionist sense this could support the argument that religious experience is only imagined neurologically, that God is physically 'all in your mind.' But a full understanding of the way in which the brain and the mind assemble and experience reality suggests a very different view. [9]

He then goes through a shopping list of brain function, demonstrating how the brain apprehends the world. He covers the autonomic system with the arousal and quiescent systems. He discusses the relation of this system to spiritual experience as the relation of the heart rate to meditation is crucial in many forms of meditation. He talks about autonomic states and spiritual experience. Hyper quiescence and hyper arousal are states of relaxation and excitation. These are results of both meditation and worship experiences. He covers the limbic system that relates emotional states to higher thoughts and concepts. He calls the limbic system "the transmitter of God."[10] This is how we can put together associations of emotional involvement with theological concepts. These same functions are connected to animal survival and finding food. Newberg is not saying that this proves there's nothing there to sense in religious experience, no more so than he is saying that there is really no food for animals to find in the forest. All of this is just describing the processes and apparatus by which God communes with us; it does not in any sense demonstrate a lack of veracity to the experiences. He talks about the hypothalamus as the "master controller" for the autonomic nervous system.[11] He does discuss other parts of the brain, but the major focus for our purpose is what he calls "cognitive operators." This is how the mind understands the world, Newberg tells us. It is significant that he speaks of "mind" here and not "brain." He's clearly saying this higher-level understanding is put together out of the bits of information gathered through all the other sensory inputs.

Newberg uses a very apt analogy; he refers to a robot constructed in one of the first robotic experiments. The robot took a whole day to perform its task of moving across the room and opening a door. The second time it tried it could not do it at all. The reason it took so long was because every time it moved it had to re-photograph the entire room and then re analyze where it was in the room. The room kept changing, as it got closer to the door, so it had to re-align itself in relation to everything every time it took a step. It couldn't open the

Joseph Hinman

door at all the second time because the researchers put a big x on the door, and it had not been programmed to understand that doors could be marked with X, so it did not recognize the door. We are like that robot except in one crucial way; we apprehend the room through sensory mechanisms that allow us to distinguish ourselves from the room. The difference is, we do not have to rethink everything we know every time we take a step, we are capable of extrapolation from our knowledge to the fact that doors could have X's on them. He does not put it this way, but one could say, we are capable of making leaps of faith all the time. We can look beyond the X and see the door, we can make the assumption that doors can have X's and be confident in it. It is these leaps of faith, metaphors for example, that enable us to put information together and understand. Newberg does put this in terms of metaphor and symbol. The empiricist might think our perceptions take literal photographs of what is there, and thus the more literal our understanding, the more accurate. Oddly enough, Newberg shows it is the opposite. Being literal, exacting, empirical, does not give us the truth of the world; being able to make metaphors, extrapolate, guess, and take leaps of faith gives us navigation skills in the world. [12]

The brain is arranged such that collective structures contain various functions that Newberg and D'Aquili call "cognitive operators." These enable us to make "leaps of faith." They speak of *the holistic operator*, which enables us to group component parts and comprehend a whole structure. The *reductionist operator* does the opposite; it allows us to see the whole broken down into component parts. "The abstractive operator, results from the operations of the parietal lobe in the brain's left hemisphere," allowing the formation of general concepts from individual facts. There's a *quantitative operator*, a *causal operator* (a binary operator that enables dichotomized perception such as "me"/"not-me"), an *existential operator* that actually allows us to judge the reality of events (this is why we can understand that jokes are pretend and hypothetical without having to be told so) and an *emotional value* operator that "exists to assign an emotional valence to all elements of perception and cognition." In other words, this one allows us to put it all together and sort it all out. This is why we can hear a joke, "A man in New York is run over by a car every fifteen minutes, and boy is he getting tired of it," without going "Oh that poor man! Why can't they stop it?"[13] All of these operations and functions come together to form man's basic myth-making ability. Through these functions we can interpret a feeling in such a way as to understand something of the divine. We are outfitted to know God. We translate early myth-making, which goes back as far as we can find traces of the Neanderthal (65,000 years). We find the evidence of concepts such as magic, afterlife, and spiritual forces. Certainly these qualities have always been present in modern human beings as we know them. It would be easy for an atheist or skeptic to write off this argument as indicative of some ancient mistake whereby mankind conjured up a lot of nonsense to explain that which he could not explain by scientific means. This outlook is commonly asserted by atheists in attempts to explain religion. Yet at this point, Newberg plugs in a much more sophisticated understanding of mythology via Joseph Campbell. As with the idea of an afterlife as a means of coping with the harsh realities of death, mythology enables us to find meaning in the world and to extrapolate and thus transcend the literal harsh realities to a point where we feel at home in the universe, a universe of value and meaning. Myth shows us "what is most important, and what in terms of the inner life is more deeply and profoundly true. The power of myth lies beneath its literal interpretation in the ability of its universal symbols and themes to connect us with the most essential parts of ourselves in ways that logic and reason alone cannot."[14] The point is that this whole myth constructing function is not just some vestige that should be discarded in favor of machine-like efficient mathematical abilities, or emotionless logic; even ordinary sense perceptions require this extrapolation ability to allow us to function in the world. That means that the most atheistic and naturalistic viewpoint of reductionism could not interpret the world for us without the myth-making function or the leaps of faith that allow us to see the door rather than the X. The situation with the "God Pod" is more complex than the original term "God part of the brain" implied (or more so than the term "God Pod" for that matter). It is not just one part of the brain; it's not just that several centers somehow "register" God talk. It's more that the overall nature of human brain architecture is "designed" or at least functions over all to use religious type thinking (metaphor, analogy, faith) even in ordinary navigation in the world.

Several writers have tried to show that religion can be accounted for naturalistically. Scott Atran *(In Gods We Trust),* Pascal Boyer *(And Man Creates God)* and David Sloan Wilson *(Darwin's Cathedral),* Matthew Alpers, *(The God Part of the Brain)*; but the most famous among them is probably Daniel Dennett, in his work *Breaking the Spell.* Dennett doesn't actually say point blank that the naturalistic nature of religion disproves it. He is sounding a call to study religion scientifically without giving it a special pass to protect people's sacred cows. I have no problem with that, per se. The problem is that atheists have a tendency to tease out an innuendo that since religion can be accounted for through evolutionary processes, this disproves any "supernatural origin" for it. Newberg as well as other researchers can account for the sense of undifferentiated unity of all things of which so many mystics speak. As Carter (2002) summarizes: the mechanism that focuses attention remains on, and the sense of the outside world is shut off, so one is in effect sensing one's self as all there is. This is the result of prolonged meditation. [15]

> There seems then to be a plausible mechanistic account for each of the core qualities of mystical or spiritual experience. Put very crudely: pure consciousness emerges when a tension is maintained in a perceptual vacuum; 'oneness' is created by the closedown of the boundary making parts of the self; ecstasy comes from turning off the right amygdala; and the sense of presence is formed by the splitting of the self system into two. [16]

Don't forget to switch off that right amygdala before you go to bed. I guess that "splitting the self system into two" is a technical term of brain anatomy. Do they really understand the self-system? Can one really switch it off or split it in two like turning on or off a light switch? Supposedly this all results from meditation, but not all RE happens in connection with meditation. Sometimes these things can be instant. Several of the examples (see the Introduction's example of the little girl and Chapter 2's example of Bucke) of mystical experiences, the experiences just came on people. One has the feeling this is not the whole story. Nevertheless, Hick (2006) compiles a short list of the major arguments proposed as to the neurological causes of RE:

1. Epileptic seizures and frontal lobe stimulation by the Presinger helmet cause religious visions.
2. Psychotropic drugs cause various forms of religious experience.
3. 'Pure Consciousness,' consciousness of the void, emptiness, *sunyata* is caused by consciousness continuing after cutting off the perceptual input.
4. The sense of unity with all reality is caused by closing down the awareness of the bodily boundaries of the individual.
5. The sense of the presence of God or other supernatural beings is caused by splitting of the self-system into two, one half seeing the other half as a distant entity. [17]

This seems like a very impressive case, and the reductionists make it sound as though they have really uncovered a one to one correspondence between brain and mind. Punch here, get this experience, and punch over there get this other experience. If you want the feeling of God's presence stimulate this area, if you want the sense of undifferentiated unity stimulate this other area over there. In reality, however, such is not the case. This is essentially Hick's argument. Such researchers are not well versed in theology or the study of mysticism, and thus they think that unusual experiences structured loosely in religious language constitutes "mystical experience." They are missing the whole nature of what RE is and what it does because they are trying to formulate this simplistic argument from sign. That's exactly what their argument is, an argument from sign. It's not a demonstration of the naturalistic causality of RE; it's a correlation between two events, one supposedly causing the other, but not necessarily producing authentic mystical experience. What is produced is an odd experience loosely structured in religious language. I don't include Newberg or D'Aquili in my broad swipe at "reductionists," but even they exhibit some of these tendencies yet to a lesser extent because they know to work with real mystics. The association between the physiological and RE is the crux of the whole naturalistic argument. It's quite common to hear skeptics say, "If you damage the brain, our body stops working, so we are just nothing more than collections of brain function and extensions of brain function." The more sophisticated argument made by scientific researchers isn't that different from the same argument. Ramachandran (1998) links seeming mystical experiences with epileptic grand mal seizures.[18] I quote a study in Chapter 3 (Studies) from Lukoff and Lu, which shows that mystical experience is not related to epilepsy.[19] Indeed, it would be absurd to assume that for all the 350 studies, all of these subjects are epileptic or have something wrong with them and no researcher thought to check that out. Newberg disregards the idea that RE is the result of epilepsy or exhaustion, drugs or hallucination or any other aspect such as this that might be triggered by any other aspect of brain dysfunction. He argues that delusional people return from such states understanding their incoherence, but mystical visions are coherent and meaningful and mystics never back off from the idea that they were shown something meaningful.[20] Ramarchandran draws no conclusion about the existence of God. He is merely giving a descriptive analysis of findings. He backs away from saying this disproves God. He also lists a host of other conditions such as temporal lobe personality that cause mystical experience (supposedly) besides epilepsy.[21] If is far-fetched, however, to assert that everyone who has such an experience is either sick or has some form of mental abnormality such that they are hallucinating or having some form of brain dysfunction. After all, the study findings show that mystics tend to be healthy both physically and mentally, to be successful, accomplished, not delusional, as demonstrated in Chapter 3.

Dr. Michael Presinger is able to produce such experiences in subjects without their having epilepsy by stimulating that part of the brain through the use of a helmet of sorts that delivers a mild stimulation.[22] This list is a set of vague generalizations that assume that mystical experiencers are doing transcendental meditation. It might hint that some experiences are the result of something related to these things, but it doesn't explain the spontaneous experiences of people not involved in meditation at all. For example, what guarantee do we have that they felt the "presence of God" in the same sense that mystics sense it, and not just any vague sense of presence that they took to be "mystically seeming" because after putting on the helmet they are told they are going to feel God? If they never had a mystical experience before, they have nothing to compare with that experience. Perhaps someone who actually had such an experience before would feel that it is entirely different. One could theorize that it's the meditative techniques that turn it on. There are two reasons not to buy this. I've already stressed that not all mystics have their experiences when they mediate or even always when they pray. The girl discussed in the Introduction had her experience just by looking out the window. Secondly, Newberg used the same methods to study nuns as well as monks. These two groups had experiences that registered on different parts of the brain. The nuns were praying and the Buddhist monks were mediating. The two sets of parishioners had both similar and very different parts of the brain activated. The major difference was the nuns had more activity in language centers, because their prayers focused attention on words. Nuns had more activity in the right hemisphere, which would be involved with meaning of words. Both groups showed activity in the frontal lobe and in a part that enables one to stay attentive. Yet the two describe their senses in very different ways. The

Joseph Hinman

Buddhists felt pure consciousness, while the nuns felt the presence of God (In case anyone is interested, the nuns were pleased with the findings, didn't particularly care what they were, and their faith was not at all shaken.[23])

Hick argues against the idea that pure consciousness (emptiness) is caused by consciousness continuing after shutting down the input (number 3 on his list above). The researchers (Newberg and D'Aquili) at this point are treating a certain part of the brain as though it were an autonomous intelligence engaged in a project to collect and interpret reality. According to Hick, who is no expert on the brain, there is no one area that is responsible for this task. He quotes Rose, who is an expert: "There is nowhere in the brain a site at which neurology becomes psychology... if there were such an area neuroscience has failed to discover it."[24] Moreover, as Hick continues, there is a further problem in that describing the Zen experience as "nothingness" is really a misconception. This means that the conclusion Newberg and D'Aquili reached is a problem in that they are matching up the wrong indications of what the brain is doing. The Zen masters don't say that they find true emptiness but actually fullness. This is a paradoxical statement, but what they mean is that there is no true nothingness but a void of cultural constructs. This state is:

> ...a deep emptying of consciousness, of the *former subjective distinction and personal attachment...* this is a zero state of the personal psyche... it means that looking out from inside the zero of this state, all things will then be perceived objectively just as they really are (Austin 1999, 570-1). (Italics Austin's preserved in Hick). There is no reason to suppose that this is caused by a slowing in the posterior superior parietal lobe, producing a blank consciousness.[25]

Again, with Newbergs's findings, the same kind of scan (SPECT) of the same areas of the brain found the same kind of changes but the results were very different. This means there is no one to one correspondence between the brain and the RE we experience. The reductionism would have us believe that if you punch part A you get the feelings that come from punching part A. This sets up a powerful argument for chemical determinism and naturalistic causes for RE. But such is not the case. While it is true not all the results were the same, the difference Newberg accounts for by understanding the verbal aspect of prayer over meditation; the nuns focused on the meaning of the words, the monks "blanked out." (see above). Nevertheless, that doesn't explain the difference in the sensations felt; the monks felt "emptiness," pure consciousness, the nuns felt "presence" the togetherness with God. That argument by Hick takes on number 3 and 4 on the list above together.

The fifth aspect dealt with by Hick (list above) is the idea that the sense of presence comes from splitting the sense of self in two, sensing the self as an objective reality apart from the first person "I" sense that we always have. "Splitting of the self-system" supposedly causes this. I'm still struck by how like a light switch it all seems to these researchers. Hick argues this is the result of Persinger's helmet stimulating certain areas; it strikes Hick as indicative of how expert these researchers are in their own areas and how inexpert they are in religious terms. Hick argues that these researchers are equating RE with unusual experiences structured in religious terms but they are not really dealing with the experiences mystics talk about. He says this is because Persinger, for example, always goes to great lengths to report visions and feelings of supernatural beings, both God and Satan and visions of Jesus and Mary; all sorts of things that his helmet-wearing subjects have seen or felt. But these are not necessarily what mystics talk about. Most mystics discount visions and few mystics have them. Most mystics don't sense an evil presence, although a subject discussed by James did feel such an evil presence but it's ambiguous what that person thought it was (see previous chapter on Proudfoot). These examples, rather than being good examples of science disproving religious experience, are really good examples of reductionism's ability to lose phenomena. This may sound like great scientific research because it uses high-tech gadgetry and advanced knowledge of brain anatomy. In reality, as a scientific study, it basically fails Social-Research Methods 101. First, because there is no control group, no administration of the M scale or any other measurement of mystical experience, there's no way to actually prove that these subjects had mystical experiences. It sounds like they had strange experiences but not necessarily "mystical" ones. The examples that Hick quotes include visions of Jesus figures. They do include a sense of divine presence. But there is no follow-up to see if their lives change or if they experienced any sort of transformative effects on a long-term basis. For that matter Newberg's work seems to suffer in that regard too, although with him, since he uses monks and nuns, one can be assured there is a much greater likelihood of such outcomes since these are authentic religious adherents who live lifestyles conductive to the mystical experience and presumably spend a great deal of their time cultivating this sort of experience. Hick makes the point that Presinger and Ramachandran are neurologists studying people who come to them because they have problems. They are not studying actual religious adherents whose lives are oriented toward cultivating the mystical, as is Newberg. This could make a profound difference. But the reductionist mentality just says the experience lines up with the stimulus. It's argument from sign: we see sign, we assume causality, case closed.They make no attempt to consider the context or nature of the experience.

The things Newberg says about myth-making and about the neurological basis of religion would be taken by many as a stark indication that religion is just another evolutionary accident that wound up benefiting us. What he says about myth-making giving us hope to face the stark realities of death, especially when we consider the nature of the brain as it began to reflect upon itself and to create the mind, furnishes a powerful argument. The problem with this kind of thinking is that it assumes that the basic reason for religion is to explain things.

The atheist approach to understanding belief is empiricist. We want to prove an idea we believe in, so we look for indications in the universe that it's true. We wish to understand why water periodically falls from the sky, and every time it does the clouds come and get black. So we invent the only reason we can think of: big guy up in the sky sends water down because he likes us. We can keep him happy by sacrificing sheep to him; he will keep raining on our crops. Of course this is too simplistic to even refute. Religion exists because people have a sense of the numinous. The atheist has to approach belief as primitive failed science. Newberg is telling us that this sense of the numinous is bound up with the very structure of our brains; we have to sense this and we have to make up myths to make sense of it. It is not an attempt to understand the physical workings of the world, although of course the early version of such attempts would draw upon religion, but it is actually an attempt to understand our place in the world, to make peace with death. Atheists tend to approach belief as empirically demonstrated by the contents of it. In other words, they look at the arguments from religious experience as justifying belief because the experience itself is a miracle. It's so amazing that anyone would sense God's presence that this must be the basis of the argument, and the reason why it would be an argument at all is because it is something wildly amazing that can't happen without miraculous intervention of the divine. That's why a naturalistic explanation is so fatal to religious belief, or so they think. Matthew Alper writes *The God Part of the Brain* and atheists react as though he's saved them from eternal fate. E. O. Wilson shows us what they think his findings prove: "Alper uses a Socratic technique to brilliantly and flawlessly argue that our concepts of spirit and God are derived from the mechanics of our brain... enormously important... full of scientific and philosophical truths."[26] It's so wonderful he bravely says what Newberg says. Except the atheists treat his work as though he is somehow answering Newberg. So again Wilson, as with Dennett, doesn't actually say "this disproves religion," but the innuendo is there. Lest anyone think this is the natural inference, it simply stands to reason they are thinking in terms of beating a miracle argument.

Demonstrating a naturalistic origin for the experience does not destroy the argument. First, let's remember that no such naturalistic origin is proven even by genetic links; all that proves is that God used genetics in creation, and that we are flesh and blood. Secondly, the argument from co-determinate or God correlate doesn't turn upon the miraculous or amazing nature of the experiences, nor does it turn upon the actual "feel" of the experiences. It turns only upon the logical nature of inference related to the content and outcome of the experiences. The content is related to ideas of the divine. The content is God-oriented. The outcome often draws one to religion; the experience is the basis for the existence of religion. It is logical to construe the existence of a state of affairs from the fitness of the organism for that state of affairs; Pinker will make this argument which I will cover below. Given the origin of religion, this is what we should expect from the divine. We should expect that God would give us a trace and a connection through a sense of presence in the world, and perhaps we should expect that it would be connected to brain chemistry and genetics since that is how our understanding works. But, the argument doesn't turn on being able to say, "This is a miracle that people have this experience because it couldn't happen unless God did this directly." That is not the argument. I will argue that there are unique aspects of religious experience that couldn't happen without divine presence being involved. We must discuss what the supernatural is in order to answer this question. The supernatural is about ontology, but it is also the power of God to vivify human nature and raise it to a higher level. These experiences do exactly what the supernatural is supposed to do. Since they are actually mystical experience itself, and that was the original conceit of the supernatural, they are literally the supernatural, no question about it. They are it.

That these experiences can be induced naturally is really not surprising nor does it undermine the argument. It would if the argument was a proof of God in an absolute sense, but since I claim only rational warrant, such experiences constitute a rational warrant for belief:

1. The content is usually religious.
2. The effects draw people into belief.
3. It fits what we should expect of God.
4. No other aspect of life produces this effect; no other aspect has the data to back it up.

When compared with other forms of support, even when smoking is controlled for, religious smokers do better than non-religious. We only get these results from religious experience. This means there is validity to religion that justifies considering these phenomena to be indicative of the co-determinate of God consciousness and, thus, rationally warrant belief. If one is determined to construe such phenomena as signs of the veracity of religion, it is not illogical to do so. The atheist reading of religious motivation turns upon the need to explain something. They assume religion came into being to explain workings of the natural world which ancient man could not account for with his limited understanding. So he made up fanciful explanations of a big powerful father in the sky. Modern atheists make those same assumptions; that's why they expect the naturalistic origin of RE to destroy the argument. But if they need some unique element for which their naturalism cannot account, this argument should be it. There is no other experience that is long-term, positive, transformational, not degenerative and not induced by a foreign substance. This is actually something they cannot account for naturalistically. Yet the argument is not that these experiences and their results are miracles. Rather the point is that they can be rationally construed as encounters with the divine due to the nature of the results of the encounter. Of course we have to discuss the concept of miracles in order to understand why I say the experiences aren't miracles per se. That's for another time; I have to save something for the next book. The final point following the four above for rational warrant is:

5. The argument does not turn upon empirical proof, but upon the nature of the decision-making paradigm

Since it is not a "proof" but the construal of a rational warrant, the only thing that really matters is to understand how and why the nature of the paradigm sets up the "God construal" as the most logical construal given the facts. The atheists want to shun the God conclusion because it requires commitment to a metaphysical construct that contradicts their "one-dimensional" worldview. I say "one-dimensional" because the naturalistic construct requires that we evade any other choices, and while harping upon empirical evidence turns upon a total lack of any empirical evidence to back its claim (yet nonetheless insists that it understands all of reality and that any other form of the real can be sawed off and done away). On the other hand, this is a straw-man argument on the atheists' part since they construct their own view of what they think "supernatural" is all about.

What are we talking about when we talk about the supernatural?

Natural and supernatural are not juxtapositions; they are not antitheses of each other. They are two sides or facets of the same harmony. We should be willing to find supernatural in the natural, and that's just what Maslow (1970) says we find:

> Now that may be taken as a frank admission of a naturalistic psychological origin, except that it involves a universal symbology which is not explicable through merely naturalistic means. How is it that all humans come to hold these same archetypical symbols? The "primitives" viewed and understood a sense of transformation, which gave them integration into the universe. This is crucial for human development. They sensed a power in the numinous, that is the origin of religion.

...I have spoken of unitive perception, i.e., fusion of the B-realm
with the D-realm, fusion of the eternal with the temporal, the sacred
with the profane, etc. Someone has called this "the measureless gap
between the poetic perception of reality and prosaic, unreal
commonsense." Anyone who cannot perceive the sacred, the eternal,
the symbolic, is simply blind to an aspect of reality, as I think I have
amply demonstrated elsewhere...[27]

Paradoxically, Maslow was an atheist, but an atheist who was aware of
other concepts of supernatural than just the atheist straw-man version.
The argument for RE turns on the rational warrant for belief found in
the believer's sense of transformation, and in the *prima facie* nature of
the warrant. That is why no amount of neurological data can reduce the
divine to the mundane or dissect the transcendent. No amount of
naturalistic ideology can empty heaven of its sacred nature. It is not that
these experiences have to be miracles and can't be understood in other
way but to resort to God as an explanation, but that if we take them to
be indicative of God we are rationally warranted to do so because they
do exactly what we expect the touch of God to do in our lives, and they
do this in a way that can't be reduced to naturalistic phenomena
without losing the phenomenon.

As said in Chapter 2, the various studies indicate that RE results in
long-term positive effects. Nothing else produces these kinds of effects;
at least, there is no data to indicate that anything does. We should
expect God to renovate lives; we should expect integration points into
meaning in life, and revitalized inner lives, as a result of contact with
the divine. This is what we find in religious experience; we do not find
it in other areas, even in areas where logically it should exist. Take the
example of social-support groups. One would theorize that if religion is
just a naturalistic development as a result of evolutionary forces (which
it is, but it is more than that, too) one would find that any sort of
positive support group should give one the same health benefits as
religious belief. Such is not the case. As shown, even when smoking is

controlled for, the religious experiencing believer is better off than people of other groups. This is true even in comparing religious believers to humanistic care groups and ideologically harmonious political groups or any other kind of group. No other support group offers the kind of long-term positive effects, as does religious participation. This is true of either participation or experience. The difference in participation and experience is that between church attendances vs. actually experiencing God's presence. Even just going to church seems to have a positive effect upon health even when one never "feels" a thing. It's not that this is a miracle; that is not the argument. The argument is that this is what we should expect from contact with the divine, transformation. Thus the argument turns upon sign. It turns upon the satisfaction of a *prima facie* burden to produce some valid reason why we should believe. We should believe because experience of the divine pans out as it fits the criteria we should expect form the co-determinate.

The extent to which atheists rely upon reductionistic assertions about consciousness and brain chemistry (any sort of experience is just chemical determinism brought on as a side-effect of brain function —i.e. a mistake and a lie) is seen in the controversy around the book by Matthew Alper, *The God Part of the Brain.* His book is hailed by no less than E.O.Wilson! "Excellent reading for every college student."[28] "All Six billion plus inhabitants of earth should be in possession of this book," claims John Scoggins Ph.D. "This is an essential book for those in search of a scientific understanding of man's religious nature," writes Elena Rusyn of Harvard Medical School. The arguments he makes are simple. He assumes at face value that if there are some physiological transitions of religious ideas in the brain, then the idea of a soul and an afterlife are disproved. "As sure as I now was that there was no such thing as a transcendent soul, I still found myself plagued by that more essential problem of God's existence."[29] What is the basis for this astounding bit of certainty that has eluded humanity for thousands of years? It is because he accepts, without referencing a single major theologian, the idea that all religious traditions around the world teach that the soul is immaterial. Yet chemicals change our perceptions and transmit ideas, thus thought is a chemical in the head, hence we can't have an immaterial soul. "The fact that I am conscious self, my allegedly immortal soul was susceptible to the effects of chemical (physical) substances convinced me that human consciousness must be a physical entity..."[30] The pioneer in the field, Newberg, tells us we can't draw such simplistic conclusions, yet where are the prominent scientific figures such as Wilson to laud Newberg? Newberg tells us that a neurological basis for RE need not be construed as disproof of any sort of religious viewpoint; one notices that there is no statement by Wilson or these other members of the atheist club raving about the greatness of Newberg's work. Yet Newberg is the one who actually did the research and made the connections. It is clear that the "new atheists" think this material (God Pod) gives them some ultimate strangle-hold on religion.

Alper's major argument is nothing more than assertion based upon argument from sign. But it's an assertion Newberg backs. The real difference is in what conclusions each man draws from the facts. Alper writes:

> For every physical characteristic that is universal to a species, there must exist some gene or set of genes responsible for the emergence of that particular trait. For example, the fact that all cats possess whiskers means that somewhere within a cat's chromosomes there must exist "whisker" genes. Of our own species, that all humans possess a nose in the middle of our face means that somewhere within our chromosomes there must exist "nose" genes that instruct our emerging bodies to develop one in that very place. It's not, for instance, as if a nose can develop anywhere on one's body, only by mere coincidence, it always ends up on our face. Apparently, humans are genetically "hard-wired" to develop in a very specific and particular way....

Actually this is not true. As will be seen below, yes there is a connection between everything we do and some form of genetic influence or some connection with genes in a very general sense, but that in no way means that "for every physical characteristic that is universal to the species there must exist a gene or a set of genes." The problem is the difference in what it means to speak of "a gene for behavior X" vs "a set of genes." There's a huge gap between chemical determinism and "a set of genes." As Newberg says:

> Essentially, what I'm suggesting is that humans are innately "hard-wired" to perceive a spiritual reality. We are "hard-wired" to believe in forces that transcend the limitations of this, our physical reality. Most controversial of all, if what I'm suggesting is true, it would imply that God is not necessarily something that exists "out there," beyond and independent of us, but rather as the product of an inherited perception, the manifestation of an evolutionary adaptation that exists within the human brain. And why would our species have evolved such a seemingly abstract trait? In order to enable us to deal with our species' unique and otherwise debilitating awareness of death.[31]

In Alper's thinking, like that of many atheists one encounters, universal means genetic and genetic means "hard-wired." That is, in Alper's view, genetic equals hard-wired. In reality, genetic does not mean hard-wired necessarily. He does not define that term; however, a behavior related to genetics has to be either an adaptation or a side-effect of an adaptation or a set of adaptations; being a side-effect of genetic behavior —also known as a "spandrel"— it is not "hard-wired." It's a side-effect of something that may or may not be "hard-wired." We humans have the ability to veto choices we make in behavior. I can decide to get up off the couch and go write on this manuscript. I can then decide I don't wish to get up. I don't get up if I choose not to. I am not compelled to get up just because the thought came into my head. If choices were hard-wired I would get up just by thinking about it. But the behaviors it takes to get up are definitely related to my genetic structure. These behaviors are not hard-wired. Moreover, there are plenty of scientists who do not think that religion is an adaptation. The adaptationist view is only one school. The counter-argument among evolutionary theorists is that religion is a "spandrel" or a side-effect of genetic structure but not produced by a gene for that behavior. There are plenty of scientists who disagree with the data on the "God pod" and don't believe that there is a "God module" or that religious behavior is inherited through a specific gene or a part of the brain. Lee A Kirkpatrick, director of graduate studies in psychology at William and Mary, tells us:

> In sum, the moderate heritability of religion, like the identification of a particular brain region, associated with religious experience, tells us virtually nothing about whether religion is the result of an adaptive evolved mechanism designed to produce it. In particular neither should be construed as evidence for an adaptive religion mechanism or system.[32]

Steven Pinker, eminent professor of psychology at MIT, does not believe the explanations offered as to why a "God pod" would be an adaptation. He opts for the notion that religion is a side-effect of adaptations. He doubts the existence of any sort of religion gene or "God pod." Both Pinker and Kirkpatrick speak in very disparaging terms of the theory that religion is an evolutionary adaptation. Pinker's logic is most instructive.

> The question is how can a powerful taste for apparently irrational beliefs evolve...? There is one way in which religious belief could be an adaptation. Many of our faculties are adaptations to enduring properties of the real world. We have depth perception because the world really is three-dimensional. We apparently have an innate fear

of snakes because the world really does have snakes and some of
them are venomous. Perhaps there really is a personal, attentive,
invisible, miracle-producing, reward-giving, retributive deity and we
have a God module to commune with him. As a scientist I like to
interpret claims as testable hypotheses, and this certainly is one. It
predicts that miracles should be observable, that success in life
should be proportionate to virtue...[33]

Of course he goes on to quibble about some typical atheistic reasons for
denying God. Having ruled out any sort of deity on the basis that he
doesn't observe a Christian fundamentalist world, he moves on to
evolution as the only valid examination for the universality of religion.
He rules out the adaptationist explanations on the grounds that they beg
the question. He then concludes that universality of religion is a
mystery at the moment, but just because it is not explained by
adaptation it could well be a side-effect of adaptation. He rejects
adaptation-oriented explanations because they beg the question. One
such explanation is that religion offers comfort, relieves fear of death
and the unknown; even Newberg offers that explanation. But this
explanation, according to Pinker, "begs the question of why the mind
should find comfort in beliefs that are false... there is no reason to think
it so when we have reason to believe it is not so."[34] What is interesting
about this is that he admits that it would be logical to assume that God
gave us the sense of the divine through a genetic link if the world
stacked up to our belief in that sort of God. But the only reason he has
for assuming it doesn't is because he begs the question in just the same
way that he accuses the adaptationists of begging the question. Do we
know that we don't see miracles? Doesn't that depend upon where you
look? I wager he has never examined the Lourdes data. Is success not
proportional to virtue? Doesn't that rather depend upon how we
measure success? Where does God promise us worldly success in
proportion to virtue? What if God doesn't work miracles? Why can't
there be a non-miracle-working God? That answer is not going to

appeal to Christian apologists, and it is not indicative of my theological commitments but forms a logical standpoint. He has hardly proven a thing regarding the world as a reflection of a creator. Yet he has hinted at a pretty good argument against the tendency to assume that religion is genetic because it gives comfort. We can add to this argument that unless the evolutionary psychologists can produce a link between the comfort religions provides and reproduction, their argument is Lamarckian because it doesn't offer any mechanism for this comfort level as genetic. It's not an adaptation (no religious genes *per se)* because there's no way to form a gene based upon the mere need for comfort.

Pinker rejects further explanations on similar grounds. I'll begin with the second argument that he takes up, that religion brings a community together. Again he charges question begging, but this time for reasons I just used; that adaptationists can't connect the behavior to a genetic level, they can't show why genes are needed to bring a community together (just as genes are not needed to comfort one on a cold night when fears of death and the unknown looms large). "But again it merely begs the question as to why. Why is there a sub goal in evolution to have people stand together to face off common enemies...?" Why, he asks, would it be necessary to have a gene to accomplish this task? Think about it. People certainly have the ability to unite, and the moment would compel unity. Why must it be genetic? It seems those who uncritically accept evolution as a catchall explanation take every opportunity to use it.[35] He then confronts a third argument, that "religion is the source of our higher ethical yearnings." He draws upon the argument made by Steven Jay Gould[36] that religion and science can co-exist; science can't tell us what ethical norms to embrace, this is religion's task. What is Pinker's answer? Religion is no good at telling us about ethical norms because in the Bible God does things that Pinker thinks are unethical. "A big problem for this hypothesis is apparent to anyone who has read the Bible, which is a manual for rape and genocide..."[37] He goes on to decry many aspects of the Old Testament which include such behaviors. His major argument against belief is the Old Testament but he doesn't consider any view but that of the Christian fundamentalist. His logic seems to be, if religion is a source of moral value, the Bible would be a source of moral value. The Bible contains certain books that have material that is hard to take and may require some sort of scholarly understanding (after all it does come from an ancient world). Rather than consult scholarly sources he just condemns it out of hand. Moreover, he's committing the fallacy of straw-man argument since he's equating religious belief of all kinds with a fundamentalist understanding of the Bible. He is willing to rule out explanations for adaptation on the basis of this sort of bad reasoning. He hasn't actually dealt with the issue of genetics in terms of religious belief but has instead pulled a bait-and-switch, attacking fundamentalist literalism of the Bible and pretending that this answers the genetic question. He roots moral philosophy not in genetics but in the work of moral philosophers such as Peter Singer and John Rawls.[38] On that basis he also rules out the possibility of God!

Pinker supports the supply-side theory of religious development. This idea says that if religion benefits someone, that's why it exists. The priest class benefits and thus they develop religion and feed it to a market where demand is greatest. Pinker is working on the assumption that religion is a by-product of other adaptations (a spandrel). The reason for choosing that is because this survives the process of elimination. Priests supply religion because it benefits them, thus "a number of anthropologists have pointed out the benefits to those causing other people to have religious beliefs."[40] He speaks this way several times. I need to talk to those priests. My task would be a lot easier if I could "cause" other people to have religious beliefs. He actually states religion is psychology running amok.[39a] This makes it a lot harder to explain because either he is unaware of the plethora of studies about how good religion is or the religious experience. It seems odd that psychology running amok could be so good for you. Stranger still is that Pinker begins his essay talking about how illogical it is to suppose the very same thing; that genetic behaviors that are good for us could be lies. That's why he connects eyesight to the three-dimensional world and fear to snakes to a world with poisonous snakes. By his own logic he undermines his own take on religion. What it means is that he actually undermines all of his explanations based upon such a view of religion. Then we are free to propose other views, such as liberal theology.[41]

Kirkpatrick (2006) also opposes the adaptation theory and thus opposes any idea of a "God module."[42] He rules out God and intelligent design as unscientific. He then proceeds to argue, "An evolution-based understanding of any psychological phenomenon, including religion, involves more than genetic speculations..."[43] According to Kirkpatrick, just finding a correlation between a behavior and a part of the brain is not enough to demonstrate a genetic adaptation for that behavior. He admits that a growing body of data validates Newberg's findings, but this is not enough to establish an adaptation. The God module would have to be an adaptation. Kirkpatrick finds the very concept dubious from the start. No one major "module" has been associated with adaptations. He uses the example of a computer. If you take your computer apart you will not find a "word processing module." Of course Newberg acknowledges that there are multiple connections in several parts of the brain, and different links for different kinds of RE: the nuns praying linked to a different section than the Buddhist monks meditating. Kirkpatrick argues that "at most it appears that brain areas have been identified that are associated with a motley collection of negligible findings and experiences that are sometimes interpreted in spiritual terms —usually by already religious research subjects."[44] So the religious subjects don't really know if they have religious feelings or not. Religious people are far too emotional and unstable to understand their own feelings. Of course the objective scientists know that their atheist presuppositions aren't getting in the way of their understanding, if that were true they would not be "objective"! Correlations always run the risk of provoking argument

Joseph Hinman

from sign. It is easy to assume that a link between genetic endowment
and behavior signals adaptation, but it's harder to understand the
complex variables of environment. He gives the analogy of calluses.
We have a genetic propensity to calluses because we have a genetic
propensity toward living epidermis. But the only determining factor of
who has more calluses is environmental. Steel and stone don't develop
calluses, skin calluses, but calluses are a function of who does the most
work. It's the environmental behavior that produces the most calluses.

There is an adaptationist argument that is not Lamarckian. Dennett
argues that those with a certain gene or a side-effect of a genetic
predisposition or combination who came to associate a certain feeling
produced by that genetic side-effect with a set of beliefs would tend to
survive not because they had comfort on cold nights, but because they
would seek shamanic help and thus have some actual chance of
overcoming illness. Dennett is assuming two things there, first that
beliefs about the power of the shaman would trigger the placebo effect,
and secondly that placebo could actually prolong life, not just stop pain.
Thirdly, he's assuming that shamans had real knowledge that would
help to some extent. His argument about placebo is more elaborate so
I'll deal with that in the next chapter on placebo and drugs. I do want to
point out here that the assumptions he makes regarding seeking
shamanic help are not supported and not logical. He makes the
argument: "Why did those with the genetic tendency survive? Because
they, unlike those who lacked the gene, had health insurance! In those
days before modern medicine shamanic healing was your only recourse
if you fell ill." [45] But animism would have been the religion of the
entire tribe, not just those who had mystical experiences. Since those
experiences would be a product of evolution alone, if Dennett is right,
then they would have been showing up in a tiny portion of the
population in the beginning, since they were merely accidents of brain
chemistry. That means they would have been confined to the shamans;
in other words the entire mystical experiences were limited to the
shamans. There's no real guarantee that shamanism would have

278

actually kept anyone alive, and no real reason why the gene would be passed on if all who had it were shamans and had not shamans to go to themselves when they fell ill. If their net effect was accomplished through placebo effect, they knew they their own tricks, so would their tricks work on themselves? How did those societies regard the shamans? Were they viewed as potential mates? Did they pass their genes on very often?

The correlation between brain and behavior doesn't always indicate adaptation. "Ironically, the existence of highly heritable individual differences can be interpreted as evidence that the trait in question is not adaptation."[46] Height is heritable as an average. Humans tend to hit a range between four to seven feet. No one particular is such an advantage in all circumstances that that one height became universal. Adaptation allows a range, just as there is a range in the level of religious attraction. Moderate habitability of religion, according to Kirkpatrick, tell us nothing about whether religion is an adaptation or a side-effect of one or more adaptations. There is no quickly available scientific data one can turn to that tells us the truth or falsehood of religion. The analysis these scientists use about the value or truth content of religion is no better than that found on message boards any night on the internet. The "God pod" may or may not be indicative of a trace of God, but the connection between God and genetics is not an argument against the hypothesis of this essay. RE can be logically construed as one trace of God to the extent that we are wiling to place confidence in it. Even if religion is a genetic side-effect of other adaptations this is no negation of the hypothesis. There is no evidence that RE and all its healing and redeeming qualities can be produced by nature alone with no divine connection.

The functionalists or chemical determinists —reductionists— really have no choice but to ascribe the phenomena of RE to genes or chemicals in the brain or brain structure. The methodology they employ, and the assumptions of chemical determinism and naturalism, necessitate losing phenomena; there's no way they could ascribe the phenomena to anything else. We see this in Dennett's dread of "wonder tissue."[47] The methodology of reduction is also accompanied by a doppelgänger, an other, a sense of ideology that uses reduction as a means of filtering out aspects of reality that count against the truth claims of the ideology. Philosophical reductionism is about relabeling reality and losing phenomena that count against its physicalism. As an ideology it must filter everything through this lens that eliminates all aspects that don't fit the ideology. William James complained of the same kind of thing in his own day. He called it 'medical materialism.'

> Medical materialism seems indeed a good appellation for the too simple-minded system of thought which we are considering. Medical materialism finishes up Saint Paul by calling his vision on the road to Damascus a discharging lesion of the occipital cortex, he being an epileptic. It snuffs out Saint Teresa as an hysteric, Saint Francis of Assisi as an hereditary degenerate. George Fox's discontent with the shams of his age, and his pining for spiritual veracity, it treats as a symptom of a disordered colon. Carlyle's organ-tones of misery it accounts for by a gastro-duodenal catarrh. All such mental over-tensions, it says, are, when you come to the bottom of the matter, mere affairs of diathesis (auto-intoxications most probably), due to the perverted action of various glands which physiology will yet discover.[48]

What is the alternative other than some sort of mysticism that refuses to yield to human investigation? James has no problem with making scientific investigations of mystical phenomena and RE. It's fairly apparent that Ralph Hood, Jr. and Robert Wuthnow and Katherine Nobel and Mohan and the others share his concern. James was not above collecting scientific data on religious experiences. That's just what he did. He calls it "existential" writing at a time before that term was used by Sartre. He means it in a way that has more to do with the modern non-Heideggerian use of the term "phenomenological." There is no problem in my view with setting forth physiological conditions that facilitate RE. The problem comes when one undertakes to use this as a means of negating the logical assumption that's one's experiences really reflect some aspect of reality. This because such assertions by their very nature demand that the phenomenon be divorced from its context and its larger picture and taken totally on the basis of its physiology.

When one strips the experience of its larger connections one forgets that these experiences form a means of navigation in the world. They are not exactly substitutes for the five senses, but they can be and are used for guidance in understanding how to deal and cope with the various trammels of life, including the need for meaning, transcendence and "higher things." One can logically dismiss this aspect as beyond the pale of one's beliefs or investigations, but to then try and reduce this aspect itself out of existence by ascribing it to the processes of physiology and placebo is nothing more than an exercise ideologically saving the paradigm.

But we need not leave it as a tie between naturalistic phenomena vs the possibility that God uses brain structure to communicate the trace. I have five tiebreakers at the end of the next chapter, "Placebo and drugs."

1   Andrew Newberg, *Why God Won't God Away: Brain Science and the Biology of Belief.* New York: Ballentine Books, 2001, 157-172.

2   *Ibid.,* 157.

3   Newberg gives a fine tribute to his late partner who was already gone by the time the book was published. p10.

4   *Ibid.,* 1-6.

5   *Ibid.,* 7.

6   *Ibid.,* 37.

7   Daniel Dennett, *Consciousness Explained.* New York: Back Bay Books, first edition, 1992.

8   Newberg. *op. cit.*,33.

9   *Ibid.,* 35-36.

10 *Ibid.,* 36-43.

11 *Ibid.,* 43.

12 he does not say where or who did the experiment., 11-14.

13 *Ibid.,* 52.

14 *Ibid.,* 56.

15 Rita Carter, *Consciousness,* London: Widenfeld and Nicholson, 2002, 288.

16 *Ibid.,* 290.

17 John Hick, *The New Frontier of Religion and Science: Religious Experience, Neuroscience and The Transcendent.* Playgrave: Macmillan, 2006, 66.

18 Ramachandran, *Phantoms in the Brain*, in John Hick, *The New Frontier of Religion and Science*, 62.

19 T. Sensky, "Religiosity, Mystical Experience and Epilepsy," summary in Lukoff, Lu, "Research Review," Op. Cit.

20 Newberg, op cit 112

21 V.S. Ramarchandran, *Phantoms in the Brain*, New York: William Marrow, 1998, 185.

22 *Ibid.,* 37.

23 Andrew Newberg, *Why We Believe What We Believe.* New York: Free Press, first edition 2006,174-177.

24 Steven Rose in Hick, *The New Frontier of Religion and Science*, 78. The original source on Rose is *The 21st Century Brain*, London: Johnathan Cape, (2005) 154

25 James H. Austin, *Zen and the Brain*, in Hick, *The New Frontier of Religion and Science*, 78-79.

26 *The God Part of the Brain*, Website, http://godpart.com/ visited 5/23/08

27 Abraham Maslow, *Religious Values...* Appendix D. *op. cit.*

28 Matthew Alper, *The God Part of the Brain*, Naperville Illinois: Sourcebook inc, originally published in 1996 by Rough Press, 2006. These quotes are stuck into the pages that come right after the dust jacket and are prior to the publication page.

29 *Ibid.,* 12.

30   *Ibid.,* 11.

31   Newberg, *op. cit.*, 37.

32   Lee A Kirckpatrick, "Religion is Not An Adaptation," in *Where God and Science Meet: How Brain and Evolutionary Studies Alter Our Understanding of Religion Vol I: Evolution, Genes, and Religious Brain.* Patrick McNamara (ed). London, Westport Connecticut: Praeger. 2006. 159-180, 164.

33   Steven Pinker, "The evolutionary psychology of Religion," in McNamara, *Where God and Science Meet,* 2.

34   *Ibid.,* 2

35   *Ibid.,* 3

36   Steven Jay Gould, *Rock of Ages.* New York: Ballantine Books 1999,1.

37   Pinker, *op. cit.,* 3.

38   *Ibid.,* 3.

39   *Ibid.,* 5.

40   *Ibid.,* 5.

41   Andrew M. Greeley and Wolfgang Jadogzinksky, "The Demand for Religion: Hard Core Atheism and the Supply Side Theory." Website, http://www.agreeley.com/articles/hardcore.html (accessed 11/25/08). Greeley is Priest and Sociologist at University of Chicago, Jadogzinksky is at University of Cologne. Greeley and Jadogzinksky have done a huge study analyzing the supply and demand for religion in Northern Europe, they disprove the supply side religion thesis, they also show Northern Europe is hard core atheist.

42   Kirkpatrick, *op. cit.*159-180.

43   *Ibid.,* 160

44   *Ibid.,* 161

45   Daniel Dennett, *Breaking the Spell: Religion as Natural Phenomena.* New York, Viking, The Penguin Group, 2006, 140.

46   *Ibid.,* 164

47   In his *Consciousness Explained,* Dennett derides any kind of implication that there is a mysterious process in our heads, or anything approaching the concept of "mind" by calling it "wonder tissue."

48   William James *The Varieties of Religious Experience: A Study in Human Nature.* Gifford Lectures on Natural Religion 1901, 1902, New York, Modern library, (1902, 1929, Random House 1936) 14-15.

7 More Alternate Causality: Placebo, Drugs and Other Issues

Placebo

An atheist on *exChristian.net* laments that his aging parents will never "know the truth." He says:

> But, religion is THE most important thing in my mom's life. It gives her "purpose." ***The placebo effect of Jesus*** makes her believe everything will be ok [sic]. Church gives her a positive social outlet. When the day comes that she passes away, religion will give her strength since she will totally believe the best is just getting ready to start. My dad is also very religious, but not quite as much. But both parents want me to "get saved". They don't overly push it, but make little comments.[1] (emphasis mine)

This sentiment is representative of that commonly exhibited by certain actively anti-religious atheists. Anything that causes one to feel good is a "placebo" meaning it's not real so the effects are not important. The illogic of this sort of thinking is apparent. It begins with the assertion that the effects of religious experience are not very impressive, as one denizen of message boards once put it, "It's just a bunch of Christians getting happy." Thus he dismissed the studies discussed in Chapter 3, as "just a bunch of pastors asking their guys to email them and say how they are getting happy." It is more than that. One's entire life is renovated. Suddenly, meaning, purpose, and joy replace frustration and longing. According to these "new" atheists, however, it's just a lie and you have to somehow "give it up" because it's not true, even though it has overhauled one's life. Apparently the greatest proof of falsehood is that something makes one fulfilled and gives meaning.

The effects are astounding and real, working even to the point of helping one survive cancer, get off heroin and reverse a lifetime of alcoholism, but "Hey it's just 'gett'n happy,' so it can't be true." What is the truth? Going back to dying of cancer, that's their "truth." Lies rarely work such good so thoroughly. It seems counterintuitive that the effectiveness of something would be an indication of its falsehood. There is no logical reason why transformational power and its effectiveness to renovate lives should not be viewed as a sign of veracity. We are made to have this experience —it's part of who we are. One can understand why this cannot be taken an indication of absolute proof of truth claims; however, it seems illogical not to understand it as a indication of veracity.

From a more serious source, Bill Taylor in *New Scientist* magazine is asking the same question:

> The special report on religious belief "Beyond Belief" seems to raise the inevitable question of how faith works (28 January, p 28). Is religion just a placebo effect, and how is belief translated into physical benefit? I recall being told during my training in clinical psychology of a study that suggested that the best predictor of the recovery of hospital patients was their own belief that they would recover.
>
> What is the biochemical mechanism triggered by belief which leads to the body's recovery? On the other hand, is there perhaps a negative placebo effect in the process involving "learned helplessness", which has been demonstrated in humans, dogs, and monkeys — even detached cockroach legs? The most dramatic examples discussed at some length in the 1975 book *Helplessness* by Martin Seligman is Voodoo or Hex Death, where individuals sentenced to death by their tribe just go off and quietly die. How does

a psychological experience have such a devastating effect on a body's natural survival processes? It is fairly easy to comprehend the feelings of distress, anguish and depression, but the link to the physical process which results in the heart stopping seems to raise questions that are awaiting further study. A controlled study would have a job getting past an ethics committee, I suppose. [2]

It's worth noting that the example Taylor gives is one of negative effects. None of the potential alternate causes of religious experience (mental illness, brain chemistry, placebos, labeling) can produce long term positive (ie transformational) effects. The only example here is for a negative. This is the only connection that can be made with anything approaching evidence; not the healing aspects of RE but the helplessness implicit in curses and voodoo. There is no data connecting placebo effects, which are medical and stem from expectations involving treatment, to the actual long-term effects of having religious experiences.

Belief Special: How Evolution found God

The issue of *New Scientist* that Taylor mentions (the "Belief Special" from January 2006) includes several articles that do a hatchet job on religious belief. Taylor describes an issue of *New Scientist*.

In the beginning religion didn't exist, so why did we feel the need to create it, asks evolutionary biologist Robin Dunbar. Several articles in the so called "belief special" demonstrate the bias of the publication. The Placebo hypothesis is a natural propaganda piece for backing up the kind of assumptions reductionists make, as seen in these articles. By the titles and their proximity in the issue one can see these assumptions back a certain perspective. They includes the following items:

Joseph Hinman

- Belief special: Glad to be gullible
  Some people believe the weirdest things - but they may just be
  onto something
- Belief special: When delusion triumphs over truth
  Belief seems intangible until you take a close look inside the brain,
  as *New Scientist* discovers
- Belief special: What's it all about?
  Why did human evolution lead to the invention of God, how does
  belief affect your brain, and why do we choose to believe in blatant
  charlatans?[3]

The one article about being gullible is about psychic powers. The
article on delusion is about healing and the suggestion of placebo:

> BELIEF has never literally moved a mountain, but it can have some
> dramatic effects. Take Madeleine Rizan: by the time she bathed in the
> waters of Lourdes in 1858 she had been paralyzed for 24 years, yet,
> according to the record, she regained her ability to move. Then there
> are the dozens of heart patients in the 1950s who were helped by a
> procedure known as internal mammary ligation - which worked just
> as well when patients simply believed it had been done. There are
> even instances of women who stop menstruating, grow a round belly
> and begin to lactate, in the firm but mistaken belief that they are
> pregnant. Equally mysterious are the paralyzed people who believe
> their limbs are still working normally, despite the evidence of their
> own eyes. What is going on inside our brains when we believe? How
> does that trigger physical changes in our bodies? ... [4]

Of course this is typical skeptical thinking; the person is really healed
but we don't dare consider a reality beyond the healing. It just must be
naturalistic, and we deny any other possibility at all cost, and expend
energy with a naturalistic song and dance to explain it away. What is
the most ready-made theory that we can put into the mix? Even though
there is no data of any kind to make it fit, we can just assert it has to

be... placebo! This is accomplished by an amazing argument from analogy, which is still a fallacy even in this day and age. Both kinds of explanation deal with brains, both deal with minds, both deal with belief.

One might wonder why the woman, in 24 years, could not find a way to make herself believe and get up and walk. I will not venture to deal with the issue of physical healing and Lourdes at this time (that is for another book). The people that go to Lourdes or who are brought Lourdes water are expecting to be healed. They have a physical ailment so they have a focus for what is to be healed. But religious experience as healing is a lot more oblique. Mystical experience is even one step more removed from these kinds of physical healings. No one seeks religious experience to be healed. The data clearly indicates it is quite common that people are not seeking such changes, or such "transformative power." There is no data to indicate that placebo works to produce the kinds of self-actualization and transformative results one finds in mystical experiences. It's probable that the studies have just not been done to link mystical experience to placebo, yet that is not proof that it is a placebo. The expectation argument is an excellent reason to rule out placebo.

There are several good arguments against the assertion that RE is "just a placebo."

1. Argument from analogy (e.g. the placebo effect)
2. There is no data linking placebo in medicine to other areas
3. RE is not often expected (converts, childhood)
4. RE often contradicts expectations of doctrine
5. Placebo is not understood

As for argument one (1), we see a tendency for people to use the concept of placebo for anything involving the mind, expectations and desire. Daniel E. Morman and Wayne B. Jonas (2002) address exactly this point:

Moreover, people frequently expand the concept of the placebo effect very broadly to include just about every conceivable sort of beneficial biological, social, or human interaction that doesn't involve some drug well-known to the pharmacopoeia. A narrower form of this expansion includes identifying "natural history" or "regression to the mean" (as we might observe them in a randomized, controlled trial) as part of the placebo effect. But natural history and regression occur not only in the control group. Nothing in the theory of regression to the mean hints that when people are selected for being extreme on some measure (blood pressure or cholesterol, for example), they are immune to regression if they receive active treatment. Such recipients are as likely (or unlikely) to move toward homeostasis as are control group patients. So, regression to the mean is in no meaningful way a "placebo effect." Ernst and Resch took an important step in trying to clarify this situation by differentiating the "true" from the "perceived" placebo effect. But "true placebo effect" hasn't really caught on as a viable concept.

The concept of the placebo effect has been expanded much more broadly than this. Some attribute the effects of various alternative medical systems, such as homeopathy or chiropractic to the placebo effect. Others have described studies that show the positive effects of enhanced communication, such as Egbert's, as "the placebo response without the placebo."[5]

This quotation speaks of the situation within the medical community. It pertains to medical practices. But this is what I find skeptics doing when they stretch the definition of placebo to include religious experience. They are not using the term in a responsible way but are merely clutching at some sloppy, rough approximation to symbolize the idea that they think the results of RE are just in one's head and have no bearing upon any external truth. The arguments I am making do not turn upon proving God. The skeptics will continue to assert, "It could be this, or it could be that," but that, however, is not the issue. Just offering a possible naturalistic explanation isn't proof and it doesn't end the discussion. The overall objective of my arguments is to show that religious belief is rational. It is not irrational to assume, on the basis of the effects of religious experience, that one has experienced the presence of the divine. This means that the power of an alternate cause must be taken in terms of likelihood and probability. But how much likelihood does one find when the argument is based upon a fallacy such as argument from analogy?

Placebo works from expectation,[6] while ME and RE are seldom expected as conscious avenues of healing; most of the transformational effects such as self-actualization are not even known to most people. The very definition of placebo in modern medicine trades upon this concept of expectation: "The 'placebo effect' —an apparent therapeutic response caused by patients' expectations— can confound the assessment of treatment efficacy, especially with subjective outcomes."[7] I've already provided evidence in the chapter on Proudfoot's labeling issue that shows a great deal of mystical experience is not expected. Most people who seek mystical experiences are not thinking of the self-actualization but of spiritual knowledge; they don't know this is a possibility. Some who experience this kind of mystical experience choose to believe and have had no belief before-hand (such as myself); then there are the children I document in the chapter on Proudfoot. The experience is commonly found in children. Certainly one would not think all those children are seeking self-authentication or self-actualization. Moreover, I've documented several examples of how RE contradicted the experiencing person's pet doctrines. In Chapter 5, I show five examples of mystics whose basic doctrine and religious orientation was contradicted by their experiences: St Teresa, Ratisboone, Arobindo and Bucke. And if I am to draw upon my meager experience —not that I call myself a mystic— it doesn't make much sense to think that RE would meet expectations of healing; my own experience contradicts the doctrines people expect to be borne out as true. Moreover, as also documented previously, mystical experience often contradicts one's expectations of doctrine. Now it is true that mystics use their experience to justify their religious tradition, but often within that tradition specific doctrines are contradicted. I gave examples from both Christianity and Hinduism. But there is even more to be examined in terms of placebo effects.

The skeptic is jumping the gun to assume that placebo is a trick, something false signifying something that doesn't work. The effects are real and the new interest in placebo as a valid therapeutic approach proves this. At the same time the placebo effect is still not really understood. The literature, both in the popular press and scientific publications, indicates a mass of conflicting theories and approaches. An article in *the British Journal of Psychiatry* by Aaron K. Vallance demonstrates the fragmented nature of our current understanding.[8] First, it's hard to even define what placebo is, and harder still to define the "effect." We can see this in what has been said above about stretching the definition to include more things. As Vallance points out: The basic split in definitions is between viewing the placebo effect as the effect of placebo administration (giving an inert compound under the guise of medicine and then defining the effects as "placebo.") vs. the difference in outcome between a group treated with placebo as opposed to one not so treated. The first is tautological, since you can't define a placebo-treated group then determine its outcome if the outcome is the definition. The second lacks explanatory power. The third option is to define it as any effect attributable to a pill, potion, or procedure, but not to its pharmacodynamic or specific properties'. The problem here is that definitions are usually given based upon properties; to base the definition upon what it is not might cause redundancy in the long run. Some skeptics try to use the underlying mechanism as the definition but we still don't know enough about the phenomena to say what that mechanism is.[9] Without a definition in the first place it seems impossible to say anyway.

New developments in understanding placebo have brought about changes in understanding how the process works. Moreman equates placebo with "meaning response." This notion of meaning as the mechanism has caught on throughout the literature.[10] Moreman's article has been much quoted and has made an influence.[11] Meaning response is not actually just the expectation of cure that makes it work but the meaning transmitted through cultural constructs that is embedded within the placebo itself. He uses a study in the *New England Journal of Medicine*[12] to illustrate. Two groups of students were given blue and red pills. They were told the red pills keep you awake and give you energy. The blue pills make you sleepy. Two pills do more of what they are supposed to do than one. All the pills were placebos. The pills had the desired effect on the each group. The administrators were equally enthusiastic about both blue pills as well as the red pills. The outcomes are explained by the colors, rather than by regression to the mean. Blue indicates sleep, soothing and comfort; red means danger, power and energy.

The Moreman article indicates several other studies that show a meaning relationship between the product and name identification. For example "Viagra" implies vital, vivacious, and "Niagara" (subliminal reference to an icon of romance and sex). In the study 835 British women were treated for headaches. One group received brand name aspirin, and another received the same aspirin in an unmarked package. The brand name aspirin (although the same product) worked better on headaches: 64% of the branded aspirin worked one hour after taking vs. 45% for the unbranded.[13] Another study used two groups of people doing aerobic exercise. One group was told that the exercises would increase their aerobic capacity and well-being (self esteem and confidence were the measure of "well-being.") The other group was just told they would increase their aerobic capacity. The group that was told they would also increase well-being did increase their well-being and responded with higher scores on tests designed to measure self esteem and confidence. The other group only increased its aerobic capacity.[14] So 'meaning' is the new understanding of placebo, but we still don't understand the mechanism by which this meaning is transfused into real action upon the body. One new approach to this problem is top-down causality.

There are effects from placebos that bear closer scrutiny. There is a new paradigm shaping up whereby placebo is used in a serious way as part of the healing regimen. In relation to this effort there is good evidence that placebo, or some aspects of placebo effects, are the result of a real connection between the central nervous system and the immune system. In other words, there's a chance the mind is really actually healing the body. No data that I've found suggests that this process can heal cancer, or mend a broken leg faster than it would heal absent of the process, but to a certain degree there may be a real effect by the mind upon the body via connections in the brain. If that is the case the analogy that skeptics draw would be negated completely, because then the arguments about God using a physical pathway for communication would apply. It is becoming increasingly possible to view the phenomena as a case of downward causation.

> Therapeutic action may now be seen as a special case of development that occurs within the interactional context of cultural evolution, personal history, and the genome. Human evolution is increasingly dominated by culture operating on the mind/brain through downward causation. This concept refers to the influence of higher organizational entities (e.g., mind) upon lower ones (e.g., brain). Although little recognized, downward causation is tacitly assumed in psychotherapeutic interventions, and is illustrated in recent fMRI studies. The clinical integration of the downward causation concept links therapeutic action to the power of cultural evolution, and facilitates reunion with traditional science. [15]

In addition, there has been a discovery illuminating a genetic link between the central nervous system and the immune system. This could be a hint, although not definite at the moment, that some meaning response could actually affect the body through top-down causality, and the link might be one between central nervous and immune systems. David Felton at the University of Rochester, a MacArthur Genius Grant recipient, has produced research results that definitely offer a link between mind and body, top-down causality. "Our grandmothers knew all along that our minds and our bodies were connected, even if the scientific community didn't. We've simply provided irrefutable data showing that it's true."[16] Using dyes he traced the first connection between blood vessels leading to cells of the immune system, when he was at Indiana in 1981. Adler, an experimental psychologist, already suspected the connection from a 1974 study. He gave rats a chemical that would retard the immune system and associated it with a sweet solution. He wanted to see how long the conditioned response would last, so he took out the immune-suppressing chemical. The rats began dying of diseases. The chemical to suppress the immune system was no longer there, but the rat brains turned off the immune system just because of the association with the sweet. The connection was clear but the link was still unknown; that was supplied by Felton.[17] He traced the pathway from spleen to immune system. The discovery was critical, as Felton says "one hundred percent quantifiable results, showing that the immune system and the central nervous system are indeed connected."[18]

This is all the skeptic needs to make the argument that RE is nothing more than the interpretation of meaning applied by the mind to turn on the neural pathways that produce religious experience and then from there the effects would follow because that's the effect such experiences have when we combine them with belief. That seems like a pretty good argument on the surface, and it's backed by empirical evidence. But the problem here is the same as it is in the case of the "God Pods." There is no way to distinguish between faith-produced healing —because it opens up to something beyond itself, in which case the chemical connections are just the route taken by God— and experiences originating totally within the brain —apart from any external cause. Meaning is embedded in religion and cultural constructs. The link from cultural constructs to religion has already been discussed: Mystical sense of the divine must be filtered through cultural constructs in order for one to be able to talk about it. One might argue that we are drawing the cultural meaning through religious belief all the time. That might make for meaning-response in a placebo fashion (although it's still an argument from analogy because there is still no definite data to connect the two), but there are also negative meanings to RE in society. People are hesitant about having religious experiences because they are seen as proof of insanity or instability, emotions out of control and that sort of thing (even though the actual data shows this is not true). Just having a bunch of associations doesn't necessarily prove anything. Certainly this argument doesn't account for the lack of expectation. Even though the placebo is shifted from expectation to "meaning response" there still has to be a certain degree of expectation or the meaning won't matter. For example, the people taking the blue pills had to expect that the pills were real medicine, even though they interpreted blue as "sleep-making." So someone who was not expecting to feel the presence of God and did not understand anything about the mystical qualities of RE reacting by finding faith is totally unaccounted for by this explanation.

Drugs

The argument for counter-causes also has in its arsenal drugs as an empirical example. There is a great deal of information about drugs as linked to religious experiences. This vast body of work is perhaps as voluminous as the body of work I deal with in the studies chapter. A great deal of data indicates that certain kinds of drugs facilitate religious experiences. That is enough for most skeptics to say it's caused by brain chemistry and case closed. If we examine it more closely, however, we see it is not caused by brain chemistry. Even major researchers don't think so. RE is made easier and enhanced by brain chemistry when it's stimulated by certain kinds of drugs. This in no way proves that the experiences originate with drugs or with brain chemistry. As with the "God Pod" and placebo effects, the contest is between localized internal origins vs. brain chemistry as a conduit of the divine. These are the two possibilities. As I will demonstrate, the latter is indicated. Specifically, the evidence would indicate that certain drugs (psilocybin in particular) opens some form of receptor in the brain such that the subject is more receptive to the divine. The formal term for the idea of using drugs to enhance religious experience is "entheogenic." These are "entheogenic" practices.

As discussed in the previous chapter, Pahnke never said that the drugs in the Good Friday experiment "caused" the experience. Rich Doblin (1991) writes: "Pahnke hypothesized that psychedelic drugs, in this case psilocybin, could facilitate a "mystical" experience in religiously inclined volunteers who took the drug in a religious setting."[19] Pahnke always thought in terms of facilitation.

In the early 1990's, Doblin did a long-term follow up to the study. Pahnke died in 1971 and the original material was destroyed (I think to protect anonymity), but Doblin[20] was able to reconstruct the sources and find the original participants, all of whom he interviewed except one who could not be found and one who had died. The study used 20 subjects, all white male seminary students. These were grouped into ten pairs, double blind, and half got the psilocybin (30mg) and half did not. They all participated in the Good Friday service. The findings indicate that almost all of the students who received the drug had mystical experiences. Of those who did not receive the drug (the control group), only two had such experiences, and these were far from being as vivid, impressive, or transformative as the experimental subjects. In Doblin's reconstruction and follow-up, almost all members of the experimental group demonstrated that they were affected their whole lives, in a positive way. Most of them were glad they participated, and the experiences stayed with them a lifetime. The two control group members who did not get the drug were not impressed by their experiences for very long. In the follow-up they could barely remember them.

This would be enough for most skeptics to claim that religious experience is caused by brain chemistry. There are some problems if one takes this route. First of all, the entire experiment was conducted with believers (seminarians) and many of the experimental group members had had religious experiences and even mystical ones prior to taking the drug, some in childhood. This means the data was contaminated and there was no control. It also might be a good indication that the drug was merely triggering experiences the subjects would have had anyway and that the experiences didn't originate with the drug or with the change in brain chemistry. But, on the other hand, it seems clear by comparison that the drug amplified the experiences.[22]

Many (in fact I can't find a major researcher who says otherwise) echo that drugs do not cause but enhance mystical experiences. Batson (1982) writes:

> If this analysis is correct, two implications follow. First, drugs can facilitate but cannot produce creative religious experience. They can facilitate it if they are used in the context of an ongoing intra-psychic process that includes not only self-surrender (incubation) and new vision (illumination) but also a preceding struggle with one or more existential questions (preparation) and a subsequent new life (verification). If the individual is not already wrestling with existential concerns, psychedelics are not likely to evoke a creative transformation. This point is underscored by the findings of Masters and Houston, of the Spring Grove project, and of Pahnke; in each study religious insight seemed limited to those actively addressing existential questions (preparation). At the same time, if the experience is to be more than psychic "fireworks," there must be positive consequences for one's everyday life (verification).[21a]

Mescaline does not produce quite the same kinds of experiences as psilocybin, J.P. Tarcher (1990) tells us:

I conclude, then, that though mescaline may occasionally give momentary ecstatic feelings, as it may have done to Mr. Mayhew, it does not typically do so and that mescaline experiences do not feel like ecstatic experiences. This is not affected by the fact that some people may believe that what they have experienced under mescaline is religious experience; but I should have thought that for anyone seeking the Beatific Vision (which was, before Mr. Huxley, granted only to Moses and St. Paul) there were surer and pleasanter ways of attaining it than by taking mescaline.[23]

These two drugs are different substances, they have different chemistry and work differently, but the effects are so similar that researchers regard them as basically interchangeable.[24] Laski compiles quite a lengthy list of differences between mescaline use and spiritual ecstasies, to summarize:

Ecstatics [are] always unanimous about the high value of their experience, mescaline users are not...[25]

Mescaline experience is always extrovertive, ecstasy of the highest type introvertive. Escstatic experience always goes either from ecstasy to ecstasy or despair to ecstasy, never the reverse. The Mystical experience may be momentary or last a half hour, but it is never hours, and it is always transformative, leaving a long-term sense of the highest value, the Mescaline user may feel a very casual approach, last for hours. Also mystics in introvertive state cannot function, Mescaline users do many ordinary things....[26]

Feelings about time are vastly different... (the) Mescaline user has a casual attitude, but the mystic senses eternity....[27]

> Major differences in triggers are recorded, the ecstatic usually taking
> the trigger from that which is found to be beautiful or valuable, the
> Mescaline user from whatever ordinary object seems enhanced.[28]

> Differences toward a sense of a transformed world...[29]

Caroline Franks Davis (1989) adds:

> There is a great deal of evidence that drugs cannot produce religious
> experiences on their own, in the way that, say, a blow to the head
> produces an experience of 'stars'. At the most, it appears they can act
> as a catalyst, and so it is open to the theist to argue that it was other,
> nonpathological factors which were crucial to the religious content of
> the experience. John Bowker informs us, for instance, that drugs do
> not introduce anything new into the mind or behavior or affect stored
> information in a discriminatory and meaningful manner, but can only
> initiate or inhibit brain activity....[30]
>
> The discussion in the previous section showed that, in some
> respects, typical drug-induced experiences are like psychotic
> experiences in the way they differ from typical mystical experiences.
> It is, moreover, clear from the literature that drug-induced mystical
> experiences are almost always extrovertive rather than the
> introvertive type extolled by most mystical traditions, and there is
> rarely a sense of personal presence or of union with another being.
> The use of drugs to induce religious experiences cannot be
> recommended, partly because of the dangers of drug use, and partly
> because experiences produced in such a way tend to be regarded as
> something separated from normal life and so may not become
> properly integrated into the subject's religious, psychological, and
> cognitive development.[31]

Davis also adds that subjects given drugs do not have mystical
experiences in sensory deprivation, another indication that the
conventional triggers have to be in place, that the drugs merely

facilitate but cannot cause the experiences; the setting has to be appropriate. Gackenbach also documents Lukoff, Alexander, and other studies which find important differences in drug-induced states and pure consciousness, such that pure consciousness is not reducible to mere drug-induced states.

Those quotes name mescaline, but what about psilocybin? The results from Good Friday and its follow-up experiment do nothing to change the argument that the drugs enhance or facilitate but do not cause the experiences. This is born out by the fact that many of the experimental subjects had such experiences before, while the follow-up shows they were profoundly affected by their Good Friday experiences, those who had such experiences before classify these as "among the greatest of my life" not "the greatest." One would expect that if the drugs themselves were the actual cause of the experience they wouldn't have other such experiences and these would be the greatest.

For the experimental group, the average score for the mystical categories at the six-month follow-up was 60.8 percent. They scored 66.8 percent at the long-term follow-up. In the six-month follow-up, the experimental group scored above 34 percent in all categories while in the long-term follow-up they scored above 48 percent in all categories. The experimental group scored the highest in those categories that typify a different state of consciousness such as transcendence of time and space, alleged ineffability and transiency.

For the control group, the average score for the eight categories of mystical experience at the six-month follow-up was 11.8 percent. They scored 12.2 percent at the long-term follow-up. The highest score of the control group at either time was 29 percent, in the sacredness category. The control group scored the highest in the categories of experience that religious services are most likely to induce, namely sense of sacredness, deeply felt positive mood and sense of objectivity and reality.[32]

But consider the comparisons of the subjects to past experience:

The discussion of Subject T.B. about the relationship between his psilocybin and his other mystical experiences illustrates how the subjects saw the validity of their psilocybin experiences.

TB: I can think of no experiences [like the Good Friday experience] quite of that magnitude. That was the last of the great four in my life. The dream state... I had no control over when it was coming. It was when I [was about nine and] had scarlet fever and rheumatic fever, apparently at either similar or at the same times. And they thought that I was going to die. And I saw a light coming out of the sky, this is in the dream, and it came toward me and it was like the figure of Christ and I said, "No, let me live and I'll serve you." And I'm alive and I've served. The prayer state when I was in seventh grade was very similar in the way it happened to me. I intentionally went for an experience with God. In seventh grade. And I also went for an experience with God at the Good Friday experience. And those were similar. The West Point experience was different. In that yes, it was prayers, it was on my knees, it was there, but the face of Christ was. .. it happened more to me than me participating in it. It was more like a saving experience kind of thing. So I've had that and can talk about "a salvation experience," a born again experience, it was that kind of dedication. [33]

The follow-up shows the lives of the experimental group were profoundly affected in a positive way by their experiences. Many went to work in the civil rights movement and all found it to be a transformative experience. For some, there are also highly negative effects that are not found with non-assisted mystical experiences. Some have also raised questions as to the religious nature of the experiences, since none of these involved the specific religious tradition in which the group participated; they were not having "Christ-centric" experiences. They were having "druggie" type experiences that may or not have pertained to some broader view of "God" but not in a Christian context.

This criticism was made by R.C. Zhaner (1972). It pertains to the questionnaire, not to the actual experiences of the subjects who may have found their experiences profoundly Christian, but the questionnaire did not explore that avenue. Pahnke just responded that it was not his aim to define the nature of religious experiences. I am not saying there are no aspects of religious experience that are not at times hard to take or are uncomfortable, or even negative in a sense; but very rarely if ever does it actually scare people in the way that an acid trip can be scary. Consider the one negative experience of Good Friday:

> Reverend L.R. had one of the most difficult experiences of all the psilocybin subjects. He described the early portion of his experience as follows:
>
> Shortly after receiving the capsule, all of a sudden I just wanted to laugh. I began to go into a very strong paranoid experience. And I found it to be scary. The chapel was dark and I hated it in there, just absolutely hated it in there. And I got up and left. I walked down the corridor and there was a guard, a person stationed at the door so individuals wouldn't go out, and he says, "Don't go outside," and I said, "Oh no, I won't. I'll just look outdoors." And I went to the door and out I went. They sent [a group leader] out after me. We [L.R. and the group leader] went back into the building and again, I hated to be in that building and being confined because there were bars on the window and I felt literally like I was in prison. One of the things that was probably happening to me was a reluctance to just flow. I tried to resist that and as soon as resistance sets in there's likely to be conflict and there's likely, I think, for there to be anxiety.[34]

In other words, on the basis of this evidence it seems clear that RE and RE enhanced by drugs are different. These are different but related phenomena. That suggests to me that drugs are opening some kind of receptor center in the "God-conduit" aspect of brain chemistry, but not creating the experience itself. They may well be also filtering the experience at the same time such that the true message is lost. That would be a matter for further investigation. It seems incumbent to include a couple of examples of the sort of positive life-changing experiences which do have some sort of connection with a generally religious outlook:

> Subject K.B.'s description of the long-term effects is representative. He remarks:
>
> It left me with a completely unquestioned certainty that there is an environment bigger than the one I'm conscious of. I have my own interpretation of what that is, but it went from a theoretical proposition to an experiential one. In one sense it didn't change anything, I didn't discover something I hadn't dreamed of, but what I had thought on the basis of reading and teaching was there. I knew it. Somehow it was much more real to me.... I expect things from meditation and prayer and so forth that I might have been a bit more skeptical about before.... I have gotten help with problems, and at times I think direction and guidance in problem solving. Somehow my life has been different knowing that there is something out there.... What I saw wasn't anything entirely surprising and yet there was a powerful impact from having seen it. [35]

A better-designed study was conducted in 2005 at Johns Hopkins University, the Griffiths study (Roland Griffiths, W.A. Richards et al, 2006). Unlike Pahnke, this study used the M scale to measure mystical experiences. [36] The M scale didn't exist when the Good Friday study was done. The conclusion: "[W]hen administered under supportive conditions, Psilocybin occasioned experiences similar to spontaneously occurring mystical experiences. The ability to occasion such experiences prospectively will allow rigorous scientific investigation of their causes and consequences." The study does not say religious experience is caused by brain chemistry alone. [37] Two or three sessions were conducted at two-month intervals. Thirty volunteers received orally administered drug (30mg/70kg) and another drug in counterbalanced order to obscure the study design. In other words they all got both drugs but they didn't know which one at which time, so it's a blind comparision. These subjects did not attend a church service but were asked to lie down blindfolded, and listen to classical music with head phones. Many commentators and researchers believe that expectation plays a large part in these experiences of the subjects; it is impossible to filter out all aspects of expectation and is deemed unethical for the researchers to give such a drug without informing the subjects.[38] Several different scales were administered, including not only the M scale but a longer version of it that is designed to take into account a person's lifetime experiences. Great care was taken to avoid the problems of the questions asked in the Good Friday study. Integrity of the double blind was assessed and verified by questionnaires for the monitors. Hallucinogen ratings were used to assess the level of "high."

The total score on the M scale and on the three states of consciousness scales were significantly higher for the psilocybin than for the other drug (methylphenidate). Sixty-seven percent of the respondents rated the experience with psilocybin to be among the most meaningful experiences of their lives; putting it in the category with the birth of a child or the death of a parent. Thirty-three percent rated the experience with the psilocybin to the single most significant spiritual event of their lives, with 38% putting it in the top five for spiritual experiences. With these findings there can be little doubt that psilocybin facilitates profound religious expenses, or that it can under the right conditions. But nothing in the Griffiths study implied that the drug was the root origin of the experiences.

It is worth noting that a third of the subjects felt a great sense of fear, and many of them reported a continuing sense of fear after the study. The Johns Hopkins blog "Medicine" quotes Griffiths:

> All of the study's authors caution about substantial risks of taking psilocybin under conditions not appropriately supervised. "Even in this study, where we greatly controlled conditions to minimize adverse effects, about a third of subjects reported significant fear, with some also reporting transient feelings of paranoia," says

Griffiths. "Under unmonitored conditions, it's not hard to imagine those emotions escalating to panic and dangerous behavior.

The researchers' message isn't just that psilocybin can produce mystical experiences. "I had a healthy skepticism going into this," says Griffiths, "and that finding alone was a surprise." But, as important, he says, "is that, under very defined conditions, with careful preparation, you can safely and fairly reliably occasion what's called a primary mystical experience that may lead to positive changes in a person. It's an early step in what we hope will be a large body of scientific work that will ultimately help people.[39]

We do read of mystics feeling a sense of fear in terms of "awe" at the sublime presence of the divine, and even of a sense of unworthiness. But we do not read of mystics who were genuinely panicking and fully afraid and continuing to have this sense of fear for long periods after their experiences. While both studies, Good Friday and Griffiths, do seem to have evoked in their subjects a long-term positive sense of meaning and transformation, we also find examples of subjects with deep abiding sense of fear and in the case of Good Friday one totally "freaking out." We don't find that in mystics, we don't find San Juan De la Cruz warning "don't try this at home; be sure and do it in controlled conditions with psychological researchers present so you won't freak out." While the Griffiths study is excellent psychological/ medical research, and while I am not disputing that Griffiths did evoke true mystical experiences, it may not be great spirituality and it may not be a perfect replica of the spiritual life.

In the previous chapter, John Hick was quoted as saying that studies that claim to evoke mystical experience often do not use the M scale. This is not true of Griffiths but it is the case for another study done in Sweden by several scientists: Psychologist Jacqueline Borg, M.Sc.; Bengt Andrée, M.D., Ph.D.; Henrik Soderstrom, M.D., Ph.D. and Lars Farde, M.D., Ph.D. The study is called "The Serotonin System and Spiritual Experiences." I will refer to this study as "Borg" or the

"Swedish serotonin study." While it claims to measure "spiritual experiences" I will show that it does no such a thing. The study determined the density of serotonin in the respondents. Those scores were compared with spiritual experience test scores to see if increased serotonin levels correlated with high spiritual experience test scores (Swedish version of the Temperament and Character Inventory self-report questionnaire).

OBJECTIVE: The serotonin system has long been of interest in biological models of human personality. The purpose of this positron emission tomography (PET) study was to search for relationships between serotonin 5-HT1A receptor density and personality traits.

METHOD: Fifteen normal male subjects, ages 20–45 years, were examined with PET and the radioligand [11C]WAY100635. Personality traits were assessed with the Swedish version of the Temperament and Character Inventory self-report questionnaire. Binding potential, an index for the density of available 5-HT1A receptors, was calculated for the dorsal raphe nuclei, the hippocampal formation, and the neocortex. For each region, correlation coefficients between 5-HT1A receptor binding potential and Temperament and Character Inventory personality dimensions were calculated and analyzed in two-tailed tests for significance.

RESULTS: The authors found that the binding potential correlated inversely with scores for self-transcendence, a personality trait covering religious behavior and attitudes. No correlations were found for any of the other six Temperament and Character Inventory dimensions. The self-transcendence dimension consists of three distinct subscales, and further analysis showed that the subscale for spiritual acceptance correlated significantly with binding potential but not with the other two subscales.

CONCLUSIONS: This finding in normal male subjects indicated that the serotonin system may serve as a biological basis for spiritual experiences. The authors speculated that the several-fold variability in 5-HT1A receptor density may explain why people vary greatly in spiritual zeal.[40]

In this test, the Swedish version of the Temperament and Character Inventory self-report questionnaire (TCI) is the major problem. If one can't determine what a mystical experience is, then it's implausable to claim that one has produced it through chemicals. This test is not a measurement of mystical experience. It was not made to be a measurement of mystical experience. Borg and her colleagues are making assumptions based upon preconceived notions of mystical experience (without consulting the literature) then back-reading those assumptions into their data based upon a similarity between one or two characteristics. The TCI is based upon Cloninger's psychobiological model of personality. According to Kose (2003):

> Cloninger developed a dimensional psychobiological model of personality that accounts for both normal and abnormal variation in two major components of personality, temperament and character. The Temperament and Character Inventory (TCI) is a self-administered dimensional questionnaire constructed to assess the seven basic dimensions of personality. TCI maintains the strong theoretical and empirical support of previously developed psychobiological models while overcoming some of their limitations for clinical use. Cloninger's model of personality has a tremendous potential to provide comprehensive insight into human personality at multiple levels of analysis, including the genetics of personality, neurobiological foundations of behavior, the cognitive emotional structure and development of personality, the behavioral correlates of individual differences in personality dimensions, and the interactions of personality constellations with developmental factors in relation to the vulnerability to psychiatric disorders. Within emerging neuroimaging technology, Cloninger's model of personality will provide novel opportunities for elucidating the characterization of neural correlates of personality, and enable a better understanding of normal and pathological states. In this article, both underlying theory and empirically valiated findings along with its potential use in both general population and psychiatric patient population were reviewed.[41]

Two issues emerge from the study by Borg et al.: The alledged measurement of mystical experience is not designed to measure mystical experiences. It's a personality test designed to validate a theory about the level of brain chemistry in personality. This also tells us that the researchers studying serotonin as a cause of mystical experience are assuming up-front that mystical experience is the result of a personality trait brought on by brain chemistry. Thus if any association is made between personality traits and serotonin, they have proved their thesis as far as they are concerned. But is this research actually measuring mystical experience? We will see by looking further at the study that this conclusion is based upon only one similar trait. In Chapter 4 (Studies), we learned that the M scale avoids the pitfalls of many scales such as MMPI because they don't correlate with Stace's categories but only rely upon the assumption that one or two characteristics correlate with mystical experiences. This same criticism seems to fit the TCI scale as well (see Chapter 4, on Studies, footnotes 73 and 74). The superiority of Hood's scale is clearly demonstrated. Other scales have been used, especially in the 1970's and 1980s before Hood made his major contributions. Other scales could have been used. One can't help but wonder if the choice of the TCI isn't the result of assumptions on the part of the researchers.

Because religious experiences vary widely, Borg and her colleagues felt that the shared qualities must have a biological explanation. They chose to explore serotonin because it is naturally occurring and drugs such as psilocybin used in previous studies such as Good Friday merely mimic what serotonin does. [42] The subjects were scanned for serotonin density using MRI. The more dense their serotonin, the more they should tend to exhibit symptoms of self-transcendence because serotonin calms you down and works on receptors that would tend to contribute to self-transcendence. The TCI is a "personality assessment." This is how they assess the mystical experience they are supposedly evoking. Borg explains:

The Swedish translation of the Temperament and Character Inventory self-report questionnaire was used. The Temperament and Character Inventory consists of 238 items covering the four temperament dimensions of novelty seeking, harm avoidance, reward dependence, and persistence and the three character dimensions of self-directedness, cooperativeness, and self-transcendence. The Temperament and Character Inventory has been developed according to a suggestion that the four temperament dimensions reflect inherited behavior, whereas the three character dimensions are thought to be influenced by environment. For the first five subjects, the Temperament and Character Inventory was administered retrospectively less than 8 months after the PET examination. For the remaining 10 subjects, the Temperament and Character Inventory was administered on the same day as the PET.[43]

The PET is given with MRI and is related to the serotonin measurement. When Borg directly addresses mystical experience in the study, the only trait she talks about that is linked to mystical expertise is "self-transcendence."

The values for binding potential correlated significantly with the self-transcendence dimension but not with any of the other six Temperament and Character Inventory dimensions[44]. The self-transcendence dimension is a composite of three distinct subscales that describe aspects of spirituality. After the demonstration of statistical significance for the self-transcendence dimension, correlations for each of the dimension's three subscales were examined. Scores for spiritual acceptance versus material rationalism correlated significantly with 5-HT1A binding potential for all three regions[45]. No significant correlations were found for any of the remaining two sub-scales.

The only control on mystical experience is a test that is not designed to determine mystical experience; the researchers appear to assume that personality traits measured by the test will correlate, but give no basis in data for those conclusions. The only trait that is correlated is self-transcendence and they break that down into subscales that describe "spirituality." But is "spirituality" necessarily the same thing as "mystical experience?" Stace's categories are derived from his reading of all the major mystics, and they are validated with the M scale by applying it to actual modern mystical experiences. But Borg is assuming that personality traits double for mystical experience. What is this "spirituality" that makes up her assumptions about self-transcendence?

Borg explains the subscales that make up the self-transcendence dimension: "The self-transcendence dimension consists of three subscales representing several aspects of religious behavior, subjective experience and individual worldview. Of interest, in the extended analysis, we found that the correlation of self-transcendence was shown to be fully dependent on the spiritual acceptance scale, whereas no correlation was found to the other two subscales."[46] The spiritual acceptance scale measures a person's acceptance of phenomena that can't be measured by demonstrative evidence. Subjects with high scores might endorse extrasensory perceptions, ideation, a named deity or a commonly unifying force. This is from Coloninger's TCI inventory.[47] The researchers are assuming that the similarities from previous studies justify the assumption that the presence of a high density of serotonin in the subjects with high scores on this scale must be causally related. What they are really measuring upon this scale is a lot of things that have nothing to do with mystical experiences and they are just assuming that they do because they sound "religious." For example ESP has nothing to do with mystical experiences. Borg, et al. contend:

> On a behavioral level, these drugs elicit perceptual distortions, illusions, a sense of insight, spiritual awareness, mystical experiences, and religious ecstasy. Of interest, such pharmacological

effects induced by hallucinogens resemble the extrasensory
perception and ideation endorsed by subjects scoring high on the
spiritual acceptance scale. [48]

This quotation would seem to suggest that they are also arguing from
analogy based upon the assumption that hallucinations and delusions
are part of mystical experience or religious experience at any rate. We
see from the previous data cited, no such connection can be made.
None of the major criteria from mystical experience includes such
things as definitive. One can only speculate that a good deal of bias had
gone into the assumptions guiding the research. She doesn't actually
say "mystical experience involves delusions" but why cite the issue at
all if she's not trying to imply a connection?

When we ask "what does this study really prove?" we can only
respond that it proves there is some relationship between serotonin
levels and certain personality traits, some of which may be linked to
religious belief in general, and religious experience in general and
maybe one of them to mystical experience. The study can't even
demonstrate that it produced any sort of mystical experience or that it
measured mystical experience because the measuring stick it used
wasn't even designed for the task and because the assumptions made
were not adequate to the task. We already knew there was a connection.
The things that Newberg was quoted as saying in the previous chapter
(on the God Pod) should relieve any fear that a link between neurology
and RE disproves a role of the divine in the process. We know that
physical processes are part of our lives and that if there is any role of
the divine in our lives it has to interact with physical processes at some
point. If serotonin calms us down and feeling God's presence illicits
serotonin, then we will calm down. Skeptics assume the argument is
about miracles. It's a miracle when we feel the presence of God. But
this may be a misguided perception on the part of the believer. It need
not be viewed as a miracle. It could be quite naturalistic. That does not
mean it's not a trace of the divine. The real bottom line of the argument

turns not upon the astounding nature of the experience as it is felt when it's had, but upon the long-term positive effects of it later. How could this Borg study demonstrate a connection when it doesn't even have the right set of characteristics to study the phenomena in the first place?

The real crux to the matter of counter-causality is this: is there anything that demonstrates a real cause of mystical experience as wholly rooted in the natural processes of the world and bearing no relation to what we should expect from the trace of the divine? We have to answer at this point, not in relation to brain chemistry and mystical experience. This is because (1) it can't be demonstrated that mystical experience has been evoked by any manipulation of or study of brain chemistry, and (2) even if it was, that would not prove the case unless all the phenomena could be accounted for wholly in naturalistic terms including the long-term results of having had the experience. This is far from being the case. But even then there's a further argument that reductionism cannot answer. It's one thing to find a correlation and suggest the possibility of counter-causes based upon association between a chemical and a sensation. But it's quite another to demonstrate that everything mystics experience and learn can be accounted for only in these terms. The inability to account for all of the phenomena includes those relating to the phenomenological upshot of the experiences themselves. When we include this kind of material, the reductionist view is inadequate to account for it. This is analogous to the argument property dualists make that consciousness is irreducible. The long-term positive effects and experiences of encounters with the divine are irreducible.[49]

Tiebreakers:

How can we distinguish RE from naturalistic misfire of neurons or brain chemistry including drugs or placebo? In all three cases: drugs, placebo and "God Pod" there's basically a tie. It could go either way

Joseph Hinman

with regards to being a trick of the brain chemistry, a natural conduit for the divine, or an aid via drugs that opens up some form of receptors. Placebo can pretty much be eliminated as a bad analogy, or a misunderstanding of the process of spiritual function. But we still need a way to tell the difference between these possibilities of naturalistic alternative causes vs. trace of the divine. There are tie breakers: factors which shed light upon the issues in such a way as to point up the trace of the divine.

- Transformational effects
- Complex effects
- Placebo neutralized
- Neurologically hard to be positive as we get older, so the experience is less likely
- Effects are real therefore the cause is real: the content of the effect is that of the divine so we can assume it's real
- It works (it does what religion is supposed to do)
- Noetic qualities
- Sense of the numinous
- Why is it positive?
- Bad evolutionary answers rule out counter-causes
- Enables meaning and navigation in life which a merely natrualsitic cause would not do

Transformational effects

The transformative effects upon the life of the subject cannot be explained by alternate causes or pop psychology. Nothing in the process of brain chemistry explains how such a "misfire" can alter one's overall view of the world, behavior, attitude and outlook in such a way as to produce the kinds of dramatic changes that occur in the subjects of these experiences.

Complex effects

Transformational effects run the gamut from better self-confidence to freedom from drug addition. They include self-actualization (which is best described as "wholeness" or coming into one's own as a well-integrated person), well-grounded psychological health, a deep sense of meaning and purpose in life, overcoming the fear of death, and overcoming physical addictions such as alcoholism and drug abuse, happiness and personal bliss. Moreover, it's not just a list of "feel-good" things, but a total re-orienting of one's overall life; a dramatic transformation of life. In fact there's even more: self-authentication; the value and meaning of the nature of life itself is affirmed and one's place in the universe is made meaningful. This sense of the numinous is the basis of religion. The origin of religion is probably found in these experiences; religion is based upon the desire to find ultimate transformative experiences to overcome the human problematic; it works. Religion works to achieve the personal goal for which it was developed so long ago: transformational effects that resolve the human problematic.

Placebo argument neutralized

There is no medical or scientific evidence to show that placebo effects can be extrapolated to such complex psychological levels as to restore or renovate one's life as a whole for a lifetime. If this could be done, everyone would have found a way to do it. It's true that confidence can accomplish a lot, and perhaps belief that an all-powerful being is contacting us with messages of love and care would create the confidence necessary to carry one through life. If such is the case, there's no real evidence to back it up. It also works for those who don't believe a supernatural being is trying to help them. Eastern-style mystics experience the same transformative effects. Something about the experience itself, perhaps believing that one has found some answer regarding the overall scheme of reality is so stimulating that it alters one's vitality or one's grasp of life. But that's not really an argument against religion; that's something one might expect religion to accomplish. It certainly speaks to the noetic quality of mystical experiences. Since the placebo argument turns on a bad analogy anyway, there's no reason to take it seriously.

Neurologically it's much harder to be positive as we get older

The idea that these effects are not important or amazing because it's all just a placebo, and anyone who thinks positively and believes that a loving God takes care of him can just snap out of any funk by the power of placebo, is operating counter to what we know about the brain. As we get older it gets harder to catch the fire of good vibes and positive thoughts, as Newberg tells us:

> Neurologically, enlightenment and peace are unlikely. Even Kohlberg admitted that only a small percentage of adults will reach a moral level at which their lives are governed by higher ethical principles. Nevertheless this level can be reached by those who choose to work diligently toward the ideas it involves, although this process can take decades of introspection and practice... at any time in life a person —through meditation, prayer, and critical thinking— might be able to transcend the narcissistic confines of adolescence and thereby alter the neural functioning of the brain.[50]

My parents had their major religious experiences after the age of 60, and for both of them these profoundly transformed their lives. People who have these experiences are not zapped into instant perfection. They are still human and they still make mistakes, but a skeptic who blithely dismisses the phenomena on the basis of "placebo" is flying in the face of the major evidence. Self-actualization cannot be reduced or minimized to "happy," nor is it an easy task that requires only a bit of "psyching yourself into it." There is no good explanation other than divine transformation.

The effects are real therefore the cause is real

This is an argument from sign, but arguments from sign are not necessarily fallacious. The only problem that would falsify an argument from sign is if some counter causality cannot be addressed. I have now answered all the major and likely counter causalities. Given all that was said in Chapter 2 about how the experiences are historically linked to the divine and lie at the root of why we even have a concept of God in the first place, the content is linked to the divine and often draws one into religious belief. The experience itself often seems to be about God, the divine, the ultimate reality or the nature of being, and the effects are real; without these counter-causalities there is no reason not to assume the cause is real.

"It works" is a reason to assume it's true

Skeptics will be inclined to answer that "just because it works doesn't mean it's true." I admit this is not a proof, but then I've never claimed to "prove" the existence of God. My argument from the beginning was that belief is rationally warranted, not proved (see Chapter 2). The fact that these experiences work to provide transformational results is a rational warrant for belief that the ultimate source of the experience is the divine. The fact that it works is a tiebreaker. The tie is that it could be naturalistic; or it could be that the naturalistic elements are just the particular working out of the divine approach to sentient life. How to decide which it is? Well, normally in most cases of epistemic judgment (when we must make judgment calls as to what we know is real) we do tend to see "it works" as the ultimate justification. I argue that this is how we determine cause and effect and it's how we decide that science is valid. We determine cause and effect by results. We can't see cause and effect happening. We don't see causal agents, we make correlations, and the tightest ones we assume to be causal relationships if we can't link them to intervening variables or alternate causes. If we have a theory of mechanism in addition to effectiveness, we deem it icing on the cake and call it "scientific." The alternate causes to mystical experience and their effects that we have discussed are stuck in the tie. So the tiebreaker is that the correlation is tight enough to assume causes; the end result delivers the goods. When we troubleshoot any sort of electronic or mechanical device, the way we tell if we fixed it is if the trouble stops. If it works, we assume our understanding of the problem was right. Working equals truth in the epistemic field of our assumptions. Science is the umpire of reality; it has come to be regarded as the major source of knowledge and the only true test. The reason for this state of affairs is because science delivers the goods. How many atheists are willing to assume there is no supernatural because the natural is demonstrated in all scientific endeavors and the supernatural is supposedly "never demonstrated" in any scientific endeavors? This approach is nothing more on the atheist's part than saying "working equals truth; if it works, we can assume it's true."

Julian Baggini, author of *A Very Short Introduction to Atheism*,[51] offers a fine example of this atheist tendency in argument. Baggini essentially argues:

- Science works to deliver the epistemic goods, its findings are empirical and demonstrable. Therefore, naturalism is deemed true.
- Religions cannot offer empirical demonstrable evidence of the supernatural (so he thinks); therefore, the supernatural is not true.

He tells us:

> This is only evidence against God's existence in a negative sense: that is to say, evidence for God's existence will be found to be lacking and so we will be left with no reason to suppose he exists.[52]
>
> The evidence of experience is that we live in a world governed by natural laws, that everything that happens in it is explained by natural phenomena.[53]

In other words, he's arguing that science works, naturalism works via scientific empiricism; therefore, it must be true. Moreover, he's arguing if something doesn't work (i.e. religion) then it must not be true. Baggini does not appear to be aware of the nature of religious experience or the huge body of data and scientific works backing it up. The supernatural is demonstrated in that religious belief accomplishes its basic task of mediating transformational experiences that overcome the human problematic. That is the supernatural. That is not just part of the supernatural or an effect of the supernatural, that's the original concept itself.[54]

Therefore RE works, so it must be true. In reality we don't see labels on rocks and trees saying, "There is no supernatural, this is a natural rock." We have no actual proof there is no supernatural. Naturalists assume so because their ideological construct tells them so. Also, science delivers the goods. In other words, "it works" is deemed to be proof of truth. The point is, for science the assumption is made that science gives us truth about reality because it delivers the goods; it works so it must be true. There is no evidence against the supernatural, but the skeptical assumption is science works so we assume science is true.

The reasons for thinking that God is behind these experiences are laid out in Chapter 2 . The construal that this is the trace of God is valid logically. It is a construal warrant for belief and not proof. The thesis that God exists does not have to be logically or scientifically proven for the construal of God as the ultimate source of the experiences to be rationally warranted. The construal works. Religious belief works to produce the effects of transformation in people's lives, which is the basic task of religious belief: overcoming the human problematic.

Of course a variety of atheists will try to minimize the effects. Experience in arguing with them shows they exhibit a range of outlooks. Some have been extremely uneducated and clueless, some have been very well educated and very intelligent, but all of them always take this approach of trying to minimize the effects. One of the worst examples was a young atheist who charged "these 'studies' are just Christian pastors asking their flock to email them and tell them how they are getting happy." I don't think Abraham Maslow was a Christian pastor. He was an atheist with Buddhist tendencies. These effects are real, as we have seen in the studies chapter, and there are just too many of them to minimize the effects. The studies are longitudinal, cross-cultural, from many different fields and areas. The studies include cancer patients, alcohol and drug addicts, the mentally ill, regular people and highly successful and accomplished people. The affects are sometimes very dramatic and far-reaching —they can last a lifetime from just one experience. Moreover, they are therapeutic; they help people get better and overcome their problems.

It is not plausable to say that these are just trivial effects that one can get from any kind of change or hobby or nice time. If that were so, why would people continue to have their problems? If you can resolve this stuff (drug addiction, depression, mental illness, meaninglessness and so forth) by collecting stamps or watching football or going to the park, why do people have problems? Obviously those pursuits, while helpful, are not transformative. As Maslow writes:

> ...My feeling is that if it were never to happen again, the power of the experience could permanently affect the attitude toward life. A single glimpse of heaven is enough to confirm its existence even if it is never experienced again. It is my strong suspicion that even one such experience might be able to prevent suicide, for instance, and perhaps many varieties of slow self-destruction, e.g., alcoholism, drug-

addiction, addiction to violence, etc. I would guess also, on theoretical grounds, that peak-experiences might very well abort "existential meaninglessness," states of valuelessness, etc., at least occasionally. (These deductions from the nature of intense peak-experiences are given some support by general experience with LSD and psilocybin. Of course these preliminary reports also await confirmation.)... ...This then is one kind of peak-knowledge of whose validity and usefulness there can be no doubt, any more than there could be with discovering for the first time that the color "red" exists and is wonderful. Joy exists, can be experienced and feels very good indeed, and one can always hope that it will be experienced again....

...Perhaps I should add here the paradoxical result —for some— that death may lose its dread aspect. Ecstasy is somehow close to death-experience, at least in the simple, empirical sense that death is often mentioned during reports of peaks, sweet death that is. After the acme, only less is possible. In any case, I have occasionally been told, "I felt that I could willingly die," or, "No one can ever again tell me death is bad," etc. Experiencing a kind of "sweet death" may remove its frightening aspect. This observation should, of course, be studied far more carefully than I have been able to. But the point is that the experience itself is a kind of knowledge gained (or attitude changed) which is self-validating. Other such experiences, coming for the first time, are true simply because experienced, e.g., greater integration of the organism, experiencing physiognomic perception, fusing primary- and secondary-process, fusing knowing and valuing, transcending dichotomies, experiencing knowing as being, etc., etc. The widening and enriching of consciousness through new perceptual experiences, many of which leave a lasting effect, is a little like improving the perceiver himself....[55]

When I have argued this tiebreaker ("it works") on the internet, atheists have responded by special pleading. Apparently they seem to think that the differences between science and religion are such that for science 'it works" is the basis for being true, but not for religion. This may be because they feel that what it works to do is invalid (they have to

Joseph Hinman

reduce self-actualization to "it makes me happy" and they have to
ignore the studies to get away with it). They try to disvalue the
transformational effects of RE; they will accept "it works" for science
but not for religion. This is nothing more than special pleading. It's not
at all the same as saying, "if the universe must have a cause, why
doesn't God have a cause?" The differences in science and religion
have no bearing on the general principle of working as an indication of
truth. No one ever says, "it works, it must be a lie." Or "it works, we
have done something wrong." That it does what it's meant to do
(provide ultimate transformational effects to resolve the human
problematic) is what religion is "meant" to do.

Noetic Qualities

"Noetic" refers to the knowledge-giving effects of mystical
experiences. Typically the sort of knowledge one derives from these
experiences is "spiritual" in nature, such as "God is love." It can also be
doctrinal such as (for some) "everything is one." The knowledge-giving
(noetic) qualities of mystical experience offer a tiebreaker because they
imply that more is going on than just some misfire of neurons or an
imbalance of brain chemistry. While I don't advocate making doctrine
solely on the basis of religious experience, the sense of the noetic
quality is important for foundational understanding of a sort that can
only be gained in "personal relationship". This is where the entire sense
of "knowing God" is found. What makes it a tiebreaker? The skeptic
will certainly say, "so what if you have a bunch of false ideas about an
imaginary entity based upon these mistaken experiences?" But the
sense of personal knowledge, first-hand knowledge of God, that comes
from such experiences fits the basic criteria we use to make epistemic
judgments. In speaking of the noetic qualities, Maslow said:

The question has to be differentiated still further. There is no doubt that great insights and revelations are profoundly felt in mystic or peak-experiences, and certainly some of these are, ipso facto, intrinsically valid as experiences. That is, one can and does learn from such experiences that, e.g., joy, ecstasy, and rapture do in fact exist and that they are in principle available for the experiencer, even if they never have been before. Thus the peaker learns surely and certainly that life can be worthwhile, that it can be beautiful and valuable. There are ends in life, i.e., experiences which are so precious in themselves as to prove that not everything is a means to some end other than itself.[56]

The previous quote from Maslow is also an example of the kind of knowledge gained; not doctrinal knowledge about the nature of God, but personal and existential knowledge about living the possibilities of transcendence.

Recall the second argument from Chapter 2. I speak of the "argument from epistemic judgment" (or "the Thomas Reid argument"). We habitually subject epistemic questions of an empirical nature to a litmus test of regularity, consistency, and inter-subjectivity ("shared"). We follow perceptions that work in terms of how they allow us to navigate in the world. We check our perceptions against others ("Did you see that?" "Do you find it hot in here too, or is it just me?"). We assume that irregularity and inconsistency are earmarks of anomaly. Mystical experiences are regular, consistent, and inter-subjective. They are regular and consistent to the extent that one can have the same kinds of experiences in prayer every time one prays. Probably there will be one major experience that won't ever be repeated but a lesser version of the same kind of thing might recur on a regular basis. The experiences are consistent to the extent that they yield the same kinds of results time after time; a loving presence, a pervading sense of peace. I can think of some counter-examples, such as the example given by James, but for the most part they are consistent. That which we identify as God's presence has a familiarity about it such that we can identify it time after time. This sense of God's presence is not wonderful one time and horrible the next. There is a sense of God's presence, which is "terrible" in that one feels convicted of sin, overwhelmed by a clearly superior greatness, over-awed by the unknown, in short, the terrible sublime; yet even in this sense the undertone of love and peace and acceptance is still pervasive. Such experiences are usually resolved with the sense of peace, love and well-being.

All of this is more complex, unified and directed, and it seems too purposeful to be a mere "misfire" or some trick of the mind. It's not based upon expectations so it can't be a placebo. It seems to have a positive end or direction, and the noetic quality gives it a sense of purpose that transcends mere brain chemistry. Why would a trick of brain chemistry lead to self-authentication and be regular, consistent, and inter-subjective? The inter-subjective qualities are important because it isn't likely that millions of people across all cultural boundaries and in different time periods would be getting the same kinds of "misfires," "accidents," mistakes in perception, do the same kind of labeling, or have the same kinds of placebos. Yet it is the case that the same kinds of experiences with the same qualities keep popping up again and again. It is also true that most of the time these experiences are noetic. They are always regular, consistent, and inter-subjective as well.

Sense of the Numinous (Holiness)

In the chapter on Proudfoot's label idea, I said that the labeling theory is leaving out an aspect to the experiences. I said that Proudfoot was losing the phenomena, which he accused the religious subject of doing. This was seen in the Bradley case that he quoted from William James where there had to be something more than just a rapid heart beat to lead Bradley to think more was happening than just a heart attack. In most of these experiences there is a sense of the numinous or "the spiritual", something more than just the normal aspects of reality. Often times that sense is the sense of the Holy that Rudolf Otto speaks of: the notion of a pervasive sense of otherness, cleanness, goodness, love, something beyond the mundane, something otherworldly that is not reducible to any mundane contrivance. This is what gives us the religious sense of the experience. Why would that happen so consistently with just some misfire of neurons or some reaction of brain chemistry? The skeptic can repeat the labeling or placebo argument, but I think that was dealt with pretty well. The skeptics are again losing the phenomena.

It doesn't seem likely that there would be this accidental misfire or chemical imbalance, which would always produce this same sense of holiness that is also always connected to the concept of God or the divine. It doesn't make sense that this could be a product of labeling or placebo because they would always have to be loading the experience into the same constructs. Yet these experiences seem to transcend time and culture. How is it that the same constructs are there in every culture to lead to the same pervasive sense of the Holy? Maslow would say this is because they are loading experiences into archetypes. While he valued mystical experience, he also reduced the sense of the numinous to everyday psychology and put the supernatural in the natural. He naturalized the archetypes but they also serve as a bridge to the divine. They are essentially the Platonic forms reduced to psychological proportions. All one need do is flip the notion over and we move into the world of Augustine. It's like one of those 3D pictures that looks like a repetitive muddle of little pictures melted into each other, but if you stare at it long enough in the right way it suddenly pops into a three-dimensional window that really does look like another world. The sense of the holy is too purposive and pervasive, too rational, to be merely a mistake of brain chemistry. The Lamarkian nonsense that tries to base genes upon the need to cope with angst is not an adequate answer. The placebo effect assumes cultural constructs that can't lend themselves to the cultural verities of the experiences.

Why is it positive?

This may seem redundant because I speak of the long-term positive effects above. But the following poses a slightly different question. If these experiences are the result of accidents, mistakes and tricks of the mind, why don't they also produce negative results as well as positive? There is no evidence at all that mystical experience is long-term negative or harmful. There have been some short-term findings of anxiety associated with TM, but there is no evidence that a mystical experience that grounds one in belief in God ever hurt anyone. These are totally positive experiences on almost every occasion. They are so strongly linked with positive results that there are no studies that show they are harmful. Why would this happen? Why would they always be so positive and never harm or lead to mental illness? Even in cases where mentally ill people have mystical experiences, the experience is good for them in that it enables faster recovery and can be distinguished from the illness itself. (See Chapter 4, on mental illness).[57]

Bad evolutionary answers

Mystical experiences are not connected to gene frequency. All of the answers about being comforted are simply non-Darwinian, and at worst Lamarckian. As pointed out in the previous chapter, such experiences are not related to gene frequency and no link has been found to connect them with reproduction. To explain the experience by some factor such as the need of early man to cope with death and the unknown, one has to assume Lamarck was right and that experiences become genetic traits. No mechanism can be produced that tells us that our existential fears can become part of our genetic endowment, or that resolving them can become a heritable trait. Thus this means that the overall experience is unaccounted for and the positive results are still mysterious (see Kirkpatrick in the chapter on "God-Pod")[58] This means the effects are unexplained, and in fact the entire phenomenon is unexplained in terms of why it would be so.

Meaning: navigation in life

These experiences form the basis of a coherent, livable, positive worldview that culminates in self-authentication. Not only do the experiences themselves produce self-actualization (the maximization of values, self definition and abilities into a holistically integrated "well" individual) but also self-authentication: the validation of one's existence in relation to the universe and one's sense of place in the universe. Self-authentication would lead one to say, "This is what my life is about, this is what it all means to me, and it's worth it to be me and live this life." To argue that this is all just imposed meaning from the labeling of quirks and characteristics that can't be explained, or it's a placebo because it involves belief, or some accidental misfire of neurons in the brain produced this by mistake (which keeps on producing it in one of four people in the world's population, across cultures and throughout history) just pushes the envelope on credulity. Why would anyone who finds this sort of bliss even care anyway? The skeptic, like Captain Kirk, has to destroy paradise after paradise to save the Prime Directive. Yet accepting the results as validating the belief is far from moving into a fantasy on mere preferences. The worldview that is fostered through these experiences is one that enables the experiencer to face the trials and trammels of life, not to pretend they are not there. There are people who have mystical experiences and decide they aren't indicative of God and go on to become skeptics; some might argue that they have not accepted the worldview of the others. While it is true they have not accepted the tradition of the others, it's not true that haven't been positively affected by their experience. There are greater complexities involved than just an experience where rejection of organized religion is concerned. The fact remains that an orientation toward the depth of being and understanding of a transcendent reality is the outcome most associated with the experiences, and that alone should tell us that there is an indication that it's pointing to some greater reality.

The skeptic will argue that meaning is just imposed. Skeptics seem to always assert that any meaning derived from anything is always imposed. Is meaning imposed? Sure it is. There is no understanding of qualia or sense data that doesn't impose meaning. We can't interpret reality without imposing meaning. All understanding is imposed meaning. That is no reason to shun meaning because if we do then we will have to shun all meaning. We cannot communicate without imposing meaning, and when we seem to make contact and actually communicate, we assume the meaning corresponds with intent. Newberg told us in the previous chapter that our brain sorts out meaning. We never see a view of the world as it is, all our senses feed the data to the brain and the brains re-writes the picture to make sense of the world for us. We operate in the world not based upon direct empirical perceptions of what is, but based upon the imposed, re-written, propagandized version of meaning we impose. Yet we can navigate and make sense of things. When this seems to work out, we assume we got it right. The fact that meanings are imposed is not a major barrier for us. We don't sweat this. We don't figure it out. We move fluidly through the world, never noticing the problem. The fact that the upshot of religious experience is a coherent, rational worldview that works in that it allows us to operate in the world and culminates in the sense of well-being and ultimate meaning that authenticates our existence is a good reason to assume that these experiences are the trace of God, that they are something more than just an accident of brain chemistry.

Furthermore, the worldview that is built upon it enables one to navigate through life in the sense of being able to cope with what comes. Pargament (1996) cites five studies showing that religious experience, devotion and spirituality enable one to cope to a greater extent with extreme conditions of hardship.[59] Moran (1990) and Patricia (1998)[60] both show that religious practices and devotion enable coping with childhood violence. De Rogario (1998) finds that spirituality enables those with handicaps and chronic illness to cope with life.[61] It seems absurd to think that all these coping mechanisms are either just the result of a chemical imbalance, which should always in other cases turn out negatively, or the result of a natural deposit of serotonin which never enables this sort of thing apart from religiosity. To each of these tie-breakers, many atheists will no doubt posit the existence of some mechanism that is entirely naturalistic but employs these effects for survival in some sense. In fact, they already posit such things in terms of the "God part of the brain" (God Pod). As I argued, they do that with Lamarckian assumptions. There is no basis for the notion that such experiences contribute to physical survival or gene frequency. Probably few early humans were drug addicts. These experiences seem too well fitted to our basic epistemic criteria, too complex, too meaningful and purposive to be attributed to an accident, and the survival mechanism theory can't hold water.

The Rogario study found that spiritual experience was essential to the ability of disabled people to build a framework around their lives which would enable them to not merely "get by" but actually grow and progress emotionally and spiritually. The people she studied are not merely imposing meaning on shattered lives to survive; they are actually going forward with a positive sense of growth. This positive movement is clearly related to the long-term positive effects of RE that I have been calling "transformation." These people's lives are transformed by their spiritual experiences. What this tells us is that this phenomenon is applicable not just to people with "disabilities" or challenges but to us all, for navigation in life. The skeptic can always theorize about counter causalities and refuse to believe, but there's no doubt that something is going on; it's more than a chemical imbalance. When you see it, when you get it, you know it's real. Rogario alludes to Victor Frankl who said of the Holocaust based upon his own experience in a Nazi concentration camp "suffering ceases to be suffering in some way at the moment it finds a meaning."[62] The skeptic can always charge that we all impose meaning, all meaning is imposed and this meaning is prompted by a chemical imbalance of the agencies that cause calm in us. The person who really experiences navigation in life living by spiritual means and fueled by RE would find this explanation missing the fact of this experience.

Rational warrant

The skeptic will no doubt reply, "but you haven't actually proven that there is a God, much less that God is doing this." We only need a rational warrant. I never claimed that my arguments proved the existence of God. I only claimed to offer rational warrant for belief, and I think I've done that. Here I want to bring in the concept of "the freedom from the need to prove". The atheists on the internet use the concept of the "default assumption". That is, they are saying that in the absence of proof (of God) they must assume as a "default" that there is no God. But if the arguments for the trace of God have met its *prima facie* burden, then we should be able to expect that *presumption has shifted and rational warrant has been established*. The freedom from the need to prove I have introduced in Chapter 2 and 4. The atheist says, "In the absence of proof I must assume there is no God." The believer's default says, "I know something is there because my life was transformed." Until it is proven otherwise, I must assume that God is real. Thus I am freed from the need to prove because I have certainty for my own life. Now the atheist is going to charge that I'm just reversing the burden of proof, but in fact this is a reasonable move according to the rules of a *prima facie* case. Once a *prima facie* case is established it becomes the other side's burden to show that more is required. We have good reason to believe that these naturalistic aspects are merely intervening variables; they are not disproof of the trace of the divine. Until that is disproved, belief is rationally warranted.

How do we know the *prima facie* burden has been met? According to the criteria that were laid out in Chapter 1:

1. Documented perceptual evidence.
   There are 200 studies or so.
2. Perception (or other evidence) that is regular (a form of replicability).
   Regularity is well-documented. One can cultivate the experiences; it may not always be exactly the same, but it can be repeated with prayer or other practices.
3. Consistency (meaning no internal contradictions).
   The experiences are consistent with themselves; the same presence can be recognized each time.
4. Inter-subjective verification (others can experience similar phenomena, share the data, observe the same kinds of qualia).
   The same commonalities show up across all cultural boundaries and throughout history.
5. Logical inference from both inductive and deductive reasoning.
   The skeptic must show that the inference is not logical; the content is about God, the experiences are real; that is a logical basis for the assumption. The content and the outcome match up and indicate the origin.
6. Tangible measurable effects.
   The M scale has demonstrated this point.
7. No counter-causality: counter-causes must be defeated, disproved, or rendered less likely
   The tie-breakers render the counter-causality less likely.
8. Must be falsifiable.
   The studies could show that the transformative effects were not

concrete but illusory, and yet that has not been the case. The M Scale makes the experiences falsifiable. These studies combined with Newberg's neurological evidence rule out the possibility of illusory effects.

Real changes occur in the brain, real behaviors (and changes of behavior) occur in the lives of the believers, and attitude changes and a new level of conscious perception accompany them. This lines up with the content of the experience, its noetic quality and its tendency to draw one to the divine. All of that indicates that we are following the trace of God; these are the effects upon the human heart and lives that we should expect from the divine.

The overall point is one of phenomenological import. The individual must realize the reality of God in his/her own life by understanding the nature of his/her own experiences. It's not a matter of "proof". It's not a matter of objective public knowledge to which all must either give assent or disprove. It is a matter of one's own subjective existential decision based upon the effect of the divine (or what is taken as the divine) on one's own life. But the objective discernable facts indicate that the effects of these experiences are real, and to that extent we are rationally justified in drawing the conclusion that the content is real, therefore, the thing experienced itself is real. To the extent that the *prima facie* burden is met the reader should be able or willing to trust to some extent and to seek for herself.

1   ExChristian.net, "letter from 'Jeff'". Website, http://exchristian.net/testimonies/2005/01/new-atheist-family-advice.php (accessed 10/28/08).

2   Bill Taylor, "Is Religion a Placebo?" *New Scientist*, 25 Feb (2006) online edition: http://www.newscientist.com/article/mg18925401.300-is-religion-a-placebo.html (accessed 10/28/08).

3   Aliceon Motluk, "Belief Special: When Delusion Triumphs over Truth." *New Scientist*, (2006) Jan 28, issue 2536

4 *Ibid.*

5 Daniel E. Morman, Wane B. Jonas, "Deconstructing the Placebo Effect and Finding the Meaning Response." *Annals of Internal Medicine,* Volume 136, Issue 6, 19 March (2002), 471-476. Dr. Moreman: Department of Anthropology, University of Michigan–Dearborn.

6 Anne Herrington, *The Placebo Effect.* Cambridge Mass.: Harvard University Press, 2000.117.

7 J. Coyle, "Seeing a Placebo Work in the Brain." Journal Watch, oct 3, vol., 293, (2001)., 1164-1166.

8 Aaron K Vallance, "Something Out of Nothing, the Placebo Effect,." *The British Journal of Psychiatry.* Advances in Psychiatric Treatment, vol 12, (2006), 287-296. This journal is also known as BJ Psych. Aaron Vallance is currently a staff-grade child and adolescent psychiatrist with the Service for Adolescents and Families in Enfield. He is also Associate Research Fellow with the Metabolic and Clinical Trials Unit, Department of Mental Health Sciences, The Royal Free Hospital, London, and a member of the Editorial Board of the *Journal of Alternative and Complementary Complimentary Medicine.*

9 *Ibid.*

10 *Ibid.*

11 Daniel E. Moreman, *op. cit.,*471-476.

12 L.D. Egbert, G.E. Battie, M.K. Bartlett, "A study of doctor-patient rapport" *New England Journal of Medicine.* 1964,270:825.

13 Moreman, Op. Cit. 471.

14 *Ibid., 471.*

15 Clay C. Whitehead, "Toward a New Paradigm of Therapeutic Action: Neuro Psychoanalysis and Downward Causation." *Journal of American Academy of Psychoanalysis,* 33, (2005), 637-656

16 *The Rochester Review,* website, University of Rochester Public Relations, Rochester, New York, 1997: http://www.rochester.edu/pr/Review/V59N3/feature2.html (accessed 10/10/08)

17 *Ibid.*

18 Ibid

19 Rick Doblin, "Pahnke's 'Good Friday Experiment' a Long Term Follow-up and Methodological Critique." *The Journal of Transpersonal Psychology,* Vol. 23, No.1, (1991), 1-28.

20 Ibid

Joseph Hinman

22 Ibid

21a 21a. C. Daniel Batson, W. Larry Ventis, *The Religious Experience: A Social-Psychological Perspective.* New York: Oxford University Press, 1982, 115.

23 M. Laski, *Ecstasy in Secular and Religious Experiences*, Los Angeles: J.P. Tarcher, publishers, 1990, oringally 1961, 271.

24 Sanford M. Unger, "Mescaline, LSD-25, Psilocybin and Personality Change*." Psychiatry Journal for the Study of Interpersonal Processes.* Vol., 26, no 2, May (1963), 111-125.

25 Laski, *op. cit.*, 263-264.

26 *Ibid.,* 264-265

27 *Ibid.,* 265

28 *Ibid.,* 267-268

29 *Ibid.,* 269-270

30 Caroline Franks Davis, *The Evidential Force of Religious Experience.* Oxford: Clarendon Press, 1989, 218.

31 *Ibid.,* 221.

32 Doblin, *Ibid.,* 12

33 *Ibid.,* 14.

34 *Ibid.,* 17.

35 *Ibid.*

36 Roland Griffiths, W.A. Richards, U. McCann, R.Jesse. "Psilocybin Can Occasion Mystical Type Experiences Having Substantial and Sustained Personal Meaning and Spiritual Significance." Psychopharmacology, Jan, 187(2006), 268-283.

37 *Ibid.,* abstract.

38 *Ibid.,* 270

39 Press release."Hopkins Scientists show Hallucinogen in Mushrooms Creates Universal Mystical Experience." Johns Hoppkins Univ. "Medicine" press release, Jul 11, 2006, http://www.hopkinsmedicine.org/Press_releases/2006/07_11_06.html (accessed 07/18/2009).

40 J. Borg et al, "The Serotonin System and Spiritual Experiences" *The American Journal of Psychiatry,* 160: (Nov 2003) 1965-1969, http://ajp.psychiatryonline.org/cgi/content/full/160/11/1965 (accessed 07/17/2009).

41   Samuel Kose. "A Psychobiological Model of Temperment and Character (TCI),"*American Journals Database.* Yeni Semposium 2003. http://www.journaldatabase.org/articles/71232/ A_psychobiological_model_.html, full text: http://www.yenisymposium.net/FULLTEXT/2003(2)/ys2003_41_2_6.pdf visted 7/17/2009.

42   Borg, Op. Cit.

43   *Ibid.,* no page number, online.

44   Table 1 online

45   Figure 1 online

46   *Ibid.,*online.

47   *Ibid.*

48   *Ibid.*

49   this has noting to do with "ID" or Intelligent Design. I am not an "ID" person.

50   Andrew Newberg, *Why We Believe What We Believe*, op cit 128.

51   Julian Baggnini, Atheism: *A Very Short Introduction.* Oxford: Oxford University press, 2003. Baggini edits Philospher Magazine,

52   *Ibid.,* 16

53   *Ibid.,* 19

54   Eugene R. Fairweather, "Christianity and the Sueprnatural" in New Theology No. 1. ed. Martin E. Marty and Dean Peerman, MacMillian, 1964, 239.

55   Abraham H. Maslow, opc cit Appendix D. "What is the Validity of Knowledge Gained in Peack Experience?"

56   Abraham H. Maslow, op cit, Appendix I. An Example of B-Analysis

57   Spiritual Emergency Mystical or Unitive Experience. Op cit

58   Lee A. Kirkpatrick. OP cit

59   K.I. Pargament, "Religious Methods of Coping: Resources for the Conversation and Transformation of Significance." In E.P. Shafnaske (ed.) *Religion and Clinical Practice of Psychology*, Washington DC: American Psychological Association, 1996, 215-239.

60   *Ibid.,* Pargament.

61   L. Do Rozario, Op. Cit. (1997) 423-427.

62   Victor Frankl in Rozario, op cit, 432

8 Traditions: The Function of Religious Tradition in Relation to Mystical Experience and its Ineffability

In this chapter I want to deal with two major arguments, both of which are related, even though they may not appear to be. Atheists or skeptics tend to argue that mystical experience is too vague to base anything upon. The ineffability of mystical experience leads the unwary to feel that there is no content, that nothing of value can be derived from it. They might tend to doubt the noetic quality of such experience. I have heard atheists say that I am trying to have it both ways, to believe in God but not have to define what that means or say anything about "him". The other issue is the problem of religious traditions. I bracketed this in Chapter 2, so it's time to deal with it now. The problem is that there are so many different religious traditions, they can't all be right; it's too parochial to maintain that just one is right and all the others are wrong. Skeptics sometimes also throw in "Don't the experiences all contradict one another?" It is true that mystics often derive confirmation of their traditional doctrines from their experiences, but as I have also documented (Chapters 5 and 8), mystics sometimes find that their experiences contradict their doctrines as well. Nevertheless we must ask "what goes on with these different traditions?" Another related topic I will pick up as a loose end: if these experiences are noetic, why have I said I won't base doctrine upon them? I am not here speaking of mystical experience in the writing of Holy Scripture. I mean that modern mystics today do not and cannot claim to supersede scripture. These three questions, but especially the first two, need to be dealt with, and this is the time to do it. Another major question that needs to be dealt with here is my own hope, expressed at the outset, that these arguments may be of use to Christian apologists (who well may be alienated by my argument by now, but since Christianity is my tradition, I would like my arguments to be of use to them).

These are the Four Issues I will address in this chapter:

1. The vague nature of the ideas (trying to have it both ways?)
2. The contradiction of many traditions
3. Why not base doctrine on these experiences if they are experiences of the divine?
4. How can these arguments be used for Christian apologetics?

As to the idea that ineffability renders the experience too vague to be of value, that depends entirely upon what one is trying to derive from the experience. In dealing with that I will also answer the third question, the one about doctrine, as well. The ineffable nature of these experiences necessitates that they be filtered through cultural constructs in order to discuss them. This basically guarantees that we cannot get it completely right, because no cultural construct can do justice to that which is transcendent and beyond our understanding. While this cannot be helped, it's not as great a problem as it seems. It's all a matter of what one expects in the way of information. All religious language is essentially analogical. Thus, all religious ideas are basically guaranteed to be wrong, that is if the precision of one-to-one correspondence is the only measure of truth. Ineffable truths, however, are not measured in this way. I would not want the heart surgeon laboring to save my life to speak in metaphor or analogical language: "clamp, scalpel, ray of hope." But while linguistic precision is possible along a narrow range of the empirical, the closer we move to anything transcendent, the more "off center" the correspondence grows. Naturalists want to pretend that this epistemic problem proves the truth of naturalism and reductionism, but all it really proves is that the limited sliver of reality that we can observe empirically is open to us along a narrow range, and anything beyond that is beyond the grasp of mere intellect and language. This in no way invalidates belief that there *is* something beyond our grasp. Just because we can't talk about it doesn't mean that we can't experience it. The reductionist balks at the process of belief based upon ineffable experiences, because there's nothing to reduce. Reductionism is in essence a method of control. Modern humans seek power over nature, and knowledge of the workings of the physical world, to an extent, is power. The reductionist seeks power through reducing phenomena and eliminating that which does not lend itself to control. If one is experiencing reality beyond our understanding, reality that can't be understood or reduced, then it cannot be controlled.

While it is true that vague notions that can't be pinned down can't bestow much rational knowledge, the matter really depends upon what one wishes to do with the knowledge. I would not attempt heart surgery by means of mystical experience. Mysticism is not engineering. I would not try to build anything based upon knowledge gleaned from the noetic aspects of mysticism. The use to which we put the experiences is not the same as that to which we put the well-defined, pinned-down knowledge that we love to gather. Mystical experience is for experiencing. Mystical experience is like love; it *is* love, in a very real sense. Love is not for reading about on paper. Those who try to do all their loving on paper are doing so out of frustration, not because it really pays off. The truth found in mystical experience is for experiencing and for living. This is truth we live by, it enables us to know how to live and to treat others, and we live through the transformational aspects —but we do not have to pin these down to tangible qualities on paper; it's not doctrinal truth. As I pointed out in the previous chapter, the kind of knowledge gleaned from mystical experience is more existential than factual. That is to say, mystical experience enables us to know life and to have the emotional strength to face life with its trials and trammels. The old saw about religious people being weak and needing crutches is off-track. In that sense, it is navigational, because it enables us to navigate life emotionally and psychologically. That characterization may illicit charges of "placebo" from skeptics, but that response seems weak when one faces the trials and tragedies of life and realizes the value of having something that does make one stronger.

Moreover, science also embraces things that are beyond our understanding. There is no real evidence of string membranes; certainly no one has ever seen one. But lots of scientifically minded people are convinced of the notion that they really exist. Yet the precise coordinates science might glean from them are as yet only as certain as that of mystical experience. In fact, our brains are wired to make metaphor a necessary part of our apparatus. We do view the world through metaphor, and we have to do so. As seen in the argument from epistemic judgment, the most basic epistemic judgments are made without empirical proof. There is no scientific evidence that enables us to know that life is real, that we exist, that other minds exist; that the past will be like the future, that this is not an illusion, that the sun will come up tomorrow, or a host of other basic assumptions we take for granted. We have no scientific evidence that answers any of these problems. Skeptics of course will argue this inductively and extrapolate from experience, but that is the point. It is only because our experiences enable us to function with the assumption of reality, that we are able to make a judgment about reality and utilize it. We do not find the lack of direct scientific verification debilitating, we just assume we perceived correctly. We do this because our experiences are regular, consistent, and to an extent inter-subjective. In the same way, religious experience fits these qualities. We should be able to trust the kinds of knowledge we gain from mystical experience to the same extent we trust our regular daily waking perceptions. When I say "to the extent," I don't mean to the same degree, but for the same reasons. Our daily waking perceptions can be inaccurate at times. Mystical experience cannot give us the kind of precision of knowledge that we get from math or science, but then we don't need that kind of precision for the types of knowledge we glean from mystical experience. For this reason (the vague nature of the experience), we must speak in metaphorical terms when speaking of religious matters. All religious language is basically analogical or metaphorical. This is not a limitation for the kind of knowledge for which mystical experience is suited.

Metaphorical language is necessary, and to some extent all perceptions of the world are metaphorical. In another chapter ("God Pod"), I quoted Newberg saying that our brains re-write our understanding of the world. We are not getting a straight one-to-one correspondence between the world and our perceptions. Without metaphor, we don't have sufficient latitude to make lateral moves and to navigate efficiently. I refer again to his example of a robot attempted at a university in the early 80s. That robot took a whole day to move across a room and close a door. When an "X" was placed upon the door, the robot could not close the door. The robot had to re-examine everything it saw every time it took a step, because with every step the world was totally different. That's why it took all day. It could not close the door with the X on it because it didn't know that doors could have X's on them. It was unable to extrapolate from what it knew to cope with the unknown, because it could not think metaphorically or analogously.[1] The assumption that the more robot-like we are, the more precise and mathematical and the more literal we are, the more truth we find, is a fallacious assumption. This is a perfect metaphor for reductionism and scientism (and a few hyper-literal religious fundamentalists might benefit from this point as well). The metaphorical nature of religious language is essential for understanding the world, because we must be able to extrapolate and to think figuratively and symbolically. The figurative nature of language enables us to extrapolate. There is an excellent quote by Newberg (already quoted in "God Pod") that speaks to just this point, and it warrants re-examination:

The medieval German mystic Meister Eckhart lived hundreds of years before the science of neurology was born. Yet it seems he had intuitively grasped one of the fundamental principles of the discipline: what we think of as reality is only a rendition of reality that is created by the brain. Our modern understanding of the brain's perceptual powers bears him out. Nothing enters consciousness whole. There is no direct, objective experience of reality. All the things the mind perceives —all thoughts, feelings, hunches, memories, insights, desires, and revelations— have been assembled piece by piece by the processing powers of the brain from the swirl of neural blimps. The idea that our experiences of reality —all our experiences, for that matter— are only "secondhand" depictions of what may or may not be objectively real, raises some profound questions about the most basic truths of human existence and the neurological nature of spiritual experience. For example, our experiment with Tibetan mediators and Franciscan nuns showed that the events they considered spiritual were, in fact, associated with observable neurological activity. In a reductionist sense this could support the argument that religious experience is only imagined neurologically, that God is physically 'all in your mind.' But a full understanding of the way in which the brain and the mind assemble and experience reality suggests a very different view.[2]

The description he gives of brain architecture is very compelling on this point: the brain re-writes the world for us; it does not deliver the world to us unvarnished. We are working through a maze of metaphor anyway. All of our understanding of reality is in a sense analogical. Even math is analogical and not literal, in the sense that we can't appreciate it literally, we can't experience the world as a computer does, wrapped entirely in mathematical terms (if we can speak of computer "experiencing").

Given the nature of brain architecture and its filtering of our perceptions of the world, a skeptic's insistence upon "objectivity" is rather pointless. There is no "objectivity." Objectivity is not an option but a chimera. There are only lesser degrees of subjectivity. We tend to think of truth as "objective," meaning it's "out there" and science discloses it all; it's so compelling in cases where scientific work is done correctly, that all must give assent. Such is not the case. The argument from Kuhn in Chapter 2 ("decision-making paradigm") indicates that scientific understanding works by paradigms. Eventually all paradigms prove false, and when they do, the ground changes; we find ourselves in another world from the one of the old paradigm. These worlds are not based upon cumulative objective knowledge but upon the relative nature of paradigms. Now Christians like to argue for "objective" morality and the "objective" nature of divine truth. That is a different matter. God is not stuck with the subjective as we are. Our understanding of God's commands and words are inter-subjective, not objective. Our language through which we describe divine truth is a cultural construct in which we load mystical apprehension (however slight). As a Christian, I believe there is "objective" truth "out there," but only God understands it objectively. Our communicating about God is analogical and inter-subjective. By analogical I mean by means of analogy: i.e., God is like a father. But all analogies have like and not-like dimensions, so God is like a father in some ways, and not like a father in other ways. By the same token, our understanding is inter-subjective, by which I mean it is apprehended by others in some sense, but each individual has her own subjective take on that apprehension. These subjective takes all relate to each other and at times can sound remarkably similar, but they will never be shared in the sense of two people having the exact same experience. Skeptics tend to dismiss inter-subjective knowledge, probably because it uses the term "subjective." But inter-subjective is the next best thing to objectivity. Examples of inter-subjective realities that can be concretely experienced are music, art, and literature. Take the Mozart effect for example. Mozart's music has been hypothesized to stimulate intellectual development in children. Yet no two children have the same experience of or feelings about the music. Take the example of *Mona Lisa,* Da Vinci's great painting. Most of its viewers in the Louvre agree it is great, but no two have the exactly the same feelings about it. This is true of any great work of art.

Phenomenology

Phenomenology is a way to understand knowledge through categories of thought suggested by the phenomenon itself, rather than pre-screening phenomena and herding them into preconceived labels. The preconception aspect is what happens under the "pretense of objectivity"; what Heidegger termed "metaphysics" includes science. Reductionists lose the phenomena, as was discussed in relation to Proudfoot, and they do this by assuming that after the reduction process cuts away all that does not fit their categories, what cannot be retained is just not important. Many forms of naturalism seek to limit reality by screening it into preconceived categories: "empirical," "objective," "quantifiable," and the like. The mystic apprehends reality at a certain level apart from these categories, and thus allows the experiences, sense data or subjective feelings, to determine their own categories. This apprehension occurs largely through the noetic quality that is suggested by the experience itself. This makes mysticism, in a certain sense, into a phenomenological attitude if not a method.

William James had a phenomenological understanding of knowledge, even though he did not use that term. That understanding is explicated by Barnard in his book *Exploring Unseen Worlds.*[3] Barnard's viewpoint is in contrast to that of most Jamesian expositors, as he says himself.[4] The issue that Barnard addresses here is James' theory of sense perception. James asserts that mystical experience is direct and immediate; he also asserts that there are similarities between mystical experience and sense experience. Thus Barnard frames the problem that "it would appear logical that he would in turn claim that sense experiences as well are direct and unmediated by our thoughts and desires."[5] This is in response to Proudfoot's attacks upon James that assume that James understands both mystical and sense experience as analogous and unmediated. James doesn't make this claim; he asserts that sense experience is immediate but is also mediated. Based upon retrospective analysis of our sense data, we can see that our sense experiences are initially independent of our conscious thought. As our sense experiences occur in daily living, they are filtered (Barnard doesn't use that term) through the system of our desires, assumptions, beliefs. Barnard says sense experiences are "inextricably interwoven" with our desires and beliefs. According to Barnard, James "emphasizes that we never have a sense experience that is not, in some way or another, affected by our conceptual schemes."[6] Barnard deals with the confusion that many scholars have felt in confronting James' claims on this matter. The major contradiction, brought out by Proudfoot (see Chapter 5, "Proudfoot"), is that James seems to claim that mystical experience is beyond sense perception, beyond words and free from concepts (Proudfoot also charges Schleiermacher with this) and yet noetic. How can it be noetic (teaching) when it is free of concepts?

Barnard argues that while the answer to this problem is absent in *The Varieties of Religious Experience*, it is present in James' earlier and latter works. In the *Principles of Psychology*[7] Knowledge-by-acquaintance is immediate and intuitive, according to Barnard. As he puts it, "this form of knowledge is operative when we see the color blue or when we taste the flavor of a pear. Knowledge-about, on the other hand, is conceptual or representational."[8] I distinguish between experiential knowledge and "book" knowledge, and this is the way I relate to this distinction James makes. Knowledge-by-acquaintance is immediate and unstructured and comes from the direct experience of a phenomenon. For example, the immediate taste of the pear. Knowledge-about would come when we give the pear a name and start collecting facts about it. An example James uses is that of schools for the blind. In schools for the blind, students are taught all the facts about light that are known to students in sighted schools, but born-blind students still do not know what light looks like.[9] Knowledge-by-acquaintance is limited to a bare impression: for example, when we first wake up and don't know where we are (or while regaining consciousness after being knocked out), we might see an object but not register any information about what it is. This is the type of knowledge we get in mystical experience. It is pre-verbal and unmediated knowledge. Barnard calls it "unmediated knowledge of the simple 'that ness' of something."[10] Knowledge-about, he goes on, is connected with the "what ness" of something. I take this to mean factual knowledge "about" something. This distinction is crucial in understanding the qualitative difference between mystical experience and other kinds of experience.

Knowledge-about is apparently factual knowledge such as one learns from books. This is the same distinction made in charismatic Christian circles when people speak of "knowing the way we know a person face to face" and "book knowledge" or "book learning." The same distinction can be found in the Greek of the New Testament, which talks about knowing God or knowing Christ in terms such as "epiginosko" —to know, to experience. Another such word is the term first used in Pauline literature, referring to proto-Gnostic groups, and "gnostic" was the Orthodox Church's term for groups they found to be less than satisfactory in their understanding of "Orthodoxy." *Ginosko,* for example, means "to experience a phenomenon first hand, to know by firsthand example."[11] The designation of "knowledge about" or "book knowledge" is the sort of knowledge required for writing doctrines. I am not advocating mystical experience as a special insight into the construction of doctrine. Mystical experience is vague; it is beyond words (at least at the deeper end of the spectrum) but it need not be the basis for doctrine. Doctrine is a matter for religious community. That is to say, it is an issue to be addressed by a community in the way that the community chooses to address it. But experience need not result in doctrinal understanding. It doesn't matter that mystical experience doesn't answer precise questions about the nature of the universe; it need not, for that is not its function. Mystical experience is not going to tell us what God is made of; it will tell us God is love. Love is a matter of experience and we can experience that. We need not make doctrines about love, we need only love. It is not a matter of spelling out truth on paper or demonstrating scientific hypotheses. The only thing religious experience need accomplish is to furnish the warrant for belief. Nothing could be a more rational warrant than personal experience of the trace of God, and nothing could be more indicative of God than the rehabilitation and transformation of one's life through the taste of the holy.

The skeptical tendency to impose the demand for understanding and demonstration is symptomatic of what Heidegger called "metaphysics". Metaphysics in this sense is the grouping of phenomena under a single rubric, an organizing principle. In this sense science is included in the definition of metaphysics. The skeptical demand for proof and clear understanding is merely the imposition of one form of metaphysics over another. It is the valuing of certain types of knowledge and the devaluation of others. Knowledge gained from empirical observation and systematically produced data is limited of necessity to that which is observable. Thus, any aspect of reality that transcends the limited framework constructed from the observable automatically violates the parameters of ideology and is disqualified for that reason. The world of reductionism, while taken to be a world of reality based upon facts, is actually a world of constructs built upon the regiments of reality reduced from the fullness of what is, to the provable and that which fits the parameters. The world of reductionism is the truncated world of surface appearance only. The world of the mystic may be impenetrable, it may be a shadow world of experience only, but it is a world of depth where the visible ends of the real imply deeper, hidden depths of the phenomenological. The ideas we articulate from this experience are metaphorical, but they are no less real and no less indicative of a deeper reality, compared with the shallow, surface illusions that pass themselves off as "empirical truth" constructed by skeptical ideology. Yet this does not mean that mystical experience cannot be studied empirically. We cannot get behind the experience to see the unmediated ("unvarnished" as it were) truth, but we can study the effects of the experience upon the "mystic". This is the basic concept of the "co-determinate"; that is to say, the flip side of the phenomenon, the thing that goes with it and is implied by it which points to the reality (i.e. the footprint in the snow must be assumed to be indicative of the foot that left the impression). The major tool for studying such experiences empirically is the M Scale, created and developed by Ralph Hood. In Chapter 4, I documented the cross-cultural verification of the M Scale.

As seen in the chapter on studies (Chapter 3), the M scale is cross-culturally validated; mystics from all over the world can sound very similar in many ways. Yet no two mystics can ever be sure they are talking about the same things. All mystics have their own takes. This is one reason why we should not try to deduce official doctrine from mystical experience. There's a better, more important reason which I will get to later. But this is reason enough. Deciding official doctrine is not the task of mysticism. Mysticism is not an end-run around religious doctrines to special revelation. It's the trace of God, not special inerrant revelation from God. It's a revelation to the individual only. Mystics are experiencing truth directly, but if they wish to speak about it (and they do), they must filter it through cultural constructs. That filtering is always going to taint the unvarnished nature of the experience. That doesn't make the experience useless: it is of inestimable value to the one having it. This fact of filtering makes the experience valuable to others — but not as a form of special revelation; mystical experience is not a means of re-obtaining the stone tablets.

What about the case of holy writ? That is a matter for another book. There is not time or space enough in this venture to discuss my views on scripture (of any religion, or of my own specifically). But there are two aspects that need to be discussed here. The first is that the concept of special revelation assumes that at some point, someone had an experience. It may not be a "mystical" experience in the special sense in which I've been using that term, but some form of "experience" has to be assumed at some point. Moreover, Schleiermacher thought that doctrines were the verbalizations of the feeling of utter dependence. That would mean that doctrines have been shaped by something akin to mystical experience. More goes into the making of doctrines than just reading a passage in the Bible. In Christianity the official depository of doctrine is the creed. Creeds began as a means of establishing Christian identity at a time when the church was beginning to spread throughout the Roman world and people were beginning to ask, "What do we really believe? Who is really of the faith and who is not?" The making of Christian doctrine is the result of a filtering process that starts with raw data that is probably drawn from experiences of some kind, such as are described in the scripture, and ends in a sifting process whereby councils work their understanding of various writings to form a definitive position. Some parts of process may have been corrupt, but as a point of faith Christians assume the Holy Spirit guided the process, which would also involve experience.

This leads to the more important reason to shy away from making doctrines based upon mystical experience. Again, I do not mean Christians should not view the Bible as inspired. I mean those who have religious experiences should not think in terms of re-writing the historical doctrines based upon modern experiences. The reason is that religious traditions come from communities. The function of a tradition is to create a vocabulary and to use that vocabulary to create a conversation that moves over time, through history, and functions as a guide for those who come after. The conversation is intra-community and is also carried on inter-communally: the communities communicate with other communities. Because "community," as understood here, is a society of like-minded believers, there must be a set of clear definitions to which all ascribe, in order to understand the terms of membership —and this is the function of the creeds. The historical value of Christian tradition and witness is found in the disposition of witnesses who are attested by the chain of succession among the leadership (i.e. Apostolic succession). Christ trained and authorized the Apostles, the Apostles trained and authorized Bishops, the Bishops passed on the word, selected the canon so that the raw data could be distilled, and selected their successors, so the chain of testimony continues. In this process a lot more is going on than just making revelations known to people. The historical integrity of the community is important. I'm not saying change can never come. But when change does come, it must be integrated into the understanding of the community so it is not a wrenching away of what has always been understood as truth in favor some new, unknown quantity or teaching. Change has to be integrated into understanding and extended from what is known of the past. In other words, new vocabulary has to be understood and integrated so that it makes sense in relation to old vocabulary. Unfortunately it doesn't always work this way; in fact, this process is never as smooth and ideal as I make it sound. This does not mean that mystics have no place in the understanding of doctrine. This is why the Catholics have saints. It's also why they make it so hard to become a saint. The role the mystic occupies in the overall life of Christianity includes acting as a source of inspiration and as a living precedent for understanding pre-ordained truths. So the two reasons that I strongly oppose basing doctrine upon modern mystical revelations are: first, that mystical experience is not intended to be a disseminating process for bestowing new, doxastic information about God; and the second, because the validity of the traditional vocabulary of the community has to be respected. What about Schliermacher's observation that doctrines are verbalizations of the feeling of utter dependence? I accept that this is true. That does not mean, however, that therefore all verbalizations of such feelings are automatically on the same level as divine revelation. I assume that "special" revelation is special for a reason: that it is not like any other form of revelation. I assume that all scripture is a human account of some sort of encounter with the divine. On the other hand, that doesn't mean that any such record is automatically fit to replace historically canonized records. A lot more goes into the making of doctrine than just a mystical experience. It's really, in a sense, something that involves the entire community. Certainly the making of doctrine involves the leaders of the community. Because there is a social/institutional aspect to organized religion, there has to be an institutional aspect to the making of doctrine. For the most part I still accept Schleiermacher's definition, that doctrine is a verbalization of the feeling of utter dependence; yet it's also more than that. All religious language is a verbalization of the sense of the numinous filtered through cultural constructs. All mystical experience is, and must be, so filtered if one is to speak of it. The level upon which we encounter God transcends the world of words or the realm of discourse. In order to speak meaningfully, we have to relate our experiences to meaningful concepts. Cultural constructs are the only concepts that are meaningful. This may give Christians pause; not only Christians, but also the adherents of any particular religious tradition. Sure, we might say, if there is actual truth that can be put into language; if a reasonable, rational God created the world and gave us minds to understand it, then there must be a connection between language and truth. Of course there is such a connection, but it is a metaphorical connection because it is not unmediated. It is mediated by concepts and ideas that come to us through culture. "Cultural construct" doesn't mean "lie." It's not a falsehood. We have seen how metaphor is necessary for navigation in the world. The relationship of transcendent truth to language must of necessity be mediated through culture, or we would have nothing to compare it to. How can we understand what is beyond our understanding unless we can compare to what we do understand?

Hood sought to construct the M scale in such a way as to reflect no one particular religious tradition. Rather than speaking of "knowing Christ in a personal relationship," he speaks of "experiencing ultimate reality." This is because Hood makes the same assumptions that W.T. Stace made in his studies of mysticism. The M scale is drawn from the categories that Stace constructed to explicate mystical experience. The school of thought that follows Stace in this move is called "'the common core", because its followers assume that there is a common core that unites all the mystics throughout time, regardless of their specific religious tradition: a common core of mystical experience. Opponents of the common core idea are called the "diversity school". The diversity school argues that there is no common basis to mystical experience. Katz, who was discussed in Chapter 6 (referred to by Proudfoot) and Proudfoot himself (Chapters 5 and 6) are both adherents of the "diversity school". While Katz gives credence to the Jewish faith, he argues that Jewish mysticism stands apart from all other mystical traditions in asserting the total and utter difference between creature and Creator. While Proudfoot is an adherent of no religious tradition, his idea of diversity could be thought of as a common core —if by that one meant the commonality of reducing all experience to labeling. That's not the way the terms are used. What the diversity group agrees upon is that experience and language are almost one and the same. As we saw with Proudfoot in Chapter 6, language is for him the basis of experience, and experience is basically an illusion set in place by the labeling effect of language.[12] The problem of language is more pervasive than one might imagine. While I reject the ideological control of reductionism in all its forms, including the "diversity school" and the labeling theory, they do make an important point. No experience is unmediated, and any time we try to talk about experience, we are automatically mediating it through language. How can we know that what one mystic describes as "ultimate reality" is the same thing another describes as "a presence?" How could we know that what one calls "Krishna" is what another calls "Christ"? For that matter, how could we know that one what one Christian calls "Jesus" is what another Christian calls "Jesus?" Hood has sought to overcome the "New-Age sounding" aspects of the common core (its seeming universalism)[13] by developing what he calls "the triple solution." To understand this solution, we must first understand the three basic assumptions that underpin all common core understanding:

1. All mystical experience is universal; the experiences are much alike even though they may be explained differently.
2. The core categories are not definitionally essential to any particular experience (in other words, they're always borderline cases).
3. Introvertive mystical experience (sense of unity with no content —pure consciousness) and extrovertive (unity in diversity —with content) are the most distinct categories.[14] "The psychometric properties of the M Scale should reflect these assumptions, and insofar as they do, they are adequate operationalizations of Stace's criteria. The question for now is this: does empirical research support a common core/perrinialist conceptualization of mysticism and its interpretation."[15]

Hood produced several special versions of the M Scale, each one directed to a different tradition: Christian, Muslim, Hindu, and secular. For each community he substituted the language of that community, "Have you felt the presence of Christ, Allah, Vishnu, or a void?" (That is not a real question from the M scale, it's just my own hypothetical version to illustrate my point, although there is a similar question that is just worded differently). The point is that all of these different traditions have the same kinds of experiences when you look at general ontological structure (in other words, if you don't look at the specific doctrines and personality of Christ, but just at the way Christ functions in the ontology of Christians). It's the same for Allah in Islam, or the void for atheists, in general terms. An atheist may think he's describing the lack of a God when he says, "I sensed the presence of a great void." But if you look at how the void functions, the place it occupies in the ontology described, it's really the same position that God occupies for the Christians or Allah for the Muslims. The one general term that names that position rather than the specific personality of a deity is a term Hood does not use; but the term we might use for this faction is *transcendental signifier*. This approach has been borne out through cross-cultural verification (see Chapter 3, "Studies").

This means that it would not be unreasonable to infer that that there is a universal reality behind all individual religious traditions. It might also tend to render some of the judgments based upon the noetic experiences of mystical consciousness as more probable. If the experience bears out as universal, and if we can eliminate counter causality emanating from within the brain of the individual (and we have done that on the basis of their lack of fit with what we know about the navigation capabilities of mystical experience), then it is not unwarranted to draw the conclusion that this universal reality exists as an other-directed formulation for the individual. In other words, "something is out there." This "something" can be understood, to some extent, in clear informational terms. We could also go so far as to say that this "something" is a positive thing. If it wants anything, it wants the best for us —because the effects of having experienced it are positive and life-transforming in the long run. This "something" stands behind all the major world religions to one degree or another. We can experience it and seem to formulate relationships of sorts with it. These may not be the only conclusions one could draw from the data. These conclusions are based upon the record of experiences left behind by mystics, as well as the results of the empirical studies. As far as this reflects experiences that people have had and have used to navigate their lives to their advantage, there is nothing irrational or unwarranted about these conclusions. But while this seems to build a pretty good case for a universalism of some sort, what about my promise to connect it with Christian apologetics?

Christian Apologetics

Of course it would be necessary to ascertain what type of apologetics one might expect to bolster with this argument. I'm not concerned with the kind of apologetics that seeks to produce some sort of hegemony over other viewpoints. I don't view other faith traditions as competitors who are taking the unwary away from God. I view my own tradition as having its own brand of efficacy. I see religious tradition as a vehicle for loading the experience of God into cultural constructs and giving meaning to that which is beyond words. Certainly, I embrace the Nicene creed, and I do believe that Jesus is the incarnate Logos. I also believe what Paul said about God working in all cultures (Acts 17:21-29) and God placing the moral law upon the heart of all people that "their hearts may excuse them…" (Romans 2:15). In my view, the purpose of apologetics is to demonstrate the human need to know God. The basis of exclusivity in Christian tradition is not the sort of exclusivity that derides other traditions. I realize it has been so construed in the past, but it need not be. It is merely the sort of exclusivity that focuses upon the efficacy of Christ in redemption and the value which that offers to the world. I am not arguing that the following argument is the only way to reconcile the seemingly universal nature of mystical consciousness with Christianity. It's the way I do it. It has to do with my own theological understanding. I am not saying it's the only possible understanding.

The phenomenological aspects of mystical consciousness are found in the Christian tradition. The idea of "knowing Christ" and the personal relationship with God, all contain the elements that William James incorporates into his "knowledge-about" and "knowledge-by-acquaintance"categories. In the New Testament this is expressed in the use of different Greek words for knowledge. The words that are used when the author speaks of "knowing Christ" invariably refer to personal knowledge, personal experience, or firsthand knowledge of something one experiences for oneself. One example of such as term is *epiginosko*. There are other Greek words that pertain to book learning and knowledge about a subject that one learns secondhand. These words are never used to describe the relationship between believers and God or Christ.

Another such word is the term first used in Pauline literature, referring to proto-Gnostic groups —and it was the Orthodox Church's term— *Ginosko:*

1. to learn to know, come to know, get a knowledge of perceive, feel

    1. to become known

2. to know, understand, perceive, have knowledge of

    1. to understand
    2. to know

3. Jewish idiom for sexual intercourse between a man and a woman
4. to become acquainted with, to know [16]

Here is how it is used in the Book of Hebrews:

> Therefore I was angry with this generation, and said, "They always go astray in their heart; And they did not *know* My ways." [17]

> And they shall not teach everyone his fellow citizen, and everyone his brother, saying, "*know* the Lord," For all shall *know* Me, from the least to the greatest of them. [18]

In that passage we see clearly the idea of firsthand knowledge through personal experience. One does not have to be taught what one experiences firsthand. "They will all know Me" means "they will all have firsthand personal knowledge of me." This means being a Christian turns upon personal experience of God at some level. That doesn't mean having mystical experiences saves someone. Many people experience God at the subliminal level, but being "saved" is a matter of recognition of what we have experienced already, the thing that draws us to Christ.

Here is the similar and related word *epiginosko:*

1. to become thoroughly acquainted with, to know thoroughly

1. to know accurately, know well
2. to know
   1. to recognize
      1. by sight, hearing, of certain signs, to perceive who a person is
   2. to know i.e. to perceive
   3. to know i.e. to find out, ascertain
   4. to know i.e. to understand [19]

Here is how it is used in the 1 Corinthians:

> For now we see in a mirror dimly, but then face to face; now I *know* in part, but then I shall *know* fully just as I also have been *fully known*.[20]

> If anyone thinks he is a prophet or spiritual, let him *recognize* that the things which I write to you are the Lord's commandment.[21]

> For they have refreshed my spirit and yours. Therefore *acknowledge* such men.[22][23]

The idea that we know "in part" might possibly include the understanding that we experience God at a subliminal level beyond words and have to encode that into cultural constructs.

The term for knowledge used by Gnostics, *Gnosis,* is contrasted in that even though it bears the notion of perfection knowledge, it deals more with the understanding of rules and facts, of knowing ideas —and doesn't seem to bear the idea of the personal face to face knowledge:

1. knowledge signifies, in general, intelligence, understanding
   1. the general knowledge of Christian religion

Joseph Hinman

2. the deeper, more perfect and enlarged knowledge of this religion, such as belongs to the more advanced
3. esp. of things lawful and unlawful for Christians
4. moral wisdom, such as is seen in right living [24]

Another word for knowledge that could be used for knowing Christ (but is not so used in the Bible), a word that carries the implication of factual knowledge, is *isemi*, which means generally just "to know." An example from Hebrews:

> For ye *know* how that afterward, when he would have inherited the blessing, he was rejected: for he found no place of repentance, though he sought it carefully with tears. [25]

Another word for knowing on a factual basis is *suneidon:*

1. to see (have seen) together with others
2. to see (have seen) in one's mind with one's self

   1. to understand, perceive, comprehend,

3. to know with another
4. to know in one's mind or with one's self, to be conscience of

Here are examples of its usage in the New Testament:

> For I *know* nothing by myself; yet am I not hereby justified: but he that judgeth me is the Lord. [26]

> ...and to know the love of Christ which surpasses *knowledge*, that you may be filled up to all the fullness of God. [27]

This passage seems to contrast the kind of knowledge known from the heart and from experiencing God, with general knowledge, including book learning.

358

The terms used in the New Testament that deal with knowing Christ are terms that relate to firsthand, personal knowledge; knowledge-by-acquaintance. The term *Ginosko*, used throughout 1 John, implies an intimate, experiential level of personal knowledge:

> 1 John 2:3-5, 13-14, 18, 29: And hereby we do *know* that we *know* him, if we keep his commandments. He that saith, I *know* him, and keepeth not his commandments, is a liar, and the truth is not in him. But whoso keepeth his word, in him verily is the love of God perfected: hereby *know* we that we are in him.... I write unto you, fathers, because ye have *know*n him that is from the beginning. I write unto you, young men, because ye have overcome the wicked one. I write unto you, little children, because ye have *know*n the Father. I have written unto you, fathers, because ye have *know*n him that is from the beginning. I have written unto you, young men, because ye are strong, and the word of God abideth in you, and ye have overcome the wicked one.... Little children, it is the last time: and as ye have heard that antichrist shall come, even now are there many antichrists; whereby we *know* that it is the last time.... If ye *know* that he is righteous, ye *know* that every one that doeth righteousness is born of him. [28]

> 1 Jo 3:1, 6, 16, 19-20, 24: Behold, what manner of love the Father hath bestowed upon us, that we should be called the sons of God: therefore the world *know*eth us not, because it knew him not.... Whosoever abideth in him sinneth not: whosoever sinneth hath not seen him, neither *know*n him.... Hereby *perceive* we the love of God, because he laid down his life for us: and we ought to lay down our lives for the brethren.... And hereby we *know* that we are of the truth, and shall assure our hearts before him. For if our heart condemn us, God is greater than our heart, and *know*eth all things.... And he that keepeth his commandments dwelleth in him, and he in him. And hereby we *know* that he abideth in us, by the Spirit which he hath given us. [29]

1 Jo 4:2, 6-8, 13, 16: Hereby *know* ye the Spirit of God: Every spirit that confesseth that Jesus Christ is come in the flesh is of God... We are of God: he that *know*eth God heareth us; he that is not of God heareth not us. Hereby *know* we the spirit of truth, and the spirit of error. Beloved, let us love one another: for love is of God; and every one that loveth is born of God, and *know*eth God. He that loveth not *know*eth not God; for God is love.... Hereby *know* we that we dwell in him, and he in us, because he hath given us of his Spirit.... And we have *know*n and believed the love that God hath to us. God is love; and he that dwelleth in love dwelleth in God, and God in him. [30]

1 Jo 5:2, 20: By this we *know* that we love the children of God, when we love God, and keep his commandments.... And we *know* that the Son of God is come, and hath given us an *understand*ing, that we may *know* him that is true, and we are in him that is true, even in his Son Jesus Christ. This is the true God, and eternal life. [31]

The nature of what it means to "know God" or "know Christ" in the Christian religion is this personal level of experiential knowledge. [32]

Traditions

According to what I've said above and in Chapter 7, mystical experience is inter-subjective. As has been documented by several researchers, the same commonalities come up over and over again. All mystical experiences have characteristics of undifferentiated unity, sense of presence, feelings of bliss, noetic aspects, ineffable nature, and so forth.

From a study by Voyle:

The contemporary interest in the empirical research of mysticism can be traced to Stace's (Stace, 1960) demarcation of the phenomenological characteristics of mystical experiences (Hood, 1975). In Stace's conceptualization, mystical experiences had five characteristics (Hood, 1985, p.176):

- The mystical experience is noetic. The person having the experience perceives it as a valid source of knowledge and not just a subjective experience.
- The mystical experience is ineffable; it cannot simply be described in words.
- The mystical experience is holy. While this is the religious aspect of the experience, it is not necessarily expressed in any particular theological terms.
- The mystical experience is profound yet enjoyable and characterized by positive effects.
- The mystical experience is paradoxical. It defies logic. Further analysis of reported mystical experiences suggests that the one essential feature of mysticism is an experience of unity (Hood, 1985). The experience of unity involves a process of ego loss and is generally expressed in one of three ways (Hood, 1 976a). The ego is absorbed into that which transcends it, or there is an inward process by which the ego gains pure awareness of self, or there is a combination of the two. [33]

Voyle demonstrates that the mystical end of the church is the mature end. That is to say, those who experience mystical consciousness represent a much more mature form of Christianity than do those who do not. He based this upon his study in which he compares the two groups for depth of understanding and commitment.

Does the universality of religious experience invalidate religious truth?

Atheists often argue this point. They will say, "They can't all be right because they are all so different. So, how can you establish that one is right and all the others wrong?" I say, "You mean aside from the fact that God manifested as Jesus and rose from the dead? I don't know." I say that sarcastically, but they do have a good point. We can be parochial and say, "well of course my tradition is the true one and all the others are damned." But that approach has some obvious drawbacks.

Religious traditions are communities of discourse. Their function is to create vocabularies in which one can receive guidance from those who have gone before and make one's own contribution to the conversation. Thus, the experiences of God are filtered through cultural constructs, and the meaningful nature of those constructs is relative to the various communities in which they take place. It is perfectly plausible that there is one truth behind all religious traditions. It is possible to maintain this position as a Christian, and to remain a Bible-believing evangelical who seeks to spread the Gospel of Jesus Christ. In fact, the Bible teaches that very thing. Paul on Mars Hill tells the Greek philosophers, "you are worshiping the right God, 'the unknown god', you just don't know enough about Him." He did not tell them "Oh, you pagans are going to hell." Other Christians, more conservative in their understanding, have told me that Paul was just using that as a trick. I can't believe that Paul was just a con man who tried to trick people. If he said it, he had to believe it. This is just my personal way of rationalizing this problem. I'm not saying this is the only valid Christian outlook, but I think it is a valid Christian outlook. "All have sinned and fallen short of the glory of God." From a human perspective, relatively speaking, from one human to another there are, of course, well-meaning people. There are good people all around us from a human perspective. Relative to the divine, however, no one is good, no one is capable of meriting salvation. We all have our sins; we all have our human frailties. We are all caught up in "height" (our ability through the image of God in which we were created to move beyond our human finitude and seek the good) and "depth" (our nature burdened in sinful wickedness to human deceit). These are Augustinian terms, and they basically mean that we are good and bad, saint and sinner. God knows the heart, He knows what we truly seek. God is merciful and is able to forgive our trespasses. But, if we are really well-meaning toward God, we will seek the truth. If we are seeking the truth, then God will make it plain to us.

World Religions

Paul said (emphasis added):

> To those who through persistence seek glory, honor and immortality *He will give eternal life.* But for those who are self-seeking and who *reject the good* and follow evil there will be wrath and anger...first for the Jew and then for the Gentile; but glory honor and peace for *everyone* who does good. *For God does not show favoritism.* All who sin apart from the law will perish apart from the law, and all who sin under the law will be judged by the law. For it is not those who hear the law who are righteous in God's sight, it is those who obey the law who will be declared righteous.
>
> Indeed when Gentiles who do not have the law, do by nature things required by the law, they are a law for themselves even though they do not have the law, since they show that the requirements of the law are *written on their hearts,* their consciences bearing witness and their hearts now accusing, *now even defending them...* [34]

The New American Standard and other translations say "their hearts accusing, *now excusing them...*" Most Christians are afraid of this conclusion and they downplay this verse. Often Evangelicals will come back and say "he makes it clear in the next passage that no one can really follow the law on their hearts." Well, if they can't, then they can't. But if they can, and do, than God will excuse them. God knows the heart but we do not. The verse clearly opens the door to the *possibility of salvation* (although by Jesus) through a *de facto* arrangement in which one is seeking the good without knowing the object one is seeking (Jesus). In other words, it is possible that people in other cultures who follow the moral law written on the heart know Jesus *de facto*, even if they don't know him overtly. Paul backs up this conclusion in Acts 17:22, in which Paul goes to Athens and is asked by the Athenian philosophers to explain his ideas to them.

These were pagan followers of another religion. Paul stood up and said to them, "Men of Athens, I see that in every way you are very religious, for as I walked around and observed your objects of worship, I even found an altar with this inscription: *'TO AN UNKNOWN GOD.'* Now *what you worship as something unknown I am going to proclaim to you.*" (Emphasis added.) He basically says that they are worshiping God; they just don't know who he is. That's why he says: "I will make it known to you." He doesn't say, "You have the wrong idea completely." Most evangelicals dismiss this as a neat rhetorical trick. But if we assume that Paul would not lie or distort his beliefs for the sake of cheap tricks, we must consider that he did not say, "You are all a bunch of pagans and you are going to hell!" He essentially told them, "God is working in your culture; you do know God, but you don't know who God is. You seek him without knowing the one you seek." He goes on (v27), "God did this [created humanity and scattered them into different cultures] so that men would seek him and perhaps reach out and find him though *he is not far from each one of us.*" This implies that God not only wants to work in other cultures, but that it is actually his plan to do things in this way. Perhaps through a diversity of insights we might come to know God better. Perhaps it means that through spreading the Gospel, people would come to contemplate better the meaning of God's love. Is it not arrogance to think that all people can be expected to just abandon the cultural constructs which frame the basis of their world-views? The reasons religions are different is because the basic experiences of God are filtered through cultural constructs.

In any case, it does mean that God is working in other cultures, and that God is in the hearts of all people, drawing them to the divine. Of their worship of idols, Paul said, "in past times God *overlooked* such ignorance but now he commands all people everywhere to repent" (v. 30, emphasis added). Now what can this mean? God never overlooks idolatry or paganism; in the Old Testament he is always commanding the Israelites to wipe the pagans out and expressly forbidding idolatry. How do we understand the contradiction between the apparent attitude of God toward idolatry we think we see throughout the OT, and this apparent excusing of it? It means that on an individual basis, when God judges the hearts of people, he looks at their desire to seek him, to seek the good. Their status as individuals in a pagan culture does not negate the good they have done, and their ignorance of idolatry does not discount their desire to seek the good or the truth. It means that "now" (which Paul defines as "since Christ came") they are following Jesus if they live in the moral life, even though they follow him as something unknown to them or as a cultural construct different from that we know. It also means that all of us should come into the truth, we should seek to know God fully, and when we do, that we find that it is Jesus all along. At this point the apologist can insert any arguments about the resurrection, prophecy or any aspect of the unique nature of Jesus. There are plenty of grounds upon which to argue the efficacy of the Christian tradition. It is not the task here to discuss soeteriology. One can plug in any theological viewpoint from the major Christian theologians at this point. The important point to make here is that the universal nature of mystical experience does not invalidate either religious truth in general or the Christian tradition. God is working all cultures, and what he's doing in all the cultures of the earth is moving people toward Christ. It's up to the Christian theologian to understand what that means. My reading of St. Paul suggests that anyone who is following the moral law placed upon the heart is following Christ *de facto*.

Joseph Hinman

Religious traditions are vehicles for creating social and cultural contexts in which the ineffable truths of mystical experience and the noetic aspects of the sense of the numinous can be loaded into cultural constructs and have concrete meaning relative to our understanding. Toward that end, doctrines are verbalizations of this sense of the numinous; they are, as Mr. Spock once said on the original *Star Trek*,[35] "conventional points of reference" for our understanding. Because these are ineffable truths loaded into constructs that only suggest meanings, religious language is metaphor. It doesn't mean the metaphors are untrue, merely that they are not literally what they seem. God is not a big man in the sky. Christ is not literally a Shepherd. The construct, the metaphor, is not a lie, nor is it a falsehood or an illusion, but it is not a literal one-to-one correspondence. This does mean that many cherished images concerning the Holy must be understood as not literal, but it does not mean they must be scrapped. As a Christian, this does not affect my relationship to Jesus Christ. I do not see the deity of Christ merely as a symbol or a construct; I don't demote the Trinity to analogical status. I embrace the Nicene Creed. I see Jesus as a real man in history, a manifestation of the divine logos but a concrete human being, not a mere cultural construct. This makes Jesus not only the most unique figure in history, but a concrete figure. While Jesus may represent symbolically many things, we can still understand him in concrete terms as the incarnate logos. What I do see as symbolic and metaphorical is the imagery pertaining to God as the potentate on the throne, the big "guy in the sky." These are obviously cultural constructs that were very meaningful to people of the late Bronze Age and on into late antiquity. God is imaged in many ways in Scripture, in which it is made clear to us that God is not a man, he does not need to be served by human hands. God is imaged by fire, storm, animals (eagle, bear, lion, lamb, mother hen) whirlwind, burning bush, darkness, light. Obviously all of these are metaphors, and it has to be significant that we are warned not to make a graven image of God. God has no fixed form. God is everywhere and nowhere. God is both and neither male and female. The translation from the Greek of the Septuagint for Exodus 3:11 is "I am being itself" rather than "I am that I am." These ideas mean the same thing: God is self-sustaining, the basis of all that is, the bottom line of all reality, transcending any form or image. It's fairly obvious that God is beyond anything we understand, and thus any image relating to God is *a priori* metaphorical. The notion of God as father is analogical, meaning God is like a father (in some ways). But all analogies have their limits, thus they all contain both like and not like aspects. So God is also not like a father. This may seem bad until we think about earthly fathers. I had a wonderful father, but everyone can't say that. For some people the realization that God is both like and not like a father is a good thing. As a Christian I have to believe that Jesus is the concrete reference point that demonstrates directly the character of God, but at the same time that which he is mirroring is also beyond our comprehension; our only real guide to God's character is Jesus.

As for the atonement, I accept the participatory model, also known as solidarity. Christ participates in our humanity, and we enter into the participation in his divine life. The death of Christ on the cross is God's statement of solidarity with humanity. Salvation is not a sale, not a financial transaction, not a public execution, not sympathetic magic, but a statement of solidarity. Jesus dies in the mode of a criminal at the bottom of society as a statement of God's willingness to identify with all people at all levels and to share with us the worst of our fates. When we return that sense of solidarity by entering into Christ's death, this creates the grounds for forgiveness because there must be forgiveness when solidarity is achieved.[36] The reality is not any less real just because one uses one metaphor as opposed to another. It may or may not matter if one accepts the Nicene Creed or rejects it (to me it matters —in so far as continuity with the orthodox tradition is concerned). But in terms of what I call "navigation in the world," it does not matter. What matters is that one has a relationship with this "transcendental signifier" —the object of ultimate concern that this sort of experience seems to be about— and that one is seeking always to know in an ever deeper and more personal way the nature of the reality that this sort of experience seems to contain. It's not about arguments on paper. We don't have to know if God is a society of occasions, or the ground of being, or the "horizon of hope," as long as we are open to the phenomenological apprehension we find present in life, and the sense of love and forgiveness that it bestows. In other words, navigation in the world is not a doctrinal matter, or a scientific question. The noetic aspects of religious experience enable navigation in the world, not by relaying accurate scientific evidence, but by imparting transformative values and experiences which give one strength and wisdom and enable one to feel loved and to love in return. This "navigation" of which I speak is not like sense data from the five senses, but it does enable navigation of a general sort that enables one to withstand the material trammels of life. One of the major noetic aspects (information imparted) of mystical experience is the deep-seated sense that God is love. The sense of God's love enables one to cope and to love others, and it gives a sense of purpose to life.

I admit this interpretation does sound a bit "New Age-like" or pie in the sky; one might go so far as to say "sunshine and candy lambs." Yet this does seem to be the upshot of the experiences — that people are able to cope with life. As with all things spiritual or religious, the skeptic loves to mock. So this interpretation will be reduced to nothing but the imposition of a pattern like finding a dog's head in the clouds. But the studies demonstrate that it works. That's really the crux of the matter: It does work, and in this sense that makes it something like navigating a ship. The acid test of the truth about the nature of one's navigation skills is whether they work when put to the test. If you set out for Jamaica and wind up in Norway, you can assume you are a bad navigator. If you get where you are going, you can assume your method of navigation works pretty well. The skeptic seeks absolute proof, though few of them will admit as much. But no level of proof ever satisfies a skeptic. In dealing with the world beyond our understanding

—and we must assume we start blank— the only real test we have is "Does it work?" Atheists will always contribute the bromide "just because it works doesn't mean it's true." Surely this is a mistake in logic. I argued in the Chapter 7 that working is always part of the acid test of the validity of any theory. Imagine if the atomic bomb hadn't worked. How unthinkable it would be for the scientists to say, "Oh, there's nothing wrong with the theory, we don't need to re-think that —just because we can't get the thing to work doesn't mean it's wrong in theory." It might mean that for the first few hundred failures, but after thousands of tries, if it never works even once, wouldn't it be re to re-evaluate the theory?

Belief in God is not merely adding a fact to the universe. Belief in God is a construal of the nature of reality given certain phenomenological and theoretical implications. RE is one of those phenomenological implications. God is not just another thing in the universe. God is the basis of reality. The point of what God is doing in the world is bound up with the nature of our lives and how we live. I don't mean that from just a moralistic standpoint. I mean in the sense that God is love *itself*; the basic motivation for all creation is love (if we can believe what Jesus said), and the upshot of mystical experience is the realization of the foundational aspects of love itself. Therefore, that it works to enable one to live better and feel better in life and to bestow that love upon others is a true test of the truth content of the ideas, the noetic component of the experience. What is taught, the information transmitted in the noetic, is this exactly: God is love, and love is the foundation of everything. That these experiences enable one to love, and that this reality enables one to be transformed and to face life (to "navigate"), is a rational warrant for belief that what is transmitted in these experiences is meaningful and that truth content can be derived from it.

The truth of religious belief is found —not in intellectual propositions through words on paper— but first and foremost in the direct experience of God. Put down the book and pray.

Joseph Hinman

1   Newberg, *Why God Wont Go Away*, Op cit, 11-14.

2   *Ibid.*, 35-36.

3   G. William Barnard, Op. Cit. 111-114.

4   *Ibid.*, 111.

5   *Ibid.*

6   *Ibid.*

7   William James, *Principles of Psychology*, vol. III, Cambridge MA: Harvard University Press, 1981.

8   Barnard, Op Cit, 111.

9   *Ibid.*, 112.

10 Ibid

11 James Strong, *Strong's Exhaustive Concordance to the Bible,* Peabody, Massachusetts: Hendrickson publishers "Ginosko" word number 1097. 2009.

12 Bernard Spilka, Ralph Hood, Bruce Hunsberger, Richard Gorsuch, *The Psychology of Religion: An Empirical Approach.* Third edition. New York, London: The Guilford Press, 2003, 321.

13 *Ibid.*, 321-324

14 *Ibid.*, 324

15 *Ibid.*, 323

16 Strong's Op. Cit. # 1097.

17 Heb 3:10 (KJV:King James Version) [Editor's Note: suggested modern translations include the ESV (English Standard Version) and NIV (New International Version]

18 Heb 8:11 (KJV)

19 - Strong's *op. cit.* # 1921

20 1 Co 13:12 (KJV)

21 1 Co 14:37 (KJV)

22 1 Co 16:18 (KJV)

23 *Ibid.*

24 *Ibid.*

25 Heb 12:17 (KJV)

26 1 Co 4:4 (KJV)

27   Eph 3:19 (KJV)

28   1 Jo 2:3-5, 13-14, 18, 29 (KJV)

29   1 Jo 3:1, 6, 16, 19-20, 24 (KJV)

30   1 Jo 4:2, 6-8, 13, 16 (KJV)

31   1 Jo 5:2, 20

32   all the material relating to Greek terms unless otherwise noted is from
      Strongs.

33   Robert J. Voyle. "The Impact of Mystical Experiences on Christian
      Maturity." http://www.voyle.com/impact.pdf. Google cache:
      http://64.233.161.104/search?q=cache:avred7zleAEJ:www.voyle.com/
      impact.pdf+Hood+scale+and+religious+experience&hl=en&gl=us&ct=clnk&cd=28
      (accessed 5/5/10)

34   Romans 2:7-15 (NIV)

35   Gene L. Coon, "Errand of Mercy," *Star Trek*, Season 1 Episode 26
      (original air date 03/23/1967). Directed by John Newland.

36   See Jurgen Moltmann *The Crucified God: The Cross as The Foundation
      and Criticism of Christian Theology*, Minneapolis Minnesota: Fortress
      Press, 1968; see also D.E.H. Whiteley *The Theology of St Paul.*
      Minneapolis, Minnesota: Fortress Press 1964. The Participatory view is
      not well known but it has an ancient history going back to Origen and
      other church fathers.

Bibliography

Abraham, William J. *Canon and Criterion in Christian Theology.*
London: Oxford University Press, 1992.

Adherents.com, "Major Religions of the World Ranked by Number of
Adherents," http://www.adherents.com/
Religions_By_Adherents.html (accessed 5/1/2013).

Alexander, Charles N., et al., quoted in "Transpersonal Childhood
Experiences of Higher States of Consciousness: Literature Review
and Theoretical Integration." Unpublished paper by Jayne
Gackenback (1992) http://www.sawka.com/spiritwatch/cehsc/
ipure.htm (accessed 3/20/2013).

Alexander, Charles N., Robert W. Boyer and Victoria K. Alexander,
"Higher states of consciousness in the Vedic Psychology of
Maharishi Mahesh Yogi: A Theoretical Introduction and Research
Review." *Journal of Modern Science and Vedic Science* Vol. 1, no. 1,
(1987), 89-126, 100.

Alexander, Charles N., Ken Chandler and Robert W. Boyer.
"Experience and Understanding of Pure Consciousness in the Vedic
Science of Maharishi Mahesh Yogi." *Higher States of
Consciousness: Theoretical and Experimental Perspectives.* New
York: Plenum Publishing, J.I. Gackenbach & H. Hunt, eds. (no date
listed), 310.

Alexander, Charles N., J.L. Davies and C.A. Dixon. "Growth of Higher
Stages of Consciousness: Maharishi's Vedic Psychology of Human
Development." In Charles N. Alexander and Ellen J. Langer *Higher
Stages of Human Development,* Oxford University Press, 1990,
286-387.

Allman, Lorraine, Olivia De La Rocha, David N. Elkins and Robert S.
Weathers. "Psychotherapist's Attitudes Toward Clients Reporting

Mystical Experiences." *Psychotherapy* Vol. 29, no 4 (1992), 564-569.

Alper, Mathew. *The God Part of the Brain*, Naperville, Illinois: Sourcebook, Inc, 2006, originally published 1996 by Rough Press.

Alper, Mathew. *The God Part of the Brain*, http://godpart.com/ (accessed 5/23/2008).

Alston, William P. *Perceiving God: The Epistemology of Religious Experience*. Ithaca and London: Cornell University Press, 1991.

Amaro, Jorge. "Psychology, Psychoanalysis and Religious Faith." *Psychology of Religion Homepage*, http://www.psywww.com/ psyrelig/amaro.html (accessed 3/27/13).

Austin, James H. "Zen and the Brain," in Hick, *The New Frontier of Religion and Science*, 78-79.

Back, K. and L. Bourque. "Can Feelings be Enumerated?" *Behavioral Science*, 15, (1970), 487-496 referenced in David Lukoff and Francis G. Lu, "Transpersonal Psychology Research Review Topic: Mystical Experience." *The Journal of Transpersonal Psychology* Vol. 20, no 2 (1988) 161-183, 171.

Baggnini, Julian. *Atheism: A Very Short Introduction*. Oxford: Oxford University Press, 2003.

Barnard, G. William. *Exploring Unseen Worlds: William James and The Philosophy of Mysticism*, Albany: SUNY Press, 1997.

Batson, C. Daniel, W. Larry Ventis. *The Religious Experience: A Social-Psychological Perspective.* New York: Oxford University Press, 1982, 115.

Benner, P. *Stress and Satisfaction on the Job: Work Meanings and Coping of Mid-Career Men.* in Rozario, Loretta Do. "Spirituality in the Lives of People with Disability and Chronic Illness: A Creative Paradigm of Wholeness and Reconstitution." *Disability and Rehabilitation: An International and Multidisciplinary Journal* Vol 19, no 10 (1997), 427-433.

Borg, Jacqueline, et al., "The Serotonin System and Spiritual Experiences," *The American Journal of Psychiatry* 160 (Nov 2003)

1965-1969, http://ajp.psychiatryonline.org/cgi/content/full/160/11/
1965 (accessed 7/17/09).

Boyatzis, Chris J. "Religious and Spiritual Development in
Childhood," *Handbook of The Psychology of Religion and
Spirituality*. New York, London: Guildford Press, Raymond F.
Paloutzian, Crystal L. Park ed., 2005, 123-143.

Brainard, F.S. *Reality and Mystical Experience*. University Park:
Pennsylvania State University Press (2000). See also D. Loy,
Nonduality: A Study in Comparative Philosophy. Amherst:
Humanities Press.

Brown, Mackenzie D. *Tillich in Dialogue*. New York: Harper and Row,
1965.

Bucke, R. *Cosmic Consciousness: A Study In The Evolution of the
Human Mind*. New York: Dutton, 1968 (originally 1901). Quoted in
Andrew Newberg, *Why We Believe What We Believe: Uncovering
Our Biological Need for Meaning, Spirituality and Truth*. New York,
London: Free Press, 2006, 168.

Bultmann, Rodolf. *Jesus Christ and Mythology*. New York: Scribner
and Sons, 1958.

Burtt, A.E. *The Metaphysical Foundations of Early Modern Science*.
Garden City, New York: Doubleday 1954.

Byrd, Randolph. "Positive Therapeutic Effects of Intercessory Prayer in
the Coronary Care Unit." *Southern Medical Journal* Vol 81 no 7
(July 1988).

Bytrentsacred.co.uk. "The Protestant Atheism of Richard Dawkins,"
Comment 1, http://www.bytrentsacred.co.uk/index.php/dawkins-
protestant-atheism/the-god-delusion-comment-1 (accessed 5/1/2013).

Caird, Dale. "The Structure of Hood's Mysticism Scale, a factor
analytic study." *Journal for the Scientific Study of Religion* 27 1
(1988), 122-127.

Cancer Research UK, "Smoking and Cancer," Cancer Research UK:
http://info.cancerresearchuk.org/healthyliving/smokingandtobacco/
(accessed 3/24/2009).

Carlson, Anton J. "Science and The Supernatural." *Science Magazine* February 27, 1937, 5.

Carter, B. *A Phenomenological Study of Survivors of Adult Cancer.* Doctoral Dissertation, University of California, San Francisco, 1989 in Rozario, Loretta Do. "Spirituality in the Lives of People with Disability and Chronic Illness: A Creative Paradigm of Wholeness and Reconstitution." *Disability and Rehabilitation: An International and Multidisciplinary Journal* Vol 19, no 10 (1997), 427-433.

Carter, Rita. *Consciousness.* London: Widenfeld and Nicholson, 2002, 288.

Council on Spiritual Practices. "State of Unitive Consciousness Research Summary." http://www.csp.org/experience/docs/unitive_consciousness.html (accessed 2/25/10).

Coyle, J. "Seeing a Placebo Work in the Brain." *Journal Watch* Vol. 293 (October 3, 2001), 1164-1166.

Davies, Paul. *The Mind of God*, New York: Simon and Schuster, 1992.

Davis, Caroline Franks. *The Evidential Force of Religious Experience.* Oxford: Clarendon Press, 1989, 218.

Dawkins, Richard. *The God Delusion.* New York: Houghton Mifflin Company, First Mariner Books edition, 2008 (originally 2006), 137.

Dennett, Daniel. *Breaking the Spell: Religion as Natural Phenomena.* New York: Viking, The Penguin Group, 2006.

Dennett, Daniel. *Consciousness Explained.* New York: Back Bay Books, first edition, 1992.

Doblin, Rick. "Pahnke's 'Good Friday Experiment' a Long Term Follow-up and Methodological Critique." *The Journal of Transpersonal Psychology* Vol. 23, no.1 (1991), 1-28.

Drob, Sanford L. *The New Kabbalah*: http://www.newkabbalah.com/home.html (accessed 9/12/2008).

Durham, John C. "Understanding the Sacred." Aberdeen University Sociology Society, 2001. http://www.bytrent.demon.co.uk/otto1.html (accessed 4/25/2013).

Egbert, L.D., G.E. Battie and M.K. Bartlett. "A Study of Doctor-Patient Rapport." *New England Journal of Medicine* 270 (1964), 825.

Elkins, D.N. "Psychotherapy and spirituality: Toward a Theory of the Soul," *Journal of Humanistic Psychology* 35 (1995), 78-98.

Elliot, D.M. "The Impact of Christian Faith on the Prevalence and Sequelae of Sexual Abuse." *Journal of Interpersonal Violence*, 9 1 (1994), 95-108.

ExChristian.net, "Letter from 'Jeff'," http://exchristian.net/testimonies/2005/01/new-atheist-family-advice.php (accessed 10/28/08).

Faidman, C., J. Savage, R. Mogar, and M. Allen. "The Effects of Psychedelic Therapy on Values, Personality and Behavior." *International Journal of Neuropsychiatry* 2 (1966), *241-254.*

Fairweather, Eugene R. "Christianity and the Supernatural." *New Theology No. 1* (1964), Martin E. Marty and Dean G. Peerman, eds., 235-256.

Fermilab. "Inquiring minds, Physics at Fermilab." http://www.fnal.gov/pub/inquiring/physics/neutrino/discovery/index.html (accessed 3/24/09).

Fermilab. "Neutrinos What are they?" http://www-donut.fnal.gov/web_pages/neutrinospg/Neutrinos.html (accessed 12/24/2009).

Forman, Robert .K.C. *Mysticism, Mind, Consciousness*. Albany: State University of New York Press, 1999.

Franks, Louis A. and Patrick Huyghe. *The Big Splash*. Avon books, 1991.

Gackenbach, Jayne. "Childhood: Transpersonal Childhood Experiences of Higher States of Consciousness: Literature Review and Theoretical Integration." *Spiritwatch,* http://www.sawka.com/spiritwatch/cehsc/ipure.htm (accessed 1/2/11)

Ghose, Aurobindo Sri. *On Himself.* Pondicherry: Sri Aurobindo Ashram, 1972.

Glik, Deborah C. "Psychosocial Wellness Among Spiritual Healing Participants." *Social Science and Medicine* 22 (1986), 579-586

Gould, Steven Jay. *Rock of Ages.* New York: Ballantine Books, 1999.

Gracely, Ed J. "Why Extraordinary Claims Demand Extraordinary Proof." *Quackwatch,* July 24, 2003, http://www.quackwatch.org/ 01QuackeryRelatedTopics/extraproof.html (accessed 5/3/13). Originally published in December 1998 issue of *Phactum*, the newsletter of the *Philadelphia Association for Critical Thinking (PhACT)*.

Greeley, Andrew M. and Wolfgang Jadogzinksky. "The Demand for Religion: Hard Core Atheism and the Supply Side Theory," http://www.agreeley.com/articles/hardcore.html (accessed 11/25/08).

Greeley, Andrew M. "Ecstasy a way of knowing." In Lukoff and Lu, "Transpersonal Psychology Research," Op. Cit. 172.

Griffiths, Roland and W.A. Richards, U. McCann, R. Jesse. "Psilocybin Can Occasion Mystical Type Experiences Having Substantial and Sustained Personal Meaning and Spiritual Significance." *Psychopharmacology* 187 (January 2006), 268-283.

Gross, Scott. "Why does God Remain so Hidden? Summary on Prehension" referenced in J.L. Hinman, "Thomas Reid Argument,"Â? http://www.doxa.ws/Reid2.html, *Doxa: Christian Thought in the 21st Century* (accessed 5/2/2013)

Hardy, A. *The Spiritual Nature of Man*, Oxford: Clarendon Press, 1979.

Hardy. A. in Lukoff, Op. Cit., 178, original research: Hardy (1979) *The Spiritual Nature of Man* Oxford: Clarendon Press.

Hawking, Steven, *A Brief History of Time*, New York: Bantam Books, 1988.

Heimelein, M.J. and J.V. McElrath, "Childhood Sexual Survivors, Cognitive Coping and Illusion." *Child Abuse and Neglect,* 20 (8), (1996) 747-758.

Herrington, Anne. *The Placebo Effect*. Cambridge: Harvard University Press, 2000.

Hick, John. *The New Frontier of Religion and Science: Religious Experience, Neuroscience and The Transcendent.* Playgrave: Macmillan, 2006.

Hinman, J.L. "How Many Atheists Are There?" *Doxa: Christian Thought in the Twenty-First Century,* http://www.doxa.ws/social/ percentage.html (accessed 5/2/2013)

Hinman, J.L. "What is the Supernatural." *Doxa: Christian Thought in the Twenty-First Century,* http://www.doxa.ws/meta_crock/ Supernature.html (accessed 3/24/2009).

Hood, Ralph W. Jr. "The Common Core Thesis in The Study of Mysticism," in *Where God and Science Meet Volume III: How Brain Evolution Studies Alter Our Understanding of Religion: Psychology of Religion,* Patrick McNamara, ed., Westport, Connecticut: Praeger, 2004, 119-138.

Hood, Ralph W. Jr., "Eliciting Mystical States of Consciousness with Semi-Structured Nature Experiences." *Journal for the Scientific Study of Religion* 16 (1977), 155-163.

Hood, Ralph W. Jr., N. Ghorbani, P.J. Waston, A.F. Ghramaleki, M.B. Bing, H.R. Davison, R.J. Morris and P. J. Williamson. "Dimensions of the Mysticism Scale: Confirming the three factor structure in the United States and Iran." *Journal for the Scientific Study of Religion* 40 (2001), 691-705.

Hood, Ralph W. Jr. and W.T. Stace quoted in Robert J. Voyle, "The Impact of Mystical Experiences Upon Christian Maturity." http://www.voyle.com/impact.pdf (accessed 1/2/11).

Hood, Ralph W. Jr. and W.P. Williamson. "An Empirical Rest of the Unity Thesis: The Structure of Mystical Descriptors in Various Faith Samples." *Journal of Christianity and Psychology* 19 (2000), 222-244.

Hume, David. *An Essay Concerning Human Understanding.* Chicago: Open Court Publishing Company, 1958.

Huyghe, Patrick. "Extraordinary Claim? Move the Goal Post," *The Anomalist* 3 (Winter 1995/6), http://www.anomalist.com/ commentaries/claim.html (accessed 7/9/08).

Idinopulos, Thomas A. "What is Religion?" *Cross Currents* Vol. 48 issue 3 (Fall 1998), http://www.crosscurrents.org/whatisreligion.htm (accessed 10/10/2008).

Idinopulos, Thomas A. "The Creation of Human Behavior: Reconciling Durkheim and the Study of religion." *Cross Currents*, "What is Religion" Vol 48, issue 3 (Fall 1998). http://www.crosscurrents.org/whatisreligion.htm (accessed 1/2/11).

Ilford, Mary. *The God's of Pre-Historic Man.* New York: Sterling Publishing Company, Inc., Johannes Maringer, trans., 2003.

Irwin, H.J. "Childhood Trauma and the Origin of Paranormal Belief: A Constructive Replication." *Psychological Reports* 74 1 (1994).

James, William. *The Varieties of Religious Experience: A Study in Human Nature.* Gifford Lectures on Natural Religion 1901, 1902. New York: Modern Library, 1902.

James, William. *Principles of Psychology* Vol. III, Cambridge MA: Harvard University Press, 1981.

James, William. *The Varieties of Religious Experience.* New York: Modern Library, 1994.

Johns Hopkins University. "Hopkins Scientists show Hallucinogen in Mushrooms Creates Universal Mystical Experience." Johns Hopkins University "Medicine" press release, July 11, 2006, http://www.hopkinsmedicine.org/Press_releases/2006/07_11_06.html (accessed 7/18/2009).

Jones, R. "Numinous," *Westminster Dictionary of Christian Theology.* Philadelphia, Pennsylvania: Westminster Press, Alan Richardson and John Bowden, eds., 1983, 405.

Kass, J.D., R. Friedman, J. Lesserman, P.C. Zuttermeister and H. Benson. "Health outcomes and a new index of spiritual experience." *Journal for Scientific Study of Religion* 30 (1991), 203-211.

Katz, Steven. quoted in Proudfoot, Op. Cit. 122.

Keith, William and David Beard, "Toulmin's Rhetorical Logic: What is the Warrant for Warrants?" *Philosophy and Rhetoric* Vol. 41, no. 1 (2008), 22.

Kilstron, John. "Tellegen Absorption Scale." http://socrates.berkeley.edu/~kihlstrm/TAS.htm (accessed 6/7/2009).

Kirckpatrick, Lee A. "Religion is Not An Adaptation" in *Where God and Science Meet: How Brain and Evolutionary Studies Alter Our*

Understanding of Religion Volume I: Evolution, Genes and Religious Brain Patrick McNamara (ed). London, Westport: Praeger, 2006. 159-180.

Kose, Samuel. "A Psychobiological Model of Temperament and Character (TCI)," Yeni Symposium 2003. http://www.journaldatabase.org/articles/71232/ A_psychobiological_model_.html full text: http://www.yenisymposium.net/FULLTEXT/2003(2)/ ys2003_41_2_6.pdf (accessed 7/17/09).

Kuhn. Thomas S. *The Structure of Scientific Revolutions*. Chicago: University of Chicago Press, 1962.

Larson, David B., Editor. *The Faith Factor: An Annotated Bibliography of Systematic Reviews And Clinical Research on Spiritual Subjects Vol. 2*, National Institute for Health Research, December 1993.

Laski, M. *Ecstasy in Secular and Religious Experiences*, Los Angeles: J.P. Tarcher, 1990 (originally 1961).

Leaky, Richard and Roger Lewin. *Origins: The Emergence and Evolution of Our Species and Its Possible Future.* New York: Penguin Books, 1991.

Lewis, C.S. *Miracles: a Preliminary Study*. New York: MacMillian, 1947, 105.

Lillegard, Norman. "On Some Differences Between Religious and Scientific Beliefs." http://www.utexas.edu/cola/depts/philosophy/ faculty/koons/ntse/papers/Lillegar.txt (accessed 10/10/08).

Linde, Andre. "The Self Reproducing Inflationary Universe." *Scientific American*, September 1999.

Lukoff, David. In Jayne Gackenback, *Spiritwatch,* http://www.sawka.com/spiritwatch/cehsc/ipure.htm (accessed 10/4/ 08).

Lukoff, David. "the Diagnosis of Mystical Experiences With Psychotic Features." *Journal of Transpersonal Psychology* 17 2 (1985), 155-81 in Lukoff and Lu, *Journal of Transpersonal Psychology* 20 2 (1988), 182.

Lukoff, David and F.G. Lu. "Transpersonal Psychology Research, Mystical Experience," *The Journal of Transpersonal Psychology* 20 2 (1988), 162-184.

Maslow, Abraham. *Religions, Values and Peak-Experiences.* New York: The Viking Press. Published by Penguin Books Limited, 1970.

Maslow, Abraham. *Toward a Psychology of Being.* Princeton,: D. Van Nostrand Company, 1962 in Robert Wuthnow "Peak Experiences: Some Empirical Tests," *Journal Humanistic Psychology* Vol. 18, no. 3 (Summer 1978), 60.

Mathes, Eugene W. "Peak Experience Tendencies." *Journal of Humanistic Psychology* Vol. 22, no. 3 (1982), 92-108.

Matt, Daniel C. *The Essential Kabbalah: the Heart of Jewish Mysticism.* New York: HarperCollins, 1995.

Mattey, G.J. "2002 Lecture notes: *Theory of Knowledge* Second Edition, Chapter 4 Foundation; Fallible Foundations." http://hume.ucdavis.edu/mattey/phi102kl/tkch4.htm (accessed 11/30/2010).

McDowell, D. and M. Galanter, L. Goldfab, H. Lifshutz, "Spirituality and the Treatment of the Dually Diagnosed: An Investigation of Patient and Staff Attitudes." *Journal of Addictive Diseases* 15 (1996), 55-68.

McFarling, Usha Lee. "Doctors Find Power of Faith Hard to Ignore," Knight Ridder News Service (December 23, 1998), http://www.tennessean.com/health/stories/98/trends1223.htm (accessed 3/27/09).

Millar, C., *A Descriptive Analysis of Psychic Opening.* Dissertation Abstracts International, (1990). 51/05, 2629B (University Microfilms No. 9027841).

Millar, C., "Developmental Characteristics of Psychic Opening," Paper presented at the Annual Meeting of the Lucidity Association, University of California Santa Cruz (June 1992), referenced in J. I. Gackenback, "Pure Consciousness, Mystical Experience," *Spirit Watch,* http://www.sawka.com/spiritwatch/cehsc/ipure.htm (accessed 2/4/2011).

Mohan, K Krishna. "Spirituality and Well Being: an Overview" presented at Second International Conference on Integral Psychology, Pondicherry India January 4-7, 2001. Published in *Consciousness and its Transformation*, M. Cornelissen, ed. Pondicherry: SAICE, 2001. http://ipi.org.in/texts/ip2/ip2-4.5-.htm (accessed 3/25/2013).

Moltmann, Jurgen. *The Crucified God: The Cross as The Foundation and Criticism of Christian Theology*. Minneapolis: Fortress Press, 1968.

Morman, Daniel E. and Wane B. Jonas, "Deconstructing the Placebo Effect and Finding the Meaning Response." *Annals of Internal Medicine* Vol. 136, issue 6 (19 March, 2002), 471-476.

Motluk, Aliceon. "Belief Special: When Delusion Triumphs over Truth." *New Scientist* Issue 2536 (January 28, 2006).

Newberg, Andrew. *Why God Won't Go Away: Brain Science and the Biology of Belief*. New York: Ballentine Books, 2001.

Newberg, Andrew and Mark Robert Waldman. *Why We Believe What we Believe*. New York, London, Toronto: Free Press, 2006.

Nielsen, Michael E. "Social Psychology and Religion on a Trip to Ukraine." *Psychology of Religion,* http://www.psywww.com/psyrelig/ukraine/ (accessed 10/10/2008).

Noble, Kathleen D. "Psychological Health and the Experience of Transcendence." *The Counseling Psychologist* 15 4 (1987), 601-614.

O'Neil, Dennis. "Early Modern Human Culture." *Evolution of Modern Humans, a Survey of Biological and Cultural Evolution of Archaic and Modern Homo Sapiens*. San Marcos, California: Behavioral Science Department, Palomar College, Anthropology Tutorials. http://anthro.palomar.edu/homo2/mod_homo_5.htm.

Otto, Rodolf. *The Idea of the Holy*. London: Oxford University Press, Trans. John W. Harvey, 1923 (first imprint).

Pailin, David. "The Religious *a priori*." *Westminster Dictionary of Christian Theology*. Louisville, Kentucky: Westminster John Knox Press, Alan Richardson and John Bowden, ed., 1983, 498.

Pargament, K.I. "Religious Methods of Coping: Resources for the Conversation and Transformation of Significance." In E.P. Shafnaske (ed.) *Religion and Clinical Practice of Psychology*, Washington D.C.: American Psychological Association, 1996, 215-239.

Pargament, K.I. in Patricia L. Ryan, "Spirituality Among Adult Survivors of Childhood Violence A Literature Review." *Journal of Transpersonal Psychology* Vol. 30, no. 1 (1998), 41.

Parker, Barry. *Creation: the Story of the Origin and Evolution of the Universe*. New York, London: Plenum Press, 1988.

Pettitt, Paul. "When Burial Begins," *British Archaeology* Issue 66 (August 2002) http://www.britarch.ac.uk/BA/ba66/feat1.shtml (accessed 10/14/08).

Pew Forum. "On Religion and Public Life: US Religious Landscape," http://religions.pewforum.org/affiliations (accessed 5/27/09).

Pinker, Steven. "The Evolutionary Psychology of Religion." In McNamara, *Where God and Science Meet* Volume I, chapter 1-2.

Poloma and Pendelton. *The Faith Factor: An Annotated Bibliography of Systematic Reviews And Clinical Research on Spiritual Subjects* Vol. II, David B. Larson M.D., National Institute for Health Research, Dec. 1993, 3290.

Plutchik, Robert. Abstract, "The Nature of Human Emotions" in *Science Week*, 3 August 2001, http://cogweb.ucla.edu/ep/ Emotions.html (accessed 9/10/08). Original: *American Scientist* 89 (2001), 344.

Proudfoot, Wayne. *Religious Experience.* Berkeley, Los Angeles, London: University of California Press, 1985.

Quack Watch, "Homeopathy," http://www.quackwatch.org/ 01QuackeryRelatedTopics/homeo.html (accessed 10/21/10).

Quack Watch, "Therapeutic Touch," http://www.quackwatch.org/ 01QuackeryRelatedTopics/tt.html (accessed 10/21/10).

Ramachandran, V.S. *Phantoms in the Brain*. New York: William Marrow, 1998.

Ramachandran, V.S. *Phantoms in the Brain*. In John Hick, *The New Frontier of Religion and Science*, 62.

Ramsey, Michael. "Evelyn Underhill," *Religious Studies* Vol 12, issue 03 (1976), Cambridge University Press, 273-279. http://journals.cambridge.org/action/ displayAbstract?fromPage=online&aid=2409960 (October 2008).

Reid, Thomas. *Essays on the Intellectual Powers of Man.* Standard text. 1785.

Reid, Thomas. *An Inquiry Into the Human Mind on the Principles of Common Sense.* Standard text. 1764.

Robinson, Edward. *The Original Vision: A Study of the Religious Experience of Childhood.* New York: The Seabury Press. 1983, 37.

Rorty, Richard. *Contingency, Irony and Solidarity.* Cambridge: Cambridge University Press, 1989.

Rose, Steven. In Hick, *The New Frontier of Religion and Science* 78. The original source on Rose is *The 21st Century Brain*, London: Johnathan Cape, (2005).

Rossano, Matt J. "The Religious Mind and the Evolution of Religion." Department of Psychology, Southeastern Louisiana University, 17-18. http://www2.southeastern.edu/Academics/Faculty/mrossano/ recentpubs/EvolOfReligionFinal.pdf (accessed 3/27/13).

Rozario, Loretta Do. "Spirituality in the Lives of People with Disability and Chronic Illness: A Creative Paradigm of Wholeness and Reconstitution." *Disability and Rehabilitation: An International and Multidisciplinary Journal* Vol 19, no 10 (1997), 427-433.

Ryan, Patricia L. "Spirituality Among Adult Survivors of Childhood Violence: A Literature Review," *The Journal of Transpersonal Psychology* Vol. 30, no. 1 (1998), 43.

Scheier, M.P. and C.S. Carver. "Dispositional Optimism and Physical Well-Being: The Influence of Generalized Outcome Expectancies on Health." *Journal of Personality* 55 (1987), 169-210.

Sensky, T. "Religiosity Mystical Experience and Epilepsy," summary of research in David Lukoff, Francis G. Lu, "Transpersonal Psychology Research Review Topic: Mystical Experience," *The Journal of Transpersonal Psychology* Vol. 20, no. 2 (1988), 161-183, 175.

Joseph Hinman

Shafranske, E.P. and H.N. Malony. "Clinical Psychologist's Religious and Spiritual Orientations and Their Practice of Psychotherapy." *Psychotherapy* Vol. 27, no. 1 (Spring 1990), 72-78.

Sloan, Richard P. *Blind Faith: the Unholy Alliance of Religion and Medicine,* New York: MacMillan Publishing, 2006.

Smelser, Neil J. "Sociology Spanning Two Centuries," *The American Sociologist* (Springer New York) Vol. 34, no. 3 (September 2003), 5-19.

Southgate, Christopher. *God, Humanity and the Cosmos.* London: T&T Clark, 1999.

Spanos, Nicholas P. and Patricia Moretti. Study Abstract "Correlates of Mystical and Diabolical Experiences in a Sample of Female University Students." *Journal For the Scientific Study of Religion* 1988. http://www.jstor.org/pss/1387405. 105-116.

Spilka, Bernard, Ralph W. Hood, Jr., Bruce Hunsberger, Richard Gorsuch, *The Psychology of Religion: An Empirical Approach.* Third edition. New York, London: The Guilford Press, 2003.

Spiritual Competency Resource Center. "Treatment: Types of Spiritual Emergency" (accessed 2/08/11).

St. Teresa of Avila. *The Life of St. Teresa of Avila by Herself.* J.M. Cohen, trans. London: Penguin, 1957.

Stace, W.T. *Mysticism and Philosophy*, New York: Palgrave Macmillan, 3rd ed. June 1960.

Steindl-Rast, David. "The Mystical Core of Organized Religion" *ReVision* 12 1 (Summer 1989). Also used on website for Council on Spiritual Practices, http://www.csp.org/experience/docs/steindl-mystical.html (accessed 10/10/2008).

Strong, James. *Strong's Exhaustive Concordance to the Bible,* Peabody, Massachusetts: Hendrickson, 2009.

Sullivan, W. "It helps me to be a Whole Person: The Role Spirituality Among the Mentally Challenged." *Psychological Rehabilitation Journal* 16 (1993), 125-134.

Swinburne, Richard. *The Existence of God,* N.Y., London: Oxford University Press, 2004.

Tart, Charles T. *Psi: Scientific Studies of the Psychic Realm,* Bloomington: IUniverse inc, 2001.

Taylor, Bill. "Is Religion a Placebo?" *New Scientist,* 25 Feb (2006). Online edition: http://www.newscientist.com/article/ mg18925401.300-is-religion-a-placebo.html (accessed 10/28/08).

Thomas, Kathy Quinn. "The Mind-BODY Connection: Granny Was Right, After All." *The Rochester Review* Spring/Summer 1995. Rochester: University of Rochester. http://www.rochester.edu/pr/ Review/V59N3/feature2.html (accessed 10/10/08).

Tillich, Paul. *The Shaking of The Foundations.* New York: Scribner and Sons, 1948.

Tomlin, Adele. Review of Jesse J. Prinz: "Gut Reactions." *Metapsychology: Online Reviews,* 2005, http://metapsychology.mentalhelp.net/poc/ view_doc.php?type=book&id=2596&cn=396 (accessed 9/10/2008).

Toulmin, Stephen E. *The Uses of Argument.* Cambridge: Cambridge University Press, Updated edition, 2003 (originally 1958).

Truzzi, Marcelo. "On Some Unfair Practices Toward Claims of the Paranormal."Â? Also found on *Skeptical Investigations*: http://www.skepticalinvestigations.org/Anomali/practices.html (accessed 10/21/10). Published in slightly edited form in Edward Binkowski, ed., *Oxymoron: Annual Thematic Anthology of the Arts and Sciences Volume 2 The Fringe,* New York: Oxymoron Media, Inc., 1998.

Unger, Sanford M. "Mescaline, LSD-25, Psilocybin and Personality Change." *Psychiatry Journal for the Study of Interpersonal Processes* Vol. 26, no. 2 (May 1963), 111-125.

Valentine, L. and LL. Feninuer. "Resistance Factors Associated With Female Survivors of Childhood Sexual Abuse." *The American Journal of Family Therapy* 21 3 (1993) 216-224.

Vallance, Aaron K. "Something Out of Nothing, the Placebo Effect." *The British Journal of Psychiatry: Advances in Psychiatric Treatment* Vol. 12, (2006), 287-296.

Voyle, Robert J. "The Impact of Mystical Experiences Upon Christian Maturity." http://www.voyle.com/impact.pdf (accessed 2/1/09).

Walsh, Roger. "The Consciousness Disciplines and the Behavioral Sciences: Questions of Comparison and Assessment." *American Journal of Psychiatry*, 137 6 (1980), 663-673.

Whitehead, Clay C. "Toward a New Paradigm of Therapeutic Action: Neuro-Psychoanalysis and Downward Causation." *Journal of American Academy of Psychoanalysis* 33 (2005), 637-656.

Whiteley, D.E.H. *The Theology of St Paul.* Minneapolis: Fortress Press 1964.

Williams, Robert R. *Schleiermacher the Theologian.* Philadelphia: Fortress Press, 1978.

Williams, Rowan. "Freudian Psychology," *Westminster Dictionary of Christian Theology.* Philadelphia, Pennsylvania: Westminster Press, Alan Richardson and John Bowden, eds., 1983, 219-22.

Wuthnow, Robert. "Peak Experiences: Some Empirical Tests." *Journal of Humanistic Psychology*, 18 3 (1978), 61-62.

Index

Joseph Hinman

Joseph Hinman

The Author

Mr. Hinman did his undergraduate work in sociology and debate at the University of Texas at Arlington. He earned a Masters degree in Theological studies where he focused upon history of doctrine at Perkins school of Theology, Southern Methodist University. He was a Ph.D. candidate in the History of Ideas (Intellectual History) and studied at the doctoral level for several years at University of Texas at Dallas. He began work focusing upon Derrida and the postmodern understanding of the self. He then switched and spent five years studying history and philosophy of science, focusing upon Newton, Boyle and the Latitudinarians. In the process of completing his dissertation, he was forced to terminate his studies ABD (all but the dissertation) due to family tragedies. Mr. Hinman published the peer-reviewed academic journal, Negations: an interdisciplinary journal of social criticism. He now works as an independent scholar.

www.ingramcontent.com/pod-product-compliance
Lightning Source LLC
Chambersburg PA
CBHW020601270326
41927CB00005B/121